Handy Reminders

To Do This Task	Here's the Best Way
Navigate (Chapter 2)	
Orbit with your mouse	Hold down scroll wheel
Zoom with your mouse	Roll scroll wheel
Pan with your mouse	Hold down Shift and the scroll wheel
Draw (Chapters 2, 4, and 6)	
Draw an edge a certain length with the Line tool	Type a length and press Enter
Snip off an edge at the last place you clicked	Press the Esc key
Lock your current direction with the Line tool	Hold down the Shift key while drawing with the tool
Change the number of sides in a circle, arc or polygon	Type a number, then type **s**, and press Enter
Draw a circle or an arc of a certain radius	Type a radius and press Enter after you draw a circle
Select with the Select tool (Chapter 2)	
Add or subtract from what you've selected	Hold down Shift
Select everything that isn't hidden	Press Ctrl+A (⌘+A on the Mac)
Select everything *inside* a selection box	Click and drag from left to right
Select everything *touched by* a selection box	Click and drag from right to left
Select all faces with the same material	Right-click and choose Select⇨All with Same Material
Move with the Move tool (Chapters 2, 4, and 6)	
Move a certain distance	After you move, type a distance and press Enter
Force Auto-Fold (tell SketchUp it's okay to fold)	Press Alt (⌘ on the Mac)
Lock yourself in the *blue* (up and down) direction	Press ↑ or ↓ key
Copy with the Move and Rotate tools (Chapters 2 and 4)	
Make a copy with the Move or Rotate tools	Press Ctrl (Option on the Mac)
Make multiple copies *in a row*	Make a copy, type a distance, type **x**, and press Enter
Make multiple copies *between*	Make a copy, type a number, type **/**, and press Enter
Hide and Smooth with the Eraser tool (Chapter 6)	
Hide something	Hold down Shift and click with the Eraser
Smooth something	Ctrl+click with the Eraser (Option+click on the Mac)
Unsmooth something	Hold down Shift+Ctrl and click with the Eraser (Shift+Option on the Mac)
Push/Pull and Offset (Chapter 4)	
Make a copy of the face you're push/pulling	Press Ctrl (Option on the Mac) and use the Push/Pull tool
Repeat the last distance you push/pulled	Double-click a face with the Push/Pull tool
Repeat the last distance you Offset	Double-click a face with the Offset tool
Scale with the Scale tool (Chapter 6)	
Scale about the center	Hold down Ctrl (Option on the Mac) while scaling
Scale uniformly (don't distort)	Hold down Shift while scaling
Scale by a certain factor	Type a number and press Enter
Make something a certain size	Type the size *and* the units and then press Enter

(continued)

Google® SketchUp®
For Dummies®

(continued)

To Do This Task	Here's the Best Way
Apply materials with the Paint Bucket tool (Chapter 2)	
Sample a material from a face	Hold down Alt (⌘ on the Mac) and click the face with the tool
Paint all faces that match the one you click	Hold down Shift while you click
Create guides (Chapters 2 and 4)	
Tell the Tape Measure or Protractor tool to create a guide	Press Ctrl (Option on the Mac) and click with the tool
Walk around your model with the Walk tool (Chapter 8)	
Walk through things	Hold down Alt (⌘ on the Mac)
Run instead of walk	Hold down Ctrl (Option on the Mac)
Get taller or shorter instead of walking	Hold down Shift
Change your eye height	Select the Look Around tool, type a height, and press Enter
Change your field of view	Select the Zoom tool, type a number, type **deg**, and press Enter

Productivity Boosts

To divide an edge into a number of shorter edges:

1. Right-click an edge with the Select tool.
2. Choose Divide from the context menu that pops up.
3. Type the number of segments you'd like and press Enter.

To resize your whole model based on one known measurement:

1. Select the Tape Measure tool.
2. Press Ctrl (Option on a Mac) until you don't see a + next to your cursor.
3. Measure a distance; click once to start measuring, and again to stop.
4. Type a dimension for the distance you just measured and press Enter.
5. Click Yes in the dialog box that pops up.

To set up your own keyboard shortcuts:

1. Choose Window⇨Preferences (File⇨Preferences on the Mac).
2. Click the Shortcuts panel.

Keyboard Shortcuts

Line	L
Eraser	E
Select	Spacebar
Move	M
Circle	C
Arc	A
Rectangle	R
Push/Pull	P
Offset	O
Rotate	Q
Scale	S
Zoom Extents	Shift+Z
Paint Bucket	B

For Dummies: Bestselling Book Series for Beginners

Google® SketchUp®

FOR DUMMIES®

by Aidan Chopra

Google® SketchUp® For Dummies®

Published by
Wiley Publishing, Inc.
111 River Street
Hoboken, NJ 07030-5774
www.wiley.com

For general information on our other products and services, please contact our Customer Care Department within the U.S. at 800-762-2974, outside the U.S. at 317-572-3993, or fax 317-572-4002.

For technical support, please visit www.wiley.com/techsupport.

Wiley also publishes its books in a variety of electronic formats. Some content that appears in print may not be available in electronic books.

Library of Congress Control Number: 2007926376

ISBN: 978-0-470-13744-4

Manufactured in the United States of America

10 9 8 7

WILEY

About the Author

Aidan Chopra has always had a thing for computers — his parents thoughtfully sent him to Apple camp instead of hockey lessons like every other eight-year-old in Montreal — but he learned to draft and build physical models the old-fashioned way, working for his architect father. These days, Aidan is a Product Evangelist at Google, where he's been since that company bought SketchUp in the first part of 2006. In the three years since he graduated with a Master of Architecture degree from Rice University, he's done a lot of writing and lecturing about the way software is used in design. Aidan writes the *SketchUpdate,* a monthly e-mail newsletter that reaches a half million SketchUp users worldwide. He has taught architecture at the university level and, at Google, works on ways to mediate between power and usability; he believes the best software in the world isn't worth a darn if nobody can figure out how it works. Aidan is based in Boulder, Colorado, even though he is what many would consider to be the diametric opposite of a world-class endurance athlete.

Dedication

For my parents, Jenny and Shab, and my brother, Quincy, because I love them very much.

Author's Acknowledgments

For helping in all the ways that it is possible to help with a book — offering technical advice, lending a critical ear, providing moral support and encouragement — I'd like to thank Sandra Winstead, with whom I live and work. It's rare to find everything you need in a single person, and I can't imagine having written this book without her.

I'd like to thank Chris Dizon for agreeing to be the Technical Editor for this volume; I can't think of anyone who brings more enthusiasm and curiosity to everything he does. As a dyed-in-the-wool SketchUpper who uses the software even more than I do, I knew he'd do a bang-up job of keeping me honest, and he did.

I thank Kyle Looper, Becky Huehls, and John Edwards, my editors at Wiley, for making what I fully expected to be a painful process not so at all. It was a delight to work with a team of such intelligent, thoughtful, and well-meaning professionals; I only hope I'm half as lucky on the next book I write.

Finally, I need to thank the very long list of individuals who provided critical help. From clearing the way for me to be able to write this book to patiently explaining things more than once, I owe the following people (and almost certainly a few more) a whole lot: Tommy Acierno, Brad Askins, John Bacus, Brian Brewington, Brian Brown, Todd Burch, Chris Campbell, Mark Carvalho, Chris Cronin, Steve Dapkus, Jonathan Dormody, Bill Eberle, Joe Esch, Rich Feit, Jody Gates, Toshen Golias, Scott Green, Barry Janzen, Tyson Kartchner, Chris Keating, Mark Limber, Allyson McDuffie, Millard McQuaid, Tyler Miller, Parker Mitchell, Alok Priyadarshi, Brad Schell, Mike Springer, Tricia Stahr, Bryce Stout, James Therrien, Mason Thrall, Nancy Trigg, Tushar Udeshi, John Ulmer, David Vicknair, Greg Wirt, and Tom Wyman.

Publisher's Acknowledgments

We're proud of this book; please send us your comments through our online registration form located at `www.dummies.com/register/`.

Some of the people who helped bring this book to market include the following:

Acquisitions, Editorial, and Media Development

Project Editor: Rebecca Huehls

Acquisitions Editor: Kyle Looper

Copy Editor: John Edwards

Technical Editor: Chris Dizon

Editorial Manager: Leah P. Cameron

Media Development and Quality Assurance: Angela Denny, Kate Jenkins, Steven Kudirka, Kit Malone

Media Development Coordinator: Jenny Swisher

Media Project Supervisor: Laura Moss-Hollister

Editorial Assistant: Amanda Foxworth

Senior Editorial Assistant: Cherie Case

Cartoons: Rich Tennant (`www.the5thwave.com`)

Composition Services

Project Coordinator: Jennifer Theriot

Layout and Graphics: Shawn Frazier, Barbara Moore, Laura Pence, Heather Ryan, Christine Williams

Proofreaders: Aptara, Jessica Kramer, Charles Spencer

Indexer: Aptara

Anniversary Logo Design: Richard Pacifico

Special Help
Jennifer Riggs, Heidi Unger

Publishing and Editorial for Technology Dummies

Richard Swadley, Vice President and Executive Group Publisher

Andy Cummings, Vice President and Publisher

Mary Bednarek, Executive Acquisitions Director

Mary C. Corder, Editorial Director

Publishing for Consumer Dummies

Diane Graves Steele, Vice President and Publisher

Joyce Pepple, Acquisitions Director

Composition Services

Gerry Fahey, Vice President of Production Services

Debbie Stailey, Director of Composition Services

Contents at a Glance

Table of Contents

· ·

Introduction

A little while ago, I was teaching a workshop on advanced SketchUp techniques to a group of extremely bright middle and high school (or so I thought) students in Hot Springs, Arkansas. As subject matter went, I wasn't pulling any punches — we were breezing through material I wouldn't think of introducing to most groups of adults. At one point, a boy raised his hand to ask a question, and I noticed he looked younger than most of the others. Squinting, I read a logo on his T-shirt that told me he was in elementary school. "You're in sixth grade?" I asked, a little stunned. These kids were *motoring*, after all. The boy didn't even look up. He shook his head, double-clicked something, and mumbled, "Third." He was 8 years old.

SketchUp was invented back in 1999 by a couple of 3D industry veterans (or refugees, depending on your perspective) to make it easier for people to see their ideas in three dimensions. That was it, really — they just wanted to make a piece of software that anyone could use to build 3D models. What I saw in Arkansas makes me think they were successful.

Before it was acquired in 2006 by Google, SketchUp cost $495 a copy, and it was already a mainstay of architects' and other designers' software toolkits. No other 3D modeler was as easy to understand as SketchUp, meaning that even senior folks (many of whom thought their CD/DVD trays were cup holders) started picking it up. These days, SketchUp is being used at home, in school, and at work by anyone with a need to represent 3D information the way it's meant to be represented: in 3D. Google SketchUp (as it's now called) is available as a free download in six languages, and is just as popular internationally as it is in North America.

About This Book

The thing I like least about software is figuring out how it works. I once saw a movie where the main character acquired knowledge by plugging a cable (a rather fat cable, actually) into a hole in the back of his head. A computer then uploaded new capabilities — languages, martial arts, fashion sense (apparently) — directly into his brain. Afterward, the character ate a snack and took a nap. *That's* how I wish I could get to know new software.

This book, on the other hand, is a fairly analog affair. In it, I do my best to guide you through the process of building 3D models with SketchUp. I wrote this book for people who are new to 3D modeling, so I don't assume you know anything about polygons, vertices, or linear arrays. The nice thing is that the people who make SketchUp don't assume you know any of those things, either. That means I don't have to spend many words explaining theoretical concepts, which I think we can both appreciate.

I don't think many people want to use software just for the sake of using software. You probably didn't learn to drive just because you thought seatbelts and turn signals were cool; I'm betting you wanted to be able to get around in a car. People use SketchUp so that they can build 3D models. As such, most of this book focuses on what *you can do* with SketchUp, and not *what SketchUp does*. Naturally, this has a few implications:

✔ **I use the word *you* a lot.** You're reading this book because you have something you want to build in 3D on your computer, and you think SketchUp can help you do that. I try to keep this in mind by letting you know how you can use the features I talk about to do what you want to do.

✔ **I err on the side of architecture.** The fact is, a lot of people want to use SketchUp to model buildings, so I'm assuming that a good many of you (the collective you, in this case) want to do the same. You can use SketchUp to build just about anything you want, but to ignore the fact that it's extra-great for architecture would be silly.

✔ **I don't cover everything SketchUp can do.** If this book were about SketchUp, and not modeling *with* SketchUp, I would list every feature, every tool, and every command in exhaustive detail. I would tell you exactly what every radio button and slider bar was for. I would, in effect, just copy the documentation that comes with SketchUp (available in the Help menu) and call it a day. In writing this book, I had to make a tough choice: I had to figure out what to show you and, more importantly, what to leave out. The Table of Contents I settled on is a list of what most people want to know, most of the time.

Just in case you're interested, here's what didn't make the cut (and why):

• **The Dimension and Label tools:** I left these out because they're so simple to use that I didn't think they needed any explanation. That's not to say they're not great — they are. It's just that this book could only be so long. . . .

• **The Sandbox tools:** These are a group of tools developed specifically for creating and editing terrain — the stuff you put buildings on if you don't live in Kansas. The trouble with the Sandbox tools is they're not simple to use, which would have meant giving them their own chapter. Because SketchUp can import terrain directly from Google Earth (see Chapter 11), I left them out.

• **The 3D Text tool:** This one is a new feature in SketchUp 6. It's fantastic, and tons of folks have been clamoring for it for years. Why isn't it in this book? Like the Dimension and Label tools, it's too easy to use. Just try it out and you'll see what I mean.

- **Ruby:** Actually, I do talk a little bit about Ruby, but only in Chapter 17, which is practically at the end of the book. Ruby is a scripting (programming) language that you (maybe) can use to code your own tools for SketchUp. I think that says it all, don't you?

One more thing: Because SketchUp is a *cross-platform* program (meaning that it's available for both Windows and Macintosh computers), I make reference to both operating systems throughout this book. In most cases, SketchUp works the same in Windows and on a Mac, but where it doesn't, I point out the differences. Just so you know, any figures in this book that show the SketchUp user interface show the Windows version.

Foolish Assumptions

I mentioned earlier that I don't presume you know anything about 3D modeling, much less 3D modeling with SketchUp, in this book. That's true — you're safe even if you call SketchUp "Sketch'em-Up" (which I've heard more than once, believe it or not). If you happen to know a thing or two about SketchUp, I think you'll still find plenty of useful stuff in this book. Even though it's written with beginners in mind, I've included a lot that definitely isn't beginner-level information. I mean for this book to be useful for people with just about any level of SketchUp skill.

That said, I assume you're familiar with a few important concepts. To begin with, I assume you know how to work your computer well enough to understand how to do basic things like saving and opening files. I don't cover those things in this book because SketchUp handles them just like every other program does. If you're trying to model with SketchUp *and* figure out how to use a computer at the same time, Wiley has some excellent books that can help you out, such as *Windows Vista For Dummies,* by Andy Rathbone, or *Mac OS X Leopard For Dummies,* by Bob LeVitus, just to name two; visit www.dummies.com for other options.

Next, I take for granted that you have, and know how to work, a mouse with a scroll wheel. If you're using Windows, you probably do, but Mac users (I'm ashamed to say) are a little late to the party when it comes to the wonders of multibutton mousing. SketchUp all but requires you to have a scroll wheel mouse — especially when you're just starting out. The good news for folks who don't have one is that they're fairly cheap. Just look for something with a left button, a right button, and a little scroll wheel in the middle.

Finally, I assume you have at least occasional access to the Internet. Don't panic! Unlike most Google applications, you don't have to be online to use SketchUp — I do most of my best work on airplanes, in fact. You can find some great resources on the Web, though, and I point them out when I think they're important.

How This Book Is Organized

Tell me if you think this is strange: I read most computer books in completely random order. I *never* start at the beginning and work my way through. In fact, I only pick them up for two reasons:

- ✔ **To figure something out:** I like to have a book on hand when I'm beginning something new because I like the way books *work*. If I need help, I look it up, but something else invariably happens — I end up reading more than I needed to, and I usually end up finding out something I didn't even know I didn't know. That almost never happens when I use digital media; it's too good at providing me with just the answer to my question. Computers are lousy for browsers like me.

- ✔ **To kill time:** I hate to admit this, but I don't usually keep my computer books anywhere near my computer. I keep them in the bathroom, because my bathroom has excellent light for reading and because I'm afraid that a television would fall in the bathtub and electrocute me. When I'm just killing time, I open my book to a random page and start reading.

Despite these two facts, this book *does* have structure. Basic concepts are grouped in the first few chapters, and more advanced material appears toward the end. Chapter 3 is entirely devoted to a step-by-step approach to getting started, just for those who like to get to know software that way.

In general, though, this book is intended to be a reference. If you keep reading from this page on, right to the end of the index, you'll have a pretty good idea of how to use SketchUp to make 3D models — but that isn't what I'm expecting you to do. I recommend that you start with Chapters 1 and 2, just to get your bearings. After that, you should use the Table of Contents or the index to find what you're looking for; then proceed from there.

To make it easier to understand how certain chapters are related, this book lumps them together into parts. Check out the following summaries to get an idea of what's in each one.

Part I: Getting Started with SketchUp

If you're completely new to SketchUp and 3D modeling, this is the most important part in this book. Start here, lest you get frustrated and decide to use these pages to line your rabbit coop. Chapter 1 talks about how SketchUp fits into the bigger 3D modeling picture. Chapter 2 lays out all — that's 100 percent — of the basic concepts you need to understand to do anything useful with SketchUp. Chapter 3 offers a basic end-to-end workflow for creating and sharing a model. You can skip it, but I think it's a nice way to ease into the program.

Part II: Modeling in SketchUp

SketchUp is a 3D modeling tool, so this part is, in Shakespeare's eternal words, "where it's at." Chapter 4 dives right into using SketchUp to make buildings, with an emphasis on drawing and extruding simple plans, modeling stairs, and constructing roofs. This isn't easy, mind you, but it's what a lot of people want to use SketchUp to do, so I put it right at the beginning.

Chapter 5 deals with tools you can use to manage big models, and Chapter 6 lays out advanced techniques for modeling things like cars, furniture, and other objects. In Chapter 7, I talk about using photographs in SketchUp. The second part of the chapter is all about Photo Match, maybe the best new feature since Follow Me came out in version 4.

Part III: Viewing Your Model in Different Ways

Making models in SketchUp is only half the fun. The chapters in this part present some of this software's truly unique presentation features. Chapter 8 dives into Styles, a brand-new feature in SketchUp 6. If you ever need to show your model to anyone, you should pay special attention to Chapter 9, which is all about using shadows. Also, don't skip the first part of Chapter 10 on using sections to create animations — it's easy and more rewarding than almost anything else you can do in SketchUp.

Part IV: Sharing What You've Made

These chapters are dedicated to getting your models out into the world. In Chapter 11, I talk about using SketchUp with Google Earth, which, if you haven't tried it, is reason in itself to have a fast Internet connection. Chapters 12 and 13 deal with printing and exporting images and movies from your model files. Chapter 14 is all about using SketchUp Pro to export files in a bunch of different formats so that you can transfer data to any number of other CAD, modeling, rendering, illustration, and animation applications. Chapter 15 is an introduction to LayOut. This whole-new program, which is also part of SketchUp Pro, is for creating 2D presentation documents that automatically link to your 3D models.

Part V: The Part of Tens

My favorite thing about books in the *For Dummies* series is the way they embrace people's love of lists. I *could* have spread the information contained in these ultra-short chapters throughout the entire book, but it's so much easier to read when it's all in one place, don't you think?

Chapter 16 is a list of ten things that you'll definitely struggle with when you're first using SketchUp; remember to check here before you do anything drastic. Chapter 17 lists great add-ons that'll make your SketchUping more enjoyable, and Chapter 18 is all about where to turn when the information you need isn't in this book.

Icons Used in This Book

This icon indicates a piece of information I think will probably save you time.

When you're working in SketchUp, you need to know a lot of things. I use the Remember icon to remind you of something I cover earlier in the book, just in case you might have forgotten (or skipped) it.

Everyone's a little bit of a nerd sometimes, and paragraphs that bear this icon indulge that nerdiness. You can skip them without fear of missing anything important, but reading them can give you something to annoy your SketchUp friends with later on.

When you see this icon, pay special attention. It occurs rarely, but when it does, something you do could harm your work.

This icon denotes a spot where you can find supporting material on this book's companion Web site, including videos, sample files, and links to helpful material, which you can find at www.dummies.com/go/SketchUpFD.

Part I

Getting Started with SketchUp

In this part . . .

This part of the book is dedicated to helping you get your bearings. It's not a step-by-step guide to starting a new file in SketchUp; instead, it provides a little bit of information about what SketchUp is, what you can use it to do, and how to get the most out of it.

Chapter 1 is a very general overview of Google SketchUp. I try not to bore you with too much background information, but here's where you can read about what the software is supposed to let you do, how it compares to other 3D modeling applications, and where everything is.

In Chapter 2, I jump right in; there are a few things about SketchUp you absolutely need to know when you're just getting started, and here's where I lay them out. I think this is the most important chapter in this book; read it, and you'll know more about SketchUp than millions of other folks who already use it every day.

The contents of Chapter 3 are included for the benefit of those readers who like to learn software by getting their hands dirty right away. The whole chapter is a workflow that takes you through the process of making a simple model, changing the way it looks, and creating an image of it that you can keep forever.

Chapter 1

Meeting Google SketchUp

*O*nce upon a time, software for building three-dimensional (3D) models of thing like buildings, cars, and other stuff was hard to use. I mean *really* hard — people went to school for years to learn it. And if that wasn't bad enough, 3D modeling software was expensive. It was so expensive that the only people who used it were professionals and software pirates (people who stole it, basically). Then along came SketchUp.

Operating under the assumption that lots of people might want — and need — to make 3D models, the folks who invented SketchUp decided to design a program that worked more intuitively. Instead of making you think about 3D models as complex mathematical constructs (the way computers think), they created an interface that lets you build models using elements you're already familiar with: lines and shapes.

So do you need to know how to draw to use SketchUp? In the latest version of the software, not really. Traditional drawing is about *translating* what you see onto a flat piece of paper: going from 3D to 2D, which is hard to do for most people. In SketchUp, you're always in 3D, so no translation is involved — you just *build,* and SketchUp takes care of stuff like perspective and shading for you.

This first chapter is about putting SketchUp in context: why Google offers it for free, how it compares to other 3D software, and what you can (and can't) use it to do. In the last part of the chapter, I give a quick tour of the program, just to let you know where things are.

Things You Ought to Know Right Away

Before I continue, here's some information you might need:

- ✓ **You get SketchUp by downloading it from the Internet.** Just type `http://sketchup.google.com` into your Web browser and read through the first page of the Google SketchUp Web site. Click the links to download the application to your computer, and then follow the installation instructions on the Web.

- ✓ **SketchUp works in Windows and Mac OS X.** Google SketchUp is available for both operating systems, and it looks (and works) about the same way on both.

- ✓ **A Pro version is available.** Google offers a Pro version of SketchUp (called Google SketchUp Pro) that you can buy if you need it. It includes a few terrific features that folks like architects, production designers, and other design professionals need for exchanging files with other software. SketchUp Pro also includes a whole new application for creating presentation documents with your SketchUp models. It's called LayOut, and it's the subject of Chapter 15. If you think you might need Pro, you can download a free trial version at `http://sketchup.google.com`.

Where SketchUp Fits in Google's World

A long time ago, somebody invented photography (hey — this isn't a history book), and all of a sudden there was a way to make pictures of things that didn't involve drawing, engraving, or painting. Nowadays, you can't throw a rock without hitting a photograph of something. *Everything* (it seems) can take pictures, including people's phones. Photography is the main way that visual information is communicated.

But what comes after photography? Google (and just about every science-fiction writer who ever lived) thinks it's 3D, and here's why: You live in 3D. The furniture you buy (or build) is 3D, and so is the route you take to work. Because so many of the decisions you need to make (buying a couch, finding your way) involve 3D information, wouldn't it be nice to be able to experience that information in 3D?

Software like SketchUp lets you see 3D information on a 2D screen, which is good, but affordable 3D printers and holography (yep, holograms) are just over the horizon. All that's left is to build a model of every single thing in the world — and guess who's going to do it?

You. By making SketchUp free for everyone, Google is leading the 3D charge. Rather than relying on a small number of 3D nerds to get around to modeling everything in the universe, Google made SketchUp available to anyone who wants to participate. After all, Google is about organizing the world's information — not creating it. By giving SketchUp away, the company has created a whole new kind of information to organize. Chapter 11 is all about SketchUp and Google Earth, as well as the Google 3D Warehouse, where the world's 3D information is being stored — at least for now.

Comparing SketchUp to Other 3D Modeling Programs

If you're reading this book, I presume you're at least interested in two things: building 3D models and using SketchUp to do so. The following sections tell you something about how SketchUp compares to other 3D modeling programs — how long it takes to figure out how to use it and what kind of models it produces.

Cruising up the shallow learning curve

When it comes to widely available 3D modeling software, it really doesn't get any easier than SketchUp. This software has been as successful as it has for one reason, and it has everything to do with how quickly people are able to get good enough at SketchUp to build something within a couple of hours of launching it for the first time. You have no thick manuals to read, no special geometric concepts to understand; modeling in SketchUp is about grabbing your mouse and jumping in.

So how long should it take you to discover how it works? It depends on your background and experience, but in general, you can expect to be able to make something recognizable in under four hours. That's not to say you'll be a whiz — it just means that SketchUp's learning curve is extremely shallow. You don't need to know much to get started, and you'll still be picking things up years from now. In fact, I've learned a couple of things just writing this book.

But is SketchUp *easy?* Lots of people say so, but I think it's all relative. SketchUp is without a doubt easi*er* than any other modeling program I've tried, but 3D modeling itself can be tricky. Some people catch on right away, and some folks take longer. But I can say this for sure: If you want to build 3D models, and you have an afternoon to spare, there's no better place to start than SketchUp.

Understanding the difference between paper and clay

Three-dimensional modeling software comes in two basic flavors: *solids* and *surfaces*. Figure 1-1 and the following points illustrate the difference:

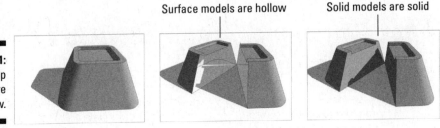

Surface models are hollow   Solid models are solid

Figure 1-1:
SketchUp
models are
hollow.

✔ **SketchUp is a "surfaces" modeler.** Everything in SketchUp is basically made up of thin (infinitely thin, actually) surfaces — these are called *faces*. Even things that look thick (like cinder-block walls) are actually hollow shells. Making models in SketchUp is a lot like building things out of paper — really, really thin paper.

Surface modelers like SketchUp are great for making models quickly, because all you really need to worry about is modeling what things *look* like. That's not to say that they're less capable; it's just that they're primarily intended for visualization.

✔ **Using a "solids" modeler is more like working with clay.** When you cut a solid model in half, you create new surfaces where you cut; that's because objects are, well, solid. Programs like SolidWorks, Form(Z, and Inventor create solid models.

People who make parts — like mechanical engineers and industrial designers — tend to work with solid models because they can use them to do some pretty precise calculations. Being able to calculate the volume of an object means that you can figure how much it will weigh, for example. Also, special machines can produce real-life prototypes directly from a solid-model file. These prototypes are handy for seeing how lots of little things are going to fit together.

An important point to reinforce here is that there's no "best" type of modeling software. It all depends on three things: how you like to work, what you're modeling, and what you plan to do with your model when it's done.

When I said (a few paragraphs ago) that 3D modeling programs come in two basic flavors, I sort of lied. The truth is, you can split them into two groups another way as well: by the kind of math they use to produce 3D models. You can find *polygonal* modelers (of which SketchUp is an example) and curves-based modelers. The former type uses straight lines and flat surfaces to define everything — even things that *look* curvy, aren't. The latter kind of modeler uses true curves to define lines and surfaces. These yield organic, flowing forms that are much more realistic than those produced by polygonal modelers, but that put a lot more strain on the computers that have to run them — and the people who have to figure out how to use them. Ultimately, it's a trade-off between simplicity and realism.

What You Should (and Shouldn't) Expect SketchUp to Do

Have you ever been to a hardware store and noticed the "multitool" gizmos on the racks next to the checkout stands? I once saw one that was a combination screwdriver, pliers, saw, tape measure, and (I swear) *hammer*. I sometimes wonder whether the hardware-store people put them there as a joke, just to make you feel better about standing in line.

I generally don't like tools that claim to be able to do everything. I much prefer *specialists* — tools that are designed for doing one thing *really* well. In the case of SketchUp, that one thing is building 3D models. Here's a list of things (all model-building-related) that you can do with SketchUp:

✔ **Start a model in lots of different ways:** With SketchUp, you can begin a model in whatever way makes sense for what you're building:

 • **From scratch:** When you first launch SketchUp, you see nothing except a little person standing in the middle of your screen. If you want, you can even delete him, leaving you a completely blank slate on which to model anything you want.

 • **In Google Earth:** Chapter 11 goes into this in detail. Basically, you can bring an aerial photograph of any place on Earth (including your home) into SketchUp and start modeling right on top of it.

 • **From a photograph:** The second part of Chapter 7 talks all about how you can use SketchUp to build a model based on a photo of the thing you want to build. It's not really a beginner-level feature, but it's there.

 • **With another computer file:** SketchUp can import images and CAD (computer-aided drawing) files so that you can use them as a starting point for what you want to make.

✔ **Work loose or work tight:** One of my favorite things about SketchUp is that you can model without worrying about exactly *how big* something is. You can make models that are super-sketchy, but if you want, you can also make models that are absolutely precise. SketchUp is just like paper in that way; the amount of detail you add is entirely up to you.

✔ **Build something real or make something up:** *What* you build with SketchUp really isn't the issue. You only work with lines and shapes — in SketchUp, they're called *edges* and *faces* — so how you arrange them is your business. SketchUp isn't intended for making buildings any more than it is for creating other things. It's just a tool for drawing in three dimensions.

✔ **Share your models:** After you've made something you want to show off, you can do a number of things, which you can discover in detail in Part IV:

- **Print:** Yep, you can print from SketchUp.

- **Export images:** If you want to generate an image file of a particular view, you can export one in any of several popular formats.

- **Export movies:** Animations are a great way to present three-dimensional information, and SketchUp can create them easily.

- **Upload to the 3D Warehouse:** This is a giant, online repository of SketchUp models that you can add to (and take from) all you want.

What *can't* SketchUp do? A few things, actually — but that's okay. SketchUp was designed from the outset to be the friendliest, fastest, and most useful modeler available — and that's it, really. Fantastic programs are available that do the things in the following list, and SketchUp can exchange files with most of them:

✔ **Photorealistic rendering:** Most 3D modelers have their own, built-in photo renderers, but creating model views that look like photographs is a pretty specialized undertaking. SketchUp has always focused on something called *nonphotorealistic rendering (NPR),* instead. NPR (as it's known) is essentially technology that makes things look hand-drawn — sort of the opposite of photorealism. If you want to make realistic views of your models, I talk about some renderers that work great with SketchUp in Chapter 17.

✔ **Animation:** A few paragraphs ago, I mentioned that SketchUp can export animations, but that's a different thing. The movies that you can make with SketchUp involve moving your "camera" around your model. True animation software lets you move the things *inside* your model around. SketchUp doesn't do that, but the Pro version lets you export to a number of different programs that do.

✔ **Building Information Modeling (BIM):** I'll try to keep this short. BIM software lets you make models that automatically keep track of things like quantities, and automatically generate standard drawing views (plans and sections) from your model. SketchUp lets you draw edges and faces, but it has no earthly idea what you're drawing — that's just not how it works. You can use SketchUp with all the major BIM packages out there (via special importers and exporters), but it won't do BIM stuff on its own.

Is it a toaster or a bungalow?

SketchUp models are made from two basic kinds of *geometry:* edges (which are straight lines) and faces (which are 2D surfaces bound by edges). That's it. When you use SketchUp to draw a bunch of edges and faces in the shape of a staircase, all SketchUp knows is how many edges and faces it has to keep track of, and where they all go. There's no such thing as a *stair* in SketchUp — just edges and faces.

Coming to this realization has the tendency to freak some people out. If you want a model of something, you have to make it out of edges and faces. SketchUp has some nice tools that let you create, delete, and otherwise arrange your geometry to make anything you want, but no Stair Tool is available to help you make stairs. Ditto for walls, windows, doors, or any of the other things that specialized architecture software programs offer. The thing to remember is that SketchUp was created to let you model *anything,* not just buildings, so its tools are designed to manipulate geometry. That's good news, believe it or not, because it means that you're not restricted in any way; you can model anything you can imagine.

Taking the Ten-Minute SketchUp Tour

The point of this portion of the chapter is to show you where everything is — kind of like the way a parent shows a new babysitter around the house before leaving for a couple of hours. It's not meant to explain what anything *does,* per se. I just want you to feel like you know where to start looking when you find yourself hunting around for something.

Just like most programs you already use, SketchUp has five main parts. Figure 1-2 shows all of them, in both the Windows and Mac versions of the program. I describe these parts, plus an additional feature, in the following list:

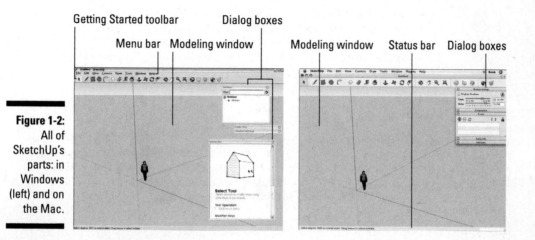

Figure 1-2: All of SketchUp's parts: in Windows (left) and on the Mac.

✔ **Modeling window:** See the big area in the middle of your computer screen? That's your modeling window, and it's where you spend 99 percent of your time in SketchUp. You build your model there; it's sort of a frame into a 3D world inside your computer. What you see in your modeling window is *always* a 3D view of your model, even if you happen to be looking at it from the top or side.

✔ **Menu bar:** For anyone who has used a computer in the last 30 years, the menu bar is nothing new. Each menu contains a long list of options, commands, tools, settings, and other goodies that pertain to just about everything you do in SketchUp.

✔ **Toolbars:** These contain buttons that you can click to activate tools and commands; they are faster than using the menu bar. SketchUp has a few different toolbars, but only one is visible when you launch it the first time: the Getting Started toolbar.

If your modeling window is too narrow to show all the tools on the Getting Started toolbar, you can click the arrow on the right to see the rest of them.

✔ **Dialog boxes:** Some programs call them palettes and some call them inspectors; SketchUp doesn't call them anything. Its documentation (the SketchUp Help document you can get to in the Help menu) refers to some of them as managers and some as dialog boxes, but I thought I'd keep things simple and just call them all the same thing: dialog boxes.

✔ **Status bar:** You can consider this your SketchUp dashboard, I suppose. It contains contextual information you use while you're modeling.

✔ **Context menus:** Right-clicking things in your modeling window usually causes a context menu of commands and options to open. These are always relevant to whatever you happen to right-click (and whatever you're doing at the time), so the contents of each context menu are different.

Although the following items aren't part of the SketchUp user interface (all the stuff I just listed in the previous list), they're a critical part of modeling in SketchUp:

✔ **A mouse with a scroll wheel:** You usually find a left button (the one you use all the time), a right button (the one that opens the context menus), and a center *scroll wheel* that you both roll back and forth and click down like a button. You should get one if you don't already have one — it'll improve your SketchUp experience more than any single other thing you could buy.

✔ **A keyboard:** This sounds silly, but some people have tried to use SketchUp without one; it's just not possible. So many of the things you need to do all the time (like make copies) involve your keyboard, so you'd better have one handy if you're planning to use SketchUp.

Hanging out at the menu bar

SketchUp's menus are a pretty straightforward affair; you won't find anything surprising like "Launch Rocket" in any of them, unfortunately. All the same, here's what they contain:

✔ **File:** Includes options for creating, opening, and saving SketchUp files. It's also where to go if you want to import or export a file, or make a printout of your model view.

✔ **Edit:** Has all the commands that affect the bits of your model that are selected.

✔ **View:** This one's a little tricky. You'd think it would contain all the options for flying around in 3D space, but it doesn't — that stuff's on the Camera menu. Instead, the View menu includes all the controls you use to affect the appearance of your model itself: what's visible, how faces look, and so on. View also contains settings for turning on and off certain elements of SketchUp's user interface.

✔ **Camera:** Contains controls for viewing your model from different angles. In SketchUp, your "camera" is your point of view, literally.

✔ **Draw:** Includes tools for drawing edges and faces in your modeling window.

✔ **Tools:** Most of SketchUp's tools are contained here, except of course for the ones you use for drawing.

✔ **Window:** If you're ever wondering where to find a dialog box you want to use, this is the place to look; they're all right here.

✔ **Plugins:** You can get extra tools for SketchUp — little programs that "plug in" to it and add functionality. Some of them show up here after they're installed. Chapter 17 has some information on these.

✔ **Help:** Chapter 18 is all about this menu, but here's the short version: Help contains some incredibly useful resources for understanding SketchUp as you go along. Pay particular attention to the video tutorials — they're great.

Where are all the tools?

The Getting Started toolbar contains a small subset of the tools that you can use in SketchUp. The thinking (which I agree with, incidentally) is that seeing all the tools right away tends to overwhelm new users, so having a limited selection helps people out.

To get access to more tools (through toolbars, anyway — you can always access everything through the menus), you do different things, depending on which operating system you're using:

✔ **Windows:** Choose View⇨Toolbars. The mother lode! I recommend starting off with the Large Tool Set to begin with, and then adding toolbars as you need them (and as you figure out what they do).

✔ **Mac:** Choose View⇨Tool Palettes⇨Large Tool Set. To add even more tools, right-click the Getting Started toolbar (the one right above your modeling window) and choose Customize Toolbar. Now drag whatever tools you want onto your toolbar, and click the Done button.

Checking the status bar

Even though the big part in the middle is the most obvious part, there's plenty more to the modeling window that you should know about:

✔ **Context-specific instructions:** Most of the time, you check here to see what options might be available for whatever you're doing. Modifier keys (keyboard strokes that you use in combination with certain tools to perform additional functions), step-by-step instructions, and general information about what you're doing all show up in one place: right here.

✔ **The Value Control Box (VCB):** The VCB is where numbers show up (to put it as simply as I can). Chapter 2 goes into more detail about it, but the basic purpose of the VCB is to allow you to be precise while you're modeling.

Taking a peek at the dialog boxes

Most graphics programs have a ton of little controller boxes that float around your screen, and SketchUp is no exception. After the dialog boxes are open, you can "dock" them together by moving them close to each other, but most people I know end up with them all over the place — me included. Dialog boxes in SketchUp contain controls for all kinds of things; here are some of the ones that I think deserve special attention:

✔ **Preferences:** While the Model Info dialog box (see the next point) contains settings for the SketchUp file you have open right now, the Preferences dialog box has controls for how SketchUp behaves *no matter what* file you have open. Pay particular attention to the Shortcuts panel, where you can set up keyboard shortcuts for any tool or command in the program.

On the Mac, the Preferences dialog box is on the SketchUp menu, which doesn't exist in the Windows version of SketchUp.

Some Preference settings changes don't take effect until you open another SketchUp file, so don't worry if you can't see a difference right away.

✔ **Model Info:** This dialog box is, to quote the bard, the mother of all dialog boxes. It has controls for everything under the sun; you should definitely open it and take your time going through it. Chances are, the next time you can't find the setting you're looking for, it's in Model Info.

✔ **Entity Info:** This little guy is small, but it shows information about *entities* — edges, faces, groups, components, and lots of other things — in your model. Keeping it open is a good idea, because it helps you see what you have selected.

✔ **Instructor:** The Instructor only does one thing: It shows you how to use whatever tool happens to be activated. While you're discovering SketchUp, you should keep the Instructor dialog box open off to the side. It's a pretty cool way to know about all the things the tool you're "holding" can do.

Chapter 2

Establishing the Modeling Mind-set

*W*hen you were learning how to drive a car, you probably didn't just get behind the wheel, step on the gas, and figure it out as you went along. (If you did, you probably have bigger things to worry about than getting started with SketchUp.) My point is, you should really know several things before you get started. This chapter is dedicated to introducing those things — concepts, really — that can make your first few hours with SketchUp a lot more productive and fun.

So here's the deal: I've divided this chapter into three main parts:

✔ The first part talks about edges and faces — the basic *stuff* that SketchUp models are made of.

✔ The second part deals with the way SketchUp lets you work in 3D (three dimensions) on a 2D (flat) surface — namely, your computer screen. Understanding how SketchUp represents depth is everything when it comes to making models. If you've never used 3D modeling software before, pay close attention to the middle part of this chapter.

✔ The final part of this chapter is all about the things you need to do all the time — things like navigating around your model, drawing lines, selecting objects, and working with accurate measurements.

It's All about Edges and Faces

In SketchUp, everything is made up of one of two kinds of things: edges and faces. They're the basic building blocks of every model you'll ever make.

Collectively, the edges and faces in your model are called *geometry*. When someone (including me) refers to geometry, we're talking about edges and faces. Other modeling programs have other kinds of geometry, but SketchUp is pretty simple. That's a good thing — there's less to keep track of.

The drawing on the left in Figure 2-1 is a basic cube drawn in SketchUp. It's composed of 12 edges and 6 faces. The model on the right is a lot more complex, but the geometry's the same: It's all just edges and faces.

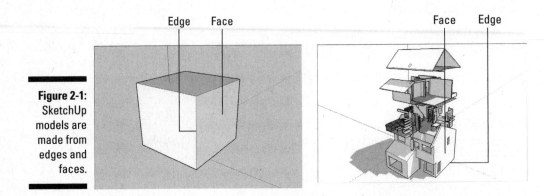

Figure 2-1: SketchUp models are made from edges and faces.

Edge   Face   Face   Edge

Living on (with, actually) the edge

Edges are lines. You can use lots of different tools to draw them, erase them, move them around, hide them, and even stretch them out. Here are some things you ought to know about SketchUp edges:

✔ **Edges are always straight.** Not only is everything in your SketchUp model made up of edges, but all those edges are also perfectly straight. Even arcs and circles are made of small straight-line segments, as shown in Figure 2-2.

✔ **Edges don't have a thickness.** This one's a little tricky to get your head around. You never have to worry about how thick the edges in your model are because that's just not how SketchUp works. Depending on how you choose to *display* your model, your edges may look like they have different thicknesses, but your edges themselves don't have a built-in thickness. You can read more about making your edges look thick in Chapter 8.

✔ **Just because you can't see the edges doesn't mean they're not there.** Edges can be hidden so that you can't see them; doing so is a popular way to make certain forms. Take a look at Figure 2-3. On the left is a model that looks rounded. On the right, I've made the hidden edges visible as dashed lines — see how even surfaces that look smoothly curved are made of straight edges?

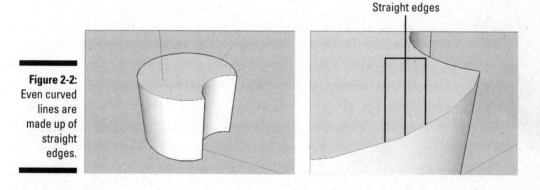

Straight edges

Figure 2-2:
Even curved
lines are
made up of
straight
edges.

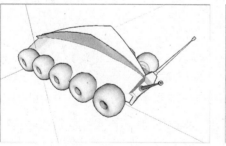

These edges are smoothed, but still there

Figure 2-3:
Even organic
shapes and
curvy forms
are made up
of straight
edges.

Facing the facts about faces

Faces are surfaces. If you think of SketchUp models as being made of toothpicks and paper (which they kind of are), faces are basically the paper. Here's what you need to know about them:

✔ **You can't have faces without edges.** To have a face, you need to have at least three *coplanar* (on the same plane) edges that form a loop. In other words, a face is defined by the edges that surround it, and those edges all have to be on the same, flat *plane*. Because you need at least three straight lines to make a closed shape, faces must have at least three sides. There's no limit to the number of sides a SketchUp face can have, though. Figure 2-4 shows what happens when you get rid of an edge that defines one or more faces.

✔ **Faces are always flat.** In SketchUp, even surfaces that look curved are made up of multiple, flat faces. In the model shown in Figure 2-5, you can see that what looks like an organically shaped surface (on the left) is really just lots of smaller faces (on the right). To make a bunch of flat faces look like one big, curvy surface, the edges between them are *smoothed;* you can find out more about smoothing edges in Chapter 6.

✔ **Just like edges, faces don't have any thickness.** If faces are a lot like pieces of paper, they're *infinitely thin* pieces of paper — they don't have any thickness. To make a thick surface (say, like a 6-inch-thick wall), you need to use two faces side by side.

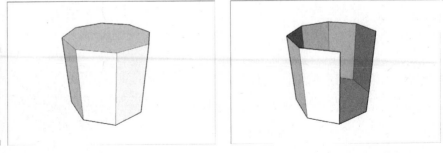

Figure 2-4:
You need a closed loop of edges to make a face.

Each of these triangles is perfectly flat

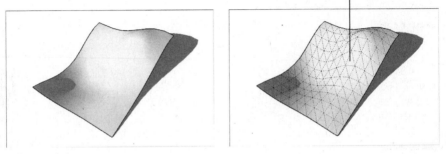

Figure 2-5:
All faces are flat, even the ones that make up larger, curvy surfaces.

Understanding the relationship between edges and faces

Now that you know that models are made from edges and faces, you're most of the way to understanding how SketchUp works. Here's some information that should fill in the gaps (and also check out additional resources on this book's companion Web site; see the Introduction for details about the site):

✔ **Every time SketchUp can make a face, it will.** There's no such thing as a "Face tool" in this software; SketchUp just automatically makes a face every time you finish drawing a closed shape out of three or more coplanar edges. Figure 2-6 shows this in action: As soon as I connect the last edge that I draw to the first one to close the "loop," SketchUp creates a face.

✔ **You can't stop SketchUp from creating faces, but you can erase them if you want.** If a face you don't want ends up getting created, just right-click it and choose Erase from the context menu. That face will be deleted, but the edges that defined it will remain. (See Figure 2-7.)

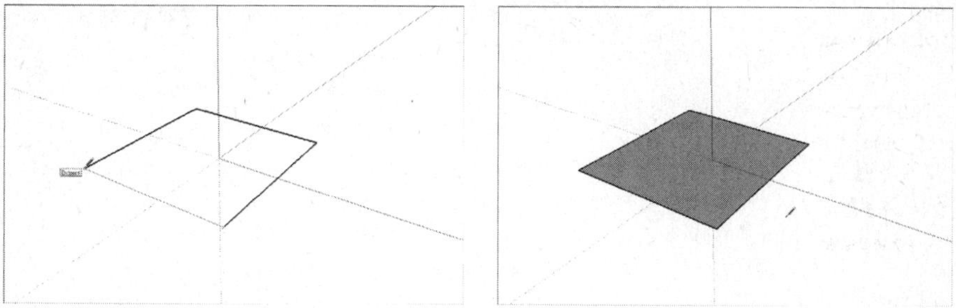

Figure 2-6:
SketchUp automatically makes a face whenever you create a closed loop of coplanar edges.

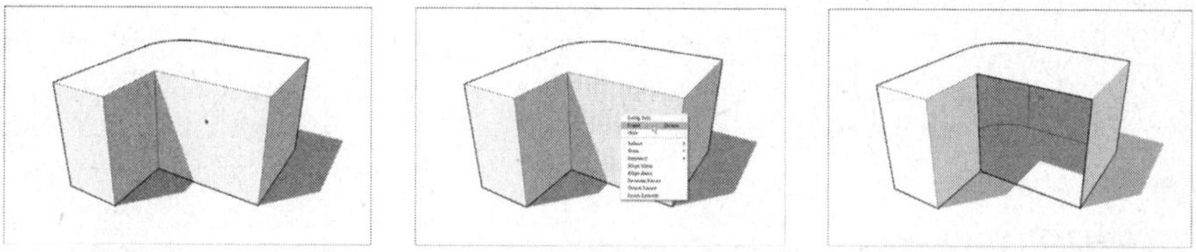

Figure 2-7:
You can delete a face without deleting the edges that define it.

✔ **If you delete one of the edges that defines a face, that face will be deleted, too.** When I erase one of the edges in the cube (with the Eraser tool, in this case), *both* of the faces that were defined by that edge disappear. This happens because it's impossible to have a face without also having all its edges.

✔ **Retracing an edge re-creates a missing face.** If you already have a closed loop of coplanar edges, but no face (because you erased it, perhaps), you can *redraw* one of the edges to make a new face. Just use the Line tool to trace over one of the edge segments, and a face will reappear. (See Figure 2-8.)

✔ **Drawing an edge all the way across a face splits the face in two.** When you draw an edge (like with the Line tool) from one side of a face to another, you cut that face in two. The same thing happens when you draw a closed loop of edges (like a rectangle) on a face — you end up with two faces, one "inside" the other. In Figure 2-9, I split a face in two with the Line tool, and then I extrude one of them out a little bit with the Push/Pull tool.

Drawing an edge from here...   ...to here...   ...causes this face to be created

Figure 2-8:
Just retrace
any edge on
a closed
loop to tell
SketchUp to
create a
new face.

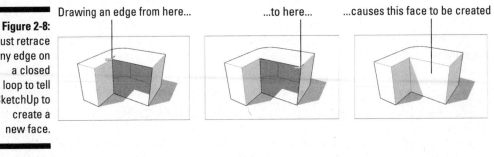

Figure 2-9:
Splitting a
face with
an edge,
and then
extruding
one of the
new faces.

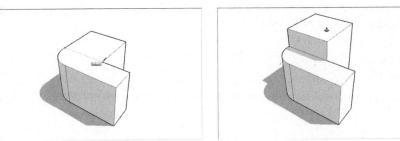

✔ **Drawing an edge that crosses another edge *doesn't* automatically split both edges.** In the left side of Figure 2-10, I draw an edge that crosses one of the edges that defines a face. Doing so doesn't split any of the edges, and more importantly, *it doesn't split the face.* If I want to make the edge I just drew into two edges, I need to retrace one of its segments with the Line tool (as shown in the middle image of Figure 2-10). When I do, I don't just end up with two edges instead of one; I also end up splitting the face (as you can see in the right side of Figure 2-10).

Figure 2-10:
Crossing
one edge
with another
doesn't cut
either one of
them. To split
an edge,
you have to
trace over
part of it with
the Line tool.

Drawing an edge from here...   ...to here splits the face

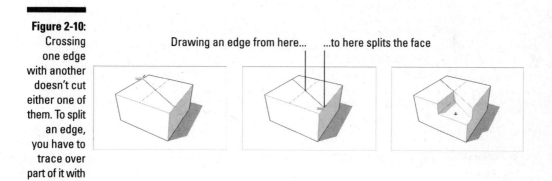

Drawing in 3D on a 2D Screen

For computer programmers, letting you draw three-dimensional objects on your screen is a difficult problem. You wouldn't think it would be such a big deal; after all, people have been drawing in perspective for a very long time. If some old guy could figure it out 500 years ago, why should it give your computer any problems?

The thing is, human perception of depth on paper is a trick of the eye. And of course, your computer doesn't have eyes that enable it to interpret depth without thinking about it. You need to give it explicit instructions. In SketchUp, this means using drawing axes and inferences, as I explain in the sections that follow.

Don't worry about drawing in perspective

Contrary to popular belief, modeling in SketchUp doesn't involve drawing in perspective and letting the software "figure out" what you mean. There are two reasons for which this turns out to be a very good thing:

✔ **Computers aren't very good at figuring out what you're trying to do.** This has probably happened to you: You're working away at your computer, and the software you're using tries to "help" by guessing what you're doing. Sometimes it works, but most of the time it doesn't, and eventually, it gets really annoying. Even if SketchUp were *able* to interpret your perspective drawings, you'd probably spend more time correcting its mistakes than actually building something.

✔ **Most people can't draw in perspective anyway.** I can see you nodding, because even if you're one of the few folks who *can*, you know darn well that most people couldn't draw an accurate 3D view of the inside of a room if their life depended on it — drawing just isn't one of the things we're taught, unfortunately. So even if SketchUp *did* work by turning your 2D perspective drawings into 3D models (which it most certainly doesn't), the vast majority of those who "can't draw" wouldn't be able to use it. And that would be a shame, because building 3D models is a real kick.

Giving instructions with the drawing axes

Color Plate 1 is a shot of the SketchUp modeling window, right after you create a new file. See the three colored lines that cross in the lower-left corner of the screen? These are the *drawing axes,* and they're the key to understanding how SketchUp works. Simply put, you use SketchUp's drawing axes to figure out where you are (and where you want to go) in 3D space. When you're working with the color axes, you need to keep two important things in mind:

✔ **When you draw, move, or copy something parallel to one of the colored axes, you're working in that "color's direction."** Take a look at Color Plate 2. In the first image, I'm drawing a line parallel to the *red* axis, so I would say I'm drawing "in the *red* direction." I'm sure that the line I'm drawing is parallel to the red axis because it turns red to let me know. In the second image, I'm moving a box parallel to the *blue* axis, so I'm "moving in the *blue* direction." I know I'm parallel to the blue axis because a dotted, blue line appears to tell me so.

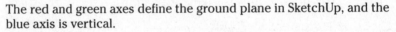

The red and green axes define the ground plane in SketchUp, and the blue axis is vertical.

✔ **The whole point of using the red, green, and blue axes is to let SketchUp know what you *mean*.** Remember that the big problem with modeling in 3D on a computer is the fact that you're working on a 2D screen. Consider the example shown in Color Plate 3: If I click the cylinder with the Move tool and move my cursor *up,* how is SketchUp supposed to know whether I mean to move it *up* in space (above the ground) or *back* in space? That's where the colored axes come into play: If I want to move it *up,* I go in the *blue* direction. If I want to move it *back,* I follow the *green* direction (because the green axis happens to run from the front to the back of my screen).

When you're working in SketchUp, you use the colored drawing axes *all the time.* They're not just handy; they're what makes SketchUp work. Having colored axes (instead of ones labeled *x, y,* and *z*) lets you draw in 3D space without having to type in commands to tell your computer where you want to draw. They make modeling in SketchUp quick, accurate, and relatively intuitive. All you have to do is make sure that you're working in your intended color direction as you model by lining up your objects with the axes and watching the screen tips that tell you what direction you're working in. After your first couple of hours with the software, paying attention to the colors becomes second nature — I promise.

Keeping an eye out for inferences

If you've spent any time fiddling with SketchUp, you've noticed all the little colored squares, dotted lines, yellow tags, and other doodads that show up as you move your cursor around your modeling window. All this stuff is referred to collectively as SketchUp's *inference engine,* and its sole purpose is to help you while you're building models. Luckily, it does. Without inferences (the aforementioned doodads), SketchUp wouldn't be very useful.

Point inferences

Generally, SketchUp's inferences help you be more precise. *Point* inferences (see Color Plate 2-4) appear when you move your cursor over specific parts of your model. They look like little colored squares, and if you pause for a second, they're accompanied by a yellow tag that says what they are. For example, watching for the little green Endpoint inference (which appears whenever your cursor is over one of the ends of an edge) helps you accurately connect an edge you're drawing to the end of another edge in your model. Here's a list of them (I don't give descriptions because I think they're pretty self-explanatory):

- ✔ Endpoint (green)
- ✔ Midpoint (cyan or light blue)
- ✔ Intersection (black)
- ✔ On Edge (red)
- ✔ Center (of a circle, green)
- ✔ On Face (dark blue)

In SketchUp, lines are called *edges,* and surfaces are called *faces.* Everything in your model is made up of edges and faces.

Linear inferences

As you've probably already noticed, color plays a big part in SketchUp's *user interface* (the way it looks). Maybe the best example of this is in the software's *linear* inferences — the "helper lines" that show up to help you work more precisely. Color Plate 5 is an illustration of all of them in action, and here's a description of what they do:

- ✔ **On Axis:** When an edge you're drawing is parallel to one of the colored drawing axes, the edge turns the color of that axis.

- ✔ **From Point:** This one's a little harder to describe. When you're moving your cursor, sometimes you'll see a colored, dotted line appear. This means that you're "lined up" with the point at the end of the dotted line. Naturally, the color of the From Point inference corresponds to whichever axis you're lined up "on." Sometimes From Point inferences show up on their own, and sometimes you have to *encourage* them; see the section "Encouraging inferences," later in this chapter, for details.

- ✔ **Perpendicular:** When you're drawing an edge that's perpendicular to another edge, the one you're drawing turns magenta (reddish purple).

- ✔ **Parallel:** When it's parallel to another edge in your model, the edge you're drawing turns magenta to let you know. You tell SketchUp which edge you're interested in "being parallel to" by *encouraging* an inference.

- ✔ **Tangent at Vertex:** This one only applies when you're drawing an arc (using the Arc tool) that starts at the endpoint of another arc. When the arc you're drawing is *tangent* to the other one, the one you're drawing turns cyan. Tangent, in this case, means that the transition between the two arcs is smooth.

One of the most important inferences in SketchUp is one that you probably didn't even realize was an inference. It's the fact that, unless you specifically start on an edge or a face in your model, you'll always be drawing on the ground plane by default. That's right — if you just start creating stuff in the middle of nowhere, SketchUp just assumes that you mean to be drawing on the ground.

Using inferences to help you model

A big part of using SketchUp's inference engine involves *locking* and *encouraging* inferences — sometimes even simultaneously. At first, it'll seem a little like that thing where you pat your head and rub your stomach at the same time, but with practice, it gets easier.

Locking inferences

If you hold down Shift when you see any of the first four types of linear inferences described previously, that inference gets *locked* — and stays locked until you release Shift. When you lock an inference, you constrain whatever tool you're using to only work in the direction of the inference you locked. Confused? Check out the following example for some clarity.

Color Plate 6 shows a situation where it would be useful to lock a blue On Axis inference while I'm using the Line tool. I want to draw a vertical line that's exactly as tall as the peak of the house's roof, so here's what I do:

1. **Click once to start drawing an edge.**

2. **Move my cursor up until I see the edge I'm drawing turn blue.**

   This is the blue On Axis inference that lets me know I'm exactly parallel to the blue drawing axis.

3. **Hold down Shift to lock the inference I see.**

   My edge gets thicker to let me know it's locked, and now I can only draw in the blue direction (no matter where I move my cursor).

4. **Click the peak of the roof to make my vertical edge end at exactly that height.**

5. **Release Shift to unlock the inference.**

Encouraging inferences

Sometimes, an inference you need doesn't show up on its own — when this happens, you have to *encourage* it. To encourage an inference, just hover your cursor over the part of your model you'd like to "infer" from, and then slowly go back to whatever you were doing when you decided you could use an inference. The following example demonstrates how to encourage an inference.

Color Plate 7 shows a model of a cylinder. I'd like to start drawing an edge that lines up perfectly with the center of the circle on top of the cylinder, but I don't want it to start at the center itself. Follow these steps:

1. **Hover (don't click) over the edge of the circle for about two seconds.**

2. **Move slowly toward the middle of the circle until the Center Point inference appears.**

3. **Hover (still don't click) over the center point for a couple of seconds.**

4. **Move your cursor slowly in the direction of where you want to start drawing your edge.**

   A dotted From Point inference should appear.

5. **Click to start drawing your edge.**

Warming Up Your SketchUp Muscles

I can think of seven activities you'll need to do every time you use SketchUp. Formal-education types would probably call them "core competencies," but I find language like that tends to put people to sleep. Whatever you care to call these activities, I'll introduce them all at the same time, in the following sections, so you can come back and get a quick refresher whenever you want.

Getting the best view of what you're doing

Using SketchUp without learning how to orbit, zoom, and pan is like trying to build a ship in a bottle. In the dark. With your hands tied behind your back. Using chopsticks. Get the picture?

Fully half of modeling in SketchUp uses the aforementioned navigation tools, which let you change your view so that you can see what you're doing. Most people who try to figure out SketchUp on their own take too long to understand this; they spend hours squinting, grunting, and having an all-around miserable time trying to "get at" what they're working on. The following sections help you avoid the headache (literally).

SketchUp has three tools that are dedicated to letting you get a better view of your model. I usually call them the Big Three, but I'm a little afraid of lawsuits from big companies in Detroit, so I'll just refer to them collectively as the navigation tools.

Going into orbit

Hold a glass of water in your hand. Now twist and turn your wrist around in every direction so that the water's all over you and the rest of the room. Stop when the glass is completely empty. I think that's a pretty memorable way to find out about the Orbit tool, don't you?

Just as your wrist helps you twist and turn a glass to see it from every angle, think of using Orbit as the way to "fly around" your work. Figure 2-11 shows Orbit in all its glory.

Here's some stuff you should know about using Orbit:

✔ **It's on the Camera menu.** By far the least productive way to use Orbit is to choose it from the Camera menu.

✔ **It's also on the toolbar.** The second-least productive way to activate Orbit is to click its button on the toolbar. It looks like two red arrows trying to form a ball.

✔ **You can orbit using your mouse.** Here's how you should *always* orbit: Click the scroll wheel of your mouse and hold it down. Now move your mouse around. See your model swiveling around? Release the scroll wheel when you're done. Using your mouse to orbit means that you don't have to switch tools every time you want a better view, which saves you *truckloads* of time.

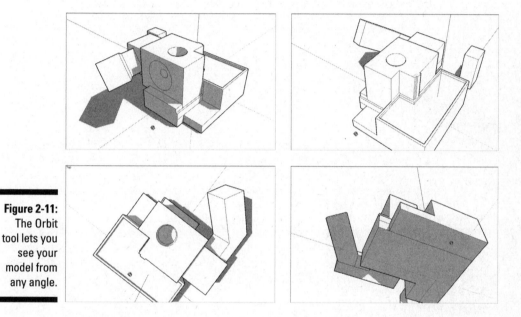

Figure 2-11: The Orbit tool lets you see your model from any angle.

Zooming in and out

Hold your empty glass at arm's length. Close your eyes, and then bring the glass rushing toward you, stopping right when it smashes you in the nose. Now throw the glass across the room, noticing how it shrinks as it gets farther away. That, in a nutshell, describes the Zoom tool.

You use Zoom to get closer to (and farther from) your model. If you're working on something small, you zoom in until it fills your modeling window. To see everything at once, zoom out. Figure 2-12 is a demonstration. I can think of a couple things to tell you about Zoom:

 ✔ **Just like Orbit, you can activate the Zoom tool in several ways.** The worst way is from the Camera menu; the next-worst way is to click the Zoom tool button in the toolbar. If you use Zoom either of these two ways, you actually zoom in and out by clicking and dragging up and down on your screen.

The best way to zoom is to roll your finger on the scroll wheel of your mouse to zoom in and out. Instead of clicking the scroll wheel to orbit, just roll your scroll wheel back and forth to zoom. And just like Orbit, using your mouse to zoom means that you don't have to switch tools — as soon as you stop zooming, you revert to whatever tool you were using before.

✔ **Use Zoom Extents to see everything.** Technically, Zoom Extents is a separate tool altogether, but I think it's related enough to mention here. If you want your model to fill your modeling window (which is especially useful when you "get lost" with the navigation tools — trust me, it happens to everyone), just choose Camera⇨Zoom Extents.

Zoomed in   Zoomed in even more

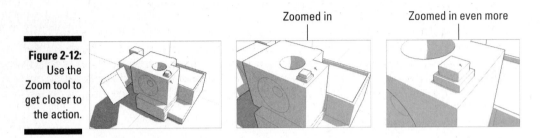

Figure 2-12:
Use the
Zoom tool to
get closer to
the action.

When you use the Zoom tool, SketchUp zooms in on your cursor; just position it over whatever part of your model you want to zoom in on (or zoom out from). If your cursor isn't over any of your model's geometry (faces and edges), the Zoom tool won't work very well — you'll end up zooming either really slowly or really quickly.

Just panning around

Using the Pan tool is a lot like washing windows — you move the paper towel back and forth, but it stays flat and it never gets any closer or farther away from you. The Pan tool is basically for sliding your model view around in your modeling window. To see something that's to the right, you use Pan to slide your model to the left. It's as simple as that. You should know these three things about Pan:

✔ **Pan is on the Camera menu.** But that's not where you should go to activate it.

✔ **Pan is also on the toolbar.** You *could* access the Pan tool by clicking its button on the toolbar (it looks like a severed hand), but there's a better way. . . .

✔ **Hold down your mouse's scroll wheel button and press Shift.** When you do both at the same time — basically, Orbit+Shift — your cursor temporarily turns into the Pan tool. When it does so, move your mouse to pan.

Drawing edges with ease

Being able to use the Line tool without having to think too much about it is *the* secret to being able to model anything you want in SketchUp. You use the Line tool to draw individual edges, and because SketchUp models are really just fancy collections of edges (carefully arranged, I'll admit), anything you can make in SketchUp, you can make with the Line tool.

SketchUp models are made up of edges and faces. Anytime you have three or more edges that are *connected* and *on the same plane,* SketchUp creates a face. If you erase one of the edges that "defines" a face (borders it), the face disappears, too. Take a look at the section "It's All about Edges and Faces," earlier in this chapter, for more information on the relationship between edges and faces.

Drawing edges is as simple. Just follow these steps:

1. **Select the Line tool (some people call it the Pencil tool).**

2. **Click where you want your line to begin.**

3. **Move your cursor to the desired endpoint for your line, and click again to end.**

   Figure 2-13 demonstrates the basic idea.

Figure 2-13:
Use the Line tool to draw edges.

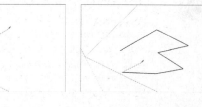

When you draw a line segment with the Line tool, notice how SketchUp automatically tries to draw another line? This is called *rubber banding* — the Line tool lets you "continue" to draw edge segments, automatically starting each new one at the end of the previous one you drew.

4. **When you want the Line tool to stop drawing lines, press Esc to "snip" the line at the last spot you clicked.**

Turning off "rubber-banding" lines

Depending on what you're making, and on how you work, you might want to turn the Line tool's rubber-banding behavior off. To do so, follow these steps:

1. **Choose Window⇨Preferences (SketchUp⇨ Preferences on the Mac).**

2. **Choose the Drawing panel from the list on the left in the Preferences dialog box.**

3. **Deselect the Continue Line Drawing check box.**

SketchUp lets you draw lines in two ways: You can either use the click-drag-release method or the click-move-click one. They both work, of course, but I highly recommend training yourself to do the latter. You'll have more control, and your hand won't get as tired. When you draw edges by clicking and *dragging* your mouse (click-drag-release), you're a lot more likely to "drop" your line accidentally. Because the Line tool only draws straight lines, think about using it less like a pencil (even though it looks like one) and more like a spool of sticky thread.

The Eraser tool is specifically designed for erasing edges; use it by clicking the edges you don't like to delete them. You can also *drag* over edges with the Eraser, but I think that's a little harder to get used to.

Injecting accuracy into your model

It's all well and fine to make a model, but most of the time, you need to make sure that it's accurate. Without a certain level of accuracy, it's not as useful for figuring things out. The key to accuracy in SketchUp is the little text box that lives in the lower-right corner of your SketchUp window — the one I point out in Figure 2-14. That little text box is called the Value Control Box, or VCB, and here are some of the things you can use it to do:

- Make a line a certain length
- Draw a rectangle a certain size
- Push/pull a face a certain distance
- Change the number of sides in a polygon
- Move something a given distance
- Rotate something by a certain number of degrees
- Make a certain number of copies
- Divide a line into a certain number of segments
- Change your field of view (how much you can see)

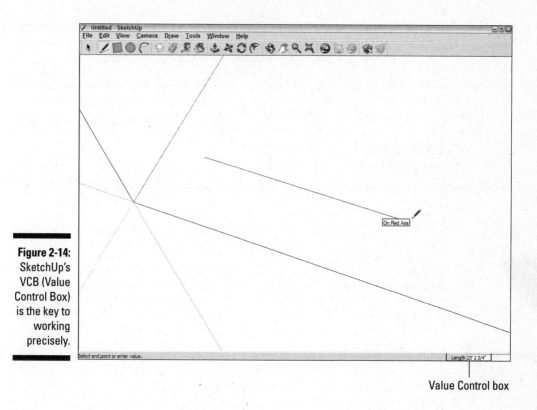

Figure 2-14:
SketchUp's
VCB (Value
Control Box)
is the key to
working
precisely.

Value Control box

Here are some things you should know about the VCB:

- **You don't have to click in the VCB to enter a number.** This one's a big one: When they're first starting out with SketchUp, people assume that they need to click in the VCB (to select it, presumably) before they can start typing. They (and you) don't — just start typing, and whatever you type shows up in the VCB automatically. When it comes to being precise, SketchUp is always "listening" for you to type something in this box.

- **The VCB is context-sensitive.** This means that what it controls depends on what you happen to be doing at the time. If you're drawing an edge with the Line tool, it knows that whatever you type is a length; if you're rotating something, it knows to listen for an angle.

- **You set the default units for the VCB in the Model Info dialog box.** Perhaps you want a line you're drawing to be 14 inches long. If you're set up to use inches as your default unit of measurement, just type **14** into the VCB and press Enter — SketchUp assumes that you mean 14 inches. If you want to draw something 14 *feet* long, you would type in **14'**, just to let SketchUp know that you mean feet instead of inches. You can override the default unit of measurement for the VCB by typing in any unit you want. If you want to move something a distance of 25 meters, type in **25m** and press Enter. You set the default units for the VCB in the Units panel of the Model Info dialog box (which is on the Window menu).

- **Sometimes, the VCB does more than one thing.** In certain circumstances, you can change the VCB's mode (what it's "listening for") by typing in a unit type after a number. For example, when you're drawing a circle, the default "value" in the VCB is the radius — if you type **6** and press Enter, you'll end up with a circle with a radius of 6 inches. But if you type in **6s**, you're telling SketchUp that you want 6 *sides* (and not inches), so you'll end up with a circle with 6 sides. If you type in **6** and press Enter, and then type in **6s** and press Enter again, SketchUp will draw a hexagon (a 6-sided circle) with a radius of 6 inches.

- **The VCB lets you change your mind.** As long as you don't do anything after you press Enter, you can always type a new value into the VCB and press Enter again; there's no limit to the number of times you can change your mind.

- **You can use the VCB *during* an operation.** In most cases, you can use the VCB to be precise *while* you're using a tool. Here's how that works:

  1. Click once to start your operation (such as drawing a line or using the Move tool).

  2. Move your mouse so that you're "going in the correct color direction." If you're using the Line tool and you want to draw parallel to the green axis, make sure that the edge you're drawing is green. Be sure not to click again.

  3. Without clicking the VCB, just type in the dimension you want; you should see it appear in the VCB.

  4. Press Enter to complete the operation.

- **You can also use the VCB *after* an operation.** Doing this revises what you've just done. These steps should give you an idea of what I'm talking about:

  1. Complete your operation. This might be drawing a line, moving something, rotating something, or any of the other things I mentioned at the beginning of this section.

  2. Before you do anything else, type in whatever dimension you *intended*, and then press Enter. Whatever you did should be redone according to what you typed in.

ON THE WEB

Resizing everything with the Tape Measure tool

Consider that you've been working away in SketchUp, not paying particular attention to how big anything in your model is, when you suddenly decide that you need what you've made to be a specific size. SketchUp has a terrific trick for taking care of this exact situation:

You can use the Tape Measure tool to resize your whole model based on a single measurement.

Here's how it works: In the following figure, I've started to model a simple staircase, and now I want to make sure that it's the right size; doing so will make it easier to keep working on it. I know I want the riser height (the vertical distance between the steps) to be 7 inches, so this is what I do:

1. **Select the Tape Measure tool (choose Tools⇨Tape Measure).**

2. **Make sure that the Tape Measure is in Measure mode by pressing Ctrl (Option on the Mac) until you don't see a plus sign (+) next to the Tape Measure cursor.**

3. **To measure the distance I want to change (in this case, the riser height), I click once to start measuring and click again to stop.**

4. **I type in the dimension I *want* what I just measured to be: 7 (for 7 inches).**

5. **In the dialog box that appears, asking me whether I want to resize my whole model, I click the Yes button.**

When I click the Yes button, my whole model is resized proportionately to the dimension I entered.

Measure from here...   ...to here

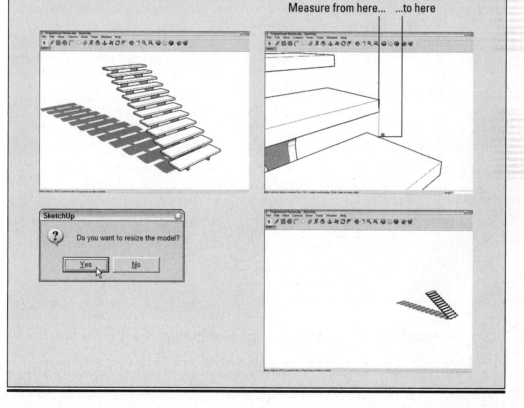

To give you a more concrete example, say I want to move my box (shown in Figure 2-15) a total of 10 meters in the red direction (parallel to the red axis). Here's what I'd do:

1. Using the Move tool, I click the box once to "pick it up."

2. I move my mouse until I see the linear inference that tells me I'm moving in the red direction.

3. I type in **10m**, and then I press Enter. My box is positioned exactly 10 meters from where I picked it up.

4. On second thought, I don't think I'm happy with the 10 meters, so I decide to change it. I type in **15m**, and then press Enter again; the box moves another 5 meters in the red direction. I can keep doing this until I'm happy (or bored).

Click to pick up the box

Move along the red axis

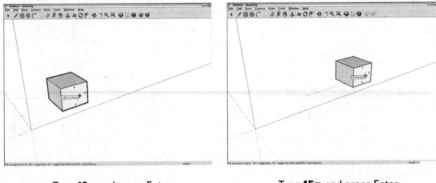

Type **10m** and press Enter

Type **15m** and press Enter

Figure 2-15: I move the box 10 meters, and then I change my mind and move it 15 meters instead.

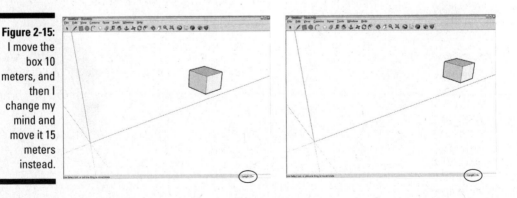

Selecting what you mean to select

If you want to move something in your model, or rotate it, or copy it, or do any number of other things to it, you need to select it first. When you select elements, you're telling SketchUp that *this* is the stuff you want to work with. To select things, you use (drum roll, please) the Select tool, which looks exactly the same as the Select tool in every other graphics program on the planet — it's an arrow. That's a good thing, because selecting isn't the sort of thing you should have to relearn every time you pick up a new program. Here's everything you need to know about selecting things in SketchUp:

✔ **Just click anything in your model to select it (while you're using the Select tool, of course).**

✔ **To select more than one thing, hold down Shift while you click all the things you want to select. (See Figure 2-16.)**

Shift works both ways when it comes to the Select tool. You can use it to *add* to your set of selected objects (which I mention above), but you can also use it to *subtract* an object from your selection. In other words, if you have a bunch of stuff selected, and you want to deselect something in particular, just hold down Shift while you click it — it won't be selected anymore.

✔ **Selected objects in SketchUp look different depending on what kind of objects they are:**

• Selected edges and guides turn blue.

• Selected faces look covered in tiny blue dots.

• Selected groups and components (which you can read about in Chapter 5) get a blue box around them.

• Selected section planes (see Chapter 10 for more info on these) turn blue.

Figure 2-16:
Click things with the Select tool to select them. Hold down Shift to select more than one thing.

Click to select a face

Shift + click to add another face to your selection

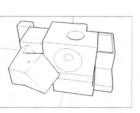 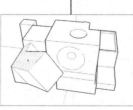 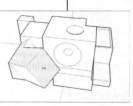

TIP

✔ **A much fancier way to select things in your model is to double- and triple-click them.** When you double-click a face, you select that face and all the edges that define it. Double-clicking an edge gives you that edge plus all the faces that are connected to it. When you *triple*-click an edge or a face, you select the whole object that it's a part of. Figure 2-17 shows what I mean.

✔ **You can also select several things at once by dragging a box around them.** You have two kinds of selection boxes; which one you use depends on what you're trying to select (see Figure 2-18):

• *Window selection:* If you click and drag from *left to right* to make a selection box, you create a window selection. In this case, only things that are *entirely* inside your selection box are selected.

• *Crossing selection:* If you click and drag from *right to left* to make a selection box, you create a crossing selection. With one of these, anything your selection box touches (including what's inside) ends up getting selected.

Figure 2-17:
Try single-, double-, and triple-clicking edges and faces in your model to make different kinds of selections.

Single click selects a face

Double-click selects the face and edges

Triple-click selects the whole object

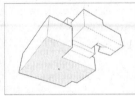 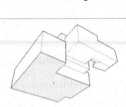 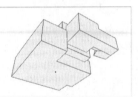

TECHNICAL STUFF

I keep saying that selected stuff turns blue in SketchUp, but you can make it turn any color you want. Blue is just the default color for new documents you create. The "selected things" color is one of the settings you can adjust in the Styles dialog box; if you're interested, you can read all about styles in Chapter 9.

WARNING!

Just because you can't see something doesn't mean it isn't selected. Whenever you make a selection, it's a very good idea to orbit around to make sure you've got only what you intended to get. Accidentally selecting too much is an easy mistake to make.

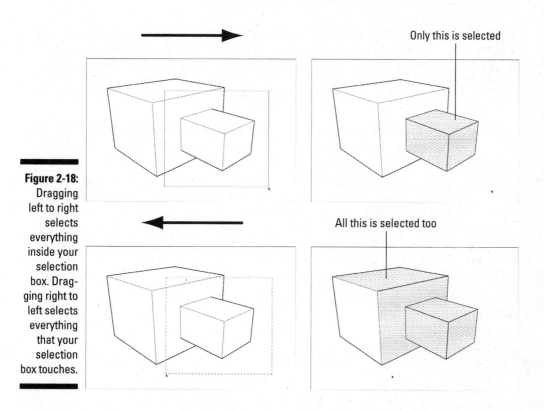

Only this is selected

All this is selected too

Figure 2-18: Dragging left to right selects everything inside your selection box. Dragging right to left selects everything that your selection box touches.

Moving and copying like a champ

To move things around in SketchUp, you use the Move tool. To make a copy of something, you use the Move tool in combination with a button on your keyboard: Ctrl in Windows and Option on a Mac. It's really that simple.

Moving things around

The Move tool is the one that looks like crossed red arrows. Using it involves clicking the entity you want to move, moving it to where you want it to be, and clicking again to drop it. It's not a complicated maneuver, but getting the hang of it takes a little bit of time. Here are some tips for using Move successfully:

✔ **Click, move, and click. Don't drag your mouse.** Just like using the Line tool, try to avoid the temptation to use the Move tool by clicking and dragging around with your mouse; doing so makes things a lot harder. Instead, practice clicking once to pick things up, moving your mouse without any buttons held down, and clicking again to put down whatever you're moving.

✔ **Click a point that will let you position it *exactly* where you want when you drop it (instead of just clicking anywhere on the thing you're trying to move to pick it up).** Figure 2-19 shows two boxes that I want precisely to stack on top of each other. If I just click anywhere on the first box and move it over the other one, I can't place it where I want; SketchUp just doesn't work that way.

To stack the boxes precisely, I have to click the *bottom corner* of the soon-to-be top box to grab it there, and then move my cursor over the *top corner* of the bottom box to drop it. Now my boxes are lined up perfectly.

✔ **Press Esc to cancel a move operation.** Here's something beginners do all the time: They start to move something (or start moving something accidentally), and then they change their minds. Instead of pressing Esc, they try to use Move to put things back the way they were. Inevitably, they don't, and things end up getting messed up.

If you change your mind in the middle of moving something, just press Esc; everything will go back to the way it was.

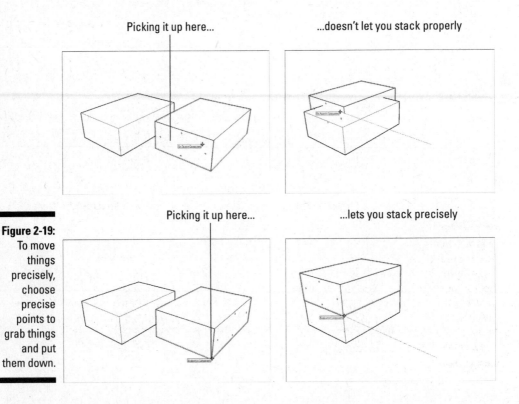

Picking it up here...   ...doesn't let you stack properly

Picking it up here...   ...lets you stack precisely

Figure 2-19: To move things precisely, choose precise points to grab things and put them down.

✔ **Don't forget about inferences.** To move something in one of the colored directions, just wait until you see the dotted On Axis linear inference appear; then hold down Shift to lock yourself in that direction. For more information about using SketchUp's inference engine, check out the section "Keeping an eye out for inferences," earlier in this chapter.

✔ **Don't forget about the VCB.** You can move things precise distances using the Value Control Box; have a look at the section "Injecting accuracy into your model," earlier in this chapter, to find out how.

Modeling with the Move tool

In SketchUp, the Move tool is very important for modeling; it's not just for moving whole objects around. You can also use it to move just about anything, including *vertices* (edges' endpoints), edges, faces, and combinations of any of these. By only moving certain *entities* (all the things I just mentioned), you can change the shape of your geometry pretty drastically. Figure 2-20 shows what I mean.

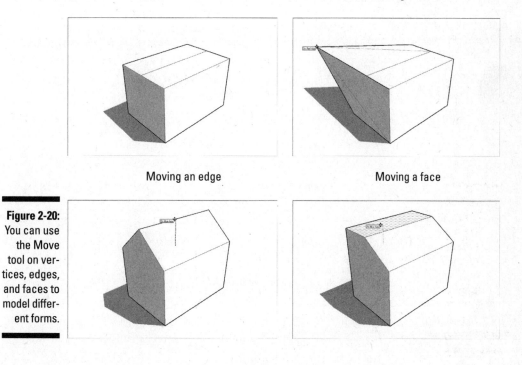

Moving a vertex

Moving an edge   Moving a face

Figure 2-20: You can use the Move tool on vertices, edges, and faces to model different forms.

Telling SketchUp who's boss with Auto-Fold

This will happen to you sooner or later: You'll be trying to move a vertex, an edge, or a face, and you won't be able to go in the direction you want. SketchUp doesn't like to let you create *folds* (when extra faces and edges are created in place of a single face) with the Move tool, so it constrains your movement to directions that won't end up adding them. If SketchUp won't let you move whatever you're trying to move, *force it* by doing one very important thing: Press and hold down Alt (⌘ on a Mac) while you're moving. When you do this, you're telling SketchUp that it's okay to proceed — to create folds if it has to. This is called Auto-Fold, and the following figure shows how it works.

Click once with the Move tool
to start moving

Hold down Alt (⌘ on a Mac)
and move your mouse

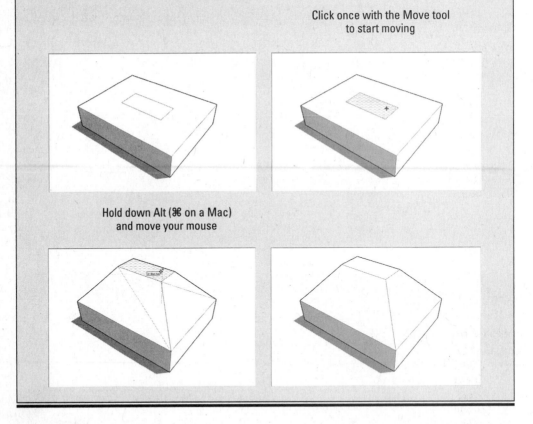

Using the Move tool to create forms (instead of just moving them around) is an incredibly powerful way to work, but isn't particularly intuitive. After all, nothing in the physical world behaves like the Move tool — you can't just grab the edge of a hardwood floor and move it up to turn it into a ramp in real life. In SketchUp, you can — and should.

To preselect or not to preselect

The Move tool works in two different ways; you'll eventually need to use both of them, depending on what you're trying to move:

- ✔ **Moving a selection:** When you have a selection of one or more entities, the Move tool only moves the things you've selected. This comes in handy every time you need to move more than one object; Figure 2-21 shows a selection being moved with the Move tool.

- ✔ **Moving without a selection:** If you don't have anything selected, you can click anything in your model with the Move tool to move it around. Only the thing you click is moved. Figure 2-22 shows what I'm talking about.

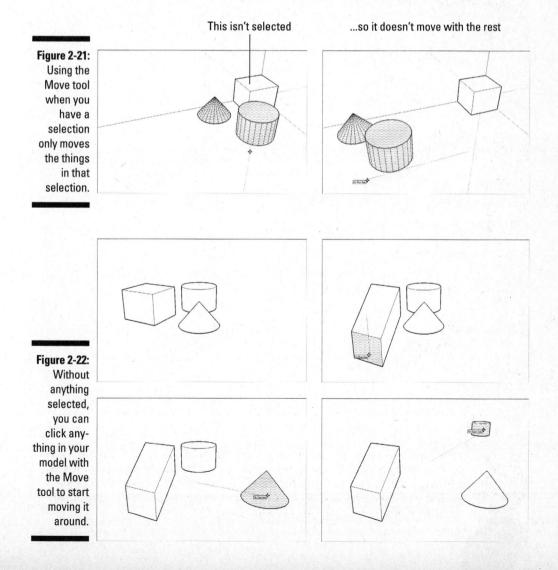

This isn't selected   ...so it doesn't move with the rest

Figure 2-21: Using the Move tool when you have a selection only moves the things in that selection.

Figure 2-22: Without anything selected, you can click any-thing in your model with the Move tool to start moving it around.

Making copies with the Move tool

Lots of folks spend time hunting around in SketchUp, trying to figure out how to make copies. It's very simple: You just press a *modifier key* (a button on your keyboard that tells SketchUp to do something different) while you're using the Move tool. Instead of moving something, you move a copy of it. Here are a couple of things to keep in mind:

- ✔ **Press Ctrl to copy in Windows, and press Option to copy on a Mac.** This tells SketchUp to switch from Move to Copy while you're moving something with the Move tool. Your cursor will get a little "+" next to it, and you'll see your copy moving when you move your mouse. Figure 2-23 shows this in action.

   If you decide you don't want to make a copy, just press Ctrl (Option) again to toggle back to Move; the "+" sign will disappear.

- ✔ **Copying is just like moving, except you're moving a copy.** This means that all the same rules that apply to using the Move tool apply to making copies, too.

- ✔ **You can make more than one copy at a time.** Perhaps I wanted to make five, equally spaced copies of a column, as shown in Figure 2-24. All I have to do is move a copy to where I want my last column to be; then I type in **5/** and press Enter. This makes five copies of my column and spaces them evenly *between* the first and last column in the row. Neat, huh?

   If I know how far apart I want my copies to be, I can move a copy that distance, type in **5x**, and press Enter. My five copies appear equally spaced in a *row*. (See Figure 2-25.)

Figure 2-23:
Press Ctrl (Option on a Mac) to tell SketchUp to make a copy while you're moving something.

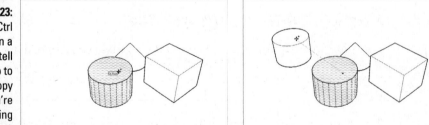

Figure 2-24:
Make evenly spaced copies by typing in the number of copies you want followed by a slash (/), and press Enter.

Move a copy

Typing **5/** yields 5 copies between

Figure 2-25:
To make multiple copies in a row, type in the number of copies you want, type an *x* and press Enter.

Move a copy

Typing **5x** creates 5 copies going away

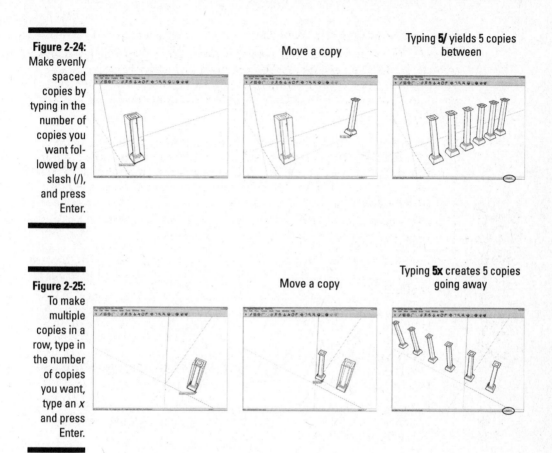

Making and using guides

Sometimes you need to draw temporary lines while you're modeling. These temporary lines, called *guides,* are useful for lining things up, making things the right size, and generally adding precision and accuracy to what you're building.

In previous versions of SketchUp, guides were called construction geometry, because that's basically what they are: a special kind of entity that you create when and where you need them. They aren't part of your model, because they're not edges or faces. This means that you can choose to hide them or delete them — they don't affect the rest of your geometry.

Figure 2-26 shows an example of guides in action. I use guides positioned 12 inches from the wall and 36 inches apart to draw the sides of a doorway. I use another guide 6 feet, 8 inches from the floor to indicate the top, and then I draw a rectangle, bounded by my guides, which I know is exactly the right size. When I'm done, I erase my guides with the Eraser tool, as I explain in a moment.

Creating guides with the Tape Measure tool

You can create three different kinds of guides, and you use the Tape Measure tool to make all of them. (See Figure 2-27.)

- **Parallel guide lines:** Clicking anywhere (except the endpoints or midpoint) along an edge with the Tape Measure tells SketchUp that you want to create a guide parallel to that edge. (See Figure 2-26.) Just move your mouse and you'll see a parallel, dashed line; click again to place it wherever you want.

- **Linear guide lines:** To create a guide along an edge in your model, click one of the endpoints or the midpoint once, and then click again somewhere else along the edge.

- **Guide points:** You might want to place a point somewhere in space; you can do exactly that with guide points. With the Tape Measure tool, click an edge's midpoint or endpoint, and then click again somewhere else in space. A little *x* appears at the end of a dashed line — that's your new guide point.

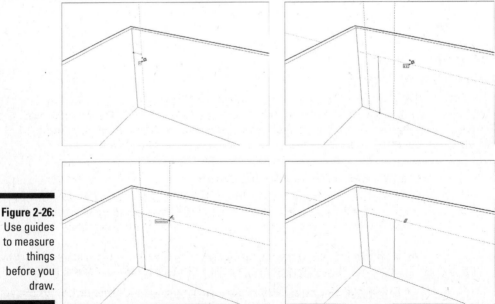

Figure 2-26:
Use guides to measure things before you draw.

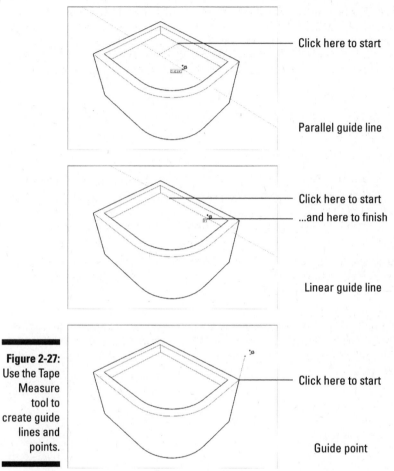

Click here to start

Parallel guide line

Click here to start
...and here to finish

Linear guide line

Figure 2-27:
Use the Tape
Measure
tool to
create guide
lines and
points.

Click here to start

Guide point

Here's an important point about the Tape Measure tool: It has two modes, and it only creates guides in one of them. Pressing Ctrl (Option on a Mac) toggles between the modes. When you see a + next to your cursor, your Tape Measure can make guides; when there's no +, it can't.

Using guides to make your life easier

As you're working along in this software, you'll find yourself using guides all the time; they're an indispensable part of the way modeling in SketchUp works. Here are some things you should know about using them:

✔ **Position guides precisely using the VCB.** Check out the section "Injecting accuracy into your model," earlier in this chapter, to find out how.

✔ **Erase guides one at a time.** Just click or drag over them with the Eraser tool to delete guides individually. You can also right-click them and choose Erase from the context menu.

✔ **Erase all your guides at once.** Choosing Edit➪Delete Guides does just that.

✔ **Hide guides individually or all at once.** Right-click a single guide and choose Hide to hide it, or deselect View➪Guides to hide all of them. It's a good idea to hide your guides instead of erasing them, especially while you're still modeling.

✔ **Select, move, copy, and rotate guides just like any other entity in your model.** Guides aren't edges, but you can treat them that way a lot of the time.

Painting your faces with color and texture

When it comes to adding colors and textures — collectively referred to in SketchUp as *materials* — to your model, there's really only one place you need to look, and one tool you need to use — the Materials dialog box and the Paint Bucket tool, respectively.

The Materials dialog box

To open the Materials dialog box (or Colors dialog box on the Mac), choose Window➪Materials. Figure 2-28 shows what you see when you do. The Materials dialog box is radically different in the Windows and Mac versions of SketchUp, but that's okay — they basically do the same thing.

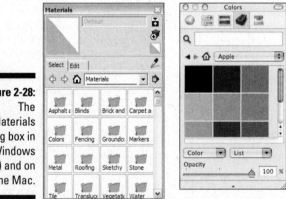

Figure 2-28: The Materials dialog box in Windows (left) and on the Mac.

In SketchUp, you can choose from two different kinds of materials to apply to the faces in your model:

✔ **Colors:** These are simple — colors are always solid colors. You can't have gradients (where one color fades into another), but you can pretty much make any color you want.

✔ **Textures:** Basically, a SketchUp texture is a tiny image — a photograph, really — that gets tiled over and over to cover the face you apply it to. If you paint a face with, say, a brick texture, what you're really doing is telling SketchUp to cover the surface with however many "brick photo" tiles it takes to do the job. The preview image you see in the Materials dialog box is actually a picture of a single texture image tile.

SketchUp comes with a whole bunch of textures, but you can get even more from the Google SketchUp Web site (`http://sketchup.google.com/bonuspacks.html`). If that's still not enough, you can go online and choose from thousands more available for sale. And if that's *still* not enough, you can make your own, though the process of doing so is well beyond the scope of this humble tome.

On the Mac, you have to click the little brick icon in the Materials dialog box to see the textures libraries that ship with SketchUp; it's the drop-down list next to the little house icon.

Here's some more interesting information about SketchUp materials:

✔ **Materials can be translucent.** Sliding the Opacity slider makes the material you've selected more or less translucent, which makes seeing through windows in your model a lot easier.

✔ **Textures can have transparent areas.** If you take a look at the materials in the Fencing library, you'll notice that a lot of them look kind of strange; they have areas of black that don't seem right. These black areas are areas of transparency — when you paint a face with one of these textures, you'll be able to see through the areas that look black.

✔ **You can edit materials, and even make your own.** I'd consider this to be a pretty advanced use of SketchUp, so I'm not going to talk about it in this book, but I thought you should at least know it's possible.

The Paint Bucket tool

The Paint Bucket tool looks just like — you guessed it — a bucket of paint. Activating it automatically opens the Materials dialog box, which is handy. Here's everything you need to know about the Paint Bucket:

✔ **You "fill it" by clicking in the Materials dialog box.** Just click a material to load your bucket, and then click the face you want to paint. It's as simple as that.

✔ **Holding down Alt (⌘ on a Mac) switches to the Sample tool.** With the Sample tool, you can click any face in your model to load your Paint Bucket with that face's material. Release the Alt key to revert to the Paint Bucket tool.

✔ **Holding down Shift paints all similar faces.** If you hold down Shift when you click to paint a face, all faces in your model that match the one you click will be painted, too. If things don't turn out the way you want, just choose Undo from the Edit menu to go back a step.

Chapter 3

Getting Off to a Running Start

· ·

In This Chapter

▶ Building a simple model

▶ Changing the way the model looks

▶ Exporting a JPEG file that you can e-mail

· ·

*I*f you can't wait to get your hands dirty (so to speak), you've come to the right chapter. Here, I help you make a simple model step by step, spin it around, paint it, and even apply styles and shadows. You don't need to read another word of this book to be able to follow along, although I do refer you to chapters where you can find out more. Above all, these pages are about *doing* and about the basics of putting together the various SketchUp features to produce a knockout model in no time.

So what are you going to build? Perhaps a doghouse. The nice thing about doghouses is that they're a lot like peoplehouses in the ways that count: They have doors and roofs, and just about everybody has seen one.

One last thing: Just about every other piece of this book is written so that you can jump around to the bits you need; you don't have to follow a particular order. I'm afraid this chapter is the exception to that rule. If you want to follow along, you should start on this page and work your way to the end. Otherwise, things just won't make sense.

Setting Things Up

I know — setup is boring. Who wants to flip through menus and options dialog boxes instead of jumping in? I completely agree, so I'll keep this short and sweet. This section is just about making sure that you're starting at the right place. That's it.

Follow these steps to get ready:

1. Launch Google SketchUp.

2. Choose your default settings.

If you've never launched SketchUp on your computer before, you'll see the Choose Default Settings dialog box. (See Figure 3-1.) Here's what to do if it pops up:

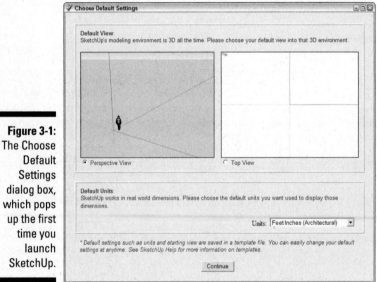

Figure 3-1:
The Choose
Default
Settings
dialog box,
which pops
up the first
time you
launch
SketchUp.

a. Choose Perspective View (on the left).

b. Choose your preferred measurement system from the Units drop-down menu.

c. Click the Continue button to close the dialog box.

If the Choose Default Settings dialog box doesn't appear, you (or someone else) have already chosen these settings. Don't worry — just follow these steps to set things straight:

a. Choose Window➪Preferences (SketchUp➪Preferences on a Mac).

b. On the left side of the System Preferences dialog box, choose Template to show the Template panel.

c. Choose one of the 3D templates from the drop-down list (see Figure 3-2).

d. If you're on a Windows machine, close the System Preferences dialog box by clicking OK. On a Mac, click the red button in the upper-left corner of the dialog box.

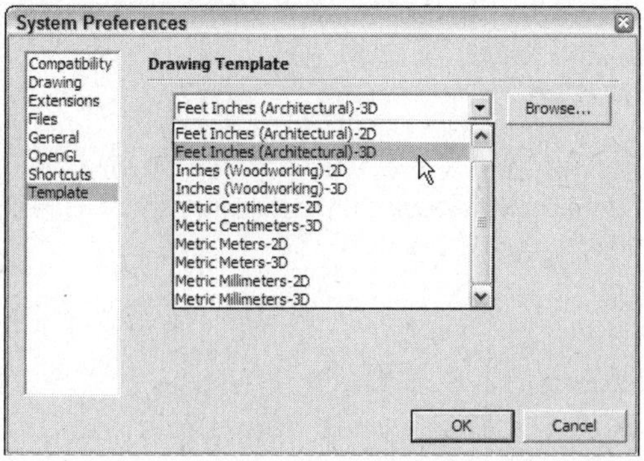

Figure 3-2:
Choose one
of the 3D
templates
from the list
in the
System
Preferences
dialog box.

    e. Open a new file by choosing File➪New.

3. Close the Learning Center dialog box (which may have opened auto-matically when you launched SketchUp) for now. If the Learning Center isn't there in the first place, skip to Step 4.

As long as the Show Tips at Startup check box has never been deselected (by you or someone else), the Learning Center dialog box will open every time you launch SketchUp. That's a good thing; don't deselect it just yet. Just close the Learning Center for now by clicking the little *X* in its upper-right corner. If you're on a Mac, click the red circle in the upper-*left* corner.

4. Make sure that you can see the Getting Started toolbar.

Figure 3-3 shows the Getting Started toolbar. If it's not visible in your modeling window, choose View➪Toolbars➪Getting Started to make it show up. If you're on a Mac, choose View➪Show Toolbar.

Figure 3-3:
The Getting
Started
toolbar lives
at the top of
your model-
ing window.

5. Clear your modeling window.

If this isn't the first time SketchUp has been run on your computer, you might see dialog boxes all over the place. If that's the case, just open the Window menu and make sure that everything is deselected to get rid of them.

Making a Quick Model

Figure 3-4 shows what your computer screen should look like at this point. You should see a row of tools across the top of your modeling window, a little man, and three colored *modeling axes* (red, green, and blue lines).

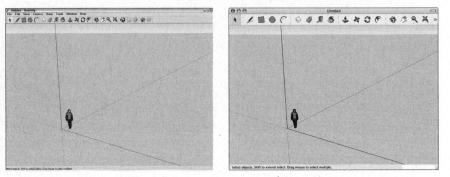

Figure 3-4:
This is what your screen should look like in Windows (left) and on a Mac (right).

Follow these steps to build a doghouse (and check this book's companion Web site for additional help; the Introduction has details about the Web site):

1. **Delete the little man on your screen.**

   Using the Select tool (the arrow on the far left of your toolbar), click the little man to select him (his name is Bryce, in case that matters to you), and then choose Edit➪Delete.

2. **Choose Camera➪Standard➪Iso.**

   This switches you to an *isometric* (3D) view of your model, which allows you to build something without having to "move around."

3. **Draw a rectangle on the ground.**

   Use the Rectangle tool (between the pencil and the circle on your toolbar) to draw a rectangle by doing the following:

   a. Click once to place one corner on the left side of your screen.

   b. Click again to place the opposite corner on the right side of your screen.

   Remember that you're in a 3D, *perspective,* view of the world, so your rectangle will look more like a diamond — 90-degree angles don't look like 90-degree angles in perspective. Figure 3-5 shows what you should be aiming for in this step.

Click here to start drawing   Finish drawing here

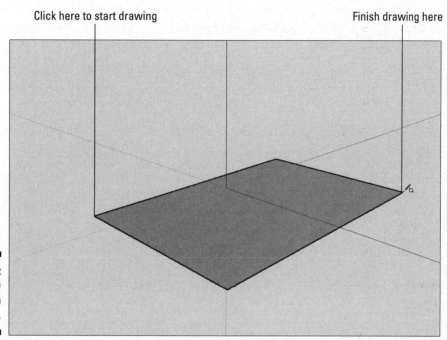

Figure 3-5:
Draw a 3D
rectangle on
the ground.

It's important to draw the right kind of rectangle for this example (or for any model you're trying to create in Perspective view), so try it a few times until it looks like the rectangle in Figure 3-5. To go back a step, choose Edit⇨Undo Rectangle; the last thing you did will be undone. You can use Undo to go back as many steps as you like, so feel free to use it anytime.

4. **Use the Push/Pull tool to extrude your rectangle into a box.**

Use this tool (it looks like a brown box with a red arrow coming out the top) to "pull" your rectangle into a box by following these steps:

a. Click the rectangle once to start the push/pull operation.

b. Click again, somewhere above your rectangle, to stop pushing/pulling.

At this point, you should have something that looks like Figure 3-6; if you don't, use Push/Pull again to make your box look about the right height.

If you are happily pushing/pulling away on your box, and everything suddenly disappears, it's because you pushed/pulled the top of your box all the way to the ground. Just choose Edit⇨Undo and keep going.

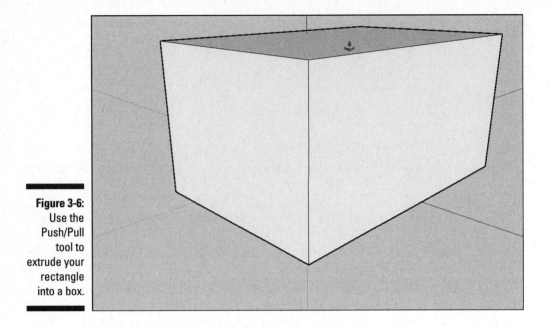

Figure 3-6:
Use the
Push/Pull
tool to
extrude your
rectangle
into a box.

5. **Draw a couple of diagonal lines for your roof.**

   Use the Line tool (it's shaped like a pencil) to draw two diagonal edges (lines) that will form your peaked roof, as shown in Figure 3-7. Follow these steps:

Click here to start drawing   Click here to finish your first edge

Figure 3-7:
Draw two
diagonal
lines that will
become your
peaked roof.

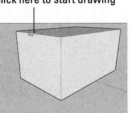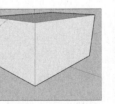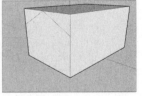

   a. Click once at the midpoint of the top of your box's front face to start your line.

   You'll know you're at the midpoint when you see a small, light-blue square and the word *Midpoint* appears. Move slowly to make sure that you see it.

   b. Click again somewhere along one of the side edges of your box's front face to end your line.

Wait until you see a red *On Edge* cue (just like the Midpoint one in the last step) before you click; if you don't, your new line won't end on the edge like it's supposed to.

c. Repeat the previous two steps to draw a similar (but opposite) line from the midpoint to the edge on the other side of the face.

Don't worry about making your diagonal lines symmetrical; for the purposes of this exercise, it's not important that they are.

6. Push/pull the triangles away to leave a sloped roof.

Use the Push/Pull tool (the same one you used back in Step 4) to get rid of the triangular parts of your box, leaving you with a sloped roof. Have a look at Figure 3-8 to see this in action, and follow these steps:

a. Select the Push/Pull tool, then click the right triangular face once to start the push/pull operation.

b. Move your cursor to the right to "push" the triangle as far as it will go (even with the end of your box).

c. Click again (on the triangle) to end the push/pull operation and to make the triangular face disappear.

d. Still using the Push/Pull tool, double-click the left triangular face to repeat the previous push/pull operation, making that face disappear as well.

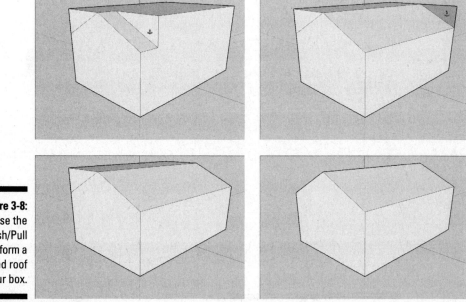

Figure 3-8:
Use the Push/Pull tool to form a peaked roof on your box.

7. Draw a rectangle on your front face.

Switch back to the Rectangle tool (which you used in Step 3) and draw a rectangle on the front face of your pointy box. Make sure that the bottom of your rectangle is flush with the bottom of your box by watching for the red On Edge hint to appear before you click. Check out Figure 3-9 to see what it should look like when you're done.

Using the Rectangle tool is a two-step process: You click once to place one corner and again to place the opposite corner. Try not to draw lines and shapes in SketchUp by *dragging* your cursor; doing so makes things more difficult. Practice clicking once to start an operation (like drawing a rectangle) and clicking again to stop.

8. Draw an arc on top of the rectangle you just drew.

Use the Arc tool (to the right of the Circle tool) to draw an arc on top of your rectangle (see Figure 3-10). Follow these steps to draw an arc:

Finish here

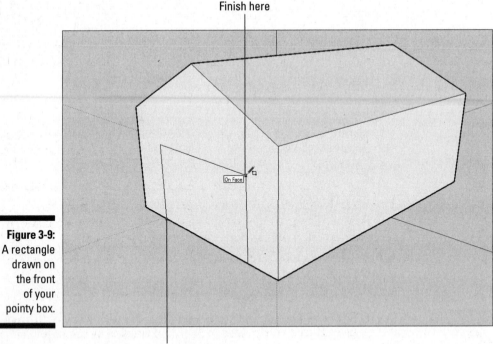

Figure 3-9:
A rectangle drawn on the front of your pointy box.

Click here to start drawing

Click here to start   Click here second

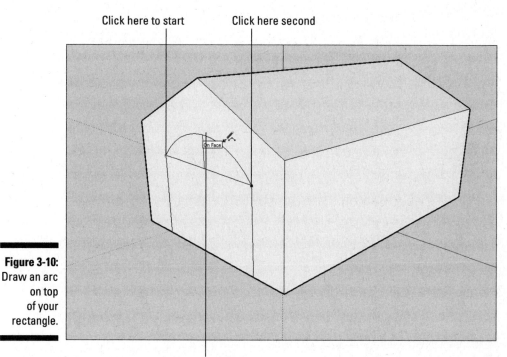

Figure 3-10:
Draw an arc
on top
of your
rectangle.

Click up here third

    a. Click the upper-left corner of the rectangle to place one endpoint of your arc. Make sure that you see the green Endpoint hint before you click.

    b. Click the upper-*right* corner of the rectangle to place the other endpoint of your arc.

    c. Move your cursor up to "bow out" the line you're drawing into an arc, and click when you're happy with how it looks.

  9. Select the Eraser tool and then click the horizontal line between the rectangle and the arc to erase that line.

10. Push/pull the doorway inward.

Use the Push/Pull tool (which you're an old hand with by now) to push the "doorway" face you created in Steps 7 through 9 in just a bit.

You use Push/Pull by clicking a face once to start, moving your cursor to "push/pull" it in or out, and then clicking again to stop.

11. **Erase the horizontal line at the bottom of the doorway by clicking it with the Eraser tool.**

    This makes the line (and the whole face above it) disappear. Figure 3-11 shows what your finished doghouse should look like.

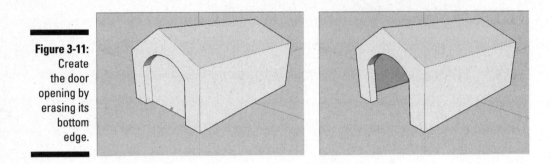

Figure 3-11: Create the door opening by erasing its bottom edge.

For a more detailed introduction to drawing lines and working with midpoints, angles, and more, flip to Chapter 2.

Slapping On Some Paint

I have an ulterior motive for getting you to paint your doghouse: To color it, you have to understand how to spin it around first. Moving around your model is *the most important* skill to develop when you're first learning SketchUp. Run through these steps to apply colors (and textures) to the faces in your model, and to find out about moving around while you're doing it:

1. **Choose Window⇨Materials to open the Materials dialog box (see Figure 3-12). Click a color or texture you like.**

    When you do, you automatically "pick up" the Paint Bucket tool and fill it with your chosen material.

2. **Paint some of the faces in your model by clicking any face you want to paint with the Paint Bucket tool.**

3. **Switch materials.**

    Choose another material from the Materials dialog box by clicking it.

4. **Paint the rest of the faces you can see. (Refer to Figure 3-13.)**

    Loop through Steps 2 to 4 for as long as you like. Finding the Materials dialog box in SketchUp is just like getting a brand new box of crayons when you were little (you know, the *big* box, with the built-in sharpener).

Click here to see your materials libraries

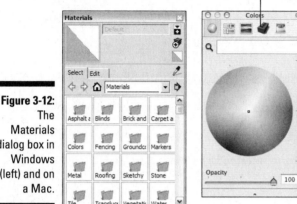

Figure 3-12:
The
Materials
dialog box in
Windows
(left) and on
a Mac.

Figure 3-13:
Use the
Paint Bucket
tool to paint
everything
you can see.

5. **Choose the Orbit tool; it's just to the left of the creepy white hand on the toolbar.**

6. **Click somewhere on the left side of your screen and *drag* your cursor over to the right. (See Figure 3-14.) Release your mouse button when you're done.**

   Your model spins! This is called *orbiting*. Orbit around some more, just to get the hang of it.

   If you're orbiting, and you've dragged your cursor over as far as it will go, and you haven't orbited as much as you wanted to, don't fret. Just release the mouse button, move your cursor over to where it was when you started orbiting, and orbit some more by clicking and dragging. You usually can't see what you want to see with a single orbit; you need a bunch of separate "drags" (separate orbits, I guess) to get things looking the way you want them to.

Figure 3-14:
Choose the
Orbit tool
and drag
your cursor
to spin your
model
around.

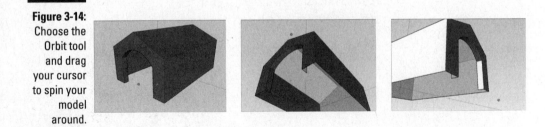

7. **Zoom in and out if you need to by selecting the Zoom tool and dragging your cursor up and down in your modeling window.**

   The Zoom tool looks like a magnifying glass, and it's on the other side of the creepy white hand. Dragging up zooms in, and down zooms out.

8. **If needed, move around in two dimensions with the Pan tool by selecting it and then clicking and dragging the Pan cursor inside your modeling window.**

   The Pan tool is the creepy white hand between Orbit and Zoom. You use Pan to "slide" your model around inside your modeling window without spinning it around or making it look bigger or smaller. You can pan in any direction.

9. **Use the Orbit, Zoom, Pan, and Paint Bucket tools to finish painting your doghouse.**

   Now that you know how to move around your model, here's how I'd like you to paint it (Color Plate 8 shows what it should look like):

   • Paint the exterior walls reddish brown

   • Paint the roof light blue

   • Paint the interior yellow-orange

When you're just starting out, it's easy to get a little lost with the navigation tools (Orbit, Zoom, and Pan); it happens to everybody. If you find yourself in a pickle, just choose Camera⇨Zoom Extents. When you do, SketchUp automatically plunks your model right in front of you; check out Figure 3-15 to see Zoom Extents in action. Just so you know, Zoom Extents is also a button on the toolbar; it's right next to the Zoom tool.

Chapter 2 is the place to look for extra tips and tricks on orbiting, zooming, and panning, as well as for details about using the Materials dialog box to paint the faces of an object.

Click Zoom Extents

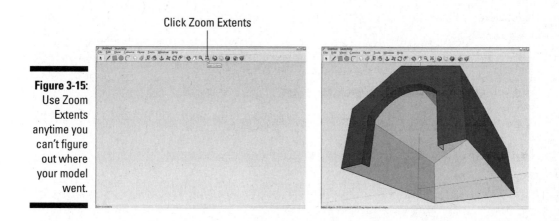

Figure 3-15:
Use Zoom
Extents
anytime you
can't figure
out where
your model
went.

Giving Your Model Some Style

SketchUp Styles allow you to change your model's appearance — the way it's drawn, basically — with just a few clicks of your mouse. You can create your own styles, of course, but SketchUp also comes with a library of pre-made ones that you can use without knowing anything about how they work.

Follow these steps to try out a couple of styles on your doghouse:

1. **Choose Window⇨Styles.**

   The Styles dialog box opens.

2. **Click the Select tab to show the Select pane.**

3. **In the Libraries drop-down menu (see Figure 3-16), choose the Assorted Styles library.**

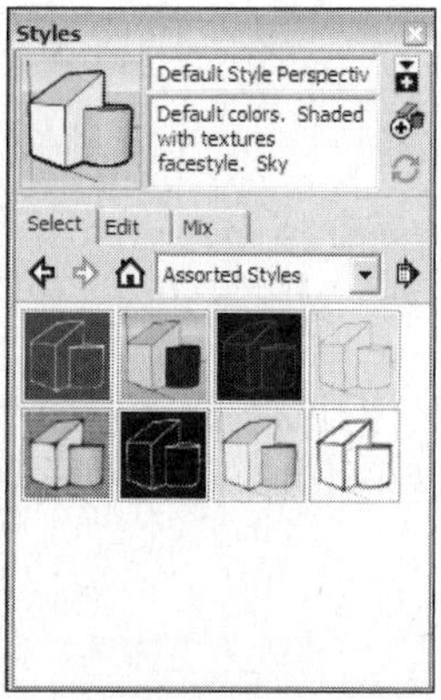

Figure 3-16:
The
Assorted
Styles
library is a
sampler of
ready-mixed
SketchUp
styles.

4. **Click through the different styles to see what they're about.**

   When you click a style in the Styles dialog box, that style is applied to your model. Figure 3-17 shows our doghouse with a few different styles applied — can you figure out which ones?

5. **Go back to the default style.**

   This is the first style in the Default Styles library.

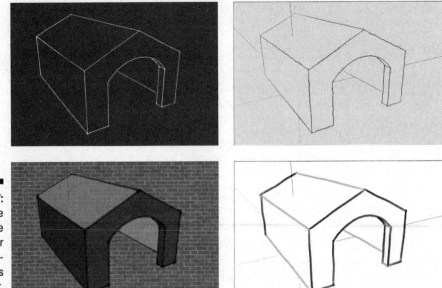

Figure 3-17: The same doghouse with four very different styles applied to it.

Switching On the Sun

You're about to use what I consider to be one of SketchUp's best features: shadows. When you turn on shadows, you're activating SketchUp's built-in sun. The shadows you see in your modeling window are *accurate* for whatever time and location you set. For the purposes of this example, though, don't worry about accuracy. Go through these steps to let the light shine in:

1. **Use Orbit, Zoom, and Pan to get an aerial, three-quarter view of your doghouse, sort of like the one shown in Figure 3-18.**

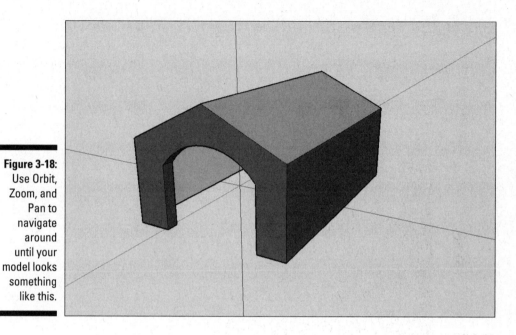

Figure 3-18:
Use Orbit,
Zoom, and
Pan to
navigate
around
until your
model looks
something
like this.

2. Choose Window⇨Shadows.

This opens the Shadow Settings dialog box (as shown in Figure 3-19).

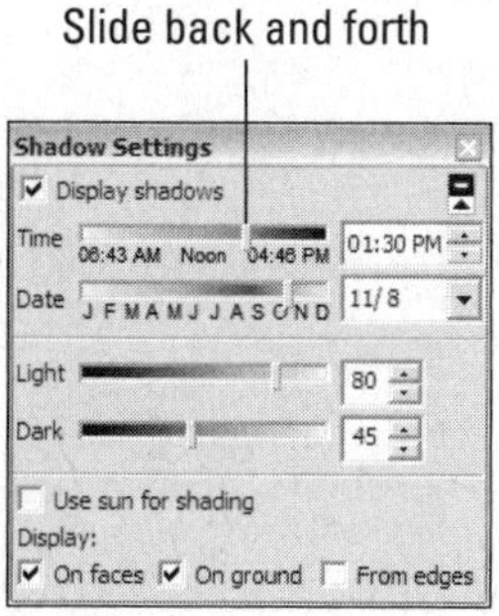

Slide back and forth

Figure 3-19:
The Shadow
Settings
dialog box
controls the
position of
SketchUp's
built-in sun.

3. Select the Display Shadows check box to turn on the sun.

Your doghouse should be casting a shadow on the ground.

4. In the Shadow Settings dialog box, move the Time slider back and forth.

Changing the time of day means that you're moving SketchUp's sun around in the sky. When the sun moves around, so do your shadows. Take a look at Figure 3-20 to see what I mean.

For more about fine-tuning light and shadows, check out Chapter 9.

7:31 a.m.   3:16 p.m.

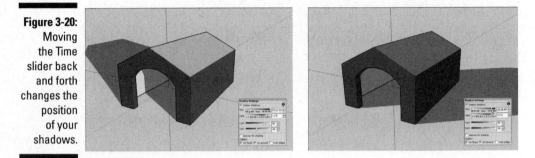

Figure 3-20:
Moving the Time slider back and forth changes the position of your shadows.

Sharing Your Masterpiece

Now that you have a model that looks about the way you want it to, you probably want to show it to someone. The easiest way to do that is by exporting a JPEG image that you can attach to an e-mail. Follow these steps and you'll be on your way:

1. **Navigate around (using Orbit, Zoom, and Pan) until you like the view of your model that you see in your modeling window.**

2. **Choose File⇨Export⇨2D Graphic.**

3. **In the Export dialog box that opens, choose JPEG from the Export Type drop-down menu.**

4. **Pick a location on your computer system, and give your exported image a name.**

5. **Click the Export button to create a JPEG image of what's visible in your modeling window.**

Exporting a JPEG file is just one way to share models. To find out about all your options, see Part IV, which explains how to share your model on Google Earth, as a printout, as an image or animation, or as a slick presentation that will (hopefully) impress all your friends.

Part II
Modeling in SketchUp

The 5th Wave   By Rich Tennant

"My brother built the barn, but the silo came from a design I did in Google SketchUp."

In this part . . .

When all is said and done, SketchUp is about making 3D models. Sure, you can paint them, make animations with them, print them, and e-mail images of them to your friends, but first you have to actually create them.

Chapter 4 makes the assumption that sooner or later, you're going to want to use SketchUp to make a model of a building. Starting with drawing simple floor plans and proceeding into the transition from 2D to 3D, modeling stairs and creating roofs, this chapter does its best to get you started.

In Chapter 5, I go over all the different ways you can organize your model; doing so improves your modeling efficiency, your computer's performance, and ultimately, your sanity. You don't have to be a tidy person to "work clean" in SketchUp — I'm living proof.

Don't want to use SketchUp to just model buildings? Chapter 6 describes how to use things like components and the Follow Me tool to create some pretty advanced models.

Chapter 7 talks about how you can use photographs in SketchUp, both to "paint" your faces, and to create whole models based on photographs of objects like buildings and furniture.

Chapter 4

Building Buildings

*E*ven though SketchUp lets you make (just about) anything you can think of, certain forms are easier to make than others. Fortunately, these kinds of shapes are exactly the ones that most people want to make with SketchUp, most of the time. That's no accident; SketchUp was designed with architecture in mind, so the whole *paradigm* — the fact that SketchUp models are made of faces and edges, and the kinds of tools it offers — is perfect for making things like buildings.

But what about curvy, swoopy buildings? You can use SketchUp to make those, too, but they're a little harder, so I don't think they're a good place to start. Because *most* of us live in boxy places with right-angled rooms and flat ceilings, that kind of architecture is relatively easy to understand.

In this chapter, I introduce you to some of the fundamentals of SketchUp modeling in terms of making simple, rectilinear buildings. By writing about how to build certain kinds of things, instead of just describing what the individual tools do, I hope to make it easier for you to get started. Even if you're not planning to use SketchUp to model any of the things I describe, you should still be able to apply these concepts to your own creations.

One more thing: Just about every page in this chapter relies heavily on the stuff I introduce in Chapter 2. Working with the colored drawing axes, selecting objects, navigating around your model, and drawing things accurately are pretty key to making anything in SketchUp, so be prepared to flip back and forth while you're getting used to how things work. I like to use paper clips as bookmarks, but I'm sure you have your own method. . . .

Drawing Floors and Walls

Most floors and walls are flat surfaces, so it's easy to model them with straight edges and flat faces in SketchUp. In fact, chances are good that the first thing you ever modeled in SketchUp looked a lot like the floor and walls of a building.

I can think of two different kinds of architectural models that most people want to create in SketchUp; how you approach modeling floors and walls depends entirely on the type of model you're making:

- ✔ **Exterior:** An exterior model of a building is basically just an empty shell; you don't have interior walls, rooms, or furniture to worry about. This type of model is a slightly simpler proposition for folks who are just starting out.

- ✔ **Interior:** An interior model of a building is significantly more complicated than an exterior-only one; dealing with interior wall thicknesses, floor heights, ceilings, and furnishings involves a lot more modeling prowess.

Here's the thing: Because everything in SketchUp is made up of super-flat faces (they have no thickness), the only way to model a wall that's, say, 8 inches thick is to use two faces side by side and 8 inches apart. For models where you need to show wall thicknesses — namely, interior models — this is what you'll have to do. Exterior models are easier to make because you can use single faces to represent walls. Figure 4-1 shows what I'm talking about.

Single-face walls   Double-face walls

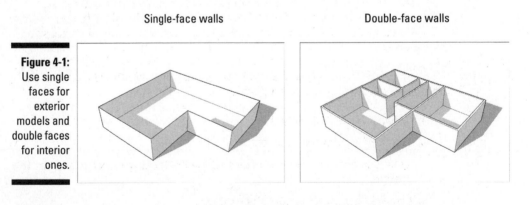

Figure 4-1:
Use single faces for exterior models and double faces for interior ones.

One of the biggest mistakes new SketchUp users make is to attempt an "inside-outside" model right off the bat. Making a model that shows both the interior and the exterior of a building at the same time is, to be honest, WAY too hard when you're just getting started. Instead, you should build two separate models if you need both interior and exterior views. If you need a combination model later on, you'll be able to build it in a quarter of the time it took you to build either of the first two — I guarantee it.

Starting out in 2D

Of course, you can make a 3D model of a building's interior in lots of different ways, but I'm going to show you the one I think makes the most sense. Basically, it involves drawing a two-dimensional floorplan that includes all your interior and exterior walls, and then extruding it up to be the right height. In my method, you don't worry about doors, windows, or stairs until after your model is extruded; you put them in afterward, which I think is an easier and more logical way to work.

If you're importing a floorplan from another piece of software like AutoCAD or VectorWorks, I think you'll appreciate this approach — it lets you take 2D information and make it 3D, regardless of where it comes from.

Even though SketchUp is a 3D modeling program through and through, it's not a bad tool for drawing simple 2D plans. The toolset is adequate and easy to use, and doing a couple of things before you get started will help a lot. The thing to keep in mind is that SketchUp isn't a full-fledged drafting program, and it probably never will be. If you're an architect-type who needs to do heavy-duty CAD (computer-aided drawing) work, you should probably be drafting in another piece of software and importing your work into SketchUp when you need 3D. If you're just drawing your house or the place where you work, look no further — SketchUp should do just fine.

Switching to a 2D view

If you're going to use SketchUp to draw a 2D plan, the first thing you need to do is to orient your point of view. It's easiest to draw in 2D when you're directly above your work, looking down at the ground plane. You also want to make sure that you're not seeing things in perspective, which distorts your view of what you have.

Follow these simple steps to set things up (and find additional help on this book's companion site; see the Introduction for details):

1. **Create a new SketchUp file.**

2. **Choose Camera➪Standard➪Top.**

   This changes your viewpoint so that you're looking directly down at the ground.

3. **Choose Camera➪Parallel Projection.**

   Switching from Perspective to Parallel Projection makes it easier to draw plans in 2D. At this point, your modeling window should look like the one shown in Figure 4-2.

TIP

Feel free to delete Bryce. That little diagonal line that's visible in your modeling window when you're in Top view is a top view of Bryce — the 2D guy who appears in every new SketchUp file you create. To get rid of Bryce, just right-click him and choose Erase from the context menu.

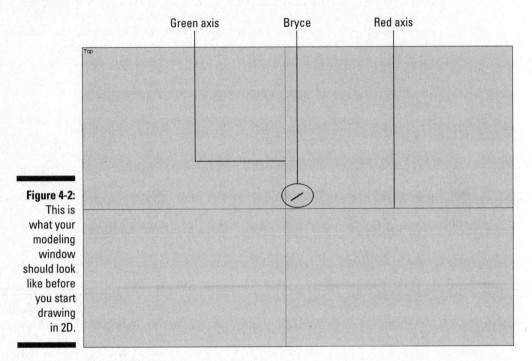

Green axis   Bryce   Red axis

Figure 4-2:
This is
what your
modeling
window
should look
like before
you start
drawing
in 2D.

ON THE WEB

Dusting off SketchUp's drafting tools

Here's some good news: You don't need many tools to draft a 2D plan in SketchUp. Figure 4-3 shows the basic toolbar; everything you need is right there:

Figure 4-3:
All the tools
you need to
draft in 2D in
SketchUp
are on the
basic
toolbar.

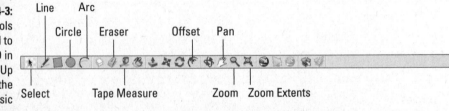

Line   Arc

Circle   Eraser   Offset   Pan

Select   Tape Measure   Zoom   Zoom Extents

✔ **Line tool:** You use the Line tool (which looks like a pencil) to draw *edges,* which are one of the two basic building blocks of SketchUp models. Fundamentally, you click to start drawing an edge and click again to finish it. (You can find lots more information about drawing lines in Chapter 2.)

✔ **Eraser tool:** You use the Eraser to erase edges (see Figure 4-4). Keep in mind that you can't use the Eraser to delete faces, though erasing one of the edges that defines a face automatically erases that face, too. Take a look at the section about edges and faces at the beginning of Chapter 2 for more detail on this. You can use the Eraser in two different ways:

 • **Clicking:** Click on edges to erase them one at a time.

 • **Dragging:** Drag over edges to erase them; this is faster if you have lots of edges you want to get rid of.

✔ **Circle tool:** Drawing circles in SketchUp is pretty easy: You click once to define the center and again to define a point on the circle (which also defines the radius). To enter in a precise radius, just draw a circle, type in a radius, and press Enter (see Figure 4-5). For more information on typing while you draw, check out the section on model accuracy in Chapter 2.

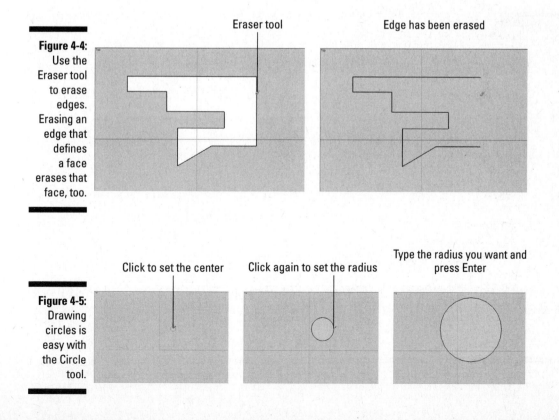

Figure 4-4: Use the Eraser tool to erase edges. Erasing an edge that defines a face erases that face, too.

Eraser tool

Edge has been erased

Figure 4-5: Drawing circles is easy with the Circle tool.

Click to set the center

Click again to set the radius

Type the radius you want and press Enter

✔ **Arc tool:** To draw an arc, you click once to define one end, again to define the other end, and a third time to define the *bulge* (how much the arc sticks out). If you want, you can type in a radius after you draw your arc by entering the radius, the units, and the letter *r.* If you want an arc with a radius of 4 feet, you would draw it however big, type in **4'r**, and press Enter. This is shown in Figure 4-6.

✔ **Offset tool:** The Offset tool helps you draw edges that are a constant distance apart from edges that already exist in your model. Pictures are usually better than words, so take a look at Figure 4-7. Using Offset on the shape I've drawn lets me create another shape that's exactly 6 inches bigger all the way around (middle image), or 6 inches *smaller* all the way around (right image). Offsetting edges is a useful way to create things like doorways and window trim.

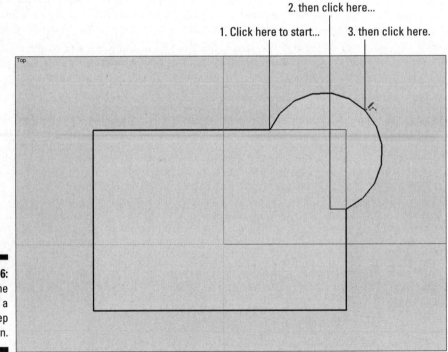

2. then click here...

1. Click here to start...   3. then click here.

Top

Figure 4-6:
Using the
Arc tool is a
three-step
operation.

Click to start drawing; then
move your cursor   6 inch *outside* offset   6 inch *inside* offset

Figure 4-7:
Offset lets
you create
edges
based on
other edges.

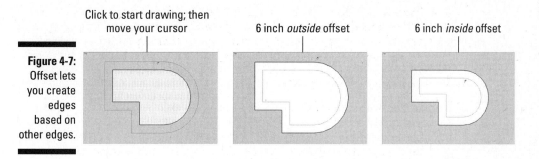

You can use Offset in two ways; with both, you click once to start offsetting and again to stop:

- **Click a face to offset all its edges.** If nothing is selected, clicking a face with the Offset tool lets you offset all that face's edges by a constant amount (as shown in Figure 4-7).

- **Preselect one or more edges, and then use Offset.** If you have some edges selected, you can use Offset on just those edges; this comes in handy for drawing things like doorframes and balconies, as shown in Figure 4-8.

✔ **Tape Measure tool:** The Tape Measure is one of those tools that does a bunch of different things. To use it for measuring distances, click any two points in your model to measure the distance between them. The distance "readout" is in the VCB, in the lower-right corner of your modeling window. You can also use it for sizing a model and for creating guides, as I explain in Chapter 2.

Select the edges you want to offset   Use Offset to create more edges

Figure 4-8:
Using Offset
on a set of
preselected
edges is
handy for
drawing
things like
doorframes.

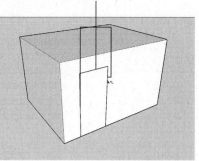

Coming up with a simple plan

If all you're trying to do is model an exterior view of a building, just measure around the perimeter, draw the outline of the building in SketchUp, and proceed from there. (See Figure 4-9.) Your walls will only be a single face thick (meaning paper-thin), but that's okay — you're only interested in the outside, anyway.

Figure 4-9:
To make an exterior model, just measure the outside of your building to draw an outline in SketchUp.

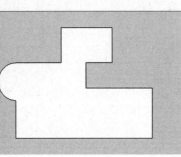 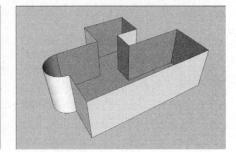

If, on the other hand, you want to create an *interior* view, your life is a little bit more complicated. The business of measuring an existing building so that you can model it on the computer is easier said than done — even experienced architects and builders often get confused when trying to create *as-builts,* as drawings of existing buildings are called. Closets, ventilation spaces, interior walls, and all kinds of other obstructions inevitably get in the way of getting good measurements; most of the time, you just have to give it your best shot and then tweak things a bit to make them right.

Drawing an interior outline

Because the main goal of making an interior model of a building is to end up with accurate interior spaces, you need to work from the inside out. If your tape measure is long enough, try to figure out a way to get the major dimensions first — this means the total interior width and length of the inside of your building. You might not be able to, but do your best. After that, it's really just a matter of working your way around, using basic arithmetic and logic to figure things out.

It really helps to make a paper drawing before you start in with SketchUp. You'll know what you need to do, leaving all your concentration for drafting on the computer. Figure 4-10 shows the paper sketch I used when modeling my own house.

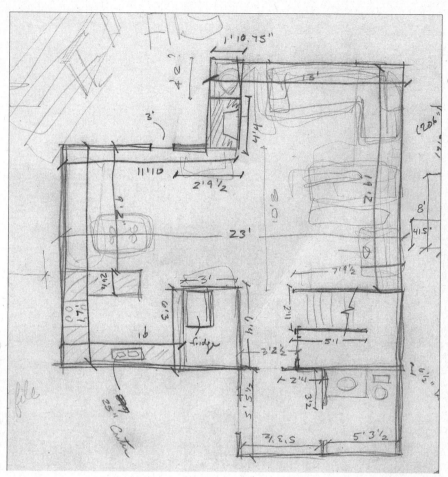

Figure 4-10:
This is the paper sketch I used to model my house in SketchUp.

From this paper drawing, here's how I would draw a basic interior outline of my house:

1. **First, I switch into a 2D, overhead view.**

   The section "Switching to a 2D view," earlier in this chapter, explains how.

2. **Using the Line tool, I draw an edge 17 feet long (see Figure 4-11, left), representing the western wall of the house.**

   To draw it, I click once to start the edge, move my cursor up until I see the green linear inference (indicating that I'm drawing parallel to the green axis), and click again to end my line. To make it 17 feet long, I type in **17'** and then press Enter — the line resizes itself automatically to be exactly 17 feet in length. If I wanted to, I could use the Tape Measure to double-check what I did.

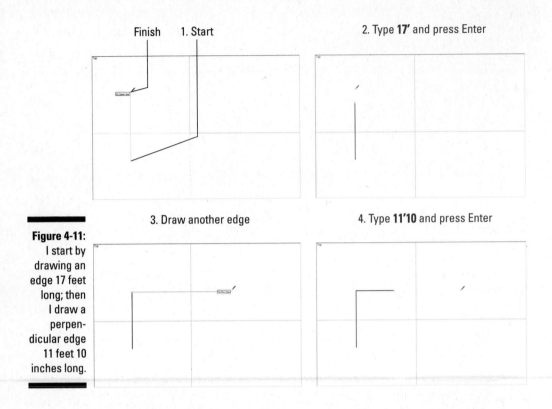

Finish   1. Start

2. Type **17′** and press Enter

3. Draw another edge

4. Type **11′10** and press Enter

Figure 4-11:
I start by
drawing an
edge 17 feet
long; then
I draw a
perpen-
dicular edge
11 feet 10
inches long.

3. **I draw an edge 11 feet 10 inches long, starting at the end of the first edge, heading to the right in the red direction. (See Figure 4-11, bottom-right.)**

   To do this, I do exactly what I did to draw the first edge, except that I move parallel to the red axis this time, type in **11′10**, and then press Enter.

4. **I keep going all the way around the house, until I get back to where I started (see Figure 4-12).**

   If I make a mistake, I either use the Eraser to get rid of edges I'm unhappy with or I choose Edit⇨Undo to go back a step or two.

5. **If all my measurements don't add up, I adjust things so that they do — a few extra inches here and there never killed anyone, after all.**

   When I complete my outline (forming a closed loop of edges that were all on the same plane), a face automatically appears. Now I have a total of 11 edges and 1 face.

Edge   Face

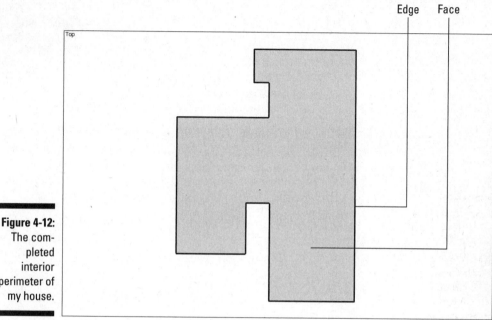

Figure 4-12:
The com-
pleted
interior
perimeter of
my house.

When you're drafting in 2D, whatever you do, don't use the Orbit tool. Because you're working in 2D, you only need to use Zoom and Pan to navigate around your drawing (see Chapter 2 for more information on this). If you accidentally end up orbiting your model into a 3D view, follow the steps in the section "Switching to a 2D view," earlier in this chapter, to get things back in order.

If you ever get lost, and no amount of zooming and panning will get you back to a view of your floorplan, choose Camera➪Zoom Extents — think of it as an emergency lever you can pull to fill your modeling window with your geometry.

Offsetting an exterior wall

Now that I've gotten this far, I decide to *offset* (using the Offset tool) an exterior wall thickness, just to make it easier to visualize my spaces. Here's how I do it:

1. **Using the Offset tool, I offset my closed shape by 8 inches to the out-side. (See Figure 4-13, left.)**

   An offset of 8 inches is a pretty standard thickness for an exterior wall, especially for houses in my neck of the woods. This is how I use the Offset tool:

a. I make sure that nothing is selected by choosing Edit⇨Select None.

b. I click once inside my shape.

c. I click again outside my shape to make a second, bigger shape.

d. I type in **8**, and then press Enter.

2. **Because I know there are no alcoves on the outside of the house, I use the Line tool to draw across them. (See Figure 4-13, middle.)**

3. **I use the Eraser tool to get rid of the extra edges. (See Figure 4-13, right.)**

   By deleting the extra edges, I go back to having only two faces: one representing the floor and one representing the exterior wall thickness. It doesn't matter that the wall is thicker in a couple of places; I can always go back and fiddle with it later on.

Figure 4-13:
I use Offset to create an exterior wall thickness, and then I do some cleanup using the Line and Eraser tools.

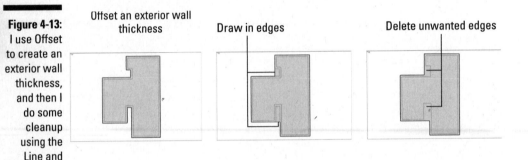

Offset an exterior wall thickness | Draw in edges | Delete unwanted edges

Putting in the interior walls

For this part of the process, I use guides a lot. If you haven't done so already, read Chapter 2 and check out the last part — you'll find a full description of guides and how to use them.

When I'm drafting a floorplan in SketchUp, I find it really helps to ignore things like doors and windows — where a doorway should be in a wall, I just draw a solid wall. I like to add in doors and windows after I've extruded my floorplan into a three-dimensional figure.

Here's how I put in the few interior walls on the first floor of my house:

1. **With the Tape Measure tool, I drag a parallel guide 5 feet, 3½ inches from the inside of my entryway. (See Figure 4-14, left.)**

   To do this, I just click the edge from which I want to draw the guide, move my cursor to the right (to tell SketchUp which way to go), type in **5'3.5**, and press Enter.

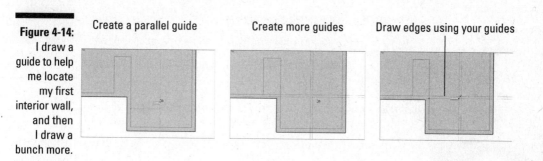

Create a parallel guide   Create more guides   Draw edges using your guides

Figure 4-14:
I draw a
guide to help
me locate
my first
interior wall,
and then
I draw a
bunch more.

2. **I draw a few more guides in the same way as I drew the first one.**

   Working from my pencil drawing, I figure out the location of each interior
   wall, and I create guides to measure off the space. (See Figure 4-14, right.)

3. **Switching to the Line tool, I draw in edges to represent the interior walls.**

   By using the guides as, er, guides, it's easy to draw my edges correctly.
   Figure 4-15 shows what I have so far.

TIP

   Don't forget to zoom! When you have a jumble of edges and guides, and
   you can't see what you're doing, just zoom in. It sounds obvious, but
   you'd be surprised how many folks forget to change their point of view
   while they're working — it makes all the difference.

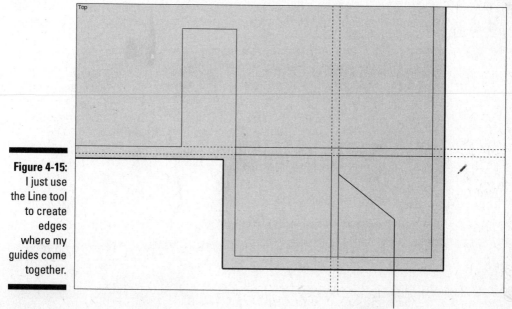

Figure 4-15:
I just use
the Line tool
to create
edges
where my
guides come
together.

Solid lines are edges

4. **I use the Eraser to delete my guides.**

5. **I use the Eraser to get rid of all the little extra edge segments. (See Figure 4-16.)**

    By doing this, I go back to only having two faces in my model (one for the floor and one for the walls). When it is time to extrude my plan into walls, as I explain in a moment, performing this step will help out a lot.

Figure 4-16:
Using the Eraser, I delete my guides and all the little edge segments left over from drawing the interior walls.

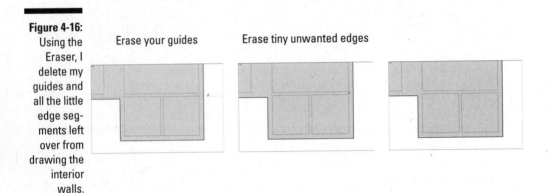

Erase your guides   Erase tiny unwanted edges

Going from 2D to 3D

With a 2D plan in hand, the next step is to extrude it into a 3D model. This is basically a one-step process, and it involves the tool that made SketchUp famous: Push/Pull. In the following sections, I take the simple floorplan I drew earlier in this chapter and turn it into three-dimensional walls.

Getting a good view

Before I pop up my plan into the third dimension, I need to change my point of view to get a better view of what I'm doing. (See Figure 4-17.) Follow these steps:

1. **Choose Camera⇨Perspective.**

    This "turns on" SketchUp's perspective engine, meaning that now I can see things more realistically — the way people really see things in 3D.

2. **Choose Camera⇨Standard⇨Iso.**

    This switches me from a top view to an isometric (three-quarter) one. I could do this with the Orbit tool, too — you always have more than one way to do everything in SketchUp.

Switch to Perspective view

Switch to Iso view

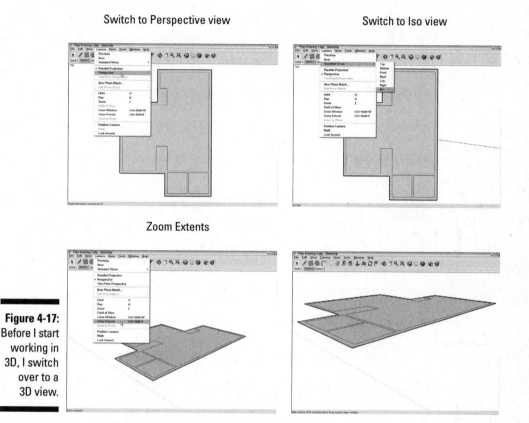

Zoom Extents

Figure 4-17:
Before I start
working in
3D, I switch
over to a
3D view.

3. **Choose Camera⇨Zoom Extents.**

   Zoom Extents has its own button on the basic toolbar, but I thought I'd
   stick with the Camera menu theme, just for consistency.

4. **Change the field of view from 35 to 45 degrees: Choose Camera⇨
   Field of View, type in 45, and press Enter.**

   By default, SketchUp's field of view is set to 35 degrees. (For more information on what this means, check out Chapter 10.)

Pushing/pulling your way to happiness

The Push/Pull tool is a simple creature; you use it to extrude flat faces into 3D
shapes. It works (like everything else in SketchUp) by clicking — you click a
face once to start pushing/pulling it, move your cursor until you like what
you see, and then click again to stop push/pulling. That's it. I doubt that any
software tool has ever been so satisfyingly easy to use and understand. For
more detail on Push/Pull, see the nearby sidebar, "More fun with Push/Pull."

Push/Pull only works on flat faces; if you need to do something to a curved face, you'll have to use something else. Read about the Intersect with Model feature in the section "Getting to know Intersect with Model," later in this chapter — it might be what you're looking for.

To use Push/Pull to extrude my house's first floorplan into a 3D model, this is what I do. (See Figure 4-18.)

Figure 4-18:
I use Push/Pull to extrude one of my faces into all the walls in my house. Presto!

Click to start Push/Pulling   Move your cursor   Type a height and press Enter

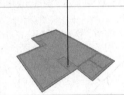 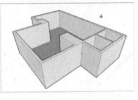

1. **Select the Push/Pull tool from the toolbar.**

   It looks like a little box with a red arrow coming out the top.

2. **Click the "wall's" face once to start extruding it.**

   If I click the "floor" face, I would end up extruding that, instead. If you choose the wrong face by accident, press Esc to cancel the operation, and try again.

3. **I move my cursor up to pull up the walls, and click to stop extruding.**

   It doesn't matter how much I extrude my face, because I'm going to add precision in the next step.

4. **I type in 8' and press Enter.**

   When I do this, my push/pull distance is revised to be exactly 8 feet — the height of the walls in my house.

If I had forgotten to erase any little edge segments before I used Push/Pull, all my walls might not have been "pulled up" at once. In this case, I would have used Push/Pull again on any faces that needed it.

Adding doors and windows

You can make openings in your walls in a couple of different ways. What you choose to do depends on what kind of building you're modeling, whether you're using single-face or double-face walls, and how much detail you plan to include in your model. You have two options:

- ✔ **Use SketchUp components that cut openings themselves.** SketchUp comes with a whole bunch of doors and windows that you can drag and drop into your model. The really cool thing about these is that they cut their own openings when you place them. Here's the catch, though: SketchUp's "Cut Opening" components only work on single-face walls, which means that they're really only useful for exterior building models. If you're building an interior model, you'll have to cut your own openings.

- ✔ **Cut openings yourself.** For double-face walls, this is your only option; luckily, it's easy to do. Basically, you draw an outline for the opening you want to create, and then you use Push/Pull to create the opening — it works the same way for doors and windows.

Using SketchUp's handy-dandy components

As long as you're making an exterior model, you can use the doors and windows that come with SketchUp. These are components, which you can read more about in Chapter 5. Without going into a ton of detail, here's what you need to know about them:

- ✔ **They're in the Components dialog box.** Choose Window⇨Components to open the dialog box, and then look in the Architecture library for the doors and windows.

- ✔ **You can find hundreds more online.** If you're connected to the Internet, choose File⇨3D Warehouse⇨Get Models. This brings up the 3D Warehouse, where you can freely download just about anything you're looking for. Chapter 11 goes into more detail about the 3D Warehouse, if you're interested.

- ✔ **They are editable.** I go into lots of detail about this in Chapter 5, but here's the gist: If you don't like something about one of SketchUp's built-in doors or windows, you can change it.

- ✔ **They cut their own openings, but the openings aren't permanent.** When you move or delete a door or window component you've placed, its opening goes with it.

ON THE WEB

Adding a hole-cutting component to your model is a piece of cake. Follow these steps to do it yourself. (See Figure 4-19.)

Figure 4-19:
Placing window and door components in your model is a breeze.

Click a component   Place it in your model

1. **In the Components dialog box, click the component that you want to place in your model.**

2. **Place the component where you want it to be.**

3. **If you don't like where it is, use the Move tool (read all about it in Chapter 2) to reposition your component.**

ON THE WEB

More fun with Push/Pull

Because Push/Pull is the tool that most people think of when they think of SketchUp, I thought you might appreciate knowing more about what it can do. The people who invented this software (back in the last millennium) *started* with the idea for Push/Pull — that's how closely linked SketchUp and Push/Pull are. Here are four things about Push/Pull that aren't immediately obvious when you first start using it:

✔ **Double-click with the Push/Pull tool to extrude a face by the last distance you pushed/pulled.** When you double-click a face, it automatically gets pushed/pulled by the same amount as the last face you used Push/Pull on.

✔ **Press Ctrl (Option on a Mac) to push/pull a *copy* of your face.** The first graphic in the following figure shows what I'm talking about here. Instead of using Push/Pull the regular way, you can use a modifier key to extrude a copy of the face you're pushing/pulling. This comes in super-handy for modeling things like multistory buildings quickly.

✔ **While pushing/pulling, hover over other parts of your geometry to tell SketchUp how far to extrude.** Take a look at the second graphic. Perhaps I want to use Push/Pull to extrude a cylinder that is exactly the same height as my box. Before I click the second time to stop pushing/pulling, I hover over a point on the top of the box; now the cylinder is exactly that tall. To complete the operation, I click while I'm still hovering over the box. It's pretty simple, and it'll save you hours of time after you're used to doing it.

✔ **Pushing/pulling a face into another, co-planar face automatically cuts a hole.** In fact, this is how you make openings (like doors and windows) in double-face walls. The last graphic shows this in action.

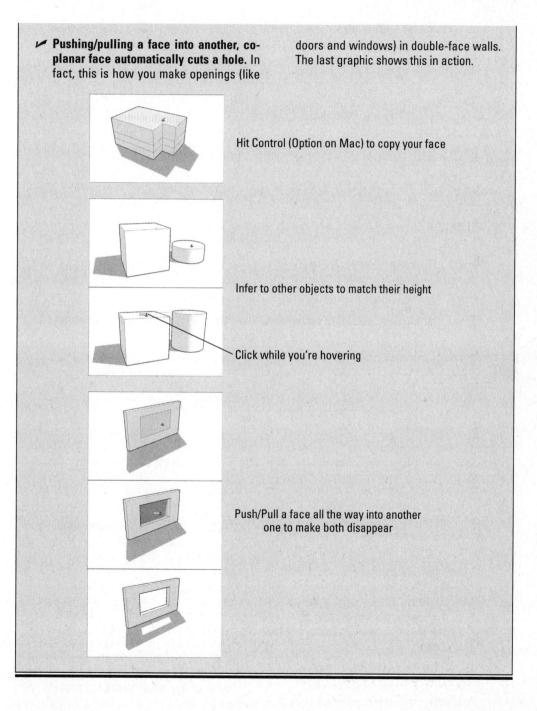

Hit Control (Option on Mac) to copy your face

Infer to other objects to match their height

Click while you're hovering

Push/Pull a face all the way into another one to make both disappear

Working through thick and thin

Pay attention to which edges look thick and which ones look thin. When you're drawing in 2D, you can tell a lot from an edge's appearance:

- ✔ **Thin edges cut *through* faces.** Edges that are thin are ones that have "sunk in"; you can think of them like cuts from a razor-sharp knife. When you successfully split a face with an edge that you draw with the Line tool, it looks thin. The first image in the following figure shows what I'm talking about.

- ✔ **Thick edges sit *on top* of faces.** If the edge you just drew looks thicker than some of the other edges in your model, it isn't actually

cutting through the face it's on — it's only sitting on top. An edge can sit on top of a face for a couple of reasons:

It has one end free. So-called "free" edges are ones that aren't connected to other edges at both ends (as in the second image).

It crosses another edge. Because edges don't automatically cut other edges where they cross, you have to manually split them. To make a thick edge thin (making it "sink in"), use the Line tool to trace over each segment, as shown in the third image.

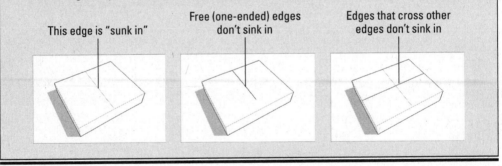

This edge is "sunk in" Free (one-ended) edges don't sink in Edges that cross other edges don't sink in

Figure 4-20 shows a simple building to which I've added a door and a couple of window components. Notice how I use guides to line things up — doing so is the best way to make sure that everything's in the right spot.

Making your own openings

Most of the time, you won't be able to get away with using SketchUp's built-in door and window components — the fact that they can't cut through two-faced walls means that they're limited to external use only. That's okay though; cutting your own holes in walls is quick and easy, and you'll always end up with exactly what you want.

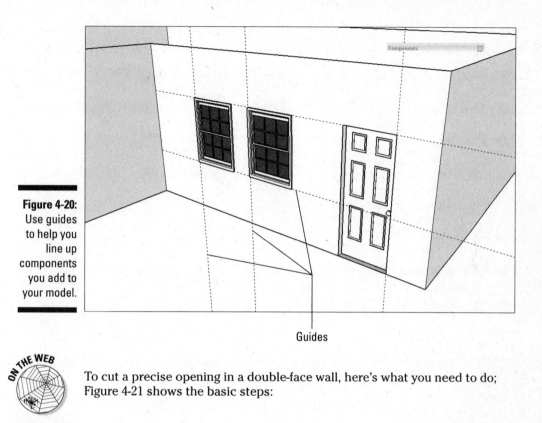

Figure 4-20:
Use guides
to help you
line up
components
you add to
your model.

Guides

ON THE WEB

To cut a precise opening in a double-face wall, here's what you need to do;
Figure 4-21 shows the basic steps:

Figure 4-21:
Use guides
to plan
where you
want an
opening,
and then
push/pull all
the way
through
both faces.

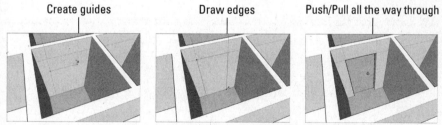

Create guides   Draw edges   Push/Pull all the way through

1. **Mark where you want your opening to be with guides.**

   For a refresher on using guides, have a look at the section "Making and
   using guides," in Chapter 2.

2. **Draw the outline of the opening you want to create, making sure to create a new face in the process.**

   You can use any of the drawing tools to do this, though I recommend sticking with the Line tool when you're starting out. You'll know you've made a new face if the edges in your outline look thin; if they don't, check out the nearby sidebar, "Working through thick and thin," for more info.

3. **Use Push/Pull to extrude your new face back into the thickness of the wall until it touches the face behind it.**

   If everything goes well, your face should disappear, taking with it the corresponding area of the face behind it. Now you have an opening in your wall. If your face doesn't disappear, and no opening is created, it's probably for one of the following reasons:

   • **Your faces aren't parallel to each other.** This technique only works if both faces are parallel. Keep in mind that just because two faces *look* parallel doesn't mean that they are.

   • **You hit an edge.** If you push/pull your face into a face with an edge crossing it, SketchUp gets confused and doesn't cut an opening. Use Undo, get rid of the pesky edge (if you can), and try again.

Don't forget to orbit! If you can't quite push/pull what you mean to push/pull, orbit around until you can see what you're doing.

Staring Down Stairs

There are probably a million different ways to make stairs in SketchUp, but (naturally) I have my favorites. In the following sections, you'll find three different methods that work equally well; take a look at all of them and then decide which works best for your situation.

Before I dive in, here's some simple stairway vocabulary, just in case you need it; take a look at Figure 4-22 for a visual reference:

✔ **Rise and run:** The *rise* is the total distance your staircase needs to climb. If the vertical distance from your first floor to your second (your *floor-to-floor* distance) is 10 feet, that's your rise. The *run* is the total *horizontal* distance your staircase takes up. A set of stairs with a big rise and a small run would be really steep.

✔ **Tread:** A *tread* is an individual step — the part of the staircase you step on. When someone refers to the size of a tread, he's talking about the *depth* — the distance from the front to the back of the tread. Typically, this is anywhere from 9 to 24 inches, but treads of 10 to 12 inches are most comfortable to walk on.

✔ **Riser:** The *riser* is the part of the step that connects each tread in the vertical direction. Risers are usually about 5 to 7 inches high, but that depends on your building. Not all staircases have actual risers (think of steps with gaps between treads), but they all have a riser *height*.

✔ **Landing:** A *landing* is a platform somewhere around the middle of a set of stairs. Landings are necessary in real life, but modeling them can be a pain; figuring out staircases with landings is more definitely more complicated. It's sometime easier if you think of your landings as really big steps.

The Subdivided Rectangles method

This is the way most people think to draw their first set of stairs. It's intuitive and simple, but it's also a bit more time-consuming than the other methods I describe in this chapter.

The key to the Subdivided Rectangles method is to use a special trick you can do with edges: Called *Divide,* it lets you pick any edge and divide it up into as many segments as you want. If you know how many steps you need to draw, but not how deep each individual tread needs to be, this comes in really handy.

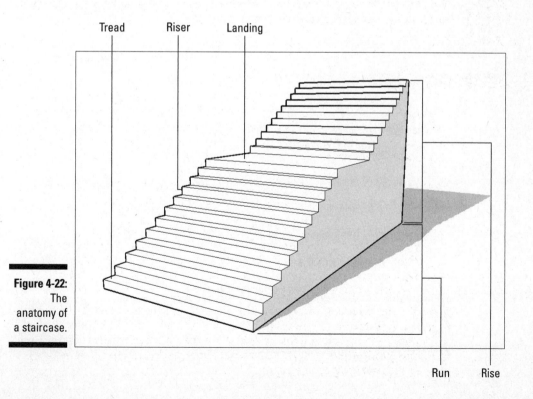

Tread   Riser   Landing

Run   Rise

Figure 4-22:
The anatomy of a staircase.

Here's how the Subdivided Rectangles method works. (See Figure 4-23.)

1. Start by drawing a rectangle the size of the staircase you want to build.

Divide edge into smaller edges,
marking off treads

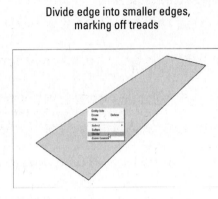

Connect new endpoints

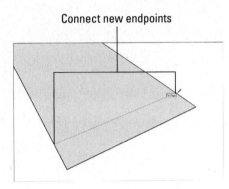

Divide vertical edge marking off vertical risers

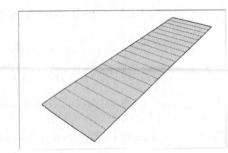

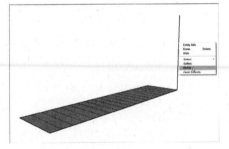

Infer to the endpoints on this divided edge

Figure 4-23:
The
Subdivided
Rectangles
method of
building
stairs.

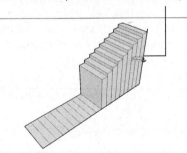

I strongly recommend modeling steps as a group, separate from the rest of your building, and then moving them into position when they're done. You can read all about groups in Chapter 5.

2. **With the Select tool, right-click one of the long edges of your rectangle and choose Divide from the context menu.**

   If your staircase is wider than it is long, right-click one of the short edges, instead.

3. **Before you do anything else, type in the number of treads you want to create and press Enter.**

   This command automatically divides your edge into many more edges, eliminating the need to calculate how deep each of your treads needs to be. Essentially, each of your new edges will become the side of one of your treads.

4. **Draw a line from the endpoint of each of your new edges, dividing your original rectangle into many smaller rectangles.**

   You can use the Line or the Rectangle tool to do this; pick whichever one you're most comfortable with.

5. **From one of the corners of your original rectangle, draw a vertical edge the height of your staircase's total rise.**

6. **Use the Divide command to split your new edge into however many risers you need in your staircase (this is generally your number of treads, plus one).**

   Repeat Steps 2 and 3 to do this. The endpoints of your new, little edges will tell you how high to make each of your steps.

7. **Push/pull the rectangle that represents your last step to the correct height.**

   Here's where you need to use the "hover-click" technique that I describe in the sidebar "More fun with Push/Pull," earlier in this chapter. Just click once to start pushing/pulling, hover over the endpoint that corresponds to the height of that tread, and click again. Your step will automatically be extruded to the right height.

   It's a good idea to start extruding your highest step first, but keep in mind that it doesn't go all the way to the top; you always have a riser between your last step and your upper floor.

8. **Repeat Step 7 for each of your remaining steps.**

9. **Use the Eraser to get rid of any extra edges you don't need.**

   Be careful not to accidentally erase geometry on the part of your staircase you can't see.

The Copied Profile method

This method for modeling a staircase relies, like the last one, on using Push/Pull to create a three-dimensional form from a 2D face, but I think you'll agree it's a lot more elegant. In a nutshell, you draw the *profile* — the side view, sort of — of a single step, and then you copy as many steps as you need, create a single face, and extrude the whole thing into shape. It's breathtakingly satisfying the first time you do it — one of those "guaranteed to make you smile" SketchUp operations you'll want to repeat for friends (assuming you have nerdy friends like me).

Follow these steps to make a staircase using the Copied Profile method. (See Figure 4-24.)

Start with a vertical face   Draw the profile of a single step   Copy it up

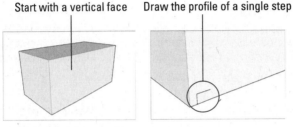

Type the number of copies, then **x**, and press Enter   Push/Pull the stair into 3D

Figure 4-24:
The Copied Profile method, in glorious grayscale.

1. **Start with a large, vertical face; make sure that it's big enough for the flight of stairs you want to build.**

   You're going to end up pushing/pulling the whole shebang out of the side of this face, just so you know.

2. **In the bottom corner of the face, draw the profile (side outline) of a single step.**

   I usually use the Line tool to do this, though you might want to use an arc or two, depending on the level of detail you need. For a refresher on drawing lines accurately, check out Chapter 2.

3. **Select all the edges that make up your step profile.**

Remember that you can hold down Shift while clicking with the Select tool to add multiple objects to your selection. Chapter 2 has lots of selection tips.

4. **Make a copy of your step profile and place it above your first one.**

   If you're unfamiliar with how to make copies using the Move tool, refer to the section on moving and copying, toward the end of Chapter 2.

5. **Type in the number of steps you'd like to make, type the letter *x*, and then press Enter.**

   For example, if you wanted ten steps, you would type in **10x**. This technique repeats the copy operation you just did by however many times you tell it to; adding an *x* at the end of the number tells SketchUp you want to make copies.

6. **Draw an edge to make sure that all your step profiles are part of a single face.**

   You don't have to do this step if your stair profiles already fit perfectly on your vertical face; if you measured carefully, they just might. If you can't seem to make things work, read the sidebar "Working through thick and thin," earlier in this chapter. That might shed some light on what's going on.

7. **Push/pull the staircase face out to be the width you need it to be.**

   This is the part that seems like magic to most folks; I don't think it ever gets old.

This method of stairway building also works great in combination with the Follow Me tool, which I talk about in Chapter 6. Figure 4-25 should whet your appetite — Follow Me is cool beans, all the way around.

Figure 4-25:
Using Follow Me (more details in Chapter 6) with the Copied Profile method produces some impressive geometry, indeed.

Profile   Extrusion path for Follow Me

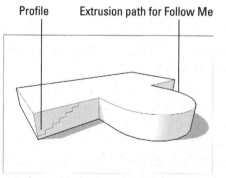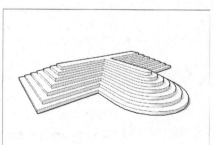

The Treads Are Components method

Nothing beats this technique for modeling stairs, but I need to warn you; this isn't really beginner-level stuff. I include it because it's something you should eventually know how to do, so don't sweat if it seems a little over your head as you get started with SketchUp — just remember it's here if you need it.

The Treads are Components method involves (you guessed it) making each tread in your staircase into an instance of the same component. Basically, you build one simple tread that's the right depth, make it into a component, and copy a bunch of instances into a full flight of stairs. Because every step is "linked," anything you do to one automatically happens to all of them. If you don't know the first thing about components, now would be a terrific time to start from the beginning of Chapter 5 — it'll fill you in.

Go through these steps to build a staircase using the Treads are Components method:

1. **Model a single step, including the tread and the riser.**

   You can make this very simple at this stage, if you want to; all that matters is that the tread depth and the riser height are correct. You can fiddle with everything else later. Figure 4-26 shows a simple example of this.

2. **Make a component out of the step you just built.**

   Chapter 5 goes on and on about making and using components, but here's the short version (see Figure 4-27):

   1. Select all the edges and faces that make up your step.

   2. Choose Edit⇨Make Component.

   3. In the dialog box that opens, name your component "Step" and then click the Create button.

   Now your step is a component instance.

3. **Move a copy of your step into position, above the first one (see Figure 4-27).**

Figure 4-26:
Model a single step, making sure that the depth and height are accurate.

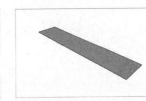

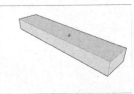

Create a component

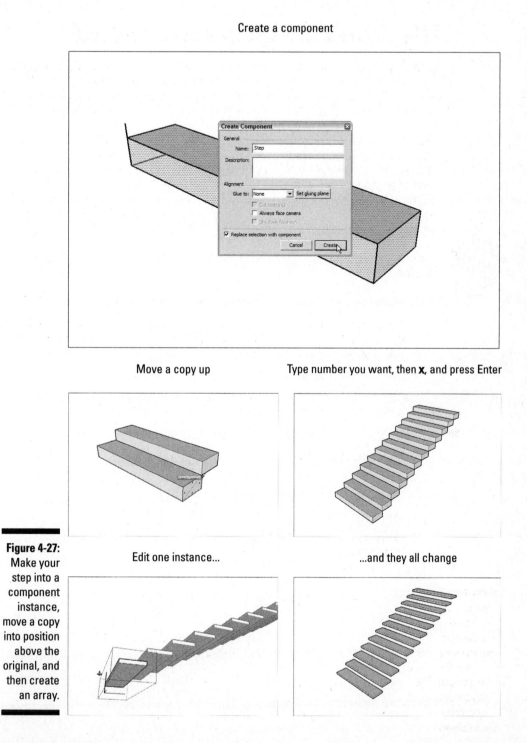

Move a copy up

Type number you want, then **x**, and press Enter

Figure 4-27:
Make your
step into a
component
instance,
move a copy
into position
above the
original, and
then create
an array.

Edit one instance...

...and they all change

4. **Type in the total number of steps you want, type an *x*, and then press Enter.**

   This is referred to as creating a *linear array,* meaning that you're making several copies at regular intervals, in the same direction you moved the first one. Typing **12x** generates 12 steps the same distance apart as the first step and its copy. The last image on the right in Figure 4-27 shows what I mean.

5. **With the Select tool, double-click any one of your steps to edit all instances of your component.**

   Everything besides the component instance you're editing should fade out a little.

6. **Go nuts.**

   This really is the fun part. Having your staircase made up of multiple component instances means that you have all the flexibility to make drastic changes to the whole thing without ever having to repeat yourself. Add a *nosing* (a bump at the leading edge of each tread), a *stringer* (a diagonal piece of structure that supports all your steps), or even a handrail by getting creative with how you modify a single component instance. Figure 4-28 shows some of what you can do. The color insert in this book shows the Treads are Components method applied to building a circular stair.

Series of component instances   A single component instance

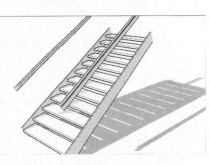 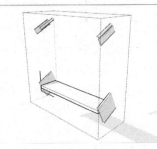

Figure 4-28: A flight of stairs with side stringers and a handrail. On the right, a single component instance.

Raising the Roof

If you're lucky, the roof you want to build is fairly simple. Unfortunately, home builders sometimes go a little crazy, creating roofs with dozens of different *pitches* (slopes), dormers, and other doodads that make modeling them a nightmare. For this reason, I'm going to keep things pretty simple: The following sections are dedicated to showing you how to identify and model some of the basic roof forms. After that, I tell you about a great tool you can use to assemble complicated roofs from less-complicated pieces — it's called Intersect with Model, and I think you'll get a kick out of it.

The tricky thing about roofs is that they're hard to see. If you want to make a model of something that already exists, it helps to be able to get a good look at it — that's not always possible with roofs. One neat way to get a better view of a roof you're trying to build is to find it in Google Earth. For more information, check out Chapter 11.

Before I dive in, what follows is a brief guide to general roof types and terminology; this might come in handy for some of the explanations I give later on. Figure 4-29 provides a visual accompaniment to my written descriptions:

- **Flat roof:** *Flat roofs* are just that, except they aren't — if a roof were really flat, it would collect water and leak. That's why even roofs that look flat are sloped very slightly.

- **Pitched roof:** Any roof that isn't flat is technically a *pitched roof.*

- **Shed roof:** A *shed roof* is one that slopes from one side to the other.

- **Gabled roof:** *Gabled roofs* have two planes that slope away from a central *ridge.*

- **Hip roof:** A *hip roof* is one where the sides and ends all slope together.

- **Pitch:** The angle of a roof surface.

- **Gable:** A *gable* is the pointy section of wall that sits under the peak of a pitched roof.

- **Eave:** *Eaves* are the parts of a roof that overhang the building.

- **Fascia:** *Fascia* is the trim around the edge of a roof's eaves where gutters are sometimes attached.

- **Soffit:** A *soffit* is the underside of an overhanging eave.

- **Rake:** The *rake* is the part of a gabled roof that overhangs the gable.

- **Valley:** A *valley* is formed when two roof slopes come together; this is where water flows when it rains.

- **Dormer:** *Dormers* are the little things that pop up above roof surfaces. They often have windows, and they serve to make attic spaces more usable.

- **Parapet:** Flat roofs that don't have eaves have *parapets:* These are extensions of the building's walls that go up a few feet past the roof itself.

Gabled roof   Dormer   Valley   Hip roof   Flat roof   Parapet   Shed roof

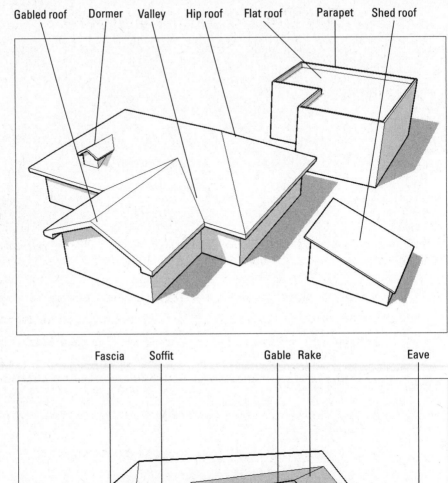

Fascia   Soffit   Gable Rake   Eave

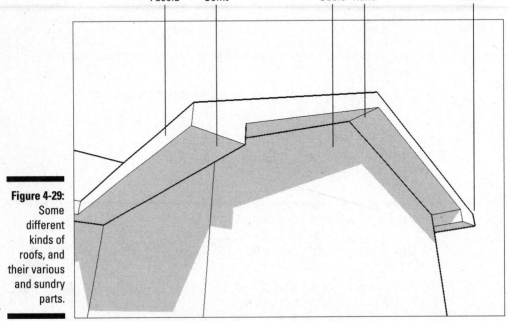

Figure 4-29: Some different kinds of roofs, and their various and sundry parts.

Building flat roofs with parapets

Good news — SketchUp was practically made for modeling these kinds of roofs. By using a combination of the Offset tool and Push/Pull, you should be able to make a parapet in under a minute. Follow these steps to see how (see Figure 4-30):

Offset to the inside   Push/Pull your parapet up

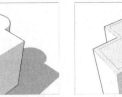  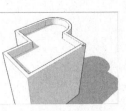

Figure 4-30:
Modeling
parapets on
flat-roofed
buildings is
easy.

1. **With the Offset tool, click the top face of your building.**

2. **Click again somewhere inside the same face to create another face.**

3. **Type in the thickness of your parapet, and then press Enter.**

   This redraws your offset edges to be a precise distance from the edges of your original face. How thick should your parapet be? It all depends on your building, but most parapets are between 6 and 12 inches thick.

4. **Push/pull your outside face (the one around the perimeter of your roof) into a parapet.**

5. **Type in the height of your parapet, and then press Enter.**

Creating eaves for buildings with pitched roofs

My favorite way to create eaves (roof overhangs) is to use the Offset tool. Follow these steps to get the general idea (see Figure 4-31):

1. **Make a group out of your whole building before you start modeling the roof.**

   This makes it easier to keep your roof separate, which in turn makes your model easier to work with.

Make a group   Retrace (or Copy and Paste) the roof line

Offset an overhang   Delete the inside face

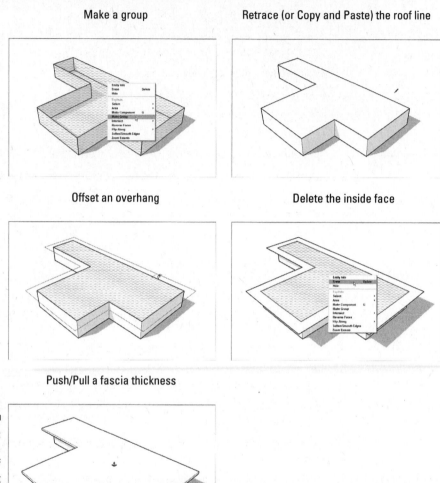

Push/Pull a fascia thickness

Figure 4-31:
Eaves are
the parts of
the roof that
overhangs a
building's
walls.

2. **Use the Line tool to create an outline of the parts of your roof that will have eaves of the same height.**

   The goal here is to end up with a single face to offset. A lot of buildings have complex roofs with eaves of all different heights; for the sake of this step, just create a face which, when offset, will create roof overhangs in the right places.

3. **Use the Offset tool to create an overhanging face.**

   For instructions on how to use Offset, see the section "Dusting off SketchUp's drafting tools," earlier in this chapter.

4. **Erase the edges of your original face.**

   A quick way to do this (with the Select tool) is to:

   a. Double-click inside your first face; this selects both it and the edges that define it.

   b. Press Delete to erase everything that's selected.

5. **Push/pull your overhanging roof face to create a thick fascia.**

   Different roofs have fasciae of different thicknesses; if you don't know yours, just take your best guess.

Constructing gabled roofs

You can approach the construction of a gabled roof in a bunch of different ways (every SketchUp expert has his or her favorite), but I've found one method in particular that works well on a consistent basis.

Follow these steps to build a gabled roof (see Figure 4-32):

1. **Create a roof overhang, following the steps in the previous section.**

   Most gabled roofs have eaves, so you'll probably need to do this for your building.

2. **Use the Protractor tool to create an angled guide at the corner of your roof.**

   See the nearby sidebar, "Pitched roofs can make you crazy," for more information about drawing angled guides with the Protractor.

   Architects and builders often express angles as *rise over run ratios*. For example, a 4:12 (pronounced four in twelve) roof slope rises 4 feet for every 12 feet it runs — a 1:12 slope is very shallow, and a 12:12 slope is very steep. When using the Protractor tool, SketchUp's VCB understands angles expressed as ratios as well as those expressed in degrees. Typing **6:12** yields a slope of 6 in 12.

3. **Use the Line tool to draw a vertical edge from the midpoint of your roof to the angled guide you created in Step 1.**

   The point at which your edge and your guide meet is the height of your roof ridge.

Create an angled guide with the Protractor   Draw a vertical edge

Complete the roof profile   Push/Pull it back

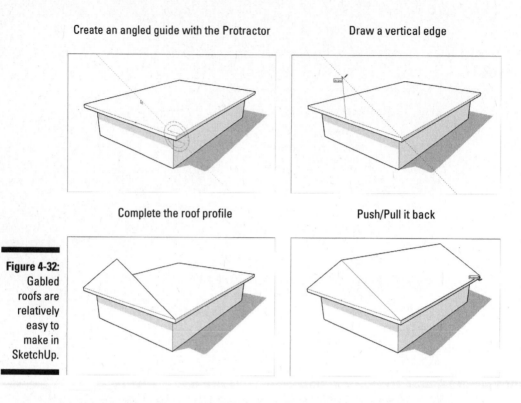

Figure 4-32:
Gabled
roofs are
relatively
easy to
make in
SketchUp.

4. **Draw two edges from the top of your vertical line to the corners of your roof.**

   This should cause two triangular faces to be created.

5. **Erase the vertical edge you drew in Step 3 and the guide you drew in Step 1.**

6. **Push/pull your triangular gable back.**

   If your gabled roof extends all the way to the other end of your building, push/pull it back that far. If your roof runs into another section of roof (as in Figure 4-33), extrude it back until it's completely "buried." The section "Sticking your roof together," later in this chapter, has more information on what to do when you're making a complex roof.

7. **Finish your eaves, fascia, soffit, and rake(s) however you want.**

   You find lots of different kinds of gabled roof details, so I can't cover them all, but Figure 4-34 shows a few common ones. Instead of writing about them (which would get confusing anyway), I'll let the pictures do the talking.

Push/Pull it all the way into the other roof pitch

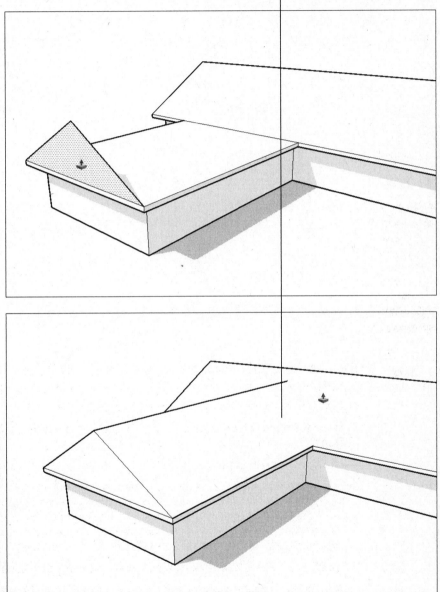

Figure 4-33:
If your
gabled roof
is part of a
larger roof
structure, it
might just
run into
another roof
pitch. Let it.

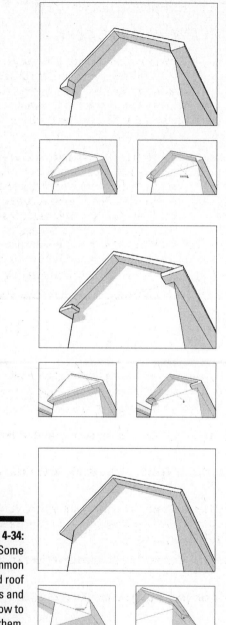

Figure 4-34:
Some
common
gabled roof
details and
how to
make them.

Pitched roofs can make you crazy

That fact notwithstanding, here are a few tips that might make building your next one a little easier:

✔ **Start by making the rest of your building a group.** Always, *always* make a group out of your whole building before you start working on your roof. If you don't, your geometry will start sticking together, you'll end up erasing walls by accident, and eventually, you'll lose your mind. On top of that, it's really handy to be able to separate your roof from the rest of your building whenever you want. You can also group your roof, if that makes sense for what you're doing. Check out Chapter 5 for a full rundown on making and using groups.

✔ **Draw a top view of your roof on paper first.** I find this really helps me figure things out. Adding measurements and angles is even better — anything so that you know what you need to do when you get around to using SketchUp.

✔ **Learn to use the Protractor tool.** This tool (which is on the Tools menu) is for measuring angles and, more importantly, creating angled guides. Because sloped roofs are all about angles, you probably need to use the Protractor sooner or later. The best way to find out how it works is to open the Instructor dialog box by choosing Window⇨Instructor and then activating the Protractor tool.

Making hip roofs

Believe it or not, building a hip roof is easier than making a gabled one. Hip roofs don't have rakes, which makes them a lot less complicated to model. Follow these steps to find out what I mean (see Figure 4-35):

1. **Follow Steps 1 through 5 in the section "Constructing gabled roofs" to begin making a hip roof.**

2. **Measure the distance from the midpoint of the gable to the corner of the roof.**

   Because hip roofs have pitches that are the same on all sides, you can use a simple trick to figure out where to locate the hip in your roof. It's a lot easier than using the Protractor; trust me.

3. **With the Tape Measure, create a guide (the distance you just measured) from the end of the gable.**

4. **Draw edges from the point on the ridge you just located to the corners of your roof.**

   This does two things: It splits the sides of your roof into two faces each and creates a new face (which you can't see yet) under the gabled end of your roof.

Measure half-width of your gable

Create a guide that distance from end of gable

Draw edges connecting ridge and corners

Erase the edges that form the gable

Now you have a hip

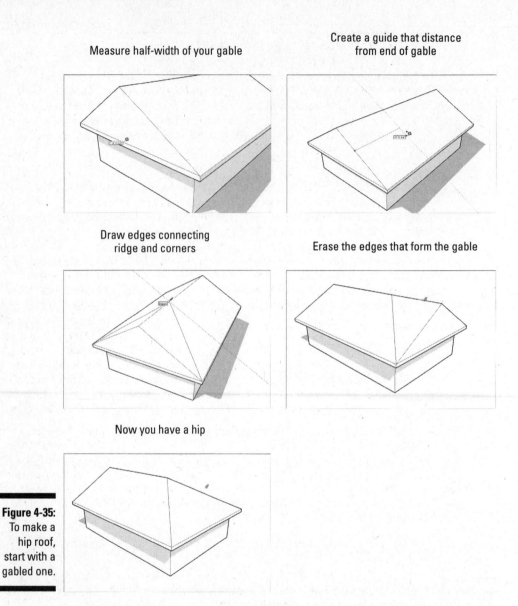

5. **Erase the three edges that form the gabled end of your roof, revealing the "hipped" pitch underneath.**

   Neat, huh? Now all three faces of your roof are the same pitch — just the way they should be.

6. **If appropriate, repeat the process on the other end of your roof.**

Sticking your roof together

In general, the newer and more expensive a house is, the more roof slopes it has. Who knows why this is the case; it probably has something to do with folks thin⟨…⟩⟨…r⟩oofed houses look more like French chateaus. Whether ⟨…⟩⟨…⟩⟨…bias⟩ showing again) are a good thing isn't rel⟨…⟩ ⟨…⟩ They're a pain in the, um⟨…⟩

Gettin⟨…⟩

Luckil⟨…⟩ often helps when it come⟨…⟩ Model. Here's what you ⟨…⟩

⟨…⟩ ⟨…x⟩isting geometry. ⟨…⟩nd creates edges ⟨…⟩del in cases where ⟨…⟩t together), *difference* ⟨…⟩y have in common) of ⟨…⟩out: Perhaps I want to ⟨…⟩d chunk taken out of it. ⟨…⟩fter positioning them ⟨…⟩ create edges where the ⟨…⟩uld use the Eraser to ⟨…⟩he cylinder, in this case.

⟨…⟩nd in hand. Anytime you ⟨…⟩ by spending some time ⟨…⟩'t a bad thing, but it does ⟨…⟩oming, and panning around ⟨…⟩ handy with the Eraser.

Figure

Int⟨…⟩

with⟨…⟩

t⟨…⟩

cyli⟨…⟩

o⟨…⟩

✔ **Most of the time, choose to Intersect with Model.** This tool has three different modes (just introduced in SketchUp 6), but the majority of the time, you'll end up using the basic one. Here's what all three of them do:

- **Intersect with Model:** Creates edges everywhere your selected faces intersect with other faces in your model — whether the other faces are selected or not.

- **Intersect Selected:** Only creates edges where *selected* faces intersect with other *selected* faces. This is handy if you're trying to be a little bit more precise.

- **Intersect with Context:** This one's a little trickier: Choosing this option creates edges where faces *within the same group or component* intersect; that's why it's only available when you're editing a group or component.

✔ **Intersect with Model doesn't have a button.** To use it, you have to either:

- Right-click and choose it from the context menu.

- Choose Edit⇨Intersect.

ON THE WEB

Complex hip roofs and the Follow Me tool

Ready to see something *really* cool? SketchUp has a tool called Follow Me, which I describe in detail in Chapter 5. You can use Follow Me to create complex hip roofs in about one-fifth the time it would normally take you to make them — sometimes even less. At its core, Follow Me works a bit like Push/Pull, except it lets you extrude faces along predetermined paths. You can use it to create very complicated geometry — the kind of stuff you probably wouldn't be able to make without it.

When it comes to hip roofs, the Follow Me technique only works if your roof meets the following conditions:

✔ The pitch needs to be the same on all roof surfaces.

✔ The roof needs to be "hipped" all the way around.

Follow these steps to use Follow Me to create a complex hip roof (the following images tell the story):

1. **Over the widest part of your building, draw a triangle that represents the slope of your roof. It should only be a *half*-gable, as shown in the images.**

2. **Select the top surface of your building.**

3. **With the Follow Me tool (available on the Tools menu), click the half-roof profile you drew in Step 1 once.**

4. **Select your whole roof by triple-clicking it with the Select tool; I like to hide the rest of my building at this point, too.**

5. **Right-click anywhere on the roof and choose Intersect⇨Intersect with Model from the context menu.**

6. **Use the Eraser to clean up your roof by erasing any geometry that isn't supposed to be part of it — you'll find plenty. You'll** probably also have to draw in edges every now and then. If you make a mistake, just use Undo and try again.

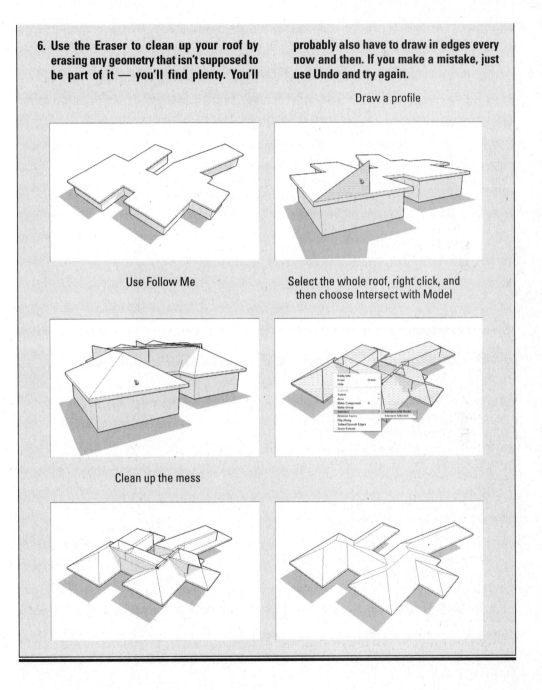

Use Follow Me

Draw a profile

Clean up the mess

Select the whole roof, right click, and then choose Intersect with Model

When all else fails, use the Line tool

Fancy tools like Follow Me and Intersect with Model are useful most of the time, but for some roofs, you just have to resort to drawing good old edges. If that's the case, you'd better get familiar with most of the stuff at the beginning of Chapter 2, because you're going to be inferencing like there's no tomorrow. SketchUp users who really know what they're doing can draw *anything* with the Line tool and the Eraser too; it's

a beautiful thing to watch. Unfortunately, it's not a beautiful thing to write (or read) about in a black-and-white book, so I can't show you as much "modeling from first principles" stuff as I'd like.

All the same, check out the following figure. In it, I use the Line tool and SketchUp's venerable inference engine to add a gabled dormer to a sloped roof surface. With practice, you can, too.

Draw an edge on the face of the roof

Draw a vertical face

Draw edges all the way back to the sloped face

Connect the edges

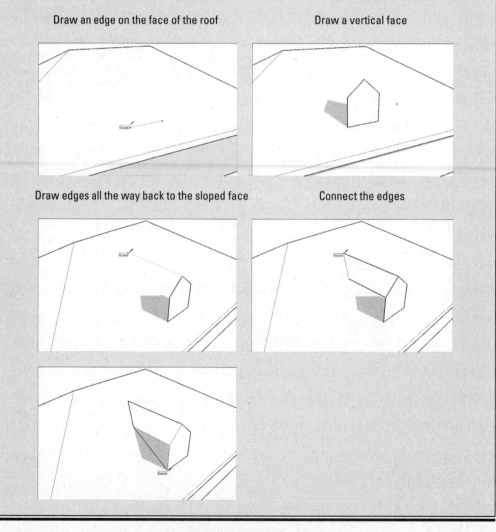

Most 3D modeling programs let you do *Boolean* operations, meaning that you're encouraged to make models by adding, subtracting, and intersecting different shapes to make new ones. For *solids* modelers (like SolidWorks, Inventor, and Form(Z), this makes sense, because this paradigm is a lot like sculpting with clay. But because SketchUp is more paper-like than clay-like (it's not clay-like at all, come to think of it), Boolean operations are not technically possible. Intersect with Model is about as close as SketchUp comes to letting you work this way.

Using Intersect with Model to make roofs

When it comes to creating roofs, you can use Intersect with Model to combine a whole bunch of gables, hips, dormers, sheds, and so on into a single roof. It's no cakewalk, and it requires a fair amount of planning, but it works great when nothing else will.

Figure 4-37 shows a complicated roof with several different elements. Gabled roofs have been pushed/pulled into the main hip roof form at all different heights, but edges don't exist where all the different faces meet. In the steps that follow, I use Intersect with Model to create the edges I want and then I use the Eraser to clean up my mess:

1. **Select the whole roof.**

   You can do this in a number of different ways, but the one that I find works the best is to first hide the group that contains the rest of your building, and then draw a big selection box around the whole roof with the Select tool.

2. **Choose Edit⇨Intersect⇨Intersect Selected.**

   This tells SketchUp to go through and create edges everywhere you have faces that intersect — everywhere they "pass through" each other without an edge.

3. **Get out your Eraser and *carefully* delete all the extra geometry on the inside of your roof.**

   I won't lie; this can be a lot of work. But it's a whole lot easier than using the Line tool and SketchUp's inference engine to figure out where everything should go. The last image in Figure 4-37 shows the end result.

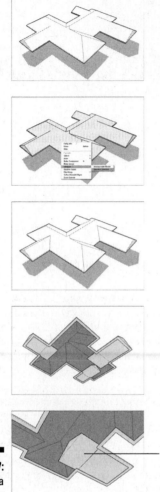

Looking at the underside

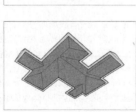

Erase the stuff that doesn't belong

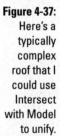

Figure 4-37:
Here's a typically complex roof that I could use Intersect with Model to unify.

Chapter 5

Keeping Your Model Organized

Starting with this chapter, I might sound like your mom: "Clean up your room! Don't leave your toys in the driveway! Put your dishes in the sink!" As everybody knows, living life can be a messy ordeal, and modeling in SketchUp is no exception. As you crank away at whatever it is you're building, you will reach a time when you stop, orbit around, and wonder how your model got to be such a pigsty. It's inevitable.

Luckily, SketchUp includes a bunch of different ways to keep your geometry (edges and faces) from getting out of control. Because big, unwieldy, disorganized models are a pain to work with — they can slow your computer, or even cause SketchUp to crash — you should definitely get in the habit of "working clean" (as cooking shows like to call it). As I said earlier, I don't mean to nag; I just want you to be familiar with the techniques experienced SketchUp modelers use to keep from going insane.

In this chapter, I present the four main tools that SketchUp provides for organizing your model. In the first section, I outline all four and talk about what they're for. Then I dive in to each one in a good amount of detail, describing how to use them and how *not* to use them (are you listening, layers?). This chapter ends with a detailed example of how all four methods can be used together to make your life easier; I show you how I organize a model of my house.

Taking Stock of Your Organization Options

When it comes to sorting out the thousands of edges and faces in your model, it's all about lumping things together into useful sets. After you've separated things out, you can name them, hide them, and even lock them so that you (or somebody else) can't mess them up. This whole chapter is dedicated to the different tools SketchUp provides to help keep your model straight, but here's a brief rundown of each of them, just to put things in perspective:

✔ **Groups:** Making a group is like gluing together some of the geometry in your model. Edges and faces that are grouped together act like mini-models inside your main model; you use groups to make it easier to select, move, hide, and otherwise work with parts of your model that need to be kept separate.

✔ **Components:** I wish there was a way to use the typography in this book to convey the relative importance of certain topics; if there was, the word *COMPONENTS* would be printed 4 inches high, and it would be colored neon green. SketchUp components are a lot like groups, but they have a lot of extra handy properties. You use components when your model includes a bunch of copies of the same thing, like windows, furniture, and trees. After you're up and running with SketchUp, you'll end up using components all the time.

✔ **Outliner:** The Outliner is a dialog box that's basically a fancy list of all the groups and components in your SketchUp model. It shows you which groups and components are nested inside other ones, lets you assign names for them, and gives you an easy way to hide parts of your model you don't want to see. If you use a lot of components (and you should), the Outliner may well become your new best friend.

✔ **Layers:** This is where a lot of people reading this book let out a big sigh of relief. "Thank goodness," they're thinking, "I was beginning to think SketchUp doesn't have layers." For people who are used to organizing content in other software programs, layers are usually where it's at — you put different kinds of things on different layers, name the layers, and then turn them on and off when you need to. It's a pretty simple concept.

In SketchUp, layers are similar, but there's a problem: Using layers the wrong way can seriously mess up your model. I'm not kidding. If you're going to use them, read the section "Discovering the Ins and Outs of Layers," later in this chapter. Not doing so could result in serious injury or even death (depending on how upset you get when your 50-hour model gets ruined).

Grouping Things Together

Anyone who's worked with SketchUp for even a short time has probably noticed something: SketchUp geometry (the edges and faces that make up your model) is *sticky*. That is to say, stuff in your model wants to stick to other stuff. The people who invented SketchUp built it this way on purpose; the reasons why would take a while to explain. Suffice it to say, making and using groups are the keys to keeping the stuff in your model from sticking together. For additional help, check out this book's companion Web site; see the Introduction for details.

You have many reasons you need to make groups; here are a few of them:

- **Grouped geometry doesn't stick to anything.** Perhaps you've modeled a building, and you want to add a roof. You want to be able to remove the roof by moving it out of the way with the Move tool, but every time you try, you end up pulling the whole top part of the house along with it (like the middle image in Figure 5-1). Making the roof a separate group allows you to let it sit on top of your house without sticking there, making it easier to deal with, as shown in the right image in Figure 5-1.

- **Using groups makes it easier to work with your model.** You can select all the geometry in a group by clicking it once with the Select tool. You can move groups around and make copies with the Move tool. To edit a group, you double-click it with the Select tool. To stop editing it, you click outside it, somewhere else in your modeling window.

- **You can name groups.** If you turn a selection of geometry in your model into a group, you can give it a name. In the Outliner (which I talk about later in this chapter) you can see a list of the groups (and components) in your model, and if you've given them names, you can see what you have.

Figure 5-1:
Making the roof into a group means that it won't stick to the rest of your building.

The house is being stretched

 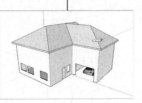 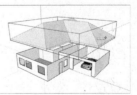

Follow these steps to create a group:

1. **Select the geometry (edges and faces) you'd like to turn into a group.**

   The simplest way to select multiple *entities* (edges and faces) is to click them one at a time with the Select tool while holding down Shift. You can also use the Select tool to drag a box around the entities you want to select, but this can be tough, depending on where they are. For more information on making selections, check out Chapter 2.

2. **Choose Edit⇨Make Group.**

   You can also right-click and choose Make Group from the context menu that pops up.

If you want to "ungroup" the geometry in a group, you need to explode it. Right-click the group and choose Explode from the context menu. The edges and faces that were grouped together aren't grouped together anymore.

Working with Components

Even though components are incredibly important, there's nothing too magical about them — they're just groupings of geometry (edges and faces) that make working in SketchUp faster, easier, and more fun. In a lot of ways, components are really just fancy groups — they do a lot of the same things. In the following sections, I talk about what makes components special and give some examples of what you can do with them. Next, I give a quick tour of the Components dialog box, pointing out where components live and how you can organize them. The last part of this section is devoted to making your own. It's not hard, and after you can make components, you'll be on your way to SketchUp stardom (check out Chapter 13 for more on sharing your SketchUp models with the world).

What makes components so great?

By now, you've probably figured out that I'm a big fan of using components whenever you can. Here's why:

✔ **Everything that's true about groups is true about components.** That's right: Components are just like groups, only better (in some ways, at least). Components don't stick to the rest of your model, you can give them meaningful names, and you can select them, move them, copy them, and edit them easily — just like you can with groups.

✔ **Components update automatically.** When you use multiple copies (these are called *instances*) of the same component in your model, they're all spookily linked. Changing one makes all of them change, which saves loads of time. Consider a window component that I created and made two copies of, as shown in Figure 5-2. When I add something (in this case, some shutters) to one instance of that component, *all* the instances are updated. Now I have three windows, and they all have shutters.

✔ **Using components can help you keep track of quantities.** You can use the Components dialog box to count, select, substitute, and otherwise manage all the component instances in your model. Figure 5-3 shows a great big (and ugly) building I designed to go with the window component I made. Because they're component instances, I have a lot more control than I would have had if they weren't.

These windows are instances
of the same component

Figure 5-2:
Changing
one instance
of a com-
ponent
changes all
the other
instances,
too.

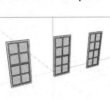   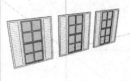

Figure 5-3:
Quickly
count all the
Window 1
instances in
your model
(left), or
even swap
them out
for another
component.
(I like
helicopters,
don't you?)

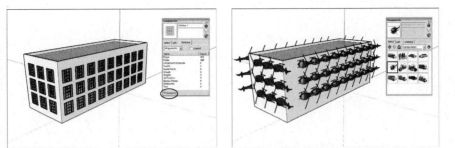

TIP

✔ **You can make a component cut an opening automatically.** Perhaps you've made a window (which I have) and you'd like that window to poke a hole through whatever surface you stick it to (which I do). SketchUp components can be set up to cut their own openings in faces. These openings are even temporary; when you delete the component, the hole disappears. Check out Figure 5-4 to see this in action.

Components that are set up to automatically cut openings can only do so through a single face. Even if your wall is two faces thick, your components will cut through only one of them.

✔ **You can use your components in other models.** It's a simple operation to make any component you build available for use whenever you're working in SketchUp, no matter what model you're working on. If you have a group of parts or other things you always use, making your own component library can save you a lot of time and effort. There's more information about creating your own component libraries later in this section.

✔ **Components are great for making symmetrical models.** Because you can flip a component instance and keep working on it, and because component instances automatically update when you change one of them, using components is a great way to model anything that's symmetrical. And if you look around, you'll notice that most of the things we use are symmetrical. Chapter 6 dives headlong into modeling symmetrical things like couches and hatchbacks; Figure 5-5 shows some examples from SketchUp's default component library.

Figure 5-4:
Components can cut their own holes in surfaces, which is handy for windows and doors.

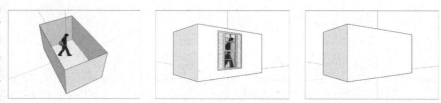

Exploring the Components dialog box

It's all fine and well that SketchUp lets you turn bits of your models into components, I suppose, but wouldn't it be nice if you had someplace to *keep* them? And wouldn't it be great if you could use components made by other people to spiff up your model, instead of having to build everything yourself? As you've probably already guessed, both of these things are possible, and both involve the Components dialog box, which you can find on the Window menu.

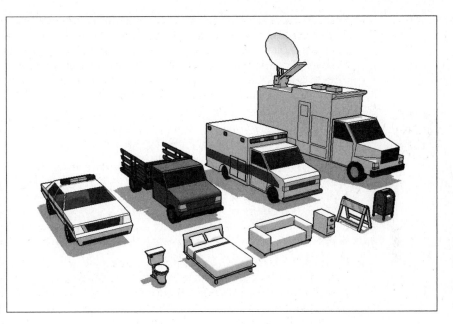

Figure 5-5:
What do all
these things
have in
common?
They're
symmetrical.

Here's something you need to realize: Any SketchUp model on your computer can be brought into your current file as a component. That's because components are really just SketchUp files embedded in other SketchUp files. When you create a component in your model, you're effectively creating a new, nested SketchUp file. Neat, huh?

The Components dialog box is made up of four major areas, which I describe in the following sections.

Info and buttons

I don't really know what to call this part of the dialog box, so I'll call it like it is: It's for information and buttons. Figure 5-6 points out its elements, and here's what everything does:

- **Name:** This is where the name of the component you select appears. If it's a component in your model, it's editable. If it's in one of the default libraries, it's not. A component is considered to be in your model if it appears in your In Model library, which you can read about in the section "The Select pane," later in this chapter.

- **Description:** Some, but not all, components have descriptions associated with them. You can write one when you're creating a new component, or you can add one to an existing component in your model. Just like the name, you can only edit descriptions for models in your In Model library.

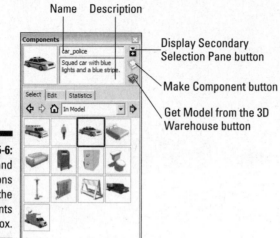

Name   Description

Display Secondary
Selection Pane button

Make Component button

Get Model from the 3D
Warehouse button

Figure 5-6:
The Info and
Buttons
area of the
Components
dialog box.

- ✔ **Display Secondary Selection Pane button:** Clicking this button opens a second view of your libraries at the bottom of the Components dialog box. You use this to manage the components on your computer system.

- ✔ **Make Component button:** Clicking this button creates a component from whatever geometry you have selected in your modeling window. You have other ways to create new components, which I explain in the next section.

- ✔ **Get Model from the 3D Warehouse button:** The 3D Warehouse is an online repository of thousands — maybe hundreds of thousands — of SketchUp components that you can use in your model. Read all about the 3D Warehouse in Chapter 11.

The Select pane

This is where your components "live" (if they can be said to live anywhere). You use the Select pane to view, organize, and choose components. Figure 5-7 shows the Select pane in all its glory.

- ✔ **Back and Forward buttons:** Use these to toggle between component libraries that you've viewed recently.

- ✔ **In Model Library button:** SketchUp automatically keeps track of the components you've used in your model and puts a copy of each of them in your In Model library. Each SketchUp file you create has its own In Model library, which contains the components that exist in that model. Clicking the In Model Library button displays the components in your In Model library, if you have any.

- ✔ **Libraries drop-down list:** Clicking this list shows a list of the component libraries you have on your computer system. SketchUp comes preinstalled with a few default libraries, but you can create you own if you want to.

Back and Forward buttons

In Model button

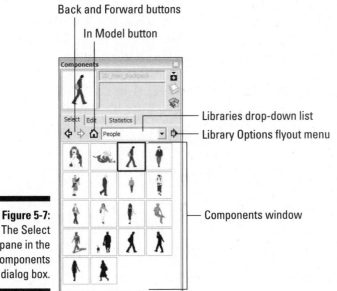

Libraries drop-down list

Library Options flyout menu

Components window

Figure 5-7:
The Select
pane in the
Components
dialog box.

Libraries are essentially folders on your computer that contain SketchUp files. When you tell SketchUp that a particular folder is a component library, it displays each SketchUp model in that folder as a component that you can use in whatever model you're working on at the moment. For more information on creating your own libraries of components, keep reading.

✔ **Components window:** This window displays the components in the currently selected component library. Click a component to use it in your model.

✔ **Library Options flyout menu:** Here's where you manage the component libraries on your computer system. A bunch of options exist, so I'd better explain what most of them mean:

  • **Open an Existing Library:** Lets you choose a folder on your computer system to use as a component library. Any SketchUp models in that folder can be used as components in your current model.

  • **Create a New Library:** Allows you to create a folder somewhere on your computer system that you can use as a component library. This is handy if you have a number of components that you use all the time; putting them all in one place makes them easier to find.

  • **Save Library As:** When you choose this option, SketchUp lets you save your In Model library (consisting of all the components in your current model) as a library all by itself. As you can imagine, this option is only available when you're viewing your In Model library.

- **Add Library to Favorites:** If you have a library you use a lot, choose this option to add it to the Favorites section of the Libraries drop-down list. That way, it'll be easier to get to in a hurry.

- **Expand:** Because components can be made up of other, nested components, a component you use in your model might really be *lots* of components. Choosing Expand displays all the components in your model, whether or not they're nested inside other components. Most of the time, you'll probably want to leave Expand deselected.

- **Purge Unused:** Choose this to get rid of any components in your In Model library that aren't in your model anymore. Be sure to use this before you send your SketchUp file to someone else; it'll seriously reduce your file size and make things a whole lot neater.

- **Get More:** Bonanza! Choosing this option sends you directly to a Google Web site (as long as you're online), where you can download extra libraries of components — thousands of them. Better yet, they're all free. All the Bonus Packs are great, but I'd definitely recommend getting Architecture (which includes furniture), Transportation (to see how experts model vehicles), and People (which includes a model of me — I'm the guy in the long, black coat).

Select and replace all your troubles away

On top of the all the buttons, menus, and windows you can immediately see in the Select pane of the Components dialog box, some hidden options exist that most people don't find until they go looking for them; they're on the context menu that pops up when you right-click a component in your In Model library:

✔ **Select Instances:** Perhaps you have 15 instances (copies) of the same component in your model, and you want to select them all. Just make sure that you're viewing your In Model library, and then right-click the component (in the Components dialog box) whose instances you want to select all of. Choose Select Instances, and your work's done. This can save you tons of time, particularly if you have component instances all over the place.

✔ **Replace Selected:** Now you might want to swap in a different component for one that's in your model. Simply select the component instances (in your modeling window) that you want to replace, and then right-click the component (in the Components dialog box) that you want to use instead. Choose Replace Selected from the context menu to perform the swap.

Ready for an even better tip? Use Select Instances and Replace Selected together to help you work more efficiently. Instead of placing 20 big, heavy tree components in your model (which can seriously slow things down), use a smaller, simpler component instead (like a stick). When you're finished modeling, use Select Instances to select all the stand-in components at once, and then use Replace Selected to swap in the real component.

The Edit pane

Because the options in this part of the Components dialog box are similar to the ones you get when you make a new component, you should check out the section "Creating your own components," later in this chapter, for the whole scoop.

You can only use the options in the Edit pane on components in your In Model library — everything will be grayed out for components that "live" in any other place.

The Statistics pane

Can you remember who won the 1975 Super Bowl? How many home runs did Hank Aaron hit in his career? Do you always check the nutrition information panel on food packaging? You might be a sucker for statistics, and if so, welcome home. . . .

Even if you're not, the Statistics pane is a useful place to spend some time. You use it to keep track of all the details related to whatever component you have selected in the Components dialog box. (See Figure 5-8.) This is especially useful for doing the following things:

✔ **Checking the size of your components:** The information in the Edges and Faces areas of this pane lets you know how much geometry is in a component. If you're worried about file size or your computer's performance, try to use small components — ones with low numbers of faces and edges.

✔ **Seeing what components are inside your components:** The Component Instances line lists how many component instances are in your selected component. If you switch from All Geometry to Components in the dropdown list at the top of the pane, you can see a list of all the constituent components: subcomponents within your main component.

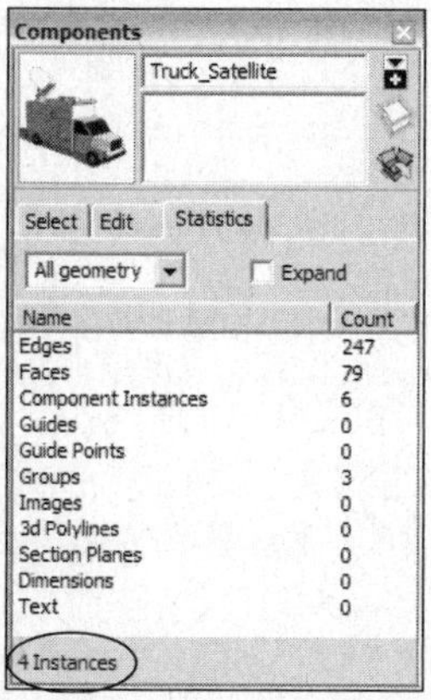

Figure 5-8:
The
Statistics
pane of the
Components
dialog box:
Geek-out on
numbers.

Components	
Truck_Satellite	

Select	Edit	Statistics

All geometry ▾   ☐ Expand

Name	Count
Edges	247
Faces	79
Component Instances	6
Guides	0
Guide Points	0
Groups	3
Images	0
3d Polylines	0
Section Planes	0
Dimensions	0
Text	0

4 Instances

The Statistics pane *doesn't* show details for components you have selected in your actual model; it only shows information about the component that's selected in the Select pane of the Components dialog box. To see information about whatever component (or other kind of object) you have selected in your modeling window, use the Entity Info dialog box (located in the Window menu).

Creating your own components

Now that I've got you all jazzed up about the wonder and mystery of using components in your models, I'll bet you can't wait to start making your own. At least I hope so — using components is probably the single best SketchUp habit you can develop. Here's why:

- **Components keep file sizes down.** When you use several instances of a single component, SketchUp only has to remember the information for one of them. This means that your files are smaller, which in turn means that you'll have an easier time e-mailing, uploading, and opening them on your computer.

- **Components show up in the Outliner.** If you're a person who's at all interested in not wasting time hunting around for things you've misplaced, you should create lots of components. Doing so means that you'll be able to see, hide, unhide, and rearrange them in the Outliner, which I go over later in this chapter.

- **Components can save your sanity.** Hooray! You've finished a model of the new airport — and it only took three weeks! Too bad the planning commission wants you to add a sunshade detail to every one of the 1,300 windows in the project. If you made that window a component, you're golden. If, on the other hand, that window *isn't* a component, you're going to be spending a very long night holding hands with your computer mouse.

Making your own doors and windows

If you're kind of nerdy like I am, nothing beats making your own window and door components. Here's what you need to know (check out the illustration that follows this sidebar for visual instructions):

1. **Start by drawing a rectangle on a vertical surface, like a wall.**

2. **Delete the face you just created to make a hole in your vertical surface.**

3. **Select all four edges of the hole you just created. Then right-click one of the edges and choose Make Component from the context menu.**

4. **Make sure that Glue to Any, Cut Opening, and Replace Selection with Component are all selected; then click the Create button to create your new component.**

5. **With the Select tool, double-click your new component (in the modeling window) to edit it; the rest of your model will appear to fade back a bit.**

6. **Use the modeling tools just like you always would to keep building your door or window any way you want.**

7. **When you're done, click outside your component to stop editing it.**

If the opening you create ever closes up, one of two things probably happened:

✔ **A new surface was created.** Try deleting the offending surface to see whether that fixes things; it usually does.

✔ **The cutting boundary was messed up.** The cutting boundary consists of the edges that define the hole your component is cutting. If you take away those edges, SketchUp doesn't know where to cut the hole anymore. Drawing them back in usually sets things straight.

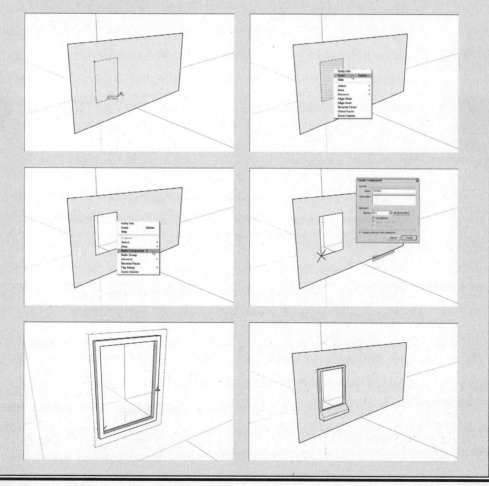

Making a new component

Creating simple components is a pretty easy process, but making more complicated ones — components that automatically cut openings, stick to surfaces, and always face the viewer — can be a little trickier. Follow these steps, regardless of what kind of component you're trying to make:

1. **Select the edges and faces (at least two) you'd like to turn into a component.**

   For more information on making selections, see Chapter 2.

2. **Choose Edit⇨Create Component.**

   The Create Component dialog box opens. (See Figure 5-9.)

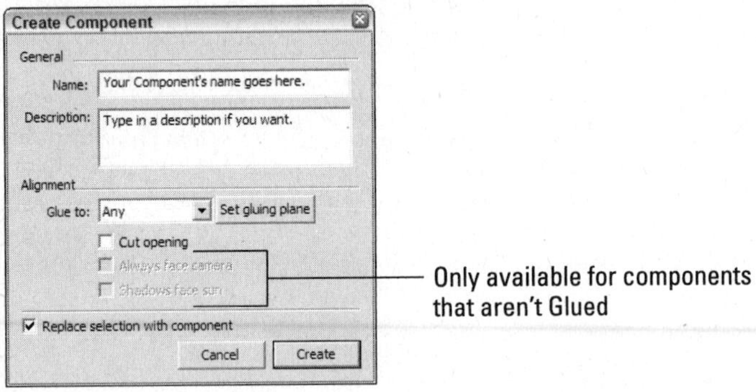

Figure 5-9:
The Create
Component
dialog box.
So many
options . . .

3. **Give your new component a name and description.**

   Of these two, the name is by far the most important. Make sure to choose one that's descriptive enough that you'll understand it when you open your model a year from now.

4. **Set the alignment options for your new component.**

   Wondering what the heck all this stuff means? I don't blame you — it can be a bit confusing the first time. For a quick introduction to each option and tips for using it, check out Table 5-1.

5. **Select the Replace Selection with Component check box, if it isn't already selected.**

   This drops your new component into your model right where your selected geometry was, saving you from having to insert it yourself from the Components dialog box.

6. **Click the Create button to create your new component.**

Table 5-1	Component Alignment Options	
Option	*What It Does*	*Tips and Tricks*
Glue To	This option makes a component automatically stick to a specific plane. For example, a chair will almost always be sitting on a floor. It will almost *never* be stuck to a wall, turned sideways. When a component is glued to a surface, using the Move tool only moves it around on that surface — never perpendicular to it (up and down, if the surface is a floor).	Use this feature for objects that you want to remain on the surface you put them on, especially objects you'll want to rearrange: Furniture, windows, and doors are prime examples. If you want to "unstick" a glued component from a particular surface, right-click it and choose Unglue from the context menu.
Set Gluing Plane	This sets a component's gluing plane, which is an invisible rectangle that tells SketchUp what part of that component should stick to things, after you select Glue To. For simple things like chairs, the gluing plane is under the chair legs. For flat-screen TVs, it's behind the back surface.	Click the Set Gluing Plane button to choose where you want your component's gluing plane to be (it looks like a gray, translucent rectangle). Click once to center your axes, again to establish the red direction, and a third time to establish the green and blue directions. Practice a few times to get it right — it's not the easiest thing to do.
Cut Opening	For components "on" a surface, select this check box to automatically cut an opening in surfaces you stick the component to.	As with pre-made components, this opening is temporary: If you delete the component instance, the opening will disappear. If you move the component instance, the opening will move, too.
Always Face Camera	This option makes a component *always* face you, no matter how you orbit around. To make your 2D Face-Me components (that's what they're called) work right, rotate your component-to-be so that it's perpendicular to your model's green axis before you choose Make Component.	Using flat, "lightweight" components instead of 3D "heavy" ones is a great way to have lots of people and trees in your model without bogging down your computer.
Shadows Face Sun	This option is only available when the Always Face Camera check box is selected, and is selected by default.	You should leave this check box selected unless your Face-Me component meets the ground in two or more separate places, as shown in Figure 5-10.

Incorrect shadow

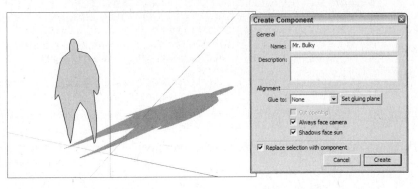

Corrected shadow

Figure 5-10:
Deselect the
Shadows
Face Sun
check box
if your
component
touches the
ground in
more than
one place.

Components can only cut through one face at a time. If your model's walls are two faces thick, you'll have to cut your window and door openings manually.

Editing, exploding, and locking component instances

Right-clicking a component instance in your modeling window opens a context menu that offers lots of useful choices; here's what some of them let you do:

✔ **Edit Component:** To edit all instances of a component at once, right-click any instance and choose Edit Component from the context menu. The rest of your model will fade back, and you'll see a dashed bounding box around your component. When you're done, click somewhere outside the bounding box to finish editing; your changes have been made in every instance of that component in your model.

✔ **Make Unique:** Sometimes you want to make changes to only one or a few of the instances of a component in your model. In this case, select the instance(s) you want to edit, right-click one of them, and choose Make Unique from the context menu. This turns the instances you selected into a separate component. Now edit any of them; only those instances you "made unique" will reflect your changes.

✔ **Explode:** When you explode a component instance, you're effectively turning it back into regular ol' geometry. Explode is a lot like Ungroup in other software programs (in SketchUp, you use Explode to "disassemble" both components and groups).

✔ **Lock:** Locking a group or a component instance means that nobody — including you — can mess with it until it's unlocked. You should use this on parts of your model you don't want to change accidentally. To unlock something, right-click on it and choose Unlock.

Falling in Love with the Outliner

I'm a person who really likes to make lists. Not only that, but I love to *look at* lists — information arranged neatly into collapsible rows is the kind of thing that brings a tear to my eye.

Now, before you decide that I ought to be locked in a small room with cushions on the walls, consider this: most halfway-complicated SketchUp models consist of dozens, if not hundreds, of groups and components. These groups and components are nested inside each other like Russian dolls, and a lot of them are heavy, computer-killing behemoths like three-dimensional trees and shrubs.

Without a list, how are you going to manage all your groups and components? How are you going to keep track of what you have, hide what you don't want to see, and (more importantly) *unhide* what you *do* want to see? I thought so — I guess it turns out I'm not so crazy after all.

Taking a good look at the Outliner

You can open the Outliner dialog box by choosing Window➪Outliner. Figure 5-11 shows what it looks like when a model consists of a simple room with some furniture in it. The individual items of furniture are all components I found in the Components dialog box (after I downloaded the Architecture Bonus Pack, that is). You can find out more about component bonus packs in the section "Working with Components," earlier in this chapter).

This symbol means this is a component instance

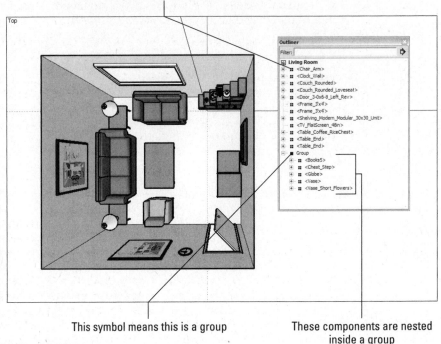

Figure 5-11:
The Outliner,
when I
have a few
components
in my model.

This symbol means this is a group

These components are nested
inside a group

The Outliner dialog box has the following features:

✔ **Search filter box:** If you type a word or phrase into this box, the
Outliner will only show the items in your model that include that word
or phrase in their name. If I were to type in **coffee**, only the coffee table
component would be visible.

✔ **Outliner Options flyout menu:** This handy little menu contains three
options:

• **Expand All:** Choose this option to have the Outliner show *all* the
nested groups and components in your model — every last one of
them (provided they're on visible layers).

It's important to note that the Outliner only shows groups and
components that exist on layers that are visible in your model.
In other words, anything on a hidden layer won't appear in the
Outliner, so you should be extra careful if you're using both the
Outliner and layers to organize your model. You can read all about
layers in the next section.

- **Collapse All:** This option collapses your Outliner view so that you only see *top-level* groups and components — ones that aren't nested inside other groups and components.

- **Sort by Name:** Select this option to make the Outliner list the groups and components in your model alphabetically.

✔ **Outliner List window:** This is where all the groups and components in your model are listed. Groups and components that have nested groups and components inside them have an Expand/Collapse toggle arrow next to their names. When they're expanded, the constituent groups and components appear as an indented list below them.

Making good use of the Outliner

If you're going to use lots of groups and components (and you should), having the Outliner open on your screen is one of the best things you can do to model efficiently. Here's why:

✔ **Use the Outliner to control visibility.** Instead of right-clicking groups and components in your model to hide them, use the Outliner instead. Just right-click the name of any element in the Outliner and choose Hide. When you do, the element is hidden in your modeling window, and its name is grayed out and italicized in the Outliner. To unhide it, just right-click its name in the Outliner and choose Unhide.

✔ **Drag and drop elements in the Outliner to change their nesting order.** Don't like having the component you just created nested inside another component? Simply drag its name in the Outliner to the top of the list. This moves it to the top level, meaning that it's not embedded in anything. You can also use the Outliner to drag groups and components "into" other ones, too.

✔ **Find and select things using the Outliner.** When you select something in the Outliner, its name gets highlighted, and it gets selected in your modeling window. This is a much easier way to select nested groups and components, especially if you're working with a complex model.

Discovering the Ins and Outs of Layers

I'm gonna give it to you straight: Layers are a very useful part of SketchUp, and they can make your life a lot easier. Layers can also be a major source of heartache, because they can *really* mess up your model if you're not careful. I'll try to get you going on the right track. . . .

What layers are — and what they're not

In a 2D program like Photoshop or Illustrator, the concept of layers makes a lot of sense: You can have content on any number of layers, sort of like a stack of transparencies. You find a distinct order to your layers, so anything that's on the top layer is visually "in front of" everything on all the other layers. Figure 5-12 shows what I'm talking about.

Figure 5-12:
In 2D software, layers are pretty straight-forward.

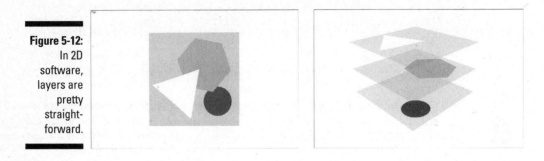

But hold on a second — SketchUp isn't a 2D program; it's a 3D program. So how can it have layers? How can objects in three-dimensional space be "layered" on top of each other so that things on higher layers appear "in front of" things on lower ones? In short, they can't — it's impossible. This means that layers in SketchUp are different from layers in most other graphics programs, and that's confusing for lots of people.

SketchUp has a layers system because some of the very first SketchUp users were architects, and many, *many* architects use drawing software called AutoCAD. Because AutoCAD uses layers extensively, layers were incorporated into SketchUp to maximize compatibility between the two products. When you import a layered AutoCAD file into SketchUp, its layers show up as SketchUp layers, which is pretty convenient.

So what are SketchUp layers for? Layers are for controlling visibility. You use them to gather particular kinds of geometry so that you can easily turn it on (make it visible) and turn it off (make it invisible) when you need to. That said, layers *don't* work the same way as groups and components; your edges and faces aren't isolated from other parts of your model, which can cause major confusion if you're not careful. Take a look at the section "Staying out of trouble," later in this chapter, to find out more.

Using layers in SketchUp

You can find the Layers dialog box on the Window menu. It's a pretty simple piece of machinery, as you can see in Figure 5-13. Here's what everything does:

✔ **Add Layer:** Clicking this button adds a new layer to your SketchUp file.

✔ **Delete Layer:** Click this button to delete the currently selected layer. If anything is on the layer you're trying to delete, SketchUp will ask you what you want to do with it; choose an option and select Delete.

✔ **Layer Options flyout menu:** This contains the following useful options:

   • **Purge:** When you choose Purge, SketchUp deletes all the layers that don't contain geometry. This is a handy way to keep your file neat and tidy.

   • **Color by Layer:** Notice how each layer in the list has a little color swatch next to it? Choosing Color by Layer temporarily changes all the colors in your SketchUp model to match the colors assigned to each layer. To see what's on each layer, this is the way to go.

✔ **Layers list:** This is a list of all the layers in your SketchUp file. You need to know about these three columns:

   • **Name:** Double-click a layer's name to edit it. Giving your layers meaningful names is a good way to quickly find what you're looking for.

   • **Visible:** This check box is the heart and soul of the Layers dialog box. When it's selected, the geometry on that layer is visible; when it's not, it's not.

   • **Color:** You can choose to view your model using Color by Layer, which I describe in the previous list. You can choose which color to assign to each layer by clicking the Color swatch.

Add Layer   Layer Options flyout menu

Delete Layer

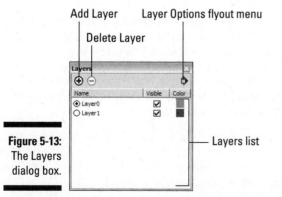

Figure 5-13:
The Layers
dialog box.

Layers list

Adding a new layer

Follow these steps to add a layer to your SketchUp file:

1. **Choose Window⇨Layers.**

   This opens the Layers dialog box.

2. **Click the Add Layer button to add a new layer to the Layers list.**

   If you want, you can double-click your new layer to rename it.

Moving entities to a different layer

Moving things from one layer to another involves using the Entity Info dialog box. Follow these steps to move an entity (an edge, face, group, or component) to a different layer:

1. **Select the entity or entities you want to move to another layer.**

   Keep in mind that you should only be moving groups and components to other layers; have a look at the next section in this chapter to find out why.

2. **Choose Window⇨Entity Info.**

   This opens the Entity Info dialog box. You can also open it by right-clicking your selected entities and choosing Entity Info from the context menu.

3. **In the Entity Info dialog box, choose a layer from the Layer drop-down list.**

   Your selected entities are now on the layer you chose from the list.

Staying out of trouble

As I said before, layers can be really helpful, but you need to know how to use them; if you don't, bad things can happen. Here's some more detail:

✔ **Do all your modeling on Layer0.** Always make sure that Layer0 is your current layer when you're working. (The current layer is the one whose radio button is selected.) Keeping all your "loose" geometry (that's not part of a group or component) together in one place is the *only* way to make sure that you don't end up with edges and faces all over the place. SketchUp, unfortunately, lets you put geometry on whatever layer you want, which means that you can end up with a face on one layer, and one or more of the edges that define it on another. When that happens, it's next to impossible to work out where everything belongs; you'll spend literally hours trying to straighten things out. This property of SketchUp's layers system is a major stumbling point for new SketchUp users; knowing to keep everything on Layer0 can save you a lot of anguish.

✔ **Don't move anything but groups and components to other layers.** If you're going to use layers, follow this rule: *Never* put anything on a layer other than Layer0 unless it's a group or a component. Doing so ensures that you don't end up with stray edges and faces on separate layers.

✔ **Use layers to organize big groups of similar things.** More complicated SketchUp models often include things like trees, furniture, cars, and people. These kinds of things are almost always already components, so they're perfect candidates for being kept on separate layers. I often make a layer called Trees and put all my tree components on it. This makes it easy to hide and show all my trees all at once. This speeds my workflow by improving my computer's performance (trees are usually big, complicated components with lots of faces).

✔ **Don't use layers to organize interconnected geometry; use the Outliner instead.** By "interconnected geometry," I mean things like building floor levels and staircases. These are parts of your model that aren't meant to be physically separate from other parts (like vehicles and people are). When you put Level 1 on one layer and Level 2 on another, more often than not, you'll get confused about what belongs where: Is the staircase part of Level 1 or Level 2? Instead, make a group for Level 1, a group for Level 2, and a group for the staircase — you'll need less headache medicine at the end of the day.

✔ **Feel free to use layers to iterate.** *Iteration* is the process of doing multiple versions of the same thing. Lots of designers work this way to figure out problems and present different options to their clients. Using layers is a great way to iterate: You can move each version of the thing you're working on to a different layer, and then turn them on and off to show each in turn. Just remember to follow the rule about only using groups and components on separate layers (mentioned previously), and you'll be fine.

Putting It All Together

In this chapter, I talk about each of SketchUp's organizational methods in isolation: discussing how they work, why they're special, and when to use them. In fact, you'll probably end up using a combination of all of them when you're working in SketchUp, so I thought it might be helpful to see an example of everything in action.

Figure 5-14 shows a model of a small house I'm building in SketchUp. I'm using all of SketchUp's organizational tools to help me manage my model's complexity while I'm working:

✔ **Each floor level is a group.** By working with each floor level as a separate group, I'm able to use the Outliner to hide whichever one I'm not working on. This makes it easier to see what I'm doing. I'm including the house's only staircase in the first floor group, because that turns out to be the easiest thing to do.

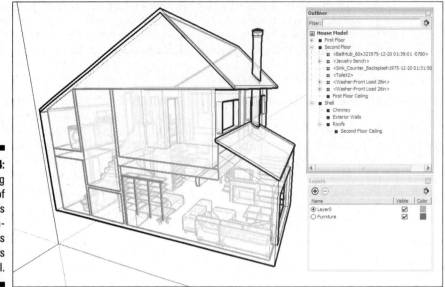

Figure 5-14:
I'm using
all of
SketchUp's
organiza-
tional tools
to build this
model.

I've decided to include the interior walls on each level of my house in that level's group. I don't think I'll ever have to hide them, so it wasn't worth making them a separate group. For what it's worth, I think the same thing probably applies to most buildings, unless you plan to study different floor plans with different interior wall arrangements.

✔ **The roof and exterior walls are groups inside of another group.** I want to be able to "remove" the roof and the exterior walls separately, so I've made each of them a group. I also want to be able to hide and unhide them both at the same time, so I made a group called "Shell" that includes both of them. Using the Outliner, I can selectively show or hide just the geometry I want. (See Figure 5-15.)

The floor levels, roof, and exterior walls of my house are groups instead of components because they're *unique* — I only have one First Floor, so it doesn't need to be a component.

✔ **All the furniture and plumbing fixtures are components.** All the components I use to furnish my house are ones I either built myself, took from the Components dialog box, or found in the 3D Warehouse. (See Chapter 11 to see what I'm referring to.)

But I only have one couch: Why make it a component instead of a group? By making every piece of furniture in my model a component, I'm able to see a list of my furniture in the In Model library of the Components dialog box. (See Figure 5-16.) I can also save that as a separate compo- nent library on my computer. The next time I move, I'll have all my furni- ture in a single place, ready to drop into a model of my new house.

✔ **All my furniture is on a separate layer.** Because furniture components can be a little heavy (they're taxing on my computer system), and because I want to be able to see my house without furniture, I created a new layer (called "Furniture") and moved all my furniture onto it. Using the Layers dialog box, I can control the visibility of that layer with a single click of my mouse.

TIP

But why not just create a group from all my furniture components and use the Outliner to hide and unhide them all, instead of bothering with layers? Good question. Because it's easier to change a component's layer than it is to add it to an existing group. To add something to a group, I would need to use the Outliner to drag and drop it in the proper place; with complex models, this can be a hassle. Changing a component's layer is just a matter of using the Entity Info dialog box to choose from a list.

Figure 5-15:
Each floor of my house, as well as the roof and the exterior walls, is a group.

All groups are visible   Shell group is hidden   Only First Floor group is visible

  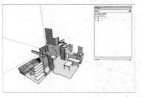

Figure 5-16:
Because all my pieces of furniture are components, I can use the Components dialog box to make my own, custom component library.

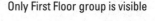
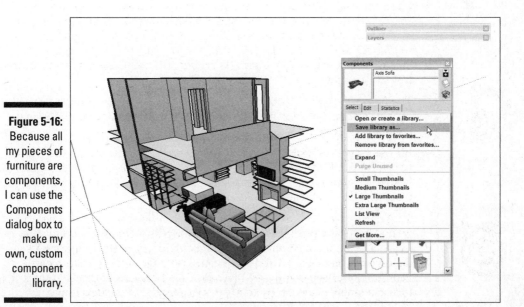

Chapter 6

Going Beyond Buildings

. . . .

. . . .

*H*ere's something you already know: There's more to life than modeling buildings. Even though SketchUp is *really good* at letting you make models of built structures, you can use it to build just about anything you can think of — all it takes is time, ingenuity, and the ability to take a step back and break things down into their basic parts. SketchUp provides some fantastic tools for creating forms that aren't in the least bit boxy, but they're not as obvious as Push/Pull and Rectangle, so most people never find them. This chapter is devoted to helping you discover SketchUp's "rounder" side.

First off, take a hard look at the shape of the things you might want to model. I want you to think about all the objects in the universe. I'll wait a couple of minutes while you do that. Done so soon? Good. Everything in the world (as I'm sure you realized) can be categorized as either of the following formal types:

✔ **Symmetrical:** Objects that exhibit *bilateral symmetry* are made of mirrored halves. You're (more or less) bilaterally symmetrical, and so is your car. Another kind of symmetry is *radial symmetry;* starfish are good examples of this, as are umbrellas and apple pies. If you were going to build a model of something that exhibits some form of symmetry, building one part and making copies would be a smarter way to do it.

✔ **Asymmetrical:** Some things — puddles, oak trees, many houses — aren't symmetrical. There's no real trick to making these things; you just have to make some coffee, settle in, and get to work.

In this chapter, I present tools, techniques, and other tips for creating forms that are distinctly unbuilding-like — my hope is that you'll use them to push the limits of what you think SketchUp can do.

Modeling Symmetrically: Good News for Lazy People

And smart people, I suppose. The fact is, a huge amount of the stuff in the galaxy exhibits some kind of symmetry. This makes modeling a heck of a lot easier, because it means you don't often have to model things in their entirety. With SketchUp's Components feature (described at length in Chapter 5), you can make a *piece* of something, copy it, flip it over (if necessary), and put it in position. Better yet, any changes you make to one part are automatically reflected in the others — that's what components do.

You can take advantage of both bilateral and radial symmetry with SketchUp components. To do so, you just assemble those components as follows, depending on what type of symmetry your object has (also take a look at Figure 6-1):

- ✔ **Bilateral symmetry:** To make a model of something that's bilaterally symmetrical, you just build half, make it into a component, and flip over a copy.

- ✔ **Radial symmetry:** Radially symmetrical objects can be (conceptually, anyway) cut into identical "wedges" that all radiate from a central axis. You can use components to model things like car wheels and turrets by building a single wedge and rotating a bunch of copies around a central point.

Axis of symmetry

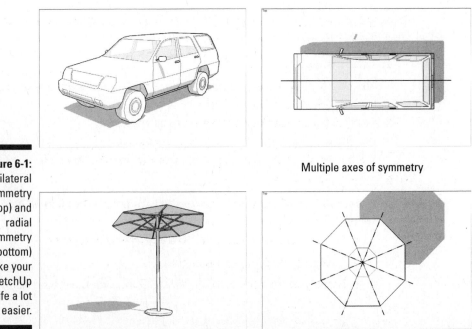

Multiple axes of symmetry

Figure 6-1: Bilateral symmetry (top) and radial symmetry (bottom) make your SketchUp life a lot easier.

The following is a list of reasons why you should work with components whenever you're building a symmetrical object:

- ✔ **It's faster.** This one's obvious. Not having to model the same things twice provides you with more time for playing golf or answering e-mail, depending on what you prefer to do.

- ✔ **It's smarter.** Everybody knows that things change, and when they do, it's nice not to have to make the same changes more than once. Using component instances means only ever having to do things once.

- ✔ **It's sexy.** Modeling something and then watching it repeat in a bunch of other places are fun to do, and the overall effect impresses the heck out of a crowd. Somehow, people will think you're smarter if they see things appearing "out of nowhere."

Working smarter by only building half

Bilaterally symmetrical forms are everywhere. Most animals you can name, the majority of the furniture in your house, your personal helicopter — they can all be modeled by building half, creating a component, and flipping over a copy.

This section (and the section that follows) talks extensively about the use of *components,* a SketchUp feature so useful it figures prominently in no fewer than three chapters of this book. If you haven't done so already, take a few minutes to read through the first part of Chapter 5 — you'll be glad you did.

Follow these steps to get the general idea of how to start building a bilaterally symmetrical model in SketchUp (see Figure 6-2):

1. **Make a simple box.**

   You can do this however you want, but I think the easiest way is to draw a rectangle and push/pull it into 3D.

2. **Draw a diagonal edge on the corner of your box.**

   The point of this step is to mark one side of your box so that when you flip it over, you don't get confused about which side is which.

3. **Turn your box into a component.**

   Chapter 5 has all the information on how to do this, but here's the mini version:

   a. Select everything you want to make into a component.

   b. Choose Edit⇨Make Component.

   c. Name your component if you want; then click the Create button.

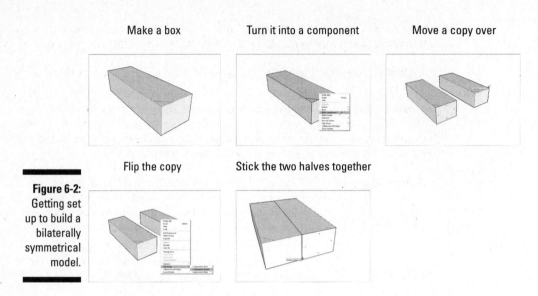

Make a box · Turn it into a component · Move a copy over

Flip the copy · Stick the two halves together

Figure 6-2:
Getting set up to build a bilaterally symmetrical model.

4. **Make a copy of your new component instance.**

   The last part of Chapter 2 has information about moving and copying objects in SketchUp, but here's a simple version:

   a. Choose the Move tool.

   b. Press Ctrl (Option on a Mac) to toggle from Move to Copy mode. You should see a little plus sign (+) next to your cursor.

   c. Click your component instance.

   d. Move your copy over beside the original, and click again to drop it. Make sure that you move in either the red or the green direction; it makes things easier in the next step.

5. **Flip the copy over.**

   To do this, right-click the copy and choose Flip Along from the context menu. If you moved your copy in the red direction in the previous step, choose Flip Along⇨Component's Red. Choose Component's Green if you moved in the green direction.

6. **Stick the two halves back together.**

   Using the Move tool (this time without Copy toggled on), pick up your copy *from the corner* and move it over, dropping it *on the corresponding corner* of the original. Take a look at the last image in Figure 6-2 to see what I mean. Doing this precisely is important, if you want your model to look right.

Now you're set up to start building symmetrically. If you want, you can do a test to make sure things went smoothly (see Figure 6-3). Follow these steps:

1. **With the Select tool, double-click one of the halves of your model to edit it.**

2. **Draw a circle on the top surface and push/pull it into a cylinder.**

If the same thing happens on the other side, you're good to go. If the same thing *doesn't* happen on the other side, it's possible that:

- ✔ **You're not really editing one of your component instances.** If you aren't, you're drawing *on top of* your component instead of *in* it. You'll know you're in Component Edit mode if the rest of your model looks grayed out.

- ✔ **You never made a component in the first place.** If your halves don't have blue boxes around them when you select them, they're not component instances. Start a new file and try again, paying particular attention to Step 3 in the preceding steps.

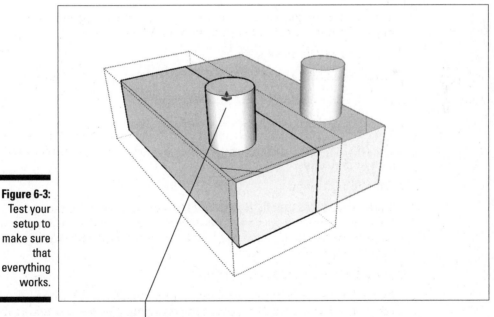

Figure 6-3:
Test your setup to make sure that everything works.

Whatever you do on this side should happen on the other side, too

Making two halves look like one whole

Looking carefully at the little boat in the figure that follows, notice how the edges in the middle clearly show that it's made out of two halves? If I were to erase those edges, my whole model would disappear, because those edges are defining faces, and without edges, faces can't exist.

Instead of erasing those unwanted edges, I can hide them by using the Eraser while pressing Shift. See the second and third images of the boat? When I hold down Shift as I drag over the edges I want to hide with the Eraser, they disappear. Two things are important to know about hidden edges:

- ✔ **Hidden edges aren't gone forever.** Actually, this applies to any hidden geometry in your model. To see what's hidden, choose View⇨Hidden Geometry. To hide it again, just choose the same thing.

- ✔ **To edit hidden edges, you have to make them visible.** If you need to make changes to your model that involves edges you've already hidden, you can either view your hidden geometry (see the previous point) or unhide them altogether. Just show your hidden geometry, select the edges you want to unhide, and choose Edit⇨Unhide⇨Selected.

Distracting edges   Use Eraser to hide

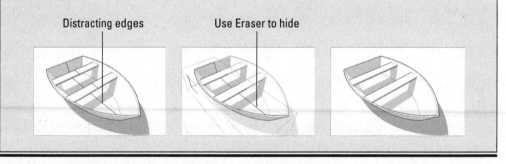

The coolest things since radially sliced bread

You can model objects that exhibit radial symmetry just as easily as those with bilateral symmetry; you just start out slightly differently. The only thing you have to decide before you start is how many "wedges" — how many identical parts — your object is made of.

To set yourself up to model something with radial symmetry, you start by modeling one wedge, then you make it into a component, and then you rotate copies around the center. Follow these steps to get the hang of it yourself:

1. **Draw a polygon with as many sides as the number of segments you need for the object you're modeling.**

Here's the easiest way to draw a polygon in SketchUp, as shown in Figure 6-4:

    a. Choose Tools⊅Polygon to select the Polygon tool.

    b. Click once to establish the center (I like to do this on the axis origin), move your cursor, and then click again to establish the radius. Don't worry about being accurate right now.

    c. Before you do anything else, type in the number of sides you'd like your polygon to have and press Enter.

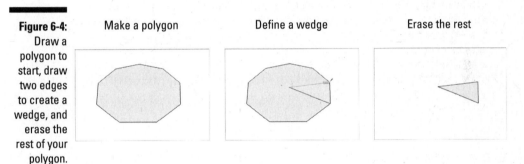

Make a polygon   Define a wedge   Erase the rest

Figure 6-4:
Draw a polygon to start, draw two edges to create a wedge, and erase the rest of your polygon.

2. **Draw edges from the center of your polygon to two adjacent vertices (endpoints) on the perimeter, creating a wedge.**

   To find the center of a polygon (or a circle), hover your cursor over the outline for a couple of seconds and move the cursor toward the middle; a center inference point should appear.

3. **Erase the rest of your polygon, leaving only the wedge.**

4. **Turn your wedge into a component.**

   Check out Step 3 in the previous section for instructions on how to do this, or read the first part of Chapter 5.

5. **Make copies of your wedge component instance with the Rotate tool (see Figure 6-5).**

   Just like with the Move tool, you can use the Rotate tool to make copies. You can even make an *array* (more than one copy at a time). Here's how to do it:

       a. Select your wedge's edges (sorry — I just wanted to say that). Select the face, too.

       b. Choose Tools⊅Rotate to select the Rotate tool.

    c. Press Ctrl (Option on a Mac) to tell SketchUp you want to make a copy; a + should appear next to your cursor.

    d. Click the pointy end of your wedge to set your center of rotation.

    e. Click one of the opposite corners of your wedge to set your rotation start point.

    f. Click the other corner to make a rotated copy of your wedge.

    g. Before you do anything else, type in the number of additional wedges you want, followed by the letter *x,* and then press Enter.

6. Test your setup, if you want.

Follow the steps at the end of the previous section in this chapter to test things out.

REMEMBER

Take a look at the sidebar "Making two halves look like one whole," earlier in this chapter, to find out about hiding the edges in your component instances. Doing so can make your finished model look a whole lot better.

Click to define center of rotation   Click to start rotating

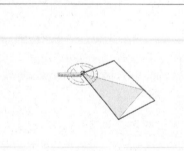
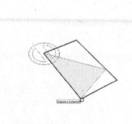

Press Ctrl (Option on Mac) to rotate copy   Make more copies

Figure 6-5:
Use the
Rotate tool
to make
copies of
your wedge
component
instance.

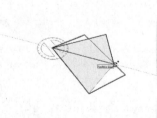

Modeling with the Scale tool

In this book, I don't spend a lot of time on the Scale tool because I don't think it's very complicated to figure out. I do, however, want to point out something that a lot of new SketchUp users don't realize: using the Scale tool to alter the *shape* of your model (instead of just the size) is an incredibly powerful way to work. The following figure shows what I'm getting at. The basic idea is to reshape your geometry by only selecting certain faces and edges, and then scaling those. You can see a good example of how this works in the Color Insert of this book, where I

create the tapered bottom of a rowboat by scaling its bottom surface. Here are some more things you should know about the Scale tool:

- Press Ctrl (Option on a Mac) to scale about the center.

- Use the corner grips (the little green cubes) to scale proportionally.

- Use the side grips to squeeze or stretch your selection.

Select the top face

Select the Scale tool and move a corner grip to scale proportionally

Scaling just the top face turns the cylinder into a bowl

Extruding with Purpose: Follow Me

Follow Me is probably the best example of a powerful SketchUp tool with kind of an underwhelming name. The problem that faced the software designers when they were trying to figure out what to call their new baby was this: It does what other 3D modeling programs dedicate two or three other tools to doing. They chose an unconventional name because it's a wholly unconventional tool.

In the following sections, I talk about how to use Follow Me to create a number of different types of shapes; examples of these are shown in Figure 6-6 and are as follows:

- **Bottles, spindles, and spheres:** These are all examples of *lathed* forms. These can be created by spinning a 2D profile (shape) around a central axis to create a 3D model.

✔ **Pipes, gutters, and moldings:** If you look closely, all three of these things are basically created by extruding a 2D face along a 3D path; the result is a complex 3D form.

✔ **Chamfers, fillets, and dados:** Without explaining what all of these things are (I get to that later in this chapter), know this: You can use Follow Me to *cut away* profiles, too.

Figure 6-6:
Follow Me
lets you
create all
kinds of
different
shapes.

Using Follow Me

At its core, Follow Me lets you create forms that are extrusions. It's a little bit like Push/Pull, except that it doesn't just work in one direction. You tell Follow Me to follow a path, and it extrudes a face all along that path. This means that you need three things to use Follow Me:

✔ **A path:** In SketchUp, you can use any edge, or series of edges, as a path. All you have to do is make sure that they're drawn before you use Follow Me.

✔ **A face:** Just like with Push/Pull, Follow Me needs a face to extrude. You can use any face in your model, but it needs to be created before you start using Follow Me.

✔ **Undo:** Imagining what a 2D face will look like as a 3D shape isn't easy — it usually takes a couple of tries to get a Follow Me operation right. That's what Undo is for, after all.

Follow these steps to use Follow Me; Figure 6-7 shows a basic example of how it works:

1. **Draw a face to use as an extrusion profile.**

   In this example, I'm creating a pipe, so my extrusion profile is a circular face.

2. **Draw an edge (or edges) to use as an extrusion path.**

   Although the edge (or edges) is touching the face in this case, it doesn't have to for Follow Me to work.

3. **Select the complete extrusion path you want to use.**

   Check out the section on making selections in Chapter 2 for pointers on using the Select tool to best advantage.

4. **Activate the Follow Me tool.**

   To do this, choose Tools➪Follow Me.

5. **Click the face you want to extrude once.**

   Magic! Your face (extrusion profile) is extruded along the path you chose in Step 3, creating a 3D form (in this case, a section of pipe).

If you want to use Follow Me all the way around the perimeter of a face, you don't need to spend time selecting all the individual edges. Just select the face and then use Follow Me; the tool automatically runs all the way around any face you have selected.

You can use Follow Me another way, too: Instead of preselecting a path (as in Step 3 of the preceding list), you can click any face with Follow Me and attempt to drag it along edges in your model. While this works on simple things, I find that preselecting a path works a lot better — it's really the only option for using Follow Me in a predictable way.

Select the whole path   Click the face with Follow Me

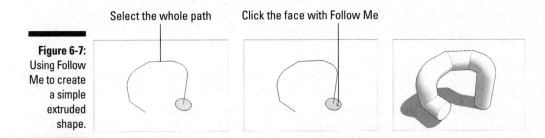

Figure 6-7:
Using Follow
Me to create
a simple
extruded
shape.

Making lathed forms like spheres and bottles

And nuclear power plant chimneys. A surprising number of things can be modeled by using Follow Me to perform a *lathe* operation. A lathe is a tool that carpenters (and machinists) use to spin a block of raw material while they carve into it — that's how baseball bats are made (the good ones, anyway).

A simple example of a lathed object is a sphere. Here's how you might make one with Follow Me:

1. **Draw a circle on the ground.**

2. **Rotate a copy of your circle up by 90 degrees, as shown in Figure 6-8:**

   If you're wondering how to do this, follow these steps:

   a. Select the face of your circle with the Select tool.

   b. Choose Tools⇨Rotate to activate the Rotate tool.

   c. Press Ctrl (Option on a Mac) to tell SketchUp you want to make a copy.

   d. Click a green endpoint inference along the edge of your circle *and hold down* your mouse button to drag. Don't let go just yet.

   e. Still dragging, move your cursor over to the endpoint on the *exact opposite* side of your circle; then release your mouse button. Now your *axis of rotation* is a line right through the center of your circle.

   f. Click anywhere on the edge of your circle, and then move your mouse over a little bit.

   g. Type in **90** and press Enter.

   You can read all about the Rotate tool in the sidebar "Wrapping your head around the Rotate tool," later in this chapter.

3. **Make sure that one of your circles is selected.**

Click and hold down mouse button   Drag here

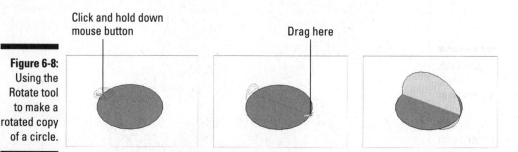

Figure 6-8:
Using the Rotate tool to make a rotated copy of a circle.

4. **With the Follow Me tool, click the circle that's not selected once (see Figure 6-9).**

   Now you have a sphere. The Follow Me tool "lathed" your circular face around the path you selected — the other circle.

If you really need a sphere, the easiest way to get one is in the Components dialog box. The Shapes library that comes installed with SketchUp has a selection of spheres (and cones and other things) you can choose from.

If you want to make your curved surfaces look smooth (hiding the edges between them), check out the sidebar "Smoothing out those unsightly edges," later in this chapter.

Under normal circumstances, you only have to model half a profile to use Follow Me to make it three-dimensional. Figure 6-10 shows a few different examples of 3D objects.

Select one circle   Click the other with Follow Me

Figure 6-9:
Clicking one
circle with
Follow Me
while the
other one is
selected
produces a
sphere.

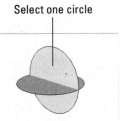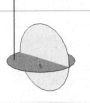

Figure 6-10:
A few
examples of
lathed
objects
created with
Follow Me.

Creating extruded shapes like gutters and handrails

A lot of the time, you'll want to use Follow Me to create geometry (edges and faces) that's attached to another part of your model. An example of this might be modeling a gutter that runs all the way around the roof of your house. In this case, you're likely to already have the path along which you want to extrude a profile (the edge of the roof).

When you're using Follow Me to extrude a face along a path that consists of edges that already exist as part of your model, there are two things you should *always* do:

- **Before using Follow Me, make the rest of your model a separate group.** Take my word for it — Follow Me can sometimes mess things up, so you want to be able to keep the geometry it creates separate, just in case.

- **Make a copy of your extrusion path outside your group.** There's a consequence to working with Follow Me on top of a group: The edge (or edges) you want to use as an extrusion path will no longer be available, because you can't use Follow Me with a path that's in a separate group or component.

   What to do? You need to make a copy of the path *outside* the group, and then use the *copy* to do the Follow Me operation. Here's the best way to make a copy of the path:

   1. With the Select tool, double-click your group to edit it.

   2. Select the path you want to use for Follow Me.

   3. Choose Edit⇨Copy.

   4. Exit (stop editing) your group by clicking somewhere else in your modeling window.

   5. Choose Edit⇨Paste in Place. Now you have a copy of the path you want to use, and it's outside your group.

Take a look at Chapter 17. You'll find a Ruby script (don't worry — I explain what that means) called "Weld" that's super-useful for creating extrusion paths for Follow Me.

When you're using an existing edge (or series of edges) as an extrusion path, the hard part is getting your profile in the right place. You have a choice of two ways to proceed; which one you use depends on what you need to model:

✔ **Draw the profile in place.** Do this only if the extrusion path is parallel to one of the colored drawing axes.

✔ **Draw the profile on the ground and then move it into position.** If your extrusion path doesn't start out parallel to a colored drawing axis, you should probably draw your profile somewhere else and move it into place later.

Why your computer is so slow

When you use Follow Me with an extrusion profile that's a circle or an arc, you're creating a piece of 3D geometry that's very big. By big, I mean that it has lots of faces, and faces are what make your computer slow down. Without going into detail about how SketchUp works (I don't really know that anyway), keep this in mind: The more faces you have in your model, the worse your computer's performance will be. At a certain point, you'll stop being able to orbit, your scenes (which I talk about in Chapter 10) will stutter, and you'll be tempted to do something terrible to someone you don't know.

The first pipe in the figure that follows has been extruded using Follow Me. It was made with a 24-sided circle as an extrusion profile, and it has 338 faces. Hidden Geometry is turned on (in the View menu) so that you can see how many faces you have.

The second pipe uses a 10-sided circle as an extrusion profile. As a result, it only has 116 faces. What an improvement!

The third pipe also uses a 10-sided circle as an extrusion profile, but the arc in its extrusion path is made up of only 4 segments, instead of the usual 12. It has a total of 52 faces. Even better.

The second image in the figure shows all three pipes with Hidden Geometry turned off. Is the difference in detail worth the exponential increase in the number of faces? Most of the time, the answer is no.

To change the number of sides in a circle or an arc, just before or just after you create it, follow these steps:

1. Type in the number of sides you'd like to have.

2. Type an *s* to tell SketchUp that you mean "sides."

3. Press Enter.

338 faces   116 faces   52 faces

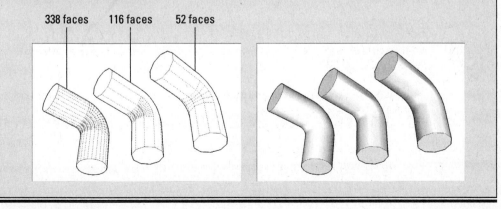

Drawing your profile in place

Consider that I have a model of a house. I want to use Follow Me to add a
gutter that goes all the way around the perimeter of the roof. I decide to draw
the profile in place (right on the roof itself) because the edges of the roof are
drawn parallel to the colored drawing axes. This means that I'll have an
easier time using the Line tool to draw "in midair."

The trick to drawing an extrusion profile that isn't on the ground is to start
by drawing a rectangular face. You then draw the profile on the face and
erase the rest of the rectangle. Figure 6-11 shows how you would draw the
profile of a gutter directly on the corner of a roof; the steps that follow
explain the same things in words:

1. **Zoom in on what you're doing.**

   I can't tell you how many people try to work without filling their modeling windows with the subject at hand. Not doing so is like trying to do a
   crossword puzzle while looking the wrong way through a pair of binoculars. Get close — SketchUp models don't bite!

2. **Using the Line tool, draw a rectangle whose face is perpendicular to
   the edge you want to use for Follow Me.**

   This involves paying careful attention to SketchUp's inference engine;
   watch the colors to make sure that you're drawing in the right direction.

3. **Use the Line tool (and SketchUp's other drawing tools) to draw your
   profile directly on the rectangle you just drew.**

   The important thing here is to make sure that your extrusion profile is
   a single face; if it's not, Follow Me won't work the way you want it to.

4. **Erase the rest of your rectangle, leaving only the profile.**

The awful thing about handrails is that they're almost always at funny angles,
not parallel to a colored axis. When it's not convenient to draw your extrusion profile in place, it's best to draw it on the ground and move it into position afterwards.

Drawing your profile somewhere else

Here's the trick: Draw a "tail" — a short edge — perpendicular to your extrusion profile. You can use this tail to help you line up your profile with the edge
you want to use as an extrusion path for Follow Me. The following steps, and
Figure 6-12, describe how you would draw and position a profile for a handrail:

1. **Draw your extrusion profile flat on the ground.**

2. **Draw a short edge perpendicular to the face you just drew.**

   This "tail" should come from the point where you want your profile to
   attach to the extrusion path.

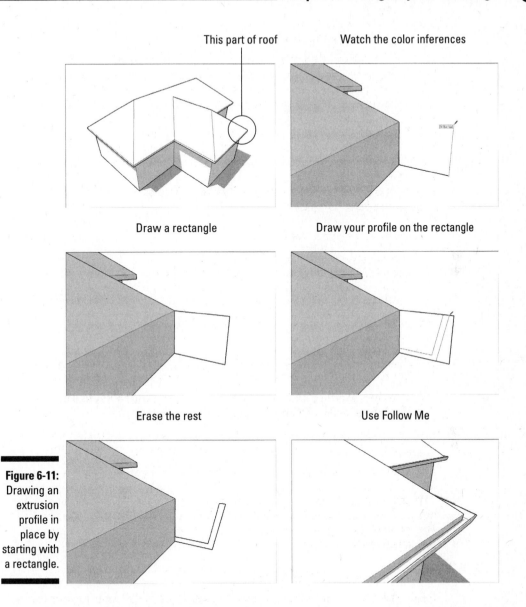

Figure 6-11: Drawing an extrusion profile in place by starting with a rectangle.

3. Make your profile and its tail into a group.

This makes it easier to move and rotate around all at once. See Chapter 5 for information on creating and using groups, if you need it.

4. Using the Move tool, place your profile at the end of the extrusion path.

To make sure that you position it accurately, pick it up by clicking the point where the tail meets the face, and drop it by clicking the end of the extrusion path.

5. **With the Rotate tool, rotate your profile into position.**

   Here's where you need to use a bit of skill. See the nearby sidebar, "Wrapping your head around the Rotate tool," for guidance. The Rotate tool is easy to use when you get the hang of it.

6. **Explode the group you created in Step 3, and delete your tail.**

   To explode a group, right-click it and choose Explode from the context menu.

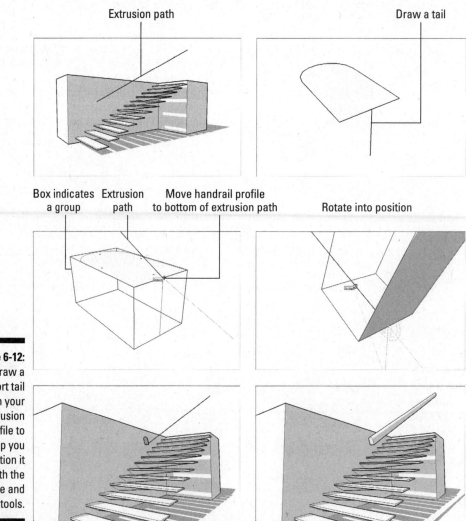

Extrusion path

Draw a tail

Box indicates a group   Extrusion path   Move handrail profile to bottom of extrusion path   Rotate into position

Figure 6-12: Draw a short tail on your extrusion profile to help you position it with the Move and Rotate tools.

Subtracting from a model with Follow Me

What if you want to model a bar of soap? Or a sofa cushion? Or anything that doesn't have a sharp edge? The best way to round off edges in SketchUp is to use Follow Me. In addition to using it to *add* to your model, you can also *subtract* from your model.

Here's how it works: If you draw an extrusion profile on the end face of a longish form, you can use Follow Me to "remove" a strip of material along whatever path you specify. Figure 6-13 demonstrates the concept on the top of a box.

If the extrusion path you want to use for a Follow Me operation consists of the entire perimeter of a face (as is the case in Figure 6-13), you can save time by just selecting the face instead of all the edges that define it.

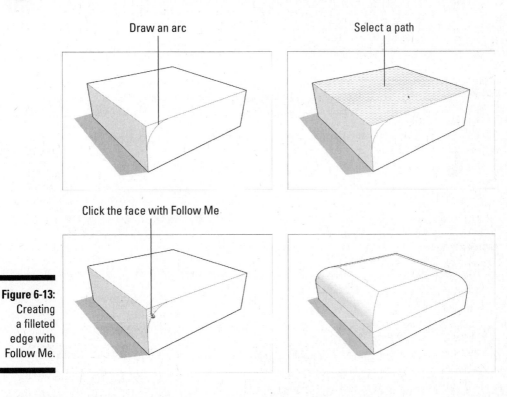

Draw an arc

Select a path

Click the face with Follow Me

Figure 6-13: Creating a filleted edge with Follow Me.

But what if you want to create a corner that's rounded in *both* directions, as so many corners are? That one's a little trickier to do in SketchUp, but because it's such a common problem, I thought I'd devote a few hundred words to explaining how to do it. The basic technique involves using Follow Me on a corner you've already rounded with the Push/Pull tool. After you have a corner that's filleted with an arc of the correct radius, you can use copies (or component instances, if you're clever) of that corner several times, wherever you need them. It's not what I'd call an elegant solution, but it's possible, and it works when you need it to.

Wrapping your head around the Rotate tool

In the last version of SketchUp, the software's designers introduced a feature that pretty much everybody realizes is great: You can establish your axis of rotation (the invisible line around which you're rotating) *while you're using the Rotate tool.* This makes it about a million times easier to rotate things around, and those of us who use SketchUp a lot danced little jigs (albeit awkwardly) when we heard the news.

By default, the Rotate tool "sticks" itself to whatever plane you happen to be hovering over — that's why it changes color as you move its big, round cursor all over your screen. When it's blue, its axis of rotation is the blue axis; the same goes for red and green. When it's black, its axis of rotation doesn't line up with any of the colored drawing axes.

If you want to show SketchUp the axis of rotation you want to use *while* you're using the Rotate tool, you can. In this case, using Rotate goes from being a three-step operation to a five-step one (check out the following figure for a visual explanation):

1. Click once to establish your center of rotation, but *don't let go* — keep your finger on your mouse button.

2. Drag your cursor around (still holding the mouse button down) until your axis of rotation is where you want it. As you drag, you'll notice your Rotate cursor changing orientation; the line from the center of the cursor to your mouse is the axis of rotation.

3. Release your mouse button to set your axis of rotation.

4. Click (but don't drag) the point at which you want to "pick up" whatever you're rotating.

5. Click again to drop the thing you're rotating where you want it.

Whew! It takes practice, but it's worth it. The efficiency you gain by being able to rotate things in free space is huge. Two more things about Rotate, while I'm on the subject:

- **Type in a rotate angle during or after you rotate something.** Check out the section about modeling with accuracy in Chapter 2 for more information on using the VCB (Value Control Box) to be precise while you're modeling.

- **Press Ctrl (Option on a Mac) to make a copy.** This works just like it does in the Move tool, which you can also read about in Chapter 2.

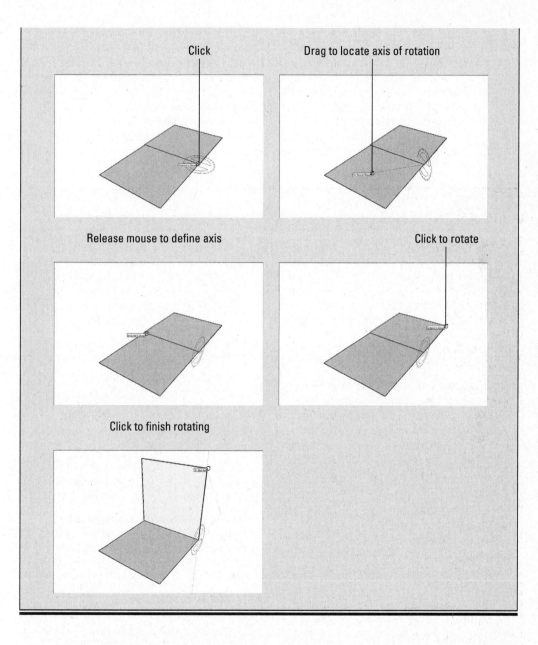

Click

Drag to locate axis of rotation

Release mouse to define axis

Click to rotate

Click to finish rotating

Figure 6-14 gives a step-by-step, visual account of the process, while I explain it in words, as follows:

1. Draw a box.

It doesn't really matter how big, as long as it's big enough for the fillet you want to apply.

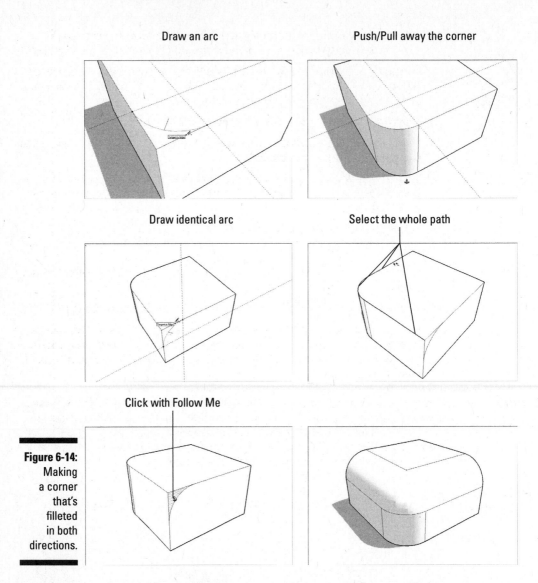

Draw an arc

Push/Pull away the corner

Draw identical arc

Select the whole path

Click with Follow Me

Figure 6-14:
Making
a corner
that's
filleted
in both
directions.

2. **With the Arc tool, draw an arc on the corner of the box.**

   When you're drawing an arc on a corner, keep an eye out for the inferences that help you draw properly:

   a. After clicking to place one endpoint of your arc, as you cut across
      the corner, the point at which your line turns magenta is where
      your endpoints are *equidistant* (the same distance) from the corner
      across which you're cutting.

   b. After clicking to place your second endpoint, you will see a point at
      which the arc you're drawing turns magenta — this means your arc

REMEMBER

is *tangent to* (continuous with) both edges it's connected to. You want this to be the case, so you should click when you see magenta.

I strongly recommend that you reduce the number of sides on your arc before you start filleting away. See the sidebar "Why your computer is so slow," earlier in this chapter, to find out why.

3. **Push/pull the new face down to round off the corner.**

4. **Draw another, *identical* arc on one of the corners directly adjacent to the corner you just rounded.**

   This is where you'll have to refer to Figure 6-14. Pictures are better than words when it comes to explaining things like which corners are adjacent to which.

5. **Select the edges shown in Figure 6-14.**

6. **Activate the Follow Me tool.**

7. **Click the arc corner face to extrude it along the path you selected in Step 4.**

8. **Hide or smooth out any edges that need hiding or smoothing.**

   For information about hiding edges, see the sidebar "Making two halves look like one whole," earlier in this chapter. Check out the nearby sidebar, "Smoothing out those unsightly edges," for the whole scoop on how to smooth edges.

After you have a fully rounded corner, you can use a bunch of them to make anything you want; it just takes a little planning. Figure 6-15 shows a simple bar of soap I created out of eight rounded corners, copied and flipped accordingly. The text (in case you're wondering) was created with SketchUp's 3D Text tool, which you can find on the Tools menu.

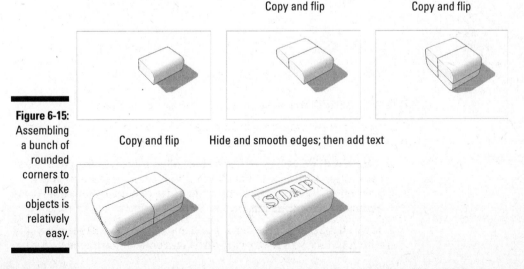

Copy and flip   Copy and flip

Copy and flip   Hide and smooth edges; then add text

Figure 6-15: Assembling a bunch of rounded corners to make objects is relatively easy.

Smoothing out those unsightly edges

If you're wondering how to get rid of all the ugly lines you end up with when you use Follow Me, the answer is pretty simple: You can *smooth* edges, just like you can hide them. (See the sidebar "Making two halves look like one whole," earlier in this chapter, for more information about hiding edges.) The difference between hiding and smoothing is illustrated by the images of the cylinders in the figure that follows:

✔ **When you *hide* an edge between two faces,** SketchUp still treats those faces as though your edge is still there — it just doesn't show the edge. Materials you've applied to each face stay separate, and each face is "lit" separately by SketchUp's sun. The latter fact is the reason why simply hiding the edges between faces that are supposed to represent a smooth curve doesn't make things look smooth — you still end up with a faceted look.

✔ **When you *smooth* an edge between two faces,** you're telling SketchUp to treat them as a single face — with a single material and smooth-looking shading. The difference is pretty huge, as you can see in the second cylinder.

You can smooth edges in two different ways:

✔ **Use the Eraser.** To smooth edges with the Eraser tool, hold down Ctrl (Option on the Mac) while you click or drag over the edges you want to smooth.

✔ **Use the Soften Edges dialog box.** Located on the Window menu, this dialog box lets you smooth a bunch of selected edges all at once, according to what angle their adjacent faces are at. It's a little complicated at first, but here's what you need to know to get started: Select the edges you want to smooth, and then move the slider to the right until things look the way you want them to.

To unsmooth edges, you need to make them visible first; turn on Hidden Geometry to do just that. Then, do the following:

1. Select the edges you want to unsmooth.

2. In the Soften Edges dialog box, move the slider all the way to the left.

Visible edges	Hidden edges	Smoothed edges

Chapter 7

Modeling with Photographs

In This Chapter

▶ Painting faces in your model with photographs

▶ Tweaking your textured faces with the Texture Tweaker

▶ Modeling on top of photo-textured faces

▶ Building a model from scratch with Photo Match

▶ Using Photo Match to match your model to a photograph

*T*hese days, it's next to impossible to meet someone who doesn't take pictures. Aside from the millions of digital cameras out there, lots of mobile phones have cameras in them, too. I expect that by the time I'm working on the next edition of this book, I'll be writing about the digital cameras we all have in our sunglasses — just wink to take a snapshot and then blink three times to e-mail it to your grandma.

You can use all these photos you're taking in SketchUp in a couple of different ways:

✔ **If you have a model you'd like to "paint" with photographs,** you can do that in SketchUp. You can apply photos to faces and then use the information in the pictures to help you model; building windows is a lot easier when they're painted right on the wall. That's what I talk about in the first part of this chapter.

✔ **If you want to use a photo to help you model something from scratch,** you can do that in SketchUp, too. New in version 6, a feature called Photo Match makes it (relatively) simple to bring in a picture, set things up so that your modeling window view matches the perspective in the photo, and then build what you see by "tracing" with SketchUp's modeling tools. Sound like fun? It is — and that's why I devote the whole second half of this chapter to it.

Neither of these techniques is what I'd call super-easy — that's why I put this chapter at the end of the modeling part of this book. If you haven't at least skimmed through Chapter 4, I recommend doing so; you'll spend less time scratching your head and thinking evil thoughts about me.

Painting Faces with Photos

Funny thing about the tool I'm about to explain: Nobody really seems to know what it's called. During its development, the SketchUp team referred to it as the Texture Tweaker, mostly because both words start with the same letter, and they thought that was catchy. For some reason, it's called the Position Texture tool in SketchUp's Help documentation, even though it's not really a tool — at least not in the traditional sense. There's no button for the Texture Tweaker/Position Texture tool; you can only get to it by choosing a command from a menu. All the same, it's one of SketchUp's coolest — and most useful — "hidden" features.

Here are some of the things you can do with the Texture Tweaker (I refer to it by its original name; I'm a sucker for alliteration):

- ✔ Stick artwork to 3D prototypes or packaging designs.
- ✔ Create photo-realistic buildings that you can *upload* (send) to Google Earth (see Chapter 11 for more detail on this).
- ✔ Figure out where things like windows, doors, signs, and ornamentation belong on your building models.

Adding photos to faces

Technically, painting surfaces with pictures using 3D software is *mapping*, as in "I mapped a photo of your face to the underside of the pile-driver model I'm building." Different software programs have different methods for mapping pictures to faces, and luckily, SketchUp's very straightforward.

Mapping photos of building facades to your building models with the Texture Tweaker/Position Texture tool has a number of benefits:

- ✔ Using photographs can make your models look more realistic.
- ✔ Taking advantage of details that are visible in a photograph (instead of modeling them) results in a smaller, easier-to-manage model.
- ✔ You can use a photograph to help you locate building elements, like doors, windows, and signs, if you plan to model them.
- ✔ Models to which you apply photo textures can be submitted to the 3D Warehouse, where they might be used on Google Earth's default Buildings layer (Chapter 11 has all the details on this).

SketchUp uses lots of different terms to refer to the stuff you can paint faces with; generically, they're all called *materials*. Materials can be colors or textures; *textures* are image-based, and *colors* are a single, solid hue. When you import an image to map it to a face, it becomes a texture — just like any of the other textures in your Materials dialog box. Read more about using materials in SketchUp at the end of Chapter 2.

Follow these steps to map an image to a face (and find additional help on this book's companion Web site; see the Introduction for details):

Before you begin, I should probably mention that you need to have at least one face in your model before you go through these steps; if you don't, you won't have anything to map your texture to.

1. **Choose File⇨Import.**

   The Open dialog box opens.

2. **Select the image file you want to use as a texture.**

   You can use JPEGs, TIFFs, PNGs, and PDFs as textures in SketchUp; all of these are common image-file formats.

3. **Select the Use as Texture option (see Figure 7-1).**

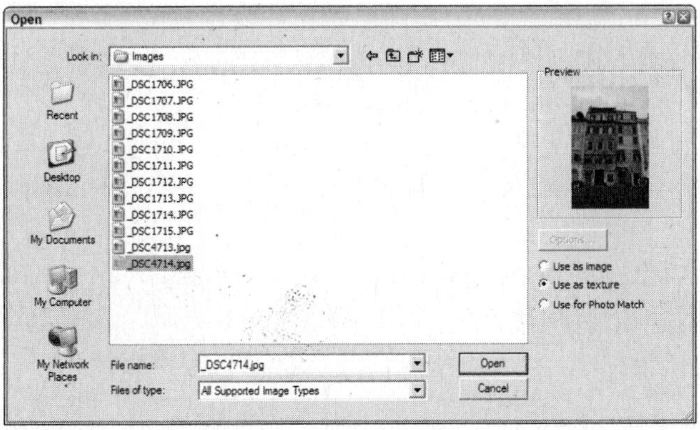

Figure 7-1:
Make sure
to pick Use
as texture.

4. **Click the Open button.**

   This closes the Open dialog box, switches your active tool to Paint Bucket, and "loads" your cursor with the image you chose to import.

5. **Click once in the lower-left corner of the face you want to "paint" (see Figure 7-2).**

   Where you click tells SketchUp where to position the lower-left corner of the image you're using as a texture. You can click anywhere on the face you're trying to paint, but I recommend the lower-left corner — it keeps things simple.

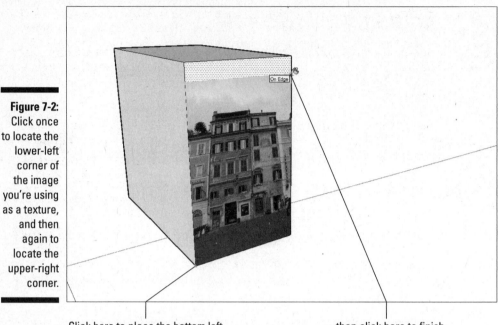

Figure 7-2:
Click once
to locate the
lower-left
corner of
the image
you're using
as a texture,
and then
again to
locate the
upper-right
corner.

Click here to place the bottom left   ...then click here to finish
corner of your image...   placing your image

6. Click somewhere else on the face you're painting to locate the upper-right corner of the image texture (see Figure 7-2).

Time for a little bit of theory: Image textures in SketchUp are made up of *tiles*. To make a large area of texture (like a brick wall), SketchUp uses a bunch of tiles right next to each other. In the case of a brick wall, it may look like there are thousands of bricks, but it's really just the same tile of about 50 bricks repeated over and over again.

Because SketchUp treats imported image textures just like any other texture, what you're really doing when you click to locate the upper-right corner of your image is this: You're telling SketchUp how big to make the tile for your new photo texture. Don't worry too much about getting it right the first time, though — you can always tweak things later on (hence the name Texture Tweaker).

Unless the proportions of your image perfectly match the face onto which it was mapped, you should see your image repeating. Don't worry — that's normal. SketchUp automatically *tiles* your image to fill the whole face. If you want to edit your new texture so that it doesn't look tiled (and you probably do), keep reading. You can scale, rotate, skew, or even stretch your texture to make it look however you want.

Editing your textures

After you've successfully mapped an image to a face, you're probably going to want to change it somehow: make it bigger, flip it over, rotate it around — you get the idea. This is where the Texture Tweaker/Position Texture tool comes in.

The Position Texture tool is actually more of a mode; I call it Texture Edit mode. Within this mode, you can be in either of two submodes: Their names are less important than what they do, so that's how I describe them:

- ✔ **Move/Scale/Rotate/Shear/Distort Texture mode:** You use this mode to move, scale, rotate, shear, or distort your texture (surprised?); it's technical name is *Fixed Pin mode* — you'll see why in a little bit.

- ✔ **Stretch Texture mode:** Stretch Texture mode lets you edit your texture by *stretching* it to fit the face it's painted on. If you want to map a photograph of a building façade to your model, this is the mode you want to use. In SketchUp's Help documentation, Stretch Texture mode is called *Free Pin mode*, just in case you're interested.

You can only edit textures on flat faces; the Texture Tweaker doesn't work on curved faces. To find out more about working with textures and curved faces, see the section, "The tricky case: Mapping photo textures to curved surfaces," later in this chapter.

Moving, scaling, rotating, shearing, and distorting your texture

The title of this section should pretty much say it all — doing the aforementioned things to your texture involves the Texture Tweaker, which is a little bit hidden, unfortunately.

Follow these steps to move, scale, rotate, or skew your texture:

1. **With the Select tool, click the face with the texture you want to edit.**

2. **Choose Edit⇨Face⇨Texture⇨Position.**

   This enables (deep breath) Move/Scale/Rotate/Shear/Distort Texture mode. You should be able to see a transparent version of your image, along with four pins, each a different color. Have a look at Color Plate 9 to see what I'm talking about. If all your pins are yellow, you're in Stretch Texture mode. Right-click your textured face and make sure there's a check mark next to Fixed Pins to switch into the correct mode.

   A quicker way to get to Edit mode is to right-click the textured face and then choose Texture⇨Position from the context menu.

3. **Edit your texture.**

   At this point, the things you can do to edit your texture are located in two different places.

   Right-clicking your texture opens a context menu with the following options:

   - **Done:** Tells SketchUp you're finished editing your texture.

   - **Reset:** Undoes all the changes you've made to your texture, and makes things look like they did before you started messing around.

   - **Flip:** Flips your texture left to right or up and down, depending on which suboption you choose.

   - **Rotate:** Rotates your texture 90, 180, or 270 degrees, depending on which suboption you choose.

   - **Fixed Pins:** When this option is selected, you're in Move/Scale/Rotate/Shear/Distort Texture mode (Fixed Pin mode). Deselecting it switches you over to Stretch Texture mode, which I talk about in the section "Stretching a photo over a face," later in this chapter.

   - **Undo/Redo:** Goes back or forward a step in your working process.

   Dragging each of the colored pins has a different effect (see Figure 7-3):

   - **Scale/Shear (Blue) pin:** Scales and shears your texture while you drag it. *Shearing* keeps the top and bottom edges parallel while making the image "lean" to the left or right.

   - **Distort (Yellow) pin:** Distorts your texture while you drag it; in this case, the distortion looks like kind of a perspective effect.

   - **Scale/Rotate (Green) pin:** Scales and rotates your texture while you drag it.

   - **Move (Red) pin:** Moves your texture around while you drag it. Of all four colored pins, I think this one's the most useful. I use it all the time to precisely reposition brick, shingle, and other building material textures in my model.

   Instead of just dragging around the colored pins, try single-clicking one of them to pick it up; this lets you place it wherever you want (just click again to drop it). This comes in especially handy when you're using the Move and Rotate pins.

4. **Click anywhere outside your texture in your modeling window to exit Edit mode.**

   You can also right-click and choose Done from the context menu, or press Enter.

Blue (Shear) pin   Yellow (Distort) pin

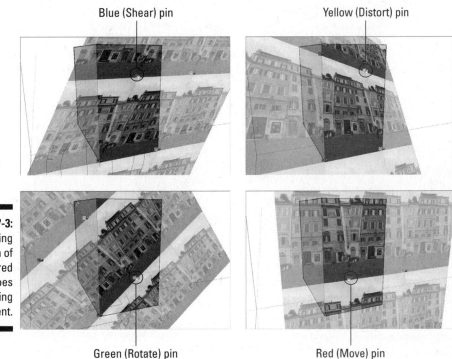

Figure 7-3:
Dragging
each of
the colored
pins does
something
different.

Green (Rotate) pin   Red (Move) pin

Stretching a photo over a face

The basic metaphor here is one of a photograph printed on a piece of really stretchy fabric. You stretch the fabric until the photo looks the way you want and then you hold it in place with pins.

Follow these steps to stretch your texture using the Texture Tweaker's Stretch Texture mode:

1. **With the Select tool, click the face with the texture you want to edit.**

2. **Choose Edit⇨Face⇨Texture⇨Position.**

   A quicker way to get to Edit mode is to right-click the textured face and choose Texture⇨Position from the context menu.

3. **Right-click your texture and *deselect* the Fixed Pins option (make sure that no check mark is next to it).**

   Deselecting Fixed Pins switches you to Stretch Texture mode (or Free Pin mode, if you're reading SketchUp's online Help). Instead of four differently colored pins with little symbols next to them, you should see four, identical yellow pins — Figure 7-4 shows you what to expect.

Figure 7-4:
You know
you're in
Stretch
Texture
mode when
all the pins
are yellow.

4. **Click a pin to pick it up.**

   Your cursor should clench up into a fist, and the pin should follow it as you move your mouse around.

   Press Esc to drop the pin you're carrying without moving it; pressing Esc cancels any operation in SketchUp.

5. **Place the pin at the corner of the building in your photograph by clicking once.**

   If the pin you're "carrying" is the upper-left one, drop it on the upper-left corner of the building in your photograph, as shown in Figure 7-5.

6. **Click and drag the pin you just moved to the corresponding corner of the face you're working on.**

   If the pin you just moved is the upper-left one, drag it over to the upper-left corner of the face whose texture you're "tweaking." Check out Figure 7-6 to see this in action.

7. **Repeat Steps 4–6 for each of the three remaining pins (see Figure 7-7).**

   If you need to, feel free to orbit, zoom, and pan around your model to get the best view of what you're doing; just use the scroll wheel on your mouse to navigate without switching tools.

   A good way to work is to pick up and drop each yellow pin in the general vicinity of the precise spot you want to place it. Then zoom in and use your better point of view to do a more accurate job.

8. **Press Enter to exit Texture Edit mode.**

Drawing axes   Sky

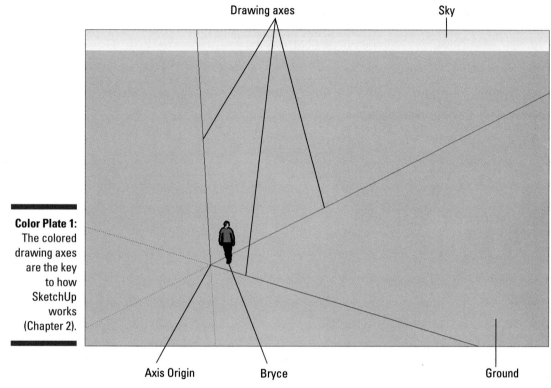

Color Plate 1:
The colored
drawing axes
are the key
to how
SketchUp
works
(Chapter 2).

Axis Origin   Bryce   Ground

Drawing in the red direction   Moving in the blue direction

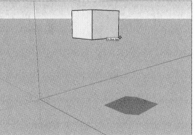

Color Plate 2:
Going in the
right color
direction
(Chapter 2).

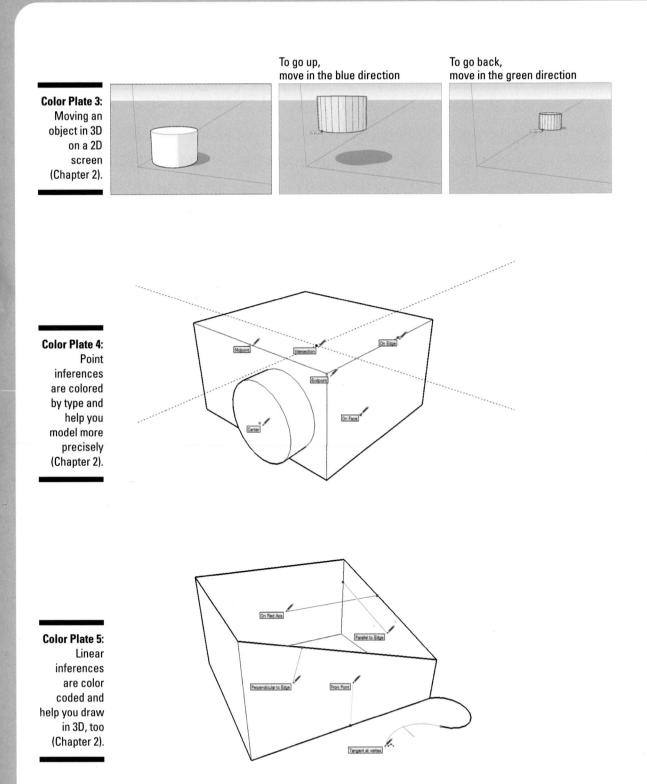

Color Plate 3:
Moving an
object in 3D
on a 2D
screen
(Chapter 2).

To go up,
move in the blue direction

To go back,
move in the green direction

Color Plate 4:
Point
inferences
are colored
by type and
help you
model more
precisely
(Chapter 2).

Color Plate 5:
Linear
inferences
are color
coded and
help you draw
in 3D, too
(Chapter 2).

Color Plate 6:
Locking an
inference
helps you
draw in the
right direction
(Chapter 2).

Hold down Shift to lock
yourself in the blue direction

Hover over the point to which
you want to infer; then click to
end your edge

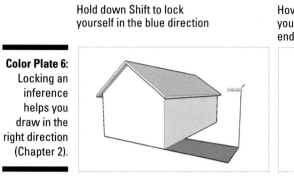

Color Plate 7:
Encouraging
an inference
(Chapter 2).

Hover over the center point
inference

Move slowly away in the red
direction

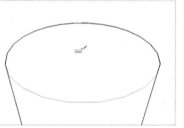

Color Plate 8:
Orbit (spin)
your model to
paint all the
faces
(Chapter 3).

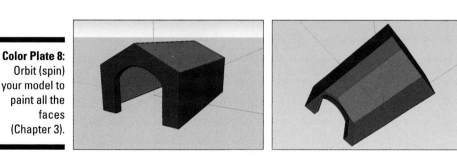

Anatomy of a Completed House Model

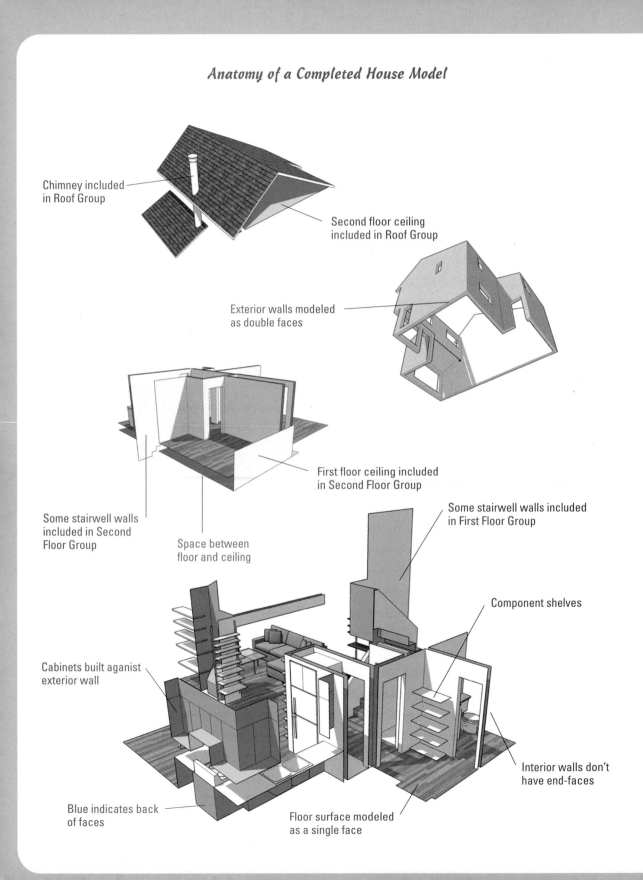

Chimney included in Roof Group

Second floor ceiling included in Roof Group

Exterior walls modeled as double faces

First floor ceiling included in Second Floor Group

Some stairwell walls included in First Floor Group

Some stairwell walls included in Second Floor Group

Space between floor and ceiling

Component shelves

Cabinets built aganist exterior wall

Interior walls don't have end-faces

Blue indicates back of faces

Floor surface modeled as a single face

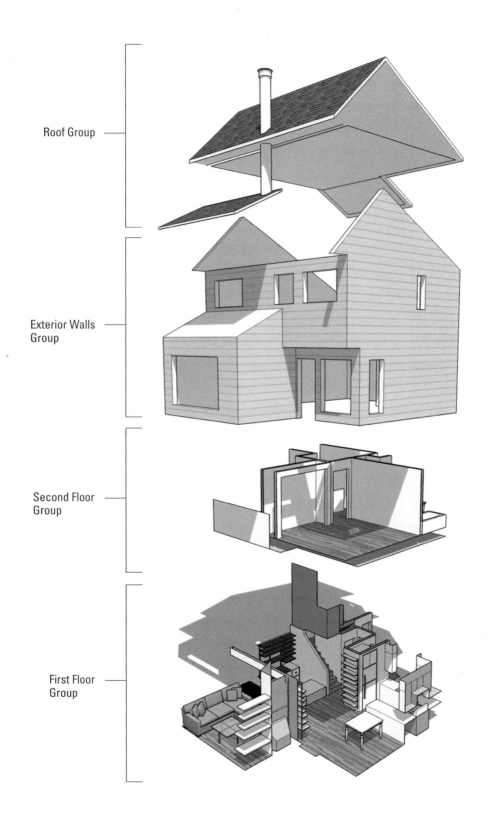

Roof Group

Exterior Walls
Group

Second Floor
Group

First Floor
Group

Building a Circular Stair with Components

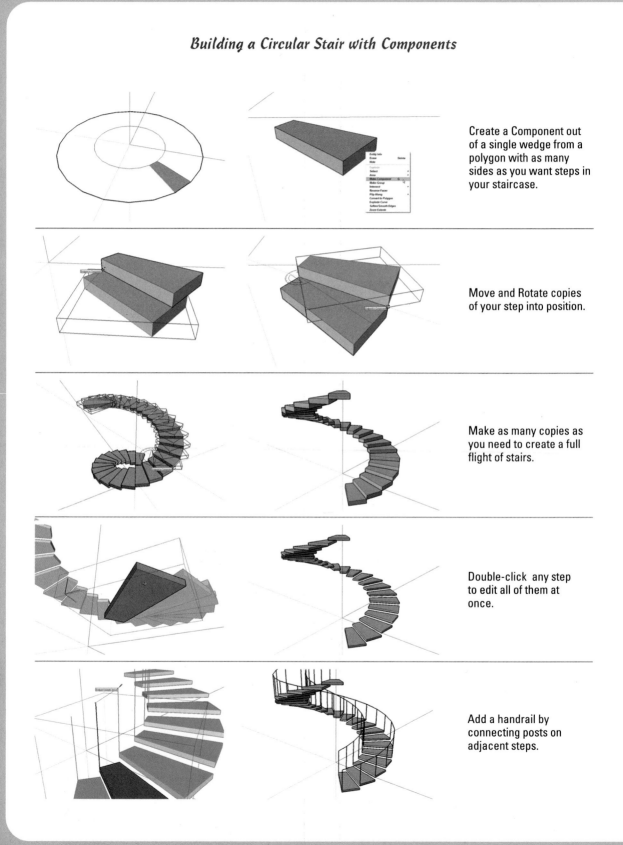

Create a Component out of a single wedge from a polygon with as many sides as you want steps in your staircase.

Move and Rotate copies of your step into position.

Make as many copies as you need to create a full flight of stairs.

Double-click any step to edit all of them at once.

Add a handrail by connecting posts on adjacent steps.

Building a Simple Boat with Mirrored Components and the Scale Tool

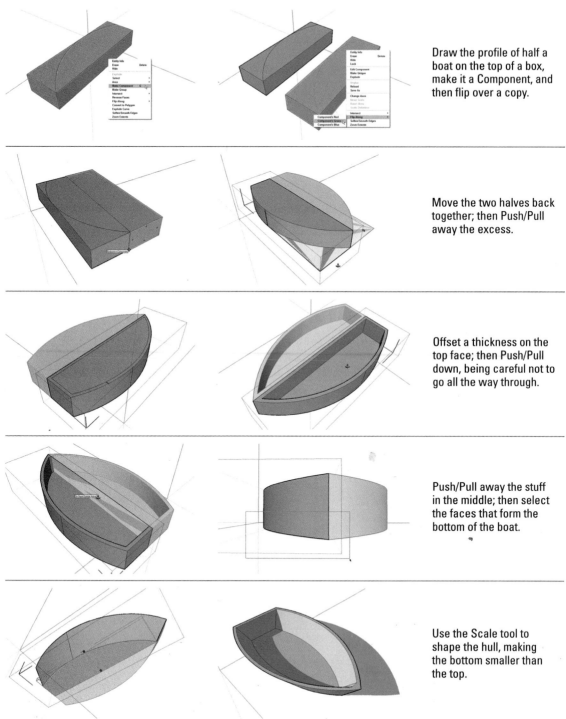

Draw the profile of half a boat on the top of a box, make it a Component, and then flip over a copy.

Move the two halves back together; then Push/Pull away the excess.

Offset a thickness on the top face; then Push/Pull down, being careful not to go all the way through.

Push/Pull away the stuff in the middle; then select the faces that form the bottom of the boat.

Use the Scale tool to shape the hull, making the bottom smaller than the top.

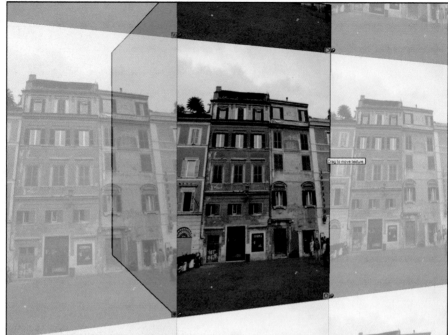

Color Plate 9:
A transparent
version of
your image,
along with
four colored
pins, appears
when editing
textures
(Chapter 7).

Perspective Bars Photograph Photo Match dialog box

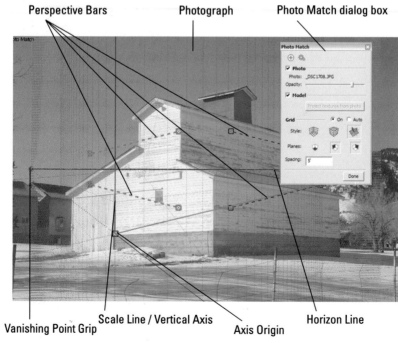

Color Plate 10:
The Photo
Match
interface
shows your
picture, plus
tools to
create a
model from it
(Chapter 7).

Vanishing Point Grip Scale Line / Vertical Axis Axis Origin Horizon Line

Line up each Perspective bar with an edge in your photograph

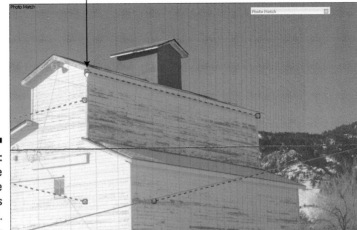

Color Plate 11:
Lining up the Perspective bars (Chapter 7).

Perspective bars lined up

Color Plate 12:
All four Perspective bars, properly lined up with edges in the picture (Chapter 7).

Move the Axis Origin to a logical place

Color Plate 13:
Placing the Axis Origin in a good spot (Chapter 7).

4 grid lines high (approx.)

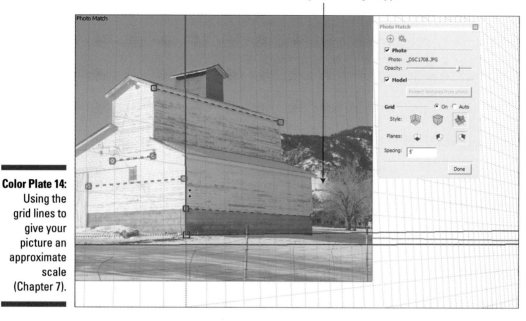

Color Plate 14: Using the grid lines to give your picture an approximate scale (Chapter 7).

Draw an edge from here...　　　　　...to here

Color Plate 15: Tracing an edge in one of the three main directions (Chapter 7).

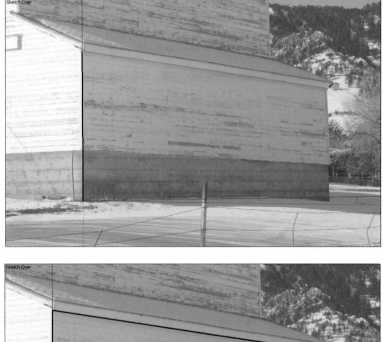

Color Plate 16: Creating a face to match a surface in the photograph (Chapter 7).

Color Plate 17: Projecting textures from a picture onto a face; then orbiting around to see the result (Chapter 7).

Color Plate 18: Using the endpoints of perpendicular edges to draw a diagonal (Chapter 7).

Draw this diagonal edge by connecting the dots

Edge

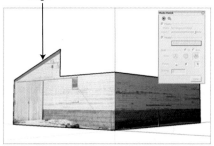

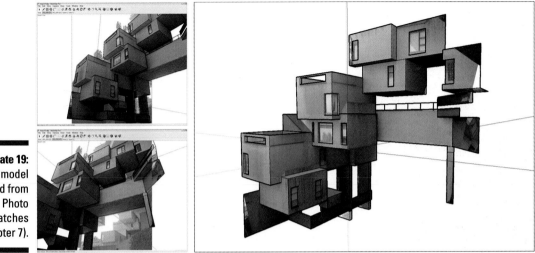

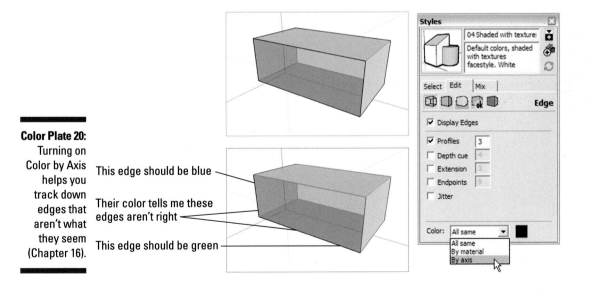

This edge should be blue

Their color tells me these edges aren't right

This edge should be green

Styles

04 Shaded with texture:

Default colors, shaded with textures facestyle. White

Select | Edit | Mix

Edge

☑ Display Edges

☑ Profiles 3
☐ Depth cue 4
☐ Extension 3
☐ Endpoints 9
☐ Jitter

Color: All same

All same
By material
By axis

Color Plate 21:
Use Styles to make your model look any way you want (Chapter 9).

Place the pin here

Figure 7-5:
Place the
pin at the
correspond-
ing corner
(upper-left
to upper-
left, for
instance) of
the building
in your
photo.

Move pin here

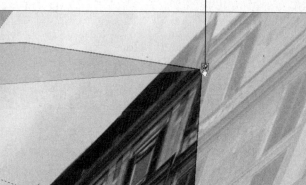

Figure 7-6:
Drag the pin
you just
placed
to the
correspond-
ing corner
of the face
you're
working on.

Figure 7-7:
Repeat
Steps 4–6
for each of
the other
three yellow
pins.

If you don't like what you see, just go back and edit the texture again; there's no limit to the number of times you can muck around.

Scaling your model until the photo looks right

When you're happy with the way your texture is stretched to fit the face, one of two things will be true:

- ✔ **The proportions are correct.** By this, I mean that the photo doesn't look stretched or squashed. This will only be the case if the face to which you applied the photo texture was already exactly the right size.

- ✔ **The proportions aren't correct.** If the photo texture you just "tweaked" looks stretched or squashed, the face it's on is the wrong size. No worries — you just need to stretch the whole face until the texture looks right. Better yet, if you know how big the face is *supposed* to be (in real life), you can stretch it until it's correct.

Follow these steps to stretch a face until the texture looks right:

1. **Use the Tape Measure tool to create guides that you can use to accurately stretch your face.**

In this case, I know the building I'm modeling is supposed to be 50 feet wide. I talk about using the Tape Measure tool and guides in Chapter 2, just in case you need a refresher.

2. **Select the face you want to stretch.**

   If your model is at a fairly early stage, just select the whole kit and caboodle. Triple-click the face with the Select tool to select it and everything attached to it. Figure 7-8 shows my whole model selected, because I'm just starting out.

3. **Choose Tools⇨Scale to activate the Scale tool.**

   When the Scale tool's active, everything that's selected in your model should be surrounded by SketchUp's Scale Box — its 27 little green cubes (they're called *grips*) and thick, yellow lines are hard to miss.

4. **Scale your selection to be the right size (see Figure 7-9).**

   Use the Scale tool by clicking on the grips and moving your cursor to stretch whatever's selected (including your texture). Click again to stop scaling.

To scale something precisely using a guide, click a scale grip to grab it and then hover over the relevant guide to tell SketchUp that's where you want to scale *to*. Click again to finish the scale operation.

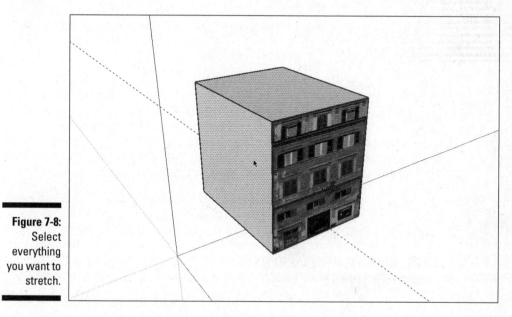

Figure 7-8:
Select everything you want to stretch.

Click here to start stretching   Click here to stretch as far as this guide

Figure 7-9:
Use the
Scale tool's
grips to
stretch your
selection
(texture and
all).

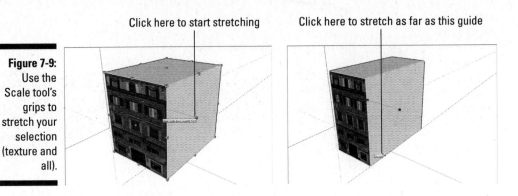

Modeling on top of photo textures

After you place a photo texture on the right face and in the right place on that face (I'm turning into Dr. Seuss), I wouldn't blame you a bit for wanting to use the information in your photograph to help you add geometry to your model. It's a great way to be more or less accurate without having to measure much, and the combination of photo textures and a few simple push/pull operations can be very convincing.

The thing you have to know

Modeling with photo-textured faces isn't hard, but you *have* to know one critical step before you can do it: You have to make sure that your texture is *projected*.

Figure 7-10 shows what happens when you try to push/pull an opening in a photo-textured face: On the left, when the texture *isn't* projected, the inside faces are painted with random parts of the texture, making your model look like a sticker-laden eye puzzle. On the right, when it *is* projected, note how the "inside" faces that are produced by the push/pull operation are a plain, easy-to-discern gray. I call this painting with "stretched" pixels, and the result is typically more appropriate for what you're doing.

It's a good idea to make sure that your face's texture is projected *before* you start drawing on top of it. Happily, telling SketchUp to make a photo texture projected is just a matter of flipping a switch. Right-click the face with the photo texture and choose Texture⇨Projected from the context menu. If you see a check mark next to Projected, your texture is already projected; don't choose anything.

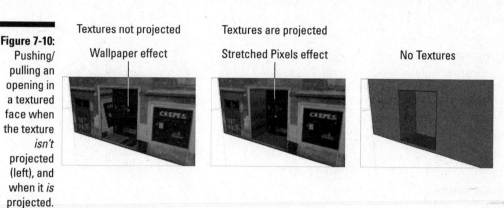

Figure 7-10:
Pushing/
pulling an
opening in
a textured
face when
the texture
isn't
projected
(left), and
when it *is*
projected.

Modeling with projected textures: A basic workflow

Follow these steps to get the hang of working with projected textures (see Figure 7-11):

1. **Make a basic rectangular box.**

2. **Apply a photo texture to one of the side faces.**

   Check out the section, "Adding photos to faces," earlier in this chapter.

3. **Right-click the textured face and choose Texture⇨Projected from the context menu.**

   Make sure that Projected has a check mark next to it.

4. **Draw a rectangle on the textured face and push/pull it inward.**

   Notice the "stretched pixels" effect?

5. **Add other angles or features to your model, if you like.**

   In Figure 7-11, I create an angled face.

6. **Switch to the Paint Bucket tool.**

7. **Hold down Alt (⌘ on a Mac) and click somewhere on the textured face to sample the texture. (Your cursor should look like an eyedropper when you do this.)**

   This "loads" your Paint Bucket with the projected texture.

8. **Release the Alt (⌘) key to switch back to the Paint Bucket cursor, and click the angled face once to paint it with the projected texture.**

   You should see the "stretched pixels" effect here, too.

Stretched pixels

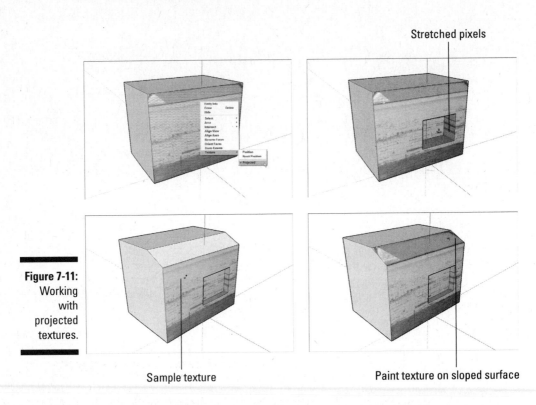

Figure 7-11:
Working
with
projected
textures.

Sample texture

Paint texture on sloped surface

The tricky case: Mapping photo textures to curved surfaces

This is always one of the first things folks ask about, and it always makes me wince a little. The thing is, mapping projected textures to curved surfaces is complicated, and in four years of SketchUping, I can count the number of times I've needed to do it on one finger. Nevertheless, you *can* do it, with a little effort.

The key is to line up a flat surface with the curved surface to which you want to apply the photo texture. You then "paint" the flat surface with the texture, make it projected, sample it, and finally, paint the curved surface with the projected, sampled texture. Whew.

Follow these steps to get the basic idea (see Figure 7-12):

1. **Create a curved surface.**

   In this case, I draw a couple of arcs on the top face of a rectangular block and then use Push/Pull to create a curved surface by "pushing" one of the top faces down to make it disappear.

2. **Create a flat surface that lines up with your curved surface.**

   I use the Line tool and SketchUp's inferencing system to draw a flat face that lines up with (and is the same size as) my curved surface.

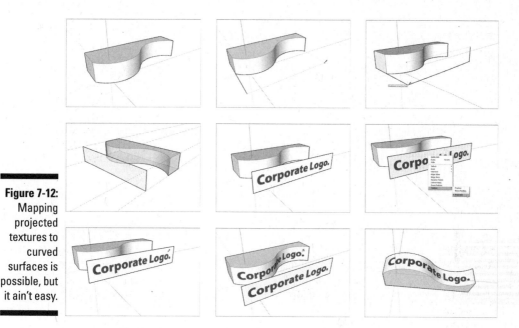

Figure 7-12:
Mapping
projected
textures to
curved
surfaces is
possible, but
it ain't easy.

3. **Apply a photo texture to your flat surface and make sure that it's positioned correctly.**

   You can refer to the earlier parts of this chapter for detailed instructions on how to do this.

4. **Right-click the textured face and choose Texture⇨Projected.**

   This ensures that the texture is projected, which is the key to this whole operation.

5. **Use the Paint Bucket tool with the Alt key (⌘ on a Mac) held down to sample the projected texture.**

   This "loads" your Paint Bucket tool with the projected texture.

6. **Use the Paint Bucket tool *without* pressing anything on your keyboard to paint the curved surface with the projected texture.**

   If everything goes as it's supposed to, the photo texture should be painted on your curved surface; the pixels in the image should look stretched in some places.

7. **Delete the flat surface that you originally mapped the image to; you don't need it anymore.**

If you're trying to do this on your own curved surface, and things don't seem to be working, your curved surface is probably part of a group or component. Either explode or double-click to edit the group or component before you do Step 6 and see if that helps.

Modeling Directly from a Photo: Introducing Photo Match

The first time I saw Photo Match in action (which wasn't very long ago — it's a new feature in SketchUp 6), I giggled and clapped my hands like a 2-year-old at a petting zoo. I'm not ashamed of it, either. Sometimes technology that's so useful, so *unexpectedly satisfying,* comes along, and you just can't help yourself. Besides — people think I'm a little strange, anyway.

So what's it do? You can use Photo Match to do a couple of things:

- ✔ **Build a model based on a photograph:** If you have a good photograph (or multiple photographs) of the thing you want to model in SketchUp, Photo Match can help you set things up so that building your model is much easier.

- ✔ **Match your model view to a photograph:** Perhaps you have a model of a building and a photograph of the spot where the building will be constructed. You can use Photo Match to position your "camera" in SketchUp to be exactly where the real-life camera was when the photograph was taken. Then, you can create a composite image that shows what your building will look like in context.

Photo Match only works on photographs of objects with at least one pair of surfaces that are at right angles to each other. Luckily, this includes millions of things you might want to build, but still, if the thing you want to Photo Match is entirely round, or wavy, or even triangular, Photo Match won't work.

Looking at all the pretty colors

Like some of SketchUp's other features, Photo Match is more of a *method* than a tool: You use it to set things up, you model a bit, you use the Photo Match dialog box a bit, and so on. If you don't know the basics of modeling in SketchUp yet, you won't have any luck with Photo Match — it's really more of an intermediate-level feature, if such a thing exists.

Color Plate 10 shows what your screen might look like when you're in the throes of Photo Match. I'll admit it's daunting, but after you've used it once or twice, it's not so bad. I include the image in the color section of this book because Photo Match (at least at the beginning of the process) uses color as a critical part of its user interface.

The following elements of Photo Match's interface show up in your modeling window:

✔ **Photograph:** The photograph you pick to create a new Photo Match shows up as a kind of background in your modeling window; it stays there as long as you don't use Orbit to change your view. To bring it back, click the Scene tab (at the top of your modeling window) labeled with the photograph's name.

✔ **Perspective bars:** These come in two pairs: one green and one red. You use them when you're setting up a new Photo Match by dragging their ends (grips) to line them up with *perpendicular* pairs of *parallel* edges in your photograph. For a clearer explanation of how this works, see the next section in this chapter.

✔ **Horizon line:** This is a yellow, horizontal bar that, in most cases, you won't have to use. It represents the horizon line in your model view, and as long as you placed the perspective bars correctly, it takes care of itself.

✔ **Vanishing point grips:** These live at both ends of the horizon line, and once again, as long as you did a good job of setting up the perspective bars, you shouldn't have to touch them.

✔ **Axis origin:** This is the spot where the red, green, and blue axes meet. You position it yourself to tell SketchUp where the ground surface is.

✔ **Scale line/vertical axis:** Clicking and dragging this blue line lets you roughly scale your photograph by using the colored Photo Match grid lines. After you're done, you can always scale your model more accurately using the Tape Measure tool (check out Chapter 2 for more information on how to do this).

You also need to work with a few things that appear outside your modeling window:

✔ **Photo Match scene tab:** When you create a new Photo Match, you create a new scene, too (you can read all about scenes in Chapter 10). Clicking a Photo Match scene tab returns your view to the one you set up when you created (or edited) that Photo Match. It also makes that Photo Match's photograph reappear — handy if you've orbited into another view.

✔ **Photo Match dialog box**. This is Photo Match Mission Control. It's where you can find almost all the controls you need for creating, editing, and working with your Photo Match.

Creating a new Photo Match

Setting up a new Photo Match is generally a step-by-step procedure. Whether you're building a new model using Photo Match or lining up an existing model with a photograph, you start by getting your modeling window ready to create a new Photo Match. How you do this depends on which one you're trying to do:

- ✔ **Use a photograph to build a model:** If this is what you want to do, open a fresh, new SketchUp file and you're good to go.

- ✔ **Line up a model you've built already with a photograph:** This case requires you to re-orient your view and then reposition your drawing axes before you're ready to create a new Photo Match.

- ✔ **Follow these steps to do this:**

    1. **Orbit around until your model view more or less matches the camera position in your photograph.**

    2. **Choose Tools⇨Axes.**

    3. **Click to place your Axis Origin (where your colored axes meet) somewhere on your model. Try to choose a spot that's also visible in your photograph, if there is one.**

    4. **Click somewhere in the lower-left quadrant of your modeling window to make sure that the red axis runs from the upper-left to the lower-right corner of your screen.**

    5. **Watch your linear inferences (more about these in Chapter 2) to be sure that your repositioned red axis is parallel to some of the edges in your model.**

    6. **Click somewhere in the upper-right quadrant of your modeling window to make sure that the blue axis is pointing up.**

After your modeling window is set up, follow these steps to create a new Photo Match in your SketchUp file:

1. **Choose Camera⇨New Photo Match.**

    This opens the New Photo Match dialog box.

2. **In the dialog box that opens, select the image on your computer that you want to use as the basis for your Photo Match and click the Open button.**

    The dialog box closes, and you see the image you chose in your modeling window. You also see a jumble of colorful techno-spaghetti all over the place. Don't worry — it's all part of the Photo Match interface. Figure 7-13 gives you an idea of what I'm referring to (Color Plate 10 shows the same image in color).

Scale Line/Vertical Axis   Perspective Bars   Photograph   Photo Match dialog box

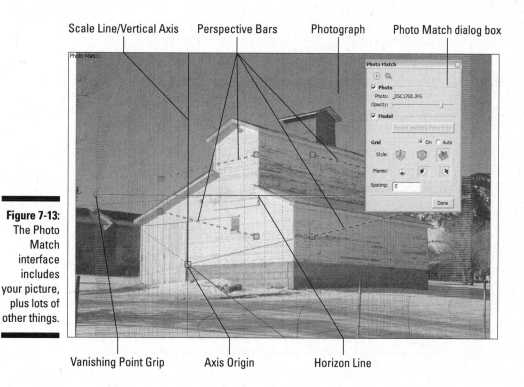

Figure 7-13:
The Photo
Match
interface
includes
your picture,
plus lots of
other things.

Vanishing Point Grip   Axis Origin   Horizon Line

Photo Match requires that you use certain kinds of photographs in order for it to work properly. See the sidebar "Taking the right kind of picture," later in this chapter, for pointers on what kinds of photos you can — and can't — use for Photo Match.

3. **In the Photo Match dialog box (which should open automatically), choose the style that matches your photograph.**

   The style buttons in the Photo Match dialog box correspond to three different types of photographs you might be using. Choose Inside if your photo is an interior view, Above if it's an aerial shot, or Outside if your photo is an exterior view taken from a human vantage point. Figure 7-14 shows examples of each of these scenarios.

4. **Begin positioning the perspective bars, starting with the two green ones, by lining them up with any two parallel edges (the tops and bottoms of windows are good candidates, as are rooflines, tabletops, and ceiling tiles).**

   Take a deep breath — this is easier than it looks. You move each perspective bar one at a time, dragging each end into position separately. Color Plate 11 shows what I mean in color.

Inside   Above   Outside

Figure 7-14:
Choose
the style
that best
describes
your
photograph's
camera
position.

The following tips can help you get the bars positioned correctly:

- Zoom in and out (using the scroll wheel on your mouse) to get a better view of your photograph while you're placing your perspective bars. The more accurate you can be, the better things will turn out.

- Pick nice, long edges in your photograph to match your bars to; you'll get better results that way.

- If you're working with an existing model, it might help to hide it while you place your perspective bars; sometimes it gets in the way. Just deselect the Model check box in the Photo Match dialog box to temporarily hide it.

5. **Line up the two red perspective bars with a different set of parallel edges — just be sure that these parallel edges are *perpendicular* (at right angles) to the first pair.**

   If they're not perpendicular, Photo Match doesn't work. Color Plate 12 shows what it looks like when all four perspective bars have been positioned properly.

6. **Drag the axis origin (the little square where the axes come together) to a place where your building touches the ground.**

   This is how you tell SketchUp where the ground plane is. Try to make sure your axis origin is right at the intersection of two perpendicular edges — it'll make things easier later on. Color Plate 13 shows what this looks like.

   If you're using Photo Match with an existing model, dragging the axis origin moves your model, too. Line up your model with the photograph so that the spot where you placed the axis origin is right on top of the corresponding spot in your photo. Don't worry about size right now; you'll deal with that in a moment.

7. **Roughly set the scale of your photograph by clicking and dragging anywhere on the blue scale/vertical axis line to zoom in or out until your photograph looks to be at about the right scale.**

   You do this by first setting your grid spacing in the Photo Match dialog box and then using the grid lines in your modeling window to "eyeball" the size of your photo until it looks about right.

   Color Plate 14 shows an example where my grid spacing is set at 5 feet (the default setting). Because I know the barn in my photo is about 20 feet tall, I zoom in or out until it's about 4 grid lines high, because 4 times 5 feet is 20 feet.

   If you're trying to match an existing model to your photo, just zoom in or out until your model looks like it's the right size.

   You don't have to be very exact at this stage of the game. You can always scale your model later by using the Tape Measure tool (Chapter 2 talks about how to do that).

8. **Click the Done button in the Photo Match dialog box.**

   When you click the Done button, you stop editing your Photo Match. All the colorful lines and grips disappear, and you're left with the photo you brought in, your model axes, and your thoughts. It might have seemed like a lot of magic, but what you did was pretty simple: You used Photo Match to create a scene (which I talk about extensively in Chapter 10) with a camera position and lens settings that match the ones used to take the picture that's on your screen. In effect, you're now "standing" exactly where the photographer was standing when the photograph was taken.

Modeling with Photo Match

Setting up a new Photo Match was just the first step. Now it's time to use SketchUp's modeling tools (with a little help from the Photo Match dialog box) to build a model based on the photograph you "matched." Here are a couple of the basic concepts:

✔ **It's not a linear process.** Building a model using a Photo Matched photo entails going between drawing edges, orbiting around, drawing some more edges, going back to your Photo Match scene, and drawing yet more edges. Every photo is different, so the ones you work with will present unique challenges that you'll (hopefully) have fun figuring out.

✔ **Don't forget the photo textures.** By far one of the coolest features of Photo Match is its ability to automatically photo-texture your model's faces using your photograph as "paint." It's a one-button operation, and it's guaranteed to make you smile.

Taking the right kind of picture

Your level of success with Photo Match depends to some extent on the photograph you start out with. Here are some tips for what kind of images are good candidates for Photo Match:

⮕ **Cropped photos won't work.** Photo Match uses your photo's center point to help figure out its perspective; if you try to use a picture that's been *cropped* (had some of the original shot cut away), the center point will be different, and things won't work properly.

⮕ **Make sure that the edges of two perpendicular surfaces are visible in the shot.** You need to be able to see planes that are at right angles to each other to be able to use Photo Match.

⮕ **Shoot at a 45-degree angle if you can.** Because of the way perspective works, you'll get a more accurate result if you use a photograph where you can see both perpendicular surfaces clearly; if one of them is sharply distorted, you'll have a harder time. The images in the following figure show what I'm talking about.

⮕ **Watch out for lens distortion.** When you take a picture with a wide-angle lens, some of the straight lines in the image "bow" a little bit, depending on where they are in the frame. Try to use photos taken with a normal or telephoto lens: 50mm to 100mm is a good bet.

Bad Photo Match candidate: bad angle

Good Photo Match candidate: you can see both sides clearly

Follow these steps to start building a model with Photo Match:

1. **Click the Photo Match scene tab to make sure that you're lined up properly.**

   If you orbit away from the vantage point you set up with Photo Match, you'll know it; your photograph will disappear. You can easily get back by clicking the scene tab for your Photo Match. It's labeled with the name of your photo, and it's at the top of your modeling window (see Figure 7-15).

2. **Trace one of the edges in your photograph with the Line tool.**

   Make sure that you're drawing in one of the three main directions: red, green, or blue. Color Plate 15 shows this in action.

   It's a good idea to start drawing at the axis origin; it'll help to keep you from getting confused.

Scene tab for this Photo Match

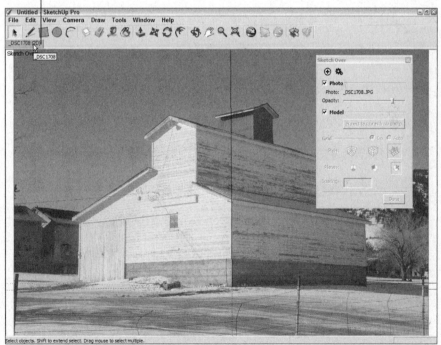

Figure 7-15:
Clicking the scene tab for your Photo Match zings you back to that vantage point (and brings back your photograph).

3. **Keep tracing with the Line tool until you have a rectangular face.**

   The key here is to make sure that you keep watching the color of your edges as you draw. You always want to see your lines turn red, green, or blue when you're starting out. Have a look at Color Plate 16 to see what this looks like.

   Be careful not to orbit while you're drawing — if you do, repeat Step 1 and keep going. You *can* zoom and pan all you want, though.

4. **Click the Project Textures from Photo button in the Photo Match dialog box.**

   Every time you do this, SketchUp paints the faces in your model with the photograph you used to create your Photo Match. The face you created in Step 3 should now be photo-textured according to the image you used to model it. Orbit around and you'll see what I mean (see Color Plate 17).

5. **Click the Photo Match scene tab to return to your Photo Match view.**

6. **Use SketchUp's modeling tools to continue to "trace" the photograph in three dimensions.**

   Here are some pointers for doing this successfully:

   • **Always start an edge at the end of an edge you've already drawn.** If you don't, your geometry won't make any sense, and you won't end up with what you expect.

   • **Never draw an edge in "midair."** Okay — this is the same as the last one, but it bears repeating: If you don't draw edges based on other edges, you won't get good results.

   • **Orbit frequently to see what's going on.** You'll be surprised what you have sometimes — tracing a 2D image in 3D is tricky business. Get in the habit of orbiting around to check on things and draw certain edges. Click the Photo Match scene tab to return to the proper view.

   • **Use other tools (like Push/Pull and Offset) when appropriate.** Nothing prevents you from using the full complement of SketchUp's modeling tools. I just prefer to stick to Line and Eraser while I'm drawing the basic skeleton of my model with Photo Match. I think it's simpler.

   • **Pay attention to the colors.** With a photograph as an underlay, it's a little harder to see what you're doing. But with Photo Match, watching to make sure that you're drawing the edge you intend to draw is critical.

- **Draw angles by "connecting the dots."** If you need to trace an edge in your photo that doesn't line up with any of the colored axes (an angled roofline, for example), figure out where the endpoints are by drawing perpendicular edges and connecting them with an angled line. Color plate 18 shows this in glorious, full-spectrum detail.

- **If you want, keep pressing the Project Textures from Photo button to use the photograph to paint your model.** Of course, using Project Textures from Photo only works on faces that are visible in the photograph. For everything else, you need to use the Paint Bucket and the Texture Tweaker (which I describe in the first part of this chapter) to do your best.

If you have more than one picture of the thing you want to model, you can use more than one Photo Match to help you build it. Just get as far as you can with the first Photo Match and then create a new one, using the geometry you created as an "existing building." Color Plate 19 shows a model I started to build of Habitat 67, in Montreal. I used two pictures to create two Photo Matches in the same SketchUp file, which let me build more of the model than I could see in a single picture.

Part III
Viewing Your Model in Different Ways

The 5th Wave   By Rich Tennant

"Oddly enough he spent nine hours organizing the layout of this room in SketchUp."

In this part . . .

Building models is actually only half of what Google SketchUp is all about. After you've actually got something built, you can do a whole bunch of things with your geometry. Chapter 8 describes Styles, a new feature in SketchUp 6 that lets you change the way your model looks. Want to make it look hand-drawn? One click. How about something more realistic? Another click. Using Styles is like having a tiny artist strapped to your clicking finger — but in a good way.

In Chapter 9, I talk about using Shadows to make your model look more realistic, and (in cases where it's relevant) to study how the sun will affect your design. Just like Styles, applying Shadows to your model is laughably easy; it's just a matter of clicking a box and moving a couple of sliders around.

Chapter 10 covers three important aspects of exploring your model: walking around, Scenes, and Sections. When it comes to seeing (and showing off) your model from inside SketchUp, this is pretty much where it begins and ends.

Chapter 8

Changing Your Model's Appearance with Styles

*I*f you're the sort of person who likes to draw, you're in for a treat. If you can't draw a straight line with a ruler, you're in for an even bigger treat. Styles (which is a new feature in SketchUp 6) are all about deciding how your geometry — all your faces and edges — will actually *look*. Take a peek at Color Plate 21 for an idea of what styles can do.

This chapter provides a complete rundown of how to use styles in SketchUp 6. First off, I talk about *why* you'd want to use styles in the first place. With so many options, I go into how you can avoid what I call *stylesitis* — an inflammation of your styles related to getting stuck trying to decide how to make your model look.

Next, I talk about the new Styles dialog box. It's a little overwhelming at first, so I spend some time talking about where everything is and what it's supposed to do. Then I dive into all the different sliders, buttons, toggles, and check boxes in enough detail that you should be able to apply existing styles, modify them to suit your taste, and make brand new ones if you need them. The last part of this chapter deals with saving the styles you want to keep.

Choosing How and Where to Apply Styles

The thing to remember about styles is that they're endless. With a million permutations of dozens of settings, you could spend all day fiddling with the way your model looks. I've found that keeping one question in mind — Does this setting help my model say what I want it to say? — helps me to focus on what's important. There's no doubt styles are cool, but making them *useful* is the key to keeping them under control.

To help you make smart decisions about using SketchUp styles, you should consider at least two factors when you're "styling" your model:

- ✓ **The subject of your model's "level of completeness":** I like to reserve "sketchy" styles for models that are still evolving. The message this sends is "this isn't permanent/I'm open to suggestions/all of this can change if it has to." As my design gets closer to its final form, the appearance of my model generally gets less rough and more polished. I use styles to communicate how much input my audience can have and what decisions still need to be made.

- ✓ **How much your audience knows about design:** When it comes to how styles are perceived, there's a big difference between an architecture-school jury and a nondesigner client who's building a house for the first time. Design professionals are more experienced at understanding 3D objects from 2D representations, so they don't need as many visual "clues" to help them along. The essence of styles is really to provide these clues, so here's a rule of thumb: The more your audience knows about design, the simpler you should keep your styles.

Before you dive in to styles, remember also that a little style goes a long way. No matter how tempting it is to go hog-wild with the styles settings, please resist the urge. Remember that the purpose of styles is to help your model communicate and *not* to make it look "pretty" or "cool." If the *style* of your work is getting noticed more than its content, tone things down. Figure 8-1 shows an example of going overboard with styles and then reining things in.

Figure 8-1: Abusing styles is altogether too easy.

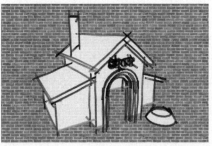 

Applying Styles to Your Models

The easiest way to get started with styles is to apply the premade styles that come with SketchUp. You find scads of them, which is great, because seeing what's been done is the best way to see what's possible. As you go through this section, you'll no doubt get ideas for your own styles, and that's where the fun begins.

Applying a SketchUp style to your model is a four-step process, and it goes like this (for additional help, see this book's companion Web site; see the Introduction for details):

1. **Choose Window⇨Styles to open the Styles dialog box.**

2. **Click the Select tab to make sure that you're looking at the Select pane.**

3. **Choose a styles library from the Styles Libraries drop-down list.**

   I introduce you to the libraries that come preinstalled with SketchUp 6 in a moment.

4. **Click a style in the Styles window to apply it to your model.**

This may come as a surprise, but it's not possible to view your model without any style at all. This is because styles are really just combinations of display settings; some styles are fancier than others, but no matter what you do, you always have to have a style applied. If you want to get a relatively neutral view of your model, I suggest choosing from the selection in the Default Styles library.

One of the best things about SketchUp is that you're rarely left out in the cold when it comes to content. Whether it's styles, components, or materials, SketchUp comes with plenty of examples to get you started. Figure 8-2 is a shot of the Styles Libraries drop-down list you'll see when SketchUp 6 is "new out of the box." Here's what everything does:

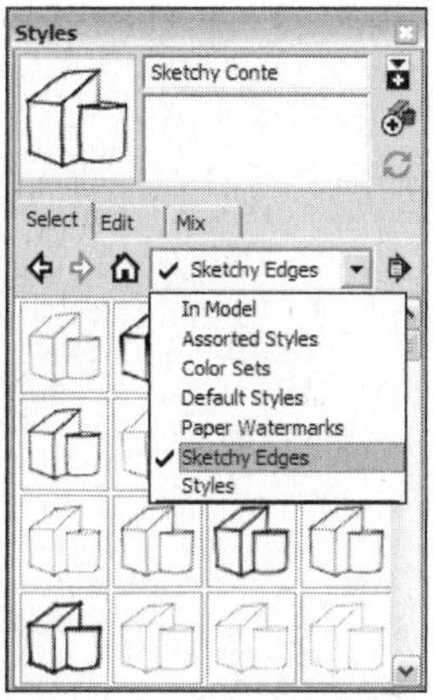

Figure 8-2:
The Styles
Libraries
drop-down
list is where
you'll find all
your styles.

✔ **In Model:** The In Model library shows you all the styles you've applied to your model. It keeps track of every style you've *ever* applied to your model, whether that style is still applied or not. To see a current list of styles in your SketchUp file:

1. Choose the In Model styles library to show a list of styles you've applied to your model.

2. Click the Library Options flyout menu and choose Purge Unused to get rid of any styles you aren't currently using.

✔ **Styles:** This is a sneaky one, because it's not actually a styles library. Instead, it's a view of your Styles folder: the place on your computer that *contains* your styles libraries. If you look carefully, this list is the same one you see in the middle section of the Styles Libraries drop-down list. Why is it there? Having it readily accessible means that you can add libraries to your Styles folder from right inside SketchUp. Convenient, huh?

✔ **Assorted Styles:** Consider this library a sampler of nifty effects that you can get with the styles settings. A couple of them are very useful, and some are just downright impressive. If you're ever trying to convince a friend to use SketchUp, head for this library of styles first.

✔ **Color Sets:** The styles in this library are different combinations of edge, face, and background colors. If you decide to depart from black and white, flip through this list to see whether any of them float your boat.

✔ **Default Styles:** Think basic. With the exception of the first one (which is the default style for all new SketchUp files you create), these styles are as minimal as it gets: white background, black edges, white-and-gray front-and-back faces, and no fancy edge effects. I use these styles to get back to a clean starting point for all my models; I like to start simple and build from there.

✔ **Paper Watermarks:** Each of the styles in this library has a different *watermark,* or background. Using one of these makes it seem like your model is drawn on a particular kind of surface. I think this concept has a lot of potential, but I'd tread lightly with these — really think about the message you're sending when you present your digital model on a piece of "canvas."

✔ **Sketchy Edges:** The Sketchy Edges styles in SketchUp 6 are the result of more than a year's work on something called *nonphotorealistic rendering* (see the nearby sidebar, "Running from realism: NPR styles," for the whole story). Basically, the miracle (okay, technological innovation) involves using real hand-drawn lines instead of digital ones to render edges. The result is that you can make your models look more like manual sketches than ever before. Before SketchUp 6, this effect has always looked unbelievably cheesy on the computer, like an anxious robot trying too hard to seem human. Not anymore, though. You can safely use the Sketchy Edges styles to convey any of the following:

- That your design is in process

- That your model is a proposal and not a finished product

- That you welcome feedback in any and all forms

✔ **Straight Lines:** All the styles in the Straight Lines library are variations on a very simple theme: The edges in these styles are rendered with progressively thicker, perfectly straight lines with square corners. You won't get a technical pen effect with these styles, though; they still make for a pretty rough (albeit anally retentive rough) rendering of your model.

Running from realism: NPR styles

In the world of 3D modeling software, the trend has been toward *photorealism*. Rays of digital light are bounced around a billion times inside your computer until you can see every glint of sunlight in every dewdrop on every blade of grass on the lawn. The standard of perfection is how close the model comes to looking like a photograph, and in a lot of cases, that standard has been met — I've seen computer renderings that look more lifelike than life itself.

But what about models of buildings or other things that aren't completely finished? Perhaps you're an architect who's designing a house for a client. If you aren't sure what kind of tile you'll end up using on your roof, how are you supposed to make a photorealistic rendering of it? You *could* just go ahead and throw any old tile up there as a placeholder, but that could backfire. Your client could hate the tile and decide not to hire you without ever telling you why, and all because of something you didn't even choose.

What you need is a way to show only the decisions you've made so far, and *that* is exactly why architects and other designers make sketches instead of photorealistic renderings. When you're designing, decisions don't all happen at once, so you need to be able to add detail as your design evolves. Sketching allows you do that because it offers a *continuum* from "cartoony" to photographic, with everything in between. The following figure is an illustration of this.

Programs like SketchUp offer what's called *NPR,* or *nonphotorealistic rendering,* as a way to solve this problem for people who design in 3D. Instead of spending processor power on making representations that look like photographs, the people who make SketchUp went in the opposite direction; they've made a tool that lets you make drawings that are useful throughout the design process. And because SketchUp's NPR engine works in real time, you can make changes on the fly, in front of your audience.

Making Changes to Styles

If you're handy in the kitchen, you've probably heard the saying that cooking is an art and baking is a science. Cooking allows you to experiment — adding a little of this and a dash of that while you're making a sauce won't wreck anything. When it comes to baking, taking liberties with a recipe can be a train wreck. What was supposed to be a cake can easily turn into a doorstop. I found this out when I made a lovely chocolate doorstop for my girlfriend's birthday not so long ago. . . .

Luckily, making your own styles has a lot more in common with cooking than it does with baking. Go ahead and fiddle around; you can't do any irreversible harm. Playing with styles doesn't affect the geometry in your model in any way, and because styles are just combinations of settings, you can always go back to the way things were before you started.

In this section, I go over the settings in the Edit and Mix panes of the Styles dialog box, explaining in detail what all the doodads and widgets are for, and providing a running commentary on *why* you might choose one setting over another.

Of the three panes in the Styles dialog box, Edit is definitely the blue whale of the group. You find more controls and settings here than you can shake a stick at, so SketchUp's designers broke the Edit pane up into five tabs. Here's a short description of each:

- ✔ **Edge:** The Edge tab contains all the controls that affect the appearance of edges in your model. This includes their visibility, their color, and other special effects you can apply.

- ✔ **Face:** This tab controls the appearance of faces in your model, including their default colors, their visibility, and their transparency.

- ✔ **Background:** The Background tab has controls for setting the color and visibility of the background, the sky, and the ground plane in your model.

- ✔ **Watermark:** New for SketchUp 6, watermarks are images that you can use as backgrounds or as overlays. The Watermark tab gives you control over these.

- ✔ **Modeling:** The Modeling tab provides controls for setting the color and visibility of a bunch of elements in your model, including section planes and guides.

The following sections explain each tab in detail; I also provide suggestions for using some of the settings.

Tweaking edge settings

The Edge tab is tricky because it changes a little bit depending on what kind of style you currently have applied to your model. NPR styles have different settings than regular, non-NPR styles. Figure 8-3 shows both versions of the Edge tab, which you open by choosing Window➪Styles, selecting the Edit tab, and then clicking the box icon on the far left.

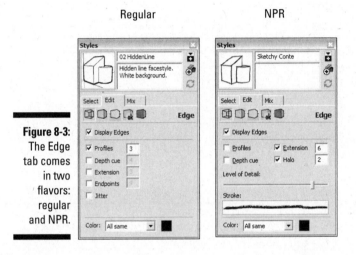

Regular   NPR

Figure 8-3: The Edge tab comes in two flavors: regular and NPR.

SketchUp 6 comes with two different kinds of styles: regular and NPR. NPR stands for *nonphotorealistic rendering,* wherein SketchUp uses digitized, hand-drawn lines to render the edges in your model. All the styles in the Sketchy Edges library, as well as all but two (Google Earth and Standard CAD) in the Assorted Styles library are NPR styles. Because you can create your own styles based on existing ones, all the styles you create using Edge settings from one of these NPR styles is an NPR style, too.

Display edges

Most of the time, you'll be viewing your model with Edges turned on. Because SketchUp is an edge-based modeler, it's hard to do any work with them turned off. Figure 8-4 shows a model with this option turned off (among other options, which I explain in a moment). Here are a couple of cases where you might not want to display edges:

✔ If you're trying to make your model look as photorealistic as possible

✔ If you plan to export your model to a program that doesn't display edges, and you want to preview how it will look

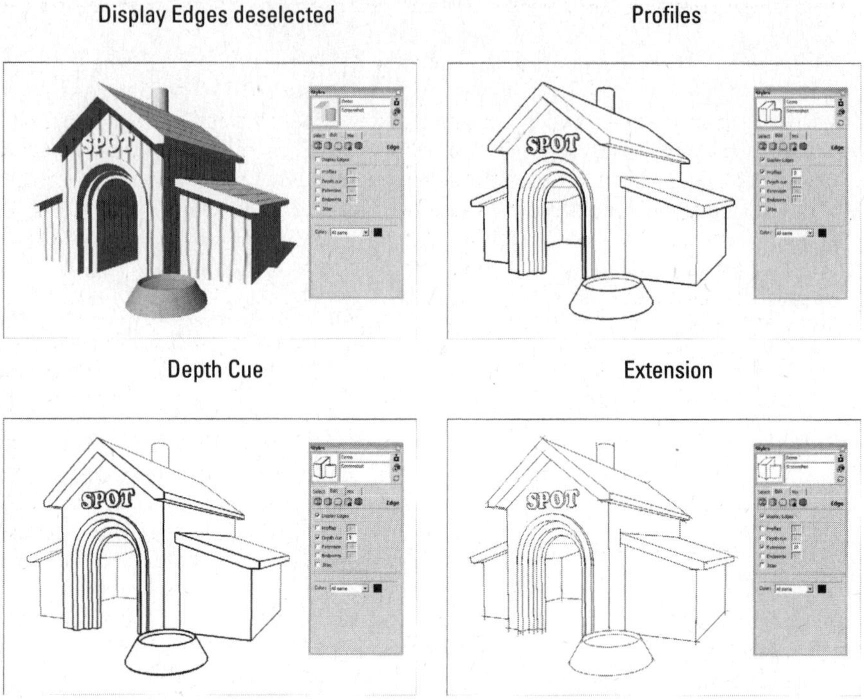

Display Edges deselected   Profiles

Depth Cue   Extension

Figure 8-4:
Choose
among the
edge
settings to
give your
model the
desired
look, from
realistic to
sketchy.

Profiles

Selecting the Profiles check box tells SketchUp to use a thicker line for edges
that outline shapes in your model. If you're using a non-NPR style, you can
type in the thickness of profile lines you'd like to see. Like all the values in
this tab, profile thickness is measured in pixels.

Using profile lines is a pretty standard drawing convention that's been
around for a long time. You use them primarily to add depth to views of
your model by making things in the foreground seem to "pop out." I think
SketchUp looks better with Profiles on, but I always have mine dialed down to
2 pixels; 3 pixels (which is the default) seems too beefy to me. Take a peek at
Figure 8-4 to see what a difference profiles can make.

Depth Cue

Using different line thicknesses to convey depth is another drawing convention that's popular. Objects closest to the viewer are drawn with the thickest
lines, whereas the most distant things in the scene are drawn with the
thinnest ones. The number of line thicknesses varies according to taste, but
it's usually somewhere between 3 and 6.

In a fog?

If you're looking for something to provide a sense of depth in your model views, look no further than the Fog feature. New for this version of SketchUp, Fog does exactly what it says — it makes your model look like it's enshrouded in fog (see the following figure). You'd think that a feature this neat would be a little complicated, but it's the opposite. Follow these three steps to let the fog roll into your model:

1. **Choose Window⇨Fog to open the Fog dialog box.**

2. **Select the Display Fog check box to turn on the fog effect.**

3. **Fool around with the controls until you like what you see.**

I wish the process of controlling how Fog looks was more scientific, but I'm afraid it's not. You just play around with the sliders until you have the amount of fog you want. But just in case you absolutely need to know, here's what the sliders do:

✔ **Top slider (0%):** This controls the point in space at which Fog begins to appear in your model. When it's all the way to the right (toward infinity), you can't see any fog.

✔ **Bottom slider (100%):** This controls the point in space at which the fog is completely opaque. As you move the slider from left to right, you're moving the "completely invisible" point farther away.

Depth Cue is SketchUp's automatic way of letting you apply this effect to your models. When its check box is selected, Depth Cue dynamically assigns line thicknesses (draftspersons call them "line weights") according to how far away from you things are in your model. In non-NPR styles, you can tell SketchUp how many line weights you want. The number you type in is both your desired number of line weights *and* the thickness of the fattest line SketchUp will use. I like to use a maximum line weight of 5 or 6 pixels. SketchUp will always make the thinnest lines 1 pixel thick because that's the finest line your computer monitor can display. Figure 8-4 shows a model with Depth Cue set to 5 pixels.

Here are some guidelines for using Depth Cue:

✔ **Depth Cue looks best on pure line drawings.** When you're using color and materials, there's usually plenty of other information in your view that can supply "depth"; my favorite use for Depth Cue is on black-and-white perspectives.

✔ **Use Depth Cue on big stuff like architecture.** In general, people who draw things like buildings use the multiple-line-weights method, and people who draw smaller things like blenders and staplers use profile lines. You can (and should) do whatever you want, but I usually like to know the conventions.

✔ **When I'm using Depth Cue, I turn off Profiles.** I don't think these two drawing conventions work well together, so I always choose to use one or the other.

Extension

This tells SketchUp to extend the edges in your model by the number of pixels you type into the Extension text box. Refer to Figure 8-4 for an idea of what this option does.

You should note that Extension is measured in pixels, which means that your extensions will appear shorter when you're zoomed in close to your model, and longer when you're zoomed out.

Extending edges is a great way to make your model look sketchy, even if you're not using one of the NPR styles. You can use edge extensions to

✔ Indicate that your model is a quick sketch and not something you slaved over

✔ Show that dimensions and proportions are still up for debate

Endpoints

When I draft "the old way," I like to begin and end my lines by grinding my pencil into my paper, just to give my drawing a little flourish. I like how it looks, and so do a lot of people who draw by hand. Emphasizing endpoints with a darker, thicker line or dot is a way of making your drawings stand out more; look at Figure 8-5 to see what I'm talking about.

SketchUp lets you achieve this effect with the Endpoints feature, which is available only in non-NPR styles. Type in the number of pixels you'd like SketchUp to emphasize at the end of each edge segment. I especially like to use Endpoints in combination with Extension and Depth Cue.

Jitter

Most people either love Jitter or hate it. With it on (it's only available for non-NPR styles), SketchUp "jitters" your edges, making it look like you rendered your model with a burnt stick while driving down a dirt road. I really like the effect. Before NPR styles came along, Jitter was the best way to make your model look hand-drawn. Use it if you want to, but be careful — not everyone will approve of your decision. I use it in the same situations where I use Extensions. Figure 8-6 shows Jitter in all its glory.

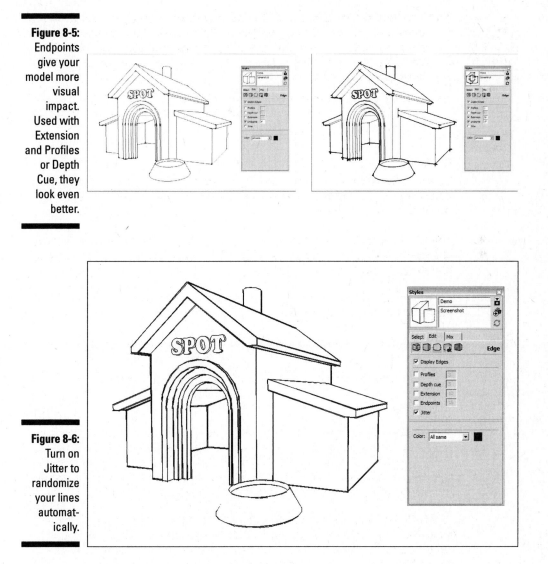

Figure 8-5: Endpoints give your model more visual impact. Used with Extension and Profiles or Depth Cue, they look even better.

Figure 8-6: Turn on Jitter to randomize your lines automatically.

Halo

I *really* wish Halo were available for non-NPR styles because it's just that great. What Halo does is very simple: It automatically ends certain lines before they run into other ones, creating a "halo" of empty space around objects in the foreground. This keeps your model looking neat and easy to read. In fact, this is a drawing trick that pencil-and-paper users have been using forever to convey depth; look closely at most cartoons and you'll see what I mean.

The number you type into the Halo box represents the amount of "breathing room" SketchUp gives your edges. The unit of measure is pixels, but there's no real science to it; just play with the number until things look right to you. For what it's worth, I like to crank it up. Take a look at Figure 8-7 to see Halo in full effect.

Figure 8-7:
Halo tells SketchUp to give your edges their space.

Level of Detail

When you slide the Level of Detail controller (which only appears when you've applied an NPR style) back and forth, you're effectively telling SketchUp how busy you want your model to look. The farther to the right you slide it, the more of your edges SketchUp displays. You should experiment with this setting to see what looks best for your model. Figure 8-8 shows what happens when I slide the Level of Detail controller from left to right.

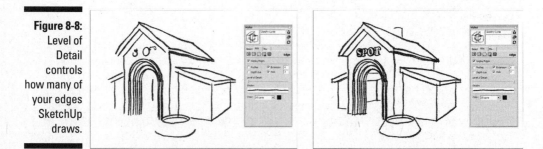

Figure 8-8:
Level of Detail controls how many of your edges SketchUp draws.

Color

You use the Color drop-down list to tell SketchUp what color to use for all the edges in your model. Here's what each of the options means:

- ✔ **All Same:** This tells SketchUp to use the same color for all the edges in your model. You tell it what color to use by clicking the color well on the right and choosing a color.

- ✔ **By Material:** Choosing this causes your model's edges to take on the color of whatever material they're painted with. Because most people don't know that you can paint edges different colors, this doesn't get used very often.

- ✔ **By Axis:** Now *here's* a useful, but hidden, gem. Choosing to color your edges "by axis" tells SketchUp to make everything that's parallel to one of the colored axes the color of that axis. Edges that aren't parallel to any of them stay black. Why is this so important? When something is screwy with your model — faces won't extrude, or lines won't "sink in" — switching your edge colors to by axis is the first thing you should do. You'll be surprised how many of your edges aren't what they seem. Have a look at Chapter 16 for more about this.

Changing the way faces look

The Face tab of the Styles dialog box is very simple — at least compared to the Edge tab (what isn't, really?). This area of the SketchUp user interface controls the appearance of faces, or surfaces, in your model. From here, you can affect their color, visibility, and translucency. Figure 8-9 shows the Face tab in vivid grayscale, and you can open it by choosing Window➪Styles, selecting the Edit tab, and clicking the box icon that's second from the left. The following sections describe each of the elements in detail.

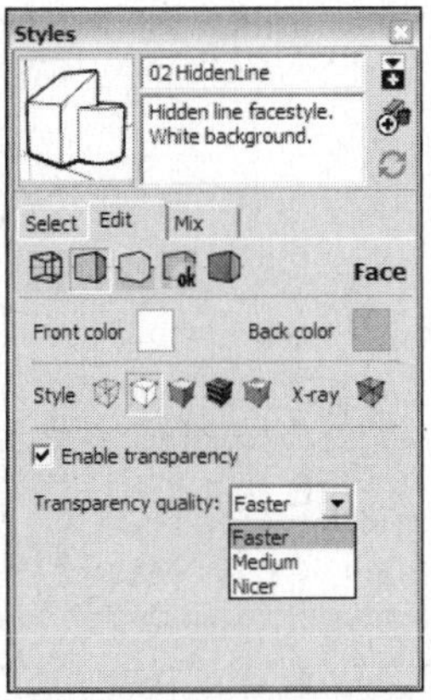

Figure 8-9:
The Face tab controls the appearance of your model's faces.

Choosing default colors for front and back faces

In SketchUp, every face you create has a back and a front. You can choose what colors to use by default for all new faces you create by clicking the Front and Back color wells and picking a color. I recommend sticking with neutral tones for your defaults; you can always paint individual faces later on.

Sometimes when you're modeling in SketchUp, a face will be turned "inside out." This happens for lots of reasons (which all have to do with programming and other nerdy pursuits), but all you need to know is how to flip them back. Follow these steps to flip a face around so that the right side is showing:

1. **Select the face you want to flip.**

2. **Right-click and choose Reverse Faces.**

Knowing which face is the front and which is the back is especially important if you plan to export your model to another program. Some of these, like 3D Studio Max, use the distinction between front and back to make important distinctions about what to display. In these cases, showing the wrong side of a face can end up producing unexpected results. I talk more about this in Part IV.

Choosing a face style

Even though these are called Face styles, they have nothing to do with styles, the major new SketchUp feature. Face styles might as well be called Face modes because that what they are: different modes for viewing the faces in your model. You can flip between them as much as you like without affecting your geometry. All they do is change the way SketchUp draws your model on the screen. Each one has its purpose, and all are shown in Figure 8-10:

✔ **Wireframe:** In Wireframe mode, your faces are invisible. Because you can't see them, you can't affect them. Only your edges are visible, which makes this mode handy for doing two things:

- When you're selecting edges, switch to Wireframe mode to make sure that you've selected what you meant to select. Because no faces block your view, this is the best way to make sure that you're getting only what you want.

- After you've used Intersect with Model, you usually have stray edges lying around. Wireframe is the quickest way to erase them because you can see what you're doing. See Chapter 4 for details on Intersect with Model.

✔ **Hidden Line:** Hidden Line mode displays all your faces using whatever color you're using for the background; it's really as simple as that. If you're trying to make a clean, black-and-white line drawing that looks like a technical illustration, make your background white. (I talk about how in the section, "Setting up the background," later in this chapter.) I like to use Hidden Line mode with Extensions and either Profiles or Depth Cue, depending on my subject matter. Shadows look great, too.

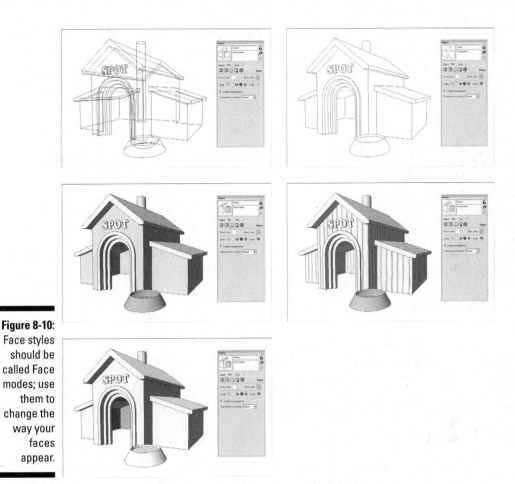

Figure 8-10:
Face styles should be called Face modes; use them to change the way your faces appear.

✔ **Shaded:** This Face style displays your faces with colors on them. Faces painted with a solid color appear that color. Faces to which you've added textures are shown with a color that best approximates their *overall color.* If your texture has a lot of brown in it, SketchUp picks a brown and uses that. For models with a lot of these textures, switching to Shaded mode can really speed up orbiting, zooming, and otherwise navigating around. Unless I absolutely need to see textures I've applied to my faces, I tend to stay in Shaded mode whenever I'm working on my model.

✔ **Shaded with Textures:** Use Shaded with Textures when you want to see your model with textures visible. Because this mode puts a lot of strain on your computer, it can also be the slowest mode to work in. I only turn it on when I'm working on a small model, or when I need to see the textures I've applied to my faces. Obviously, if you're going for a photorealistic effect, this is the mode to choose. It's also the mode that best approximates what your model will look like when (and if) you export it to Google Earth.

✔ **Display Shaded Using All Same:** When you want to quickly give your model a simplified color scheme, use this Face style; it uses your default front and back face colors to paint your model. Think of it as a compromise between the Hidden Line and Shaded modes — color, but not *too much* color.

Seeing through walls with x-rays

Ever wonder what it would be like to be Superman? X-Ray mode is a simple on-off proposition; you use it when you want to be able to see through faces by making them translucent (see Figure 8-11). Unlike using translucent materials on some of your faces (like glass and water), flipping on X-Ray lets you see through *all* your faces. I tend to use it when I want to see through a wall or a floor to show what's behind it. If you're in a plan (overhead) view, it's a great way to demonstrate how a floor level relates to the one below it.

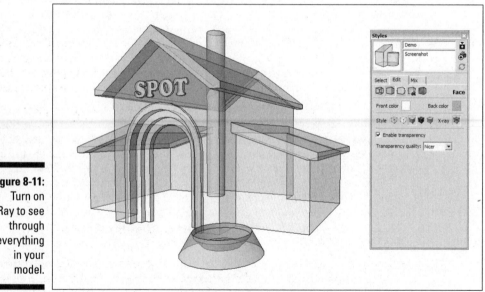

Figure 8-11:
Turn on
X-Ray to see
through
everything
in your
model.

Adjusting transparency

Because how well SketchUp runs on your computer depends on what's in your model, and because displaying transparency (as in translucent materials) is an especially taxing operation for SketchUp and your computer to handle, you can decide how to display translucent materials:

✔ **Enable transparency:** Deselect this check box to display translucent materials as opaque. You should turn off transparency to speed SketchUp's performance if you find that it's slowed down.

✔ **Transparency quality:** If you decide to display transparency, you can further fine-tune your system's performance by telling SketchUp how to render that transparency: You have the choice of better performance, nicer graphics, or an average of the two. Which one you choose depends on the size and complexity of your model, the speed of your computer, and the nature of your audience.

Setting up the background

In the Background tab of the Styles dialog box, you choose colors and decide whether you want to be able to see a sky and a ground plane. It doesn't get less complicated than this folks. Check out Figure 8-12 to get a view of the Background tab, along with an idea of how it works. To open these options in your own copy of SketchUp, choose Window➪Styles, select the Edit tab, and click the middle icon, at the top of the tab. You have the following options on the Background tab:

✔ **Background:** Click the color well to choose a color for the background of your model. If you're going for a blueprint or blackboard effect, pick a dark color and then change your edge color to white in the Edge tab. For most models, I set the background to white — I guess I'm a traditionalist.

✔ **Sky:** If you turn on the Sky feature, SketchUp paints everything above the horizon with any color you want; click the color well to choose one. The sky is rendered as a *gradient* that gets lighter the closer it gets to the horizon. This makes things slightly more realistic, but the real purpose of the Sky tool is to provide a point of reference for your model. In 3D views of big things like architecture, it's nice to be able to see the horizon. Another reason for turning on the sky is to "set the mood" — keep in mind that the sky isn't always blue. I've seen some beautiful SketchUp renderings wherein the sky was sunset (or maybe nuclear winter) orange. Play around and see what you like.

✔ **Ground:** Just like the Sky tool, you can choose to display a ground plane in your model. You can pick the color by clicking the color well, and you can even choose to have the ground be translucent. I have to admit that I'm not a big fan of turning on the Ground feature, and here's why: It's *very* hard to find a ground color that looks halfway good, no matter what you're building. I also don't like the fact that you can't dig into the earth to make sunken spaces (like courtyards) with the ground turned on. Instead of turning on this feature, I prefer to make my own ground planes with faces and edges. It's more flexible, and I think it looks better.

If you find that you need to see the ground, or that you want to, you can choose to *not* be able to see it when you're below it, which is a useful option. Just deselect the Show Ground from Below check box to make this happen.

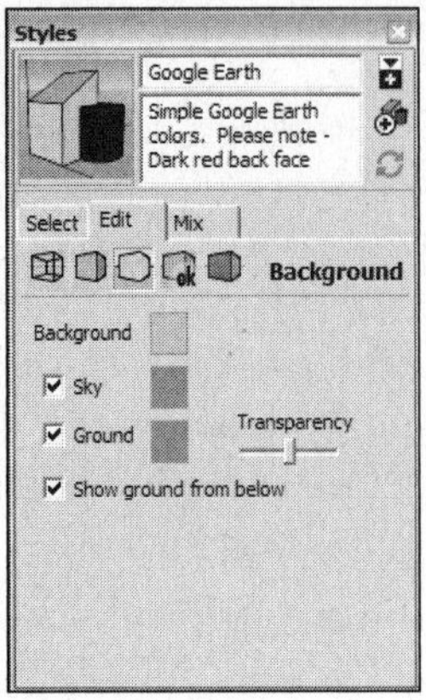

Figure 8-12:
Use the
Background
tab to turn
on the sky
and the
ground, and
to choose
colors.

Working with watermarks

It's time to put your thinking cap back on. Watermarks, which are brand new for SketchUp 6, are much easier to understand if you don't think about them as actual watermarks. They're not anything like watermarks, in fact — they're much more useful. If I had to define them (and because I'm writing this book, I guess I do), I'd put it this way: *Watermarks* are graphics that you can apply either *behind* or *in front of* your model to produce certain effects. Here are a few of the things you can do with SketchUp watermarks:

✔ Simulate a paper texture, just like the styles in the Paper Watermarks library

✔ Apply a permanent logo or other graphic to your model view

✔ Layer a translucent or cutout image in the foreground to simulate looking through a frosted window or binoculars

✔ Add a photographic background like "Outer Space" or "Inside My Colon" to create a unique model setting

Eyeing the watermark controls

Figure 8-13 shows the Watermark tab of the Styles dialog box. Here's a brief introduction to what the controls do:

✔ **Display Watermarks:** Displaying watermarks is an all-or-nothing proposition; if you have more than one, you can turn them all on or all off.

✔ **Add Watermark:** Click this button to add a new watermark to your model view. You're asked to select an image file on your computer and then you're taken through the Choose Watermark procedure to set things up.

✔ **Remove Watermark:** Select the watermark you want to delete and then click this button to remove it.

✔ **Edit Watermark:** Selecting a watermark and then clicking this button opens the Edit Watermark dialog box, where you can change your watermark's properties. Editing a watermark is similar to creating a new one; I cover that in the next section.

✔ **Watermark List:** This list shows all your watermarks in relation to something called Model Space, which is the space occupied by your model. All watermarks are either in front of or behind your model, making them overlays or underlays, respectively.

✔ **Move Up or Down:** Use these buttons to change the "stacking" order of the watermarks in your model view. Select the watermark you want to move in the list and then click one of these buttons to move it up or down in the order.

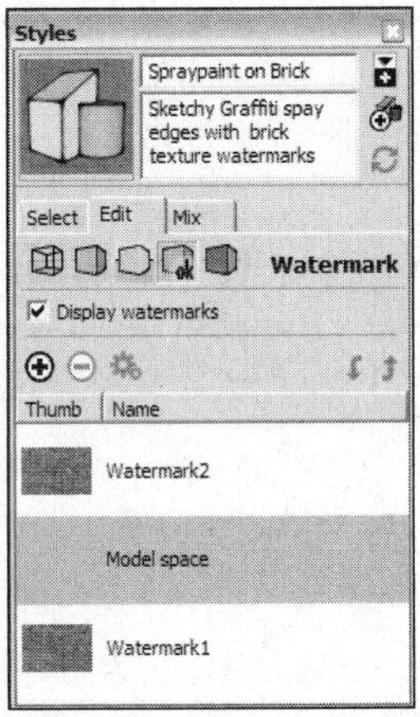

Figure 8-13:
The
Watermark
tab, new for
SketchUp 6.

Adding a watermark

Watermarks are by no means simple, but working with them, miraculously enough, is. Follow these steps to add a watermark to your model view:

1. **Click the Add Watermark button to begin the process of adding a watermark.**

   The Open dialog box appears.

2. **Find the image you want to use as a watermark and then click the Open button to open the first Choose Watermark dialog box (see Figure 8-14).**

   You can use any of these graphics file formats: TIFF, JPEG, PNG, and GIF.

This is *way* beyond the scope of this book, but I think it's worth mentioning because you're bound to need this sooner or later: If you want to make a watermark out of an image that isn't a solid rectangle (like a logo), you need to use a graphics file format, like PNG or GIF, that supports alpha channels. An *alpha channel* is an extra layer of information in a graphics file that describes which areas of your image are supposed to be transparent. It sounds complicated, but it's really a straightforward concept. To make an image with an alpha channel, you need a piece of software like Photoshop. Try searching for "alpha channels" on Google for more information.

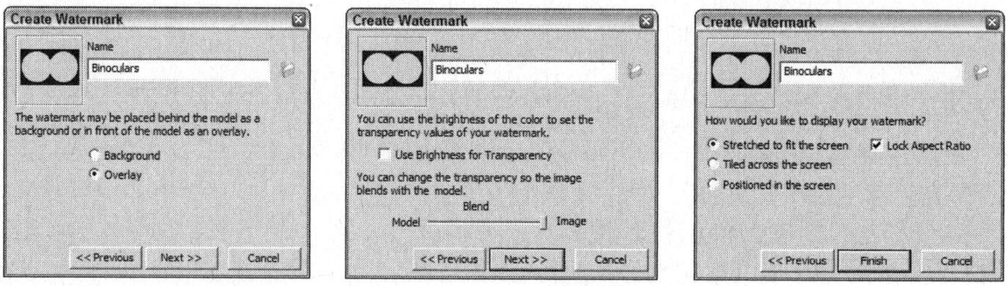

Figure 8-14:
The Choose Watermark series of dialog boxes.

3. **Type in a name for your watermark in the Name box.**

4. **Choose whether you want your new watermark to be in the background or in the foreground as an overlay and click the Next button.**

5. **Decide whether to use brightness for transparency.**

   Selecting this check box tells SketchUp to make your watermark transparent, which kind of simulates a real watermark. *How* transparent each part becomes is based on how bright it is. White is the brightest color, so anything white in your watermark becomes completely transparent. Things that are black turn your background color, and everything in between turns a shade of your background color.

6. **Adjust the amount that your watermark blends with what's behind it, and click the Next button.**

   In this case, Blend is really just a synonym for Transparency. By sliding the Blend slider back and forth, you can adjust the transparency of your watermark.

Blend comes in handy for making paper textures because that process involves using the same watermark twice: once as an overlay and once as an underlay. The overlay version gets "blended" in so that your model appears to be drawn on top of it. To see how this works, apply one of the Paper Texture styles to your model, and then edit each of the watermarks to check out its settings.

7. **Decide how you want your watermark to be displayed and then click the Finish button.**

   You have three choices for how SketchUp can display your watermark: stretched to fit the entire window, tiled across the window, and positioned in the window. Each is illustrated in Figure 8-15. If you select Stretched to Fit the Entire Window, be sure to select the Locked Aspect Ratio check box if your watermark is a logo that you don't want to appear distorted.

Editing a watermark

You can edit any watermark in your SketchUp file at any time. Follow these simple steps to edit a watermark:

1. **Select the watermark you want to edit in the Watermark list.**

   You can find the Watermark list on the Watermark tab, in the Edit pane of the Styles dialog box.

2. **Click the Edit Watermark button to open the Edit Watermark dialog box.**

   The Edit Watermark button looks like a couple of little gears; it's right next to the Add and Delete Watermark buttons above the Watermark list.

Stretched to fit

Tiled

Positioned in lower right

Figure 8-15: You can display watermarks stretched, tiled, or positioned in your modeling window.

3. **Use the controls in the Edit Watermark dialog box and click the OK button when you're done.**

   For a complete description of the controls in this dialog box, see the previous section in this chapter.

Tweaking modeling settings

All you need to know about the controls in the Modeling tab (see Figure 8-16) of the Styles dialog box is that there's not much to know. You use the controls to adjust the color and visibility of all the elements of your model that aren't geometry. To open these options, choose Window⇨Styles, select the Edit tab, and click the box icon on the far right, at the top of the tab. The controls are described as follows:

✔ **Controls with color wells:** Click the wells to change the color of that type of element.

✔ **Section cut width:** This refers to the thickness of the lines, in pixels, that make up the section cut when you're using a section plane. For more about this, have a look at the information on cutting sections in Chapter 10.

✔ **Controls with check boxes:** Use these to control the visibility of that type of element in your model. Three of them are a little confusing:

  • **Color by Layer:** Tells SketchUp to color your geometry according to the colors you've set up in the Layers dialog box. Check out Chapter 8 for more on this.

  • **Section Planes:** This refers to the section plane objects that you use to cut sections. They're gray with four arrows on their corners.

  • **Section Cuts:** Unlike section planes, this setting controls the visibility of the section cut effect itself. With this deselected, your section planes won't appear to be cutting anything.

Mixing styles to create new ones

You can make new styles in two very different ways; which you choose depends on what kind of style you're trying to make. If you've been reading through this chapter from the beginning, you're already familiar with the first method of creating your own styles:

✔ **Use the Edit pane to change settings until you like what you see.** This method is handy and quick, especially if you already know what all the controls do. You can *almost always* use the Edit pane to make your style adjustments. There's only one exception: It's impossible to switch from a regular to an NPR (Sketchy Edges) Edge style (or vice versa) using only the Edit pane; for that, you need to use the next method of creating new styles.

✔ **Use the Mix pane to combine features of multiple styles.** Instead of working through the tabs of the Edit pane, flipping controls on and off, sliding sliders, and picking colors, the Mix pane lets you build new styles by dropping existing ones onto special "category" wells. This is the only way you can switch a style's edge settings between NPR and non-NPR lines.

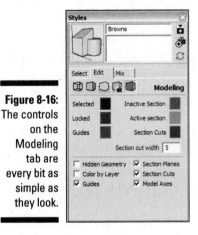

Figure 8-16:
The controls on the Modeling tab are every bit as simple as they look.

NPR refers to the styles in the Assorted Styles and Sketchy Edges Styles libraries. These nonphotorealistic rendering styles use scanned, hand-drawn lines to draw the edges in your model. You *can't* make your own NPR styles from lines you draw and scan in yourself, but you can adapt the existing ones by editing them and saving the changed versions as new styles.

The basic principle of the Mix pane is that you use the *secondary selection pane* (which appears automatically when you choose the Mix pane) to choose styles from which you want to sample certain settings. The secondary selection pane is the lower part of the Styles dialog box, from the word "Select" down, as you can see in Figure 8-17. You drag (on a Mac) or sample (in Windows) these styles onto one or more of the *category wells* to apply the settings you want to your current style. The category wells are the five, long "Settings" rectangles in the middle of the Styles dialog box, as shown in Figure 8-17.

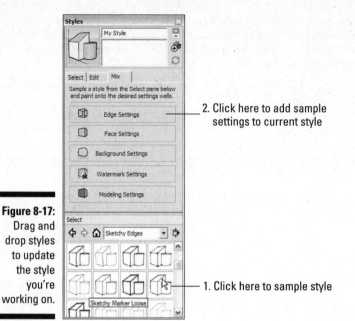

Figure 8-17: Drag and drop styles to update the style you're working on.

Follow these steps to change a style using the Mix pane:

1. **Choose Window⇨Styles and click the Mix tab in the Styles dialog box to open the Mix pane.**

   As part of the Mix pane, the secondary selection pane opens at the bottom of the dialog box. This provides you with a way to view your styles without having to switch from the Mix pane to the Select one.

2. **Find the style you want to sample *from* in the secondary selection pane. You can call this your *source* style.**

   Say that you're working on a new style, and you want your edges to look just like those in the Sketchy Marker Loose style that came with SketchUp. In this example, choose the Sketchy Edges library from the Styles Libraries drop-down list, where you'll find the Sketchy Marker Loose style.

3. **Windows users: Click the source style from the Styles list in the secondary selection pane to sample it and then click the category well that corresponds to the style setting you want to apply.**

   Mac users: Drag your source style from the Styles list in the secondary selection pane to the category well that corresponds to the style setting you want to apply.

In this case, sample the Sketchy Marker Loose style from the secondary selection pane and drop it on the Edge Settings Category well because you want the edge settings from that style to be applied to the style you're working on.

4. **To save your style after you're done adding all the bits and pieces, see the following section.**

Saving and Sharing Styles You Make

As you're working along in SketchUp, you'll want to create your own styles. You'll also want to save those styles so that you can use them in other models. If you're part of a team, it's likely that everyone will want to have access to the same styles so that all your models look consistent. The following sections describe how to do all of these things, and more.

Saving the styles you've made

When it comes to creating your own styles, you can approach things in two different ways. Each of these ways gets its own button (see Figure 8-18):

 ✔ **Create new style:** Clicking this button creates a new style with the settings you currently have active. When you create a new style, it shows up in your In Model library of styles and is saved with your model. The Create button can be found in the upper-right corner of the dialog box, and looks like a couple of objects with a "+" sign on it.

 ✔ **Update style with changes:** This button updates the current style with any settings changes you've made in the Edit or Mix panes. If you want to modify an existing style without creating a new one, this is the way to go. You can find the Update button right below the Create button in the upper-right corner of the dialog box; it looks like two arrows chasing each other around in a circle.

Updating an existing style

To make adjustments to a style in your model, you need to update it. Follow these steps to update a style:

1. **Apply the style you want to update to your model.**

   If you need help with this, follow the steps in the section, "Applying Styles to Your Models," earlier in this chapter.

2. **Use the controls in the Edit pane to make changes to the style.**

   For a complete description of how to modify a style, check out the section "Making Changes to Styles," earlier in this chapter.

3. **Click the Update Style with Changes button in the Styles dialog box to update the style with your changes.**

You use the Update Style with Changes button to rename existing styles, too. Just type the new name into the Name box (at the top of the Styles dialog box), press Enter, and then click the Update button.

Create New Style

Update Style with Changes

Figure 8-18:
The Update and Create buttons in the Styles dialog box.

When you update a style, only the copy of the style that's saved with your model is updated. You aren't altering the copy of the style that shows up in every new SketchUp file you create.

Creating a new style

Creating a new style adds it to your In Model library of styles, which means that you can come back and apply it to your model anytime you like. Follow these steps to create a new style:

1. **Click the Create New Style button in the Styles dialog box.**

   This duplicates the style that was applied to your model before you clicked the Create New Style button. Your new style appears in your In Model library as [*name of the original style*]1.

2. **Use the controls in the Edit pane to set up your style the way you want.**

   Have a look at the section "Making Changes to Styles," earlier in this chapter, for a rundown on using the controls in the Edit pane of the Styles dialog box.

   Frequently, you'll want to make a new style *after* you've already made changes to an existing one. If you want to create a new style that reflects modifications you've already made, just switch Steps 1 and 2 around.

3. **Use the Name box (at the top of the Styles dialog box) to give your new style a name and press Enter.**

   If you want, you can also give your new style a description in the Description box, though you might want to wait until later. After all, it's hard to describe something you haven't made yet.

4. **Click the Update button.**

   This updates your new style with all the changes you made in Steps 2 and 3.

5. **Check the In Model library in the Select pane to make sure that your new style is there.**

   Click the In Model button (which looks like a little house) to see your In Model Styles library. Your new style should appear alphabetically in the list.

If a bunch of styles exist in your In Model library that you aren't using anymore and you want to clean things up, right-click the Library Options flyout menu and choose Purge Unused. This gets rid of any styles that aren't currently applied to any scenes in your model. Have a look at Chapter 10 to find out more about scenes.

Creating a new style *doesn't* automatically make it available for use in other SketchUp files. To find out how to do this, have a look the section "Sharing styles with other models," later in this chapter.

Working with Style Library options

After you've updated or created a style, you'll probably want to make that style available for use in other SketchUp models. To make this happen, you need to understand styles *libraries:* how to make them, how to use them, and how to share them with other people. This section explores your many library options; the next section explains how to save and share a library for yourself or on a network.

To see how you can use libraries to manage your styles, take a closer look at the Library Options flyout menu in the Select pane of the Styles dialog box (click the arrow icon to the right of the Libraries drop-down list). On that menu, you see the following options:

- ✔ **Open or Create a Library (Windows users):** Lets you either choose a library that already exists or make a new one. Whichever you do, the library you end up with is added to your Libraries drop-down list.

- ✔ **Open an Existing Library (Mac users):** Lets you choose an existing styles library from anywhere on your computer or network. A styles library isn't a special kind of file; it's any folder that contains one or more styles. You can keep your styles libraries anywhere you want on your computer or network.

- ✔ **Create a New Library (Mac users):** Lets you create a new styles library anywhere on your computer or network. Because libraries are really just folders, this is a nifty shortcut for creating a new folder without having to leave SketchUp. After you've created a new library, you can put styles in it. Select the Add to Favorites check box in the Add New Library dialog box to automatically add your new library to the Libraries drop-down list.

- ✔ **Save Library As:** Allows you to save copies of the styles in your In Model library to a location on your computer or network. If you don't see this option, make sure that your In Model library is selected in the Libraries drop-down list.

- ✔ **Add Library to Favorites:** Adds the currently selected library to the Favorites section of the Libraries drop-down list. Your Favorite Styles libraries are available in every SketchUp model you're working on, which makes this a great way to gather together libraries that might exist anywhere on your computer or network.

- ✔ **Remove Library from Favorites:** Pops open a dialog box that lets you choose which libraries to remove from the Favorites section of your Libraries drop-down list.

- ✔ **Thumbnails and List View:** Allows you to view your styles in a number of different ways. List view is particularly important if you have styles with subtle differences that don't show up in the Preview Thumbnail view.

- ✔ **Get More:** Opens a Web browser window and takes you to a place on the Internet where you can download more styles. You need to be online for this option to work.

Creating and sharing a library for the styles you make

Follow these steps to create a library to contain your styles:

1. **Choose Window⇨Styles to open the Styles dialog box.**

2. **Click the Select tab to make sure that you're looking at the Select pane.**

3. **Click the Library Options flyout menu and choose Create a New Library.**

   This opens the Add New Library dialog box.

4. **Navigate to the folder on your computer or network where you would like to create your library.**

   You can locate your new library anywhere you like, but I recommend putting it in the same folder as the other styles libraries on your computer:

   • **Windows:** C:/Program Files/Google/Google SketchUp 6/Styles

   • **Mac:** Hard Drive/Library/Application Support/Google SketchUp 6/ SketchUp/Styles

5. **Click Make New Folder if you're on a Windows computer, or New Folder if you're on a Mac.**

   The new folder you create will become your new library.

6. **Type in a name for your new library.**

   Call your new library "Josephine's Library." You can call it something else if your name isn't Josephine.

7. **If you're on a Mac, make sure that the Add to Favorites check box is checked.**

8. **Click the Save button.**

   The Add New Library dialog box closes, and your library is added to the Favorites section of the Libraries drop-down list. It will be there in every SketchUp model you open on this computer.

Sharing styles with other models

Follow these steps to make a style available for use in other SketchUp files:

1. **Choose Window⇨Styles, and in the Style dialog box that appears, click the Select tab.**

2. **Click the In Model button to display your In Model library.**

   The In Model button looks like a little house. The In Model library contains all the styles you've used in your model, including the ones you've created.

3. **Click the Show Secondary Selection Pane button.**

   When you click this button, which looks like a black-and-white rectangle and is in the upper-right corner of the Styles dialog box, a second copy of the Select pane pops out of the bottom of the Styles dialog box (see Figure 8-19). You use this pane to drag and drop styles between folders on your computer, which makes it easier to keep them organized.

4. **In the secondary selection pane, choose the library to which you want to add your style.**

   If you've created a library specifically for the styles you make, choose that one, or you can pick any of the libraries in the Libraries drop-down list.

5. **Drag your style *from* the In Model styles list *to* the Styles list in the secondary selection pane (see Figure 8-20).**

   By dragging and dropping your style from the upper list to the lower one, you're making it available to anyone who has access to that library. This means that you can use it in other SketchUp models you build on your computer. To share it with other members of your team, copy your style to a library somewhere where other people can get to it, like on a network.

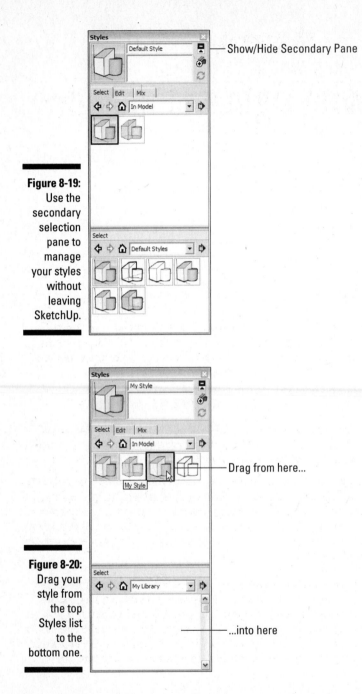

Show/Hide Secondary Pane

Figure 8-19:
Use the secondary selection pane to manage your styles without leaving SketchUp.

Drag from here...

Figure 8-20:
Drag your style from the top Styles list to the bottom one.

...into here

Chapter 9

Working with Light and Shadow

You can always rely on a few features in SketchUp to make people's jaws drop, and the ability to cast shadows is definitely one of them. Displaying shadows is an easy operation — it's a matter of clicking a single button — and the Shadows feature offers lots of ways to make your models look more realistic, more accurate, and more readable.

Typically, you add shadows to a SketchUp drawing for two key reasons:

✔ **To display or print a model in a more realistic way:** Turning on shadows adds depth and realism and gives your model an added level of complexity that makes it look like you worked harder than you really did.

✔ **To study the effect of the sun on what you've built (or plan to build) in a specific geographic location:** Shadow studies are an integral part of the design of any built object. If you're making a sunroom, you need to know that the sun is actually going to hit it, no? You can use SketchUp to show exactly how the sun will affect your creation, at every time of day, on every day of the year.

In this chapter, I start out with a brief, nuts-and-bolts description of how all the controls work, without diving too much into why you'd want to pick one setting instead of another. The middle portions are devoted to running through each of the above scenarios and using the controls to make SketchUp do exactly what you want it to. In the last part of the chapter, I dive into some more advanced material — how to animate your shadows to see how they change over time.

Discovering SketchUp's Shadow Settings

The basic thing to understand about shadows in SketchUp is that, just like in real life, they're controlled by changing the position of the sun. If SketchUp were another kind of program, you might have to type in a bunch of information about azimuths and angles, but luckily, it's not. Because the sun moves in exactly the same way every year, you just pick a date and time, and SketchUp automatically displays the correct shadows by figuring out where the sun should be. Hooray for math!

Luckily for us, using shadows in SketchUp is something you can figure out without fear of messing anything up. Turning on shadows and fiddling with them can never do anything to your model except change the way it's displayed. None of the stuff you've built can be affected in any way, so go ahead and experiment with shadow settings to your heart's content — I promise you'll never break anything.

You do all these simple maneuvers in the Shadow Settings dialog box, shown in Figure 9-1. The sections that follow introduce how the controls work so that you can apply to them to your model.

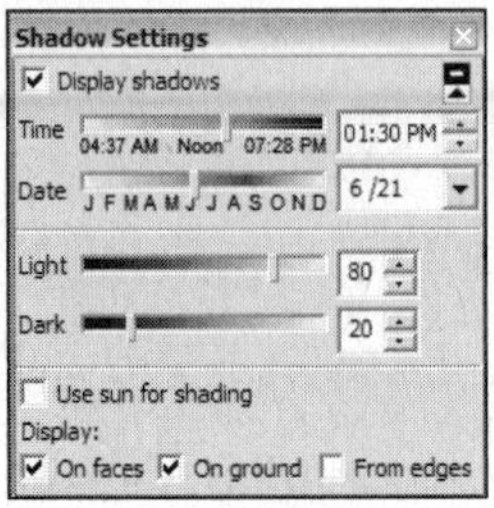

Figure 9-1:
The Shadow
Settings
dialog box.

Turning on the sun

Shadows aren't on by default, so the first thing you need to know about applying shadows is how to turn them on. Follow these simple steps (and check out this book's companion Web site for additional help; see the Introduction for details about the site):

1. **Choose Window⇨Shadows to display the Shadow Settings dialog box.**

2. **At the top of the dialog box, select the Display Shadows check box.**

   Clicking it "turns on" the sun in SketchUp, casting shadows throughout your model and, generally speaking, making everything much more exciting.

Setting a shadow's time and date

The Shadow Settings dialog box has time and date controls, which you use to change the position of the SketchUp "sun." The time and date you choose, in turn, controls the appearance of shadows in your model:

- ✔ **Setting the time:** You don't have to be Copernicus to figure out how to set the time of day; move the Time slider back and forth, or type a time into the little box on the right. Use a colon (:) to separate the hours from the minutes, and type in **AM** or **PM** if you're using 12-hour time. Notice the little times at each end of the slider? These represent sunrise and sunset for the day of the year you've set in the Date control, described in the next point.

- ✔ **Setting the date:** Just like the time of day, you set the day of the year by moving the Date slider back and forth, or by typing in a date in the little box on the right. Use a forward slash (/) to separate the month from the day, entering the month first. If you slide the Date control back and forth, notice that the sunrise and sunset times change in the Time control, in the previous point.

To toggle the extra shadow controls open or closed, click the triangular Expand button in the upper-right corner of the Shadow Settings dialog box.

Controlling contrast

You can use the Shadow Settings dialog box to control the overall contrast in your model view, as shown in Figure 9-3. The Light and Dark sliders seem simple, but it's not immediately obvious to most people how they work. Most of the time, you'll want to leave these settings the way they are, but here's what they do, just in case you want to work with them:

- ✔ **The Light slider controls the lightness of surfaces that are not in shadow.** Sliding it all the way to the left is like a solar eclipse — everything looks like it's in the shade. The default setting for Light is 80.

- ✔ **The Dark slider controls the darkness of shadows cast both on surfaces and on the ground.** Sliding it all the way to the right is like having no shadows. The default setting for Darkness is 20.

The Use Sun for Shading check box is confusing because it doesn't actually control shadows, even though it's in the Shadow Settings dialog box. It has a big effect on the appearance of your model, though:

- ✔ **When it's selected, you see more contrast in your model view.** That's because SketchUp is lighting surfaces as if shadows are turned on, regardless of whether they are. You should leave this check box selected most of the time; things look better with it on.

- ✔ **When it's deselected, things look flatter.** You should deselect this check box when you're working with photos mapped onto faces; doing so makes it easier to see what you're doing. Select the Use Sun for Shading check box again when you're ready to present your work.

Choosing where shadows are displayed

The Display check boxes in the Shadow Settings dialog box enable you to control *where* shadows are cast. Depending on your model, you may want to toggle these on or off. Figure 9-2 shows shadows only on faces (top), only on the ground (middle), and from the edges of the model (bottom):

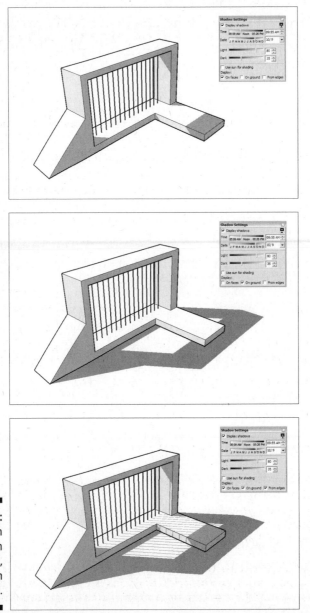

Figure 9-2:
Shadows on faces, on the ground, and from edges.

✔ **On Faces:** Deselecting the On Faces check box means that shadows will be not be cast on faces in your model. This is on by default, and should probably be left on, unless you only want to cast shadows on the ground. For what it's worth, I always have it selected.

✔ **On Ground:** Deselecting the On Ground check box causes shadows not to be cast on the ground plane. Again, this is on by default, but sometimes you'll want to turn it off. A prime example of this is when something you're building extends underground.

✔ **From Edges:** Selecting the From Edges check box tells SketchUp to allow edges to cast shadows. This applies to single edges that are not associated with faces — things like ropes, poles, and sticks are often modeled with edges like these.

Using Shadows to Add Depth and Realism

The neat thing about shadows in SketchUp is how easy they are to apply — and how easy they are to adjust. In the previous sections, I give a dry rundown of the basic controls in the Shadow Settings dialog box. In the following sections, I show you how to use those controls to add depth, realism, and delicious nuance to your models. If only Caravaggio had had it so good. . . .

There are lots of times when you'll need to use shadows to make your drawings read better; most of them fit into one of the following three categories:

✔ **Indoor scenes:** The sun is the only source of lighting that SketchUp has, so any shadows you use in interior views have to come from it.

✔ **Objects that aren't in any particular location:** For things like cars and furniture, it doesn't matter that the shadows are *geographically accurate;* all that matters it that they help to make your model look good.

✔ **2D views:** Without shadows, it's next to impossible to read depth in 2D views of 3D space.

Lighting indoor spaces

Adding shadows to interior views presents an interesting problem: There are no lights besides the sun in SketchUp, so how are you supposed to make anything that looks halfway realistic? With a ceiling in your room, everything's dark. If you leave off the ceiling, your model looks ridiculous. Don't despair — here are some tricks I've learned:

✔ **Decrease the darkness of the shadows.** Sliding the Dark slider to the right brightens your view considerably. You'll still be able to see the shadows cast by the sun coming through windows and other openings, but the whole room won't look like something bad is about to happen. Check out Figure 9-3 to see what I mean.

✔ **Make an impossible ceiling.** As long as you haven't modeled anything on top of the interior you're planning to show, you can tell the ceiling not to cast a shadow. That way, sunlight will shine directly onto your furniture, casting gloriously complex shadows all over everything.

Figure 9-3: Brighten the room by decreasing the Dark setting.

Figure 9-4 shows this ceiling method in action; follow these steps to do it yourself:

Figure 9-4:
Tell the ceiling not to cast a shadow.

1. **Adjust the settings in the Shadow Settings dialog box until the sun is shining through one or more windows in your view.**

   This ensures that shadows cast by objects in your room look like they're caused by light from the windows.

   To make it seem like overhead lighting is in your space, set the time of day to about noon. The shadows cast by furniture and similar objects will be directly below the objects themselves. One more thing: If you have lighting fixtures on the ceiling, remember to set them not to cast shadows in the Entity Info dialog box (read on).

2. **Choose Window⇨Entity Info.**

   This opens the Entity Info dialog box.

3. **Select any faces that make up the ceiling.**

   Hold down Shift to select more than one thing at a time.

4. **In the Entity Info dialog box, deselect the Cast Shadows check box.**

   The ceiling now no longer casts a shadow, brightening your space considerably.

5. **Repeat Steps 3 and 4 for the following faces and objects:**

   • The wall with the windows in it

   • The windows themselves

   • Any walls in your view that are casting shadows on the floor of your space

6. **Move the Dark slider over to about 50.**

   This brightens things even more and makes your shadows more believable.

If you try the first two methods and shadows just don't seem to be working, *don't bother turning on shadows.* Instead, try this:

1. **In the Shadow Settings dialog box, deselect the Display Shadows check box to turn off shadows.**

2. **Select the Use Sun for Shading check box to add some contrast.**

3. **Slide the Dark slider all the way to the left and the Light slider all the way to the right to add even more contrast.**

4. **Move the Time slider around until things look good.**

   Try to make walls with windows in them darker than walls that might be "lit" by those windows. Figure 9-5 demonstrates this technique.

Figure 9-5:
Increase the contrast in your view without using shadows.

Making 3D objects "pop"

Adding shadows to freestanding things like tables and lamps and pineapples is a mostly aesthetic undertaking; just fiddle with the controls until things look good to you, and you'll be okay. Here are some things to keep in mind, (which are illustrated in Figure 9-6):

✔ **Take it easy on the contrast** — especially when it comes to very complex shapes or faces with photos mapped to them. When your model is too contrasty and dramatic, it can be hard to figure out what's going on. To decrease the contrast:

 1. Move the Dark slider over to about 40.

 2. Move the Light slider down to 60 or 70.

✔ **Shorten your shadows.** It's strange to see objects lit as though the light source is very far away; overhead lighting looks more natural. To make your shadows look better, follow these steps:

 1. Set the Date slider to a day in the early autumn.

 2. Set the Time slider to a time between 10 a.m. and 2 p.m.

✔ **Don't be afraid to rotate your model around.** Remember that you can't get every possible shadow position by using only the controls in the Shadow Settings dialog box; to get the effect you want, you might have to rotate your model by selecting it and using the Rotate tool.

✔ **Select the From Edges check box.** Lots of times, modelers use free edges to add fine detail to models (think of a harp or a loom). Selecting the From Edges check box tells SketchUp to allow those edges to cast shadows, which makes complex objects look about 900 percent cooler.

✔ **Pay attention to the transparency of faces.** When you have a face painted with a transparent material, you can decide whether that face should cast a shadow — chances are that it shouldn't. In SketchUp, the rule is that materials that are more than 50-percent transparent cast shadows. So, if you don't want one of your transparent-looking faces to cast a shadow, do one of the following:

 • Select the face, and then deselect the Cast Shadows check box in the Entity Info dialog box.

 • Adjust the opacity of the face's material to be less than 50 percent in the Materials dialog box. For more information on how to do this, have a look at Chapter 2.

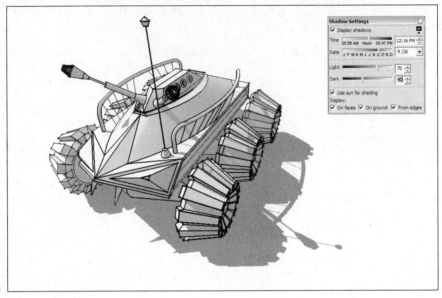

Figure 9-6:
Tips for making objects stand out with shadows.

Conveying depth in 2D views

Have you ever looked at a roof plan or building elevation (a straight-on view of the exterior) and wondered what the heck was going on? One of the main reasons that 2D drawings are so hard to read is that they usually don't convey *depth*. Without knowing how close or far away things are, everything turns into a flat jumble of lines. Of course, experienced draftspersons can use line weight (thickness) and tone to convey depth — SketchUp's style settings, which you can read about it Chapter 8, provide some help, but your best bet is to use shadows.

Take a look at Figure 9-7 to see what a difference the addition of shadows can make to a 2D overhead view of a row of buildings. In Parallel Projection mode, which is how 99 percent of 2D drawings are made, there's no way to know how high any of the buildings are. Turning on shadows reveals a whole new layer of information.

Figure 9-7:
Adding shadows to a 2D view provides important extra information.

When adding shadows to 2D views of your model, here are some things to keep in mind:

- ✔ **The convention in architecture is to cast shadows at a 45-degree angle.** If you want your views to look somewhat official, play with the Time and Date sliders until your shadows are cast at about 45 degrees from your model. There are probably ways to be super-accurate about this, but I wouldn't worry; the point is to make your drawings readable.

- ✔ **Lighten your shadows.** Because the purpose of this exercise is to increase the legibility of your 2D views, you don't need to be dramatic. To be able to see what's happening in your shadows, crank the Dark slider in the Shadow Settings dialog box up to about 50.

- ✔ **The same goes for elevations.** An elevation is a 2D view of the side of a building. Feel free to use shadows to make these drawings clearer, too. Architects do it all the time, and it makes a huge difference.

Creating Accurate Shadow Studies

One of the most useful features in SketchUp is the ability to display accurate shadows. To do this, three pieces of information are necessary:

- ✔ The time of day
- ✔ The day of the year
- ✔ The latitude of the building site

The sun's position (and thus the position of shadows) depends on geographic location — that is to say, latitude. The shadow cast by a building at 3:00 on March 5 in Minsk is very different from that cast by a similar building, at the same time of day, on the same date in Nairobi.

If you're displaying shadows on a model of a toaster oven, geographic location probably doesn't matter to you; the shadows are just there for effect. But if you're trying to see how much time your pool deck will spend in the sun during the summer months, you need to tell SketchUp where you are.

Telling SketchUp where you are

How many of people know the precise latitude of where they live? I sure don't. It's a good thing SketchUp makes it easy to *geolocate* your model — that is, you can tell the model where in the world it's supposed to be. How you do so depends on which version of SketchUp you're using:

- ✔ **Google SketchUp 6 (free):** With SketchUp 6, you geolocate your model by importing a Google Earth snapshot, as I explain in Chapter 11.

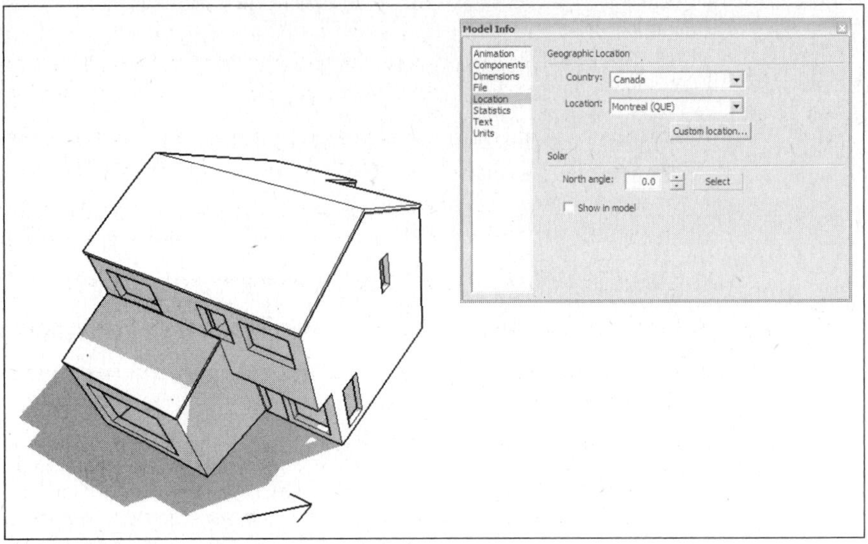

Figure 9-8:
Giving your
model a
geographic
location
with
SketchUp
Pro.

✔ **Google SketchUp Pro 6:** Users of SketchUp Pro have access to some nifty additional functionality. If you're using Pro, you have a choice of methods for geolocating your model:

• You can import a Google Earth snapshot (see Chapter 11).

• You can use the Location panel in the Model Info dialog box, as shown in Figure 9-8. Read following section to find out more.

To give your model a geographic location using the Location panel in SketchUp Pro, follow these steps:

1. **Somewhere on the ground in your model, draw a short line to indicate the direction of north.**

   If you're working with imported geometry (from AutoCAD, for instance) you might already have a north indicator.

2. **Choose Window➪Model Info to open the Model Info dialog box.**

3. **On the left side of the Model Info dialog box, choose Location.**

   If the Country drop-down list says Custom or N/A, stop here. Your model has already been geographically located by importing a Google Earth snapshot, and you don't need to go through any of the following steps. Shadows will be accurate for wherever you were in Google Earth when you imported a snapshot. Close the Model Info dialog box, make yourself some coffee, and waste the time you just saved.

4. **Choose a country from the Country drop-down list.**

5. **Choose a location from the Location drop-down list.**

   If the location you want isn't listed, choose the closest one, or click the Custom Location button to enter a set of coordinates.

To find coordinates for just about anywhere in the world, try searching for "city, country coordinates" on Google; something usually pops up.

6. **Instead of typing in a north angle (which I find overly complicated), click the Select button to the right of the North angle box.**

   Back in your model window, your cursor will have become a biggish circle with four lines radiating out from the center, as shown in Figure 9-9.

7. **Click the southern end of the line you drew in Step 1.**

8. **Click the northern end of the same line, finishing the operation.**

9. **If you want, select the Show in Model check box to display the direction of north as a yellow line.**

10. **Close the Model Info dialog box.**

    The shadows in SketchUp are now specific to the geographic location you've just set up. If you like, you can erase the line you drew in Step 1.

Displaying accurate shadows for a given time and place

After you tell SketchUp where your model is, it's a pretty simple process to study how the sun will affect your project, as shown in Figure 9-10. This is the fun part; all you have to do is move some sliders around. If you have an audience, get ready for some completely undeserved praise.

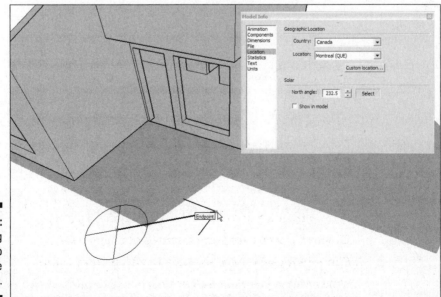

Figure 9-9: Telling SketchUp where north is.

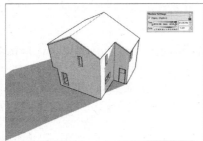

Figure 9-10:
Studying the
effect of the
sun on your
model.

To study how the sun will affect your project, follow these steps:

1. **Orbit, zoom, and pan around until you have a good view of the part of your project you want to study.**

2. **Choose Window⇨Shadows to open the Shadow Settings dialog box.**

3. **Select the Display Shadows check box to turn on SketchUp's sun.**

4. **Type a month and day into the box to the right of the Date slider, and press Enter.**

5. **Move the Time slider back and forth to see how the shadows will move over the course of that day.**

6. **Pick a time of day using the Time controls.**

7. **Move the Date slider back and forth to see how the sun will affect your project at that time of day over the course of the year.**

Animating a shadow study

As if playing with the shadow settings weren't sexy enough, it's a relatively easy next step to create a simple animation that shows shadows moving over time. To do this, you'll use scenes, a feature so impressive and relevant to this topic I mention it here as well as in Chapter 10, where you'll find more detailed coverage of scenes in general.

Uses for shadows

Even if you're not an architect, you might want to study shadows accurately for these reasons:

✔ To figure out where to locate the plants in your garden that need the most light (or the most shade)

✔ To see when sunlight will be coming straight through the skylight you're thinking of installing

✔ To make sure that the overhang behind your house will provide enough shade at lunchtime in the summer

✔ To plan and build a 50-foot stone sundial as a birthday gift for your Druidic neighbor

To create a simple animation showing the movement of shadows in your model over time, follow these steps:

1. **If you haven't already done so, give your model a geographic location by following the steps in the section "Telling SketchUp where you are," earlier in this chapter.**

2. **Orbit, zoom, and pan around until you're happy with the way your model looks in the modeling window.**

3. **If you haven't already done so, open the Shadow Settings dialog box by choosing Window⇨Shadows.**

4. **Turn on the sun (and thus the shadows) by making sure that the Display Shadows check box is selected.**

5. **Use the controls to pick a time and date.**

   Try picking a time early in the morning — it'll make for a better animation when you're done (see Figure 9-11).

6. **Choose Window⇨Scenes to open the Scenes dialog box.**

7. **Click the Add button (which looks like a plus sign in a circle) in the Scenes dialog box.**

   This adds a scene to the list in the Scenes dialog box, and a tab at the top of your modeling window (see Figure 9-12). If it's the first scene you've created in this model, it will be called Scene 1.

8. **Back in the Shadows dialog box, choose a different time of day.**

   A time late in the afternoon works well.

Figure 9-11:
Pick a time
in the
morning.

9. **Back in the Scenes dialog box, click the Add button again.**

   This adds Scene 2 to the list in the dialog box and another tab at the top of your modeling window.

10. **Click the tab you created in Step 7.**

   See the shadows moving? Clicking back and forth between the tabs causes the shadows to animate between the times of day you set up in the Shadow Settings dialog box. You can keep changing the date and time, adding more scenes if you like; it's your weekend, after all.

11. **When you're ready to animate all the scenes you've created, flip to Chapter 13 to find how to export the animation you just created as a movie file.**

To do a proper shadow study, you need to see where the shadows fall on the longest and shortest days of the year. In the Northern Hemisphere, these days are June 21 and December 21, respectively. In the Southern Hemisphere, it's the opposite. I think it has something to do with gravity.

Remember that SketchUp does not support daylight savings time. When you do a shadow study over the course of a year, mentally adjust the shadows an hour forward if daylight savings time will be in effect.

Scene tab   Add button

Figure 9-12:
Click the
Add button
to add a
scene to
your model.

Chapter 10

Presenting Your Model Inside SketchUp

● ●

In This Chapter

▶ Walking around inside your model

▶ Creating scenes to capture particular views

▶ Making animations with scenes

▶ Cutting slices through your model with section planes

▶ Generating plans and sections

● ●

After you've made a model, you're probably going to want to show it to someone. How you present your work depends on the idea you're trying to convey. The tricky part about using SketchUp to present a model isn't actually using the tools; it's choosing the *right* tools to get your idea across without distracting your audience with a bunch of extra information. Most 3D models have so much to look at that the real challenge is to figure out a presentation method that helps you focus on the stuff you want to talk about.

In this chapter, I talk about three different ways to show off your models without ever leaving SketchUp. If you've made a building, you can walk around inside it. You can even walk up and down stairs and ramps — just like in a video game. You can create animated slide shows by setting up scenes with different camera views, times of day, and even visual styles. If you want to talk about what's *inside* your model, you can cut sections through it without taking it apart.

As you're reading through this chapter, keep in mind what you want your model to communicate. Think about how you might use each method to make a different kind of point, and think about the order in which you'd like those points to be made. As with everything else in SketchUp (and in life, I suppose), a little bit of planning goes a long way. That said, presenting a model live in SketchUp is undeniably sexy; you can't really go wrong, so have fun.

Exploring Your Creation on Foot

Few experiences in life are as satisfying as running around inside your model. After you've made a space, you can drop down into it and explore by walking around, going up and down stairs, bumping into walls, and even falling off of ledges. You can check to make sure that the television is visible from the kitchen, say, or experience what it would be like to wander down the hall. In a potentially confusing building (like an airport or a train station), you could figure out where to put the signs by allowing someone who's never seen your model to explore the space "on foot."

These tools were made for walking

A couple of tools in SketchUp are dedicated to moving around your model as if you were actually inside it. The first step (no pun intended) is to position yourself so that it seems like you're standing inside your model. This can be tricky with just the Orbit, Pan, and Zoom tools, so SketchUp provides a tool just for this: Position Camera. After you're standing in the right spot (and at the right height), you use the Walk tool to move around. It's as simple as that.

Standing in the right spot: The Position Camera tool

The essence of the Position Camera tool is its ability to precisely place your viewpoint in SketchUp in a particular spot. That's really all it does, but it works in two different ways (see this book's Web site for more details; the Introduction tells you all about the Web site):

✔ **I want to be standing right here.** Choose Camera⇨Position Camera from the menu bar and then single-click anywhere in the modeling window to automatically position your viewpoint 5 feet, 6 inches above wherever you clicked. Because this is the average *eye-height* of an adult human being, the result is that you are, for all intents and purposes, standing on the spot where you clicked (see Figure 10-1). After using Position Camera, SketchUp automatically switches to the Look Around tool, assuming that, now that you're where you want to be, you might want to have a look around. I talk about Look Around in the next section of this chapter.

You're not stuck being five-and-a-half-feet tall forever. After you use Position Camera, type in the height you'd rather "be" and press Enter. Type **18"** to see a golden retriever's view of the world, or type **7'** to pretend you play for the L.A. Lakers. Keep in mind that the VCB (the spot in the lower-right corner where numbers appear) displays your eye height as a distance from the ground, and not from whatever surface you're "standing on." To set your eye height to be 5 feet above a platform that's 10 feet high, you'd type in **15'**.

✔ **I want my eyes to be right here, and I want to be looking in this direction.** Select Position Camera, click the mouse button while in the spot where you want your eyes to be, drag over to the thing you want to be looking at (you'll see a dashed line connecting the two points), and release the mouse button (as shown in Figure 10-2). Try this technique a couple of times; it takes a bit of practice to master. You'd use Position Camera in this way if you wanted to be standing in a particular spot *and* looking in a particular direction. This technique works great with scenes, which I talk about later in this chapter.

Figure 10-1: Drop yourself into your model with the Position Camera tool.

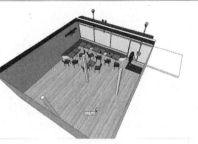

Figure 10-2: "Aim" your view by using Position Camera in another way.

Stepping out with the Walk tool

After you've used Position Camera to place yourself in your model, use the Walk tool to move through it. (Again, find out more on this book's companion Web site.) To walk around, click and drag the mouse in the direction you want to move:

✔ Straight up is forward.

✔ Straight down is backward.

✔ Anything to the left or right causes you to turn while you're walking.

The farther you move your cursor, the faster you walk. Release the mouse button to stop. If you've ever played video games, you'll get used to it quickly. If Scrabble is more your speed, it'll take a few minutes to get used to things.

You can even use the Walk tool to walk up and down stairs and ramps. Keep in mind that the highest step you can "climb" is 22 inches — anything higher and you get the "bump" cursor, just like you walked into a wall. Also, if you walk off a high surface, you'll fall to the surface below. It's times like these that I wish SketchUp had cartoon sound effects. . . .

Using modifier keys in combination with the Walk tool makes SketchUp even more like a video game:

- ✔ Hold down Ctrl (Option on a Mac) to run instead of walking. This might be useful if you're trying to simulate what it would be like if a werewolf were chasing you through your model.

- ✔ Hold down Shift to move straight up (like you're growing), straight down (like you're shrinking), or sideways (like a crab).

- ✔ Hold down Alt (⌘ on a Mac) to disable collision detection, which allows you to walk through walls instead of bumping into them. Burglars find this handy for entering models without having to break any windows.

Stopping to look around

Look Around is the third tool in SketchUp that's dedicated to exploring your model from the inside. If using Position Camera is like swooping in to be standing in a particular spot, and Walk is like moving around while maintaining a constant eye-height, Look Around is like turning your head while standing in one spot. It's pretty well named, I think; it does exactly what it says.

Using Look Around is so simple it hardly merits these steps:

1. **Choose Camera⇨Look Around from the menu bar to activate the Look Around tool.**

2. **Click and drag around in the modeling window to turn your virtual head.**

   Don't move too fast or you'll strain your virtual neck, though. Just kidding.

While in any of the navigation tools, you can right-click to access any of the other navigation tools; this makes switching between them a little easier.

When you use Look Around with the field of view tool I discuss in the next section, you get a pretty darned realistic simulation of what it would be like to be standing in your model.

Setting your field of view

Field of view is the amount of your model you're able to see in your modeling window at one time. Imagine your eyesight kind of like a cone, with the pointy end pointing at your eyes and the cone getting bigger as it gets farther away from you. Everything that falls inside the cone is visible to you, and everything outside the cone isn't.

If you increase the angle of the cone at the pointy end, the cone gets wider, and you see more of what's in front of you. If you decrease the angle, the cone gets narrower, and you see less (see Figure 10-3).

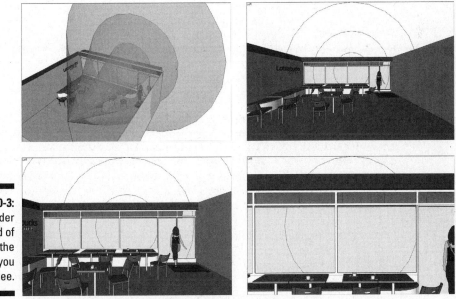

Figure 10-3: The wider your field of view, the more you can see.

Measured in degrees, a wide field of view means that you can see more of your model without having to move around. The bigger the angle, the more you can see. This comes in handy when you're inside a SketchUp model you're working on, because it's hard to work on things you can't see.

It's a good idea to fiddle with your field of view while walking around inside your model. Follow these steps to do so:

1. **Choose Camera⇨Field of View.**

   Notice that the Value Control Box in the lower-right corner of your modeling window says Field of View and that the default value is 35 deg. This means that you currently have a 35-degree cone of vision, which is kind of narrow.

2. **Type** 60 **and press Enter.**

   Your field of view is increased, and you now have a wider view of your model. The trade-off is that you see more distortion at the edges of your modeling window as more information is being displayed in the same amount of space.

A good rule of thumb for setting your field of view is to strike a balance between quantity and quality; a wider view always means more distortion. For views of the *outside* of something I've built, I like to use a field of view of 35 to 45 degrees. For interior views, I use 60 or 70 degrees.

If you happen to know something about photography, you can also express field of view in millimeters, just like you're using a camera lens. Typing in **28mm** gives you a wide-angle view, just like you're looking through a 28-mm lens. For people who think about field of view in these terms, this can be a lot more intuitive than trying to imagine cones of vision.

Taking the Scenic Route

Wouldn't it be great if you could save a particular view of your model so that you could come back to that view whenever you wanted to? And wouldn't it be even greater if that saved view could also save things like styles and shadow settings? What if you could come back to any of these saved views by clicking a button on your screen? What if this whole paragraph were just a series of questions?

SketchUp scenes are (you guessed it) saved views of your model. It's probably easiest to think of scenes as cameras, except that scenes can save much more than just camera positions. Although they don't get a lot of space in this book (they don't even get their own chapter), scenes are one of the most important features in SketchUp, for three reasons:

✔ **Scenes can save you hours of time.** It's not always easy to get back to exactly the right view by using Orbit, Zoom, and Pan. Sometimes a view involves shadows, styles, sections (you'll read about those later), and even hidden geometry. It can be a pain to set up everything the way you need it, every time you need it. It's not that SketchUp's *hard* — it's just that you have a lot of different ways to view your model. Making a scene reduces the process of changing dozens of settings to a single click of your mouse.

✔ **Scenes are *by far* the most effective way of presenting your model.** Saving a scene for each point that you'd like to make in a presentation allows you to focus on what you're trying to say. Instead of fumbling around with the navigation tools, turning on shadows, and making the roof visible, you can click a button, and SketchUp will automatically transition to the next scene (which you've already set up exactly the way you want it). Figure 10-4 shows a set of scenes I created to present a house I designed for my dog, Savannah.

✔ **Scenes are the key to making animations.** You make animations by creating a series of scenes and telling SketchUp to figure out the transitions between them. The process, which is explained in later sections, is as simple as clicking a button.

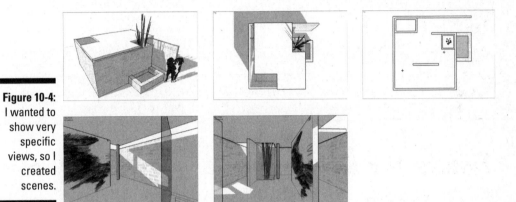

Figure 10-4:
I wanted to show very specific views, so I created scenes.

After you get used to them, you'll find yourself using scenes all the time. Here are some of the most common uses for scenes:

✔ Showing shade conditions for the same area at different times of the day

✔ Saving scenes for each floorplan, building section, and other important view of your model

✔ Building a walk-through or flyover animation of your design

✔ Creating scenes to show several views of the same thing with different options (the pointy roof or the flat one, Madam?)

✔ Demonstrating change over time by showing or hiding a succession of components

Creating scenes

Let's get one thing straight: Making a scene in SketchUp is *not* like taking a snapshot of your model. If you create a scene to save a view, then do some more modeling, and then return to that scene, your model will not go back to the way it was when you created the scene. The camera position will be the same and the settings will the same, but your geometry won't be. This is a pretty important concept, and one that makes using scenes so powerful.

A scene is just a set of view settings, which means that they're automatically updated to reflect your changes every time you edit your model. You can make some scenes and use them all the way through your process, from when you start modeling to when you present your design to the president. Or to your mother.

Creating scenes is a simple process. The basic idea is that you add a scene to your SketchUp file whenever you have a view you want to return to later. You can always delete scenes, so there's no downside to using lots of them. Follow these steps to make a new scene (and check this book's companion Web site for additional help):

1. **Choose Window⇨Scenes to open the Scenes dialog box.**

   When it first opens, it doesn't look like there's much to the Scenes dialog box. Expanding it by clicking the expansion toggle in the upper-right corner reveals more options, which I cover in the next section, but don't worry about that right now.

2. **Set up your view however you want.**

   Navigate around until you're happy with your point of view. If you want, use the Shadows and Styles dialog boxes to change the way your model looks.

3. **Click the Add button to make a new scene with your current view settings.**

   At this point, a new scene is added to your SketchUp file. If this is the first scene you've created, it will be called Scene 1 and will appear in two places (see Figure 10-5):

   • As a list item in the Scenes dialog box, right underneath the Add button

   • As a tab at the top of your modeling window, labeled Scene 1

Nothing is generated outside of SketchUp when you add a scene; it's not like exporting a JPEG or a TIFF. Scenes are just little bits of programming code that "remember" the view settings in effect when they were created. Scenes also don't add much to your file size, so you don't have to worry about using too many of them.

Moving from scene to scene

Activate a scene you've added earlier by doing one of three things:

- ✔ Double-clicking the name of the scene in the Scenes dialog box.

- ✔ Single-clicking the tab for that scene at the top of the modeling window.

- ✔ Right-clicking any scene tab and choosing Play Animation to make SketchUp automatically flip through your scenes. (Choose Play Animation again to make the animation stop.)

Notice how the transition from one scene to the next is animated? You don't have to do anything special to make this happen; it's something SketchUp automatically does to make things look better (and ultimately, to make *you* look better).

You can adjust the way SketchUp transitions between scenes, which is handy for customizing your presentations. Follow these steps to access these settings:

1. **Choose Window⇨Model Info to open the Model Info dialog box.**

2. **On the left side of the Model Info dialog box, choose Animation.**

   The Animation settings panel in the Model Info dialog box (see Figure 10-6) isn't very complicated, but it can make a huge difference in the appearance of your scene-related presentations.

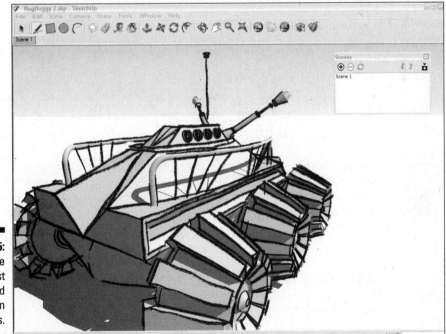

Figure 10-5:
The scene you just added shows up in two places.

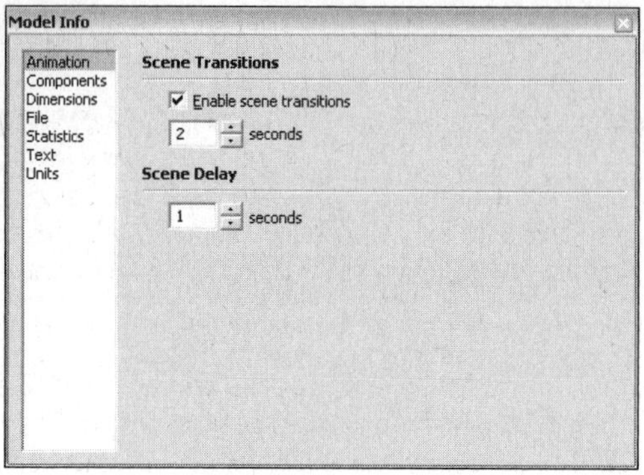

Figure 10-6:
The
Animation
settings
panel is a
big help in
customizing
your
presen-
tations.

Model Info

Animation
Components
Dimensions
File
Statistics
Text
Units

Scene Transitions

☑ Enable scene transitions

2 ⏶ seconds

Scene Delay

1 ⏶ seconds

3. **In the Scene Transitions area, set how SketchUp transitions from one scene to another.**

These settings apply to both manual (clicking on a page tab) and automatic (playing an animation) scene transitions:

- **Enable Scene Transitions:** Deselect this check box to make SketchUp change scenes without animating the transitions between them. You'll probably want to do this if your model is so complex (or your computer is so slow) that animated transitions don't look good.

- **Seconds:** If you've selected the Enable Scene Transitions check box, the number of seconds you enter here will be the amount of time it takes SketchUp to transition from one scene to the next. If you're "moving the camera" very far between scenes, it's a good idea to bump up the transition time so that your audience doesn't get sick. I find three seconds to be a good compromise between nausea and boredom.

If you're presenting an incomplete model (perhaps you've thought about the garage and the living room, but nothing in between), it can be helpful to turn off scene transitions. That way, your audience won't see the things you haven't worked on when you click a tab to change scenes. It's sneaky, but effective.

4. **In the Scene Delay area, set the length of time SketchUp pauses on each slide before it moves to the next one.**

If you want it to seem like you're walking or flying, set this to 0. If you want time to talk about each scene in your presentation, bump this up a few seconds.

Modifying scenes after you've made 'em

After you create a whole bunch of scenes, it's inevitable that you're going to need to fiddle with them in some way. After all, modifying something is almost always easier than making it all over again, and the same thing holds true for scenes. Because your SketchUp model will change a million times, understanding how to make changes to your existing scenes can save you a lot of time in the long run.

Certain aspects of the scene-modification process can get a little tricky. This is kind of surprising, given how simple the rest of working with scenes can be, but I think it's inevitable. You deal with a lot of complexity when working in SketchUp, and this is just one of the places where that complexity rears its ugly head. The upshot: Pay special attention to the section on updating scenes, and don't worry if it takes a little while to figure things out. It happens to the best of us.

Reordering, renaming, and removing scenes

Making simple modifications to scenes, such as reordering, renaming, and removing them, is easy. You can accomplish each of these in two ways: You either use the Scenes dialog box, or you right-click the scene tabs at the top of your modeling window. Figure 10-7 is an illustration.

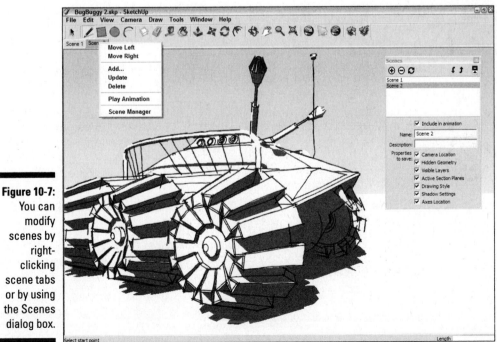

Figure 10-7:
You can modify scenes by right-clicking scene tabs or by using the Scenes dialog box.

To access the modification controls in the Scenes dialog box, click the arrow-shaped expansion button in the upper-right corner.

Here's how to reorder, rename, or remove scenes:

✔ **Reordering scenes:** You can change the order in which scenes play in a slide show. If you're using scenes, you'll need to do this often — trust me. Use one of the following methods:

- Right-click the tab of the scene you want to move (in the modeling window) and choose Move Right or Move Left.

- In the expanded Scenes dialog box, click the name of the scene you want to move to select it, and then click the up or down arrows to the right of the list to change the scene's position in the scene order.

✔ **Renaming scenes:** It's a good idea to give your scenes meaningful names: "Living Room," "Top View," and "Shadows at 5:00 p.m." are descriptive enough to be useful. "Scene 14," I find, lacks a certain *je ne sais quoi*. Use one of the following methods:

- Right-click the scene tab and choose Rename.

- In the Scenes dialog box, select the scene you want to rename and type something into the Name field below the list. If you're feeling really organized, go ahead and give it a description, too — more information never hurts.

✔ **Removing scenes:** If you don't need a scene anymore, feel free to delete it. However, if you have a scene that you don't want to appear in slide shows, you don't have to get rid of it. Use one of the following methods to remove a scene:

- Right-click the scene tab and choose Delete to get rid of it permanently.

- In the Scenes dialog box, select the scene you want to ax and click the Delete button.

To exclude a scene from slide shows without getting rid of it, select its name in the list and deselect the Include in Animation check box.

Making walk-throughs

A really great way to use scenes is to pretend you're walking or flying through your model. By setting up your scenes sequentially, you can give a seamless tour without having to mess around with the navigation tools. This is especially handy

when you need to be able to "walk and talk" at the same time.

Here are some tips that can help you to simulate a person walking or flying through your model with scenes:

✔ **Adjust your field of view.** For interior animations, make your camera "see" a wider area by setting your field of view to 60 degrees. I like to set my field of view between 30 and 45 degrees for exterior views, but there's no hard and fast rule. I talk about how to do this in the section "Setting your field of view," earlier in this chapter.

✔ **Make sure that your scenes aren't too far apart.** Instead of racing through a room like it's on fire, don't be afraid to add more scenes. Your audience will thank you by not throwing up on your conference table.

✔ **Add scenes at equal distance intervals.** Because SketchUp only lets you control the scene transition timing for all your scenes at once, it's best to make sure that your scenes are set up about the same distance apart. If you don't, your walk-through animations will be jerky and strange, like my dancing.

✔ **Don't forget the animation settings in the Model Info dialog box.** Set the scene delay to 0 seconds so that your animation doesn't pause at every scene. For a normal walking speed, set your scene transitions so that you're moving about 5 feet per second. If your scenes are about 20 feet apart, set your scene transition time to 4 seconds. This gives your audience time to look around and notice things. For flying animations, pick a scene transition time that looks good.

✔ **Slide around corners.** When you're setting up a walking animation, you have an easy, reliable way to turn corners without seeming too robotic. The method is illustrated in the following figure. Basically, the trick is to add a scene just short of where you want to turn — in this case, a few feet ahead of the doorway. The key is to angle your view *into* the turn slightly. You should set up your next scene just past the turn, close to the inside and facing the new view. This technique makes it seem like you're turning corners naturally.

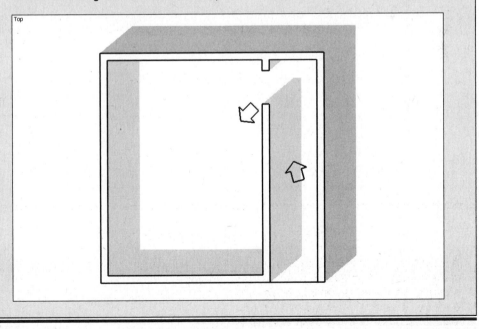

Updating scenes

Okay. Turn off the television. Send the kids outside to play. Do whatever you need to do to be able to concentrate, because the process of updating scenes isn't altogether straightforward. I'll do my best to explain it.

Basically, a scene is just a collection of saved viewing *properties*. Each of these properties has something to do with how your model looks. A scene can save one, some, or all of the following properties, depending on what you need to do:

- ✔ **Camera location:** Camera location properties include the position of the camera, or viewpoint, and the field of view. I discuss field of view earlier in this chapter.

- ✔ **Hidden geometry:** Hidden geometry properties are really just one thing: what elements are hidden and what elements aren't. These properties keep track of the visibility of the lines, faces, groups, components, and axes in your model.

- ✔ **Visible layers:** Visible layer properties keep track of the visibility of layers in your model.

- ✔ **Active section planes:** Active section plane properties include the visibility of section planes and whether they are active. I talk about sections in the last part of this chapter.

- ✔ **Style and fog:** Style and fog properties are all the settings in the Styles and Fog dialog boxes, and there are a lot of them.

- ✔ **Shadow settings:** Shadow settings properties include whether shadows are turned on and the time and date for which the shadows are set. They also include all the other settings in the Shadow Settings dialog box.

- ✔ **Axes locations:** Axes location properties are very specific. They keep track of the visibility of the main SketchUp red, green, and blue axes in your modeling window. Because you'll often want to hide the axes when you're giving a presentation, these elements get their own properties.

Updating all the scene properties at once

The simplest way to modify a scene is to not worry about individual properties. If all you want to do is update a scene after you've made an adjustment to the appearance of your model, you're in luck. Follow these steps:

1. **Go to the scene you want to update by clicking its tab at the top of the modeling window.**

2. **Make whatever styles, shadows, camera, or other display changes you want to make to your model.**

3. **Right-click the current scene tab and choose Update.**

   Be careful not to accidentally double-click the tab or you'll reactivate the scene and lose all the changes you made. The old scene properties are replaced by the new ones, and you're home free.

After you update a scene, you can't use Undo to revert things back to the way they were. I suggest saving your SketchUp file right before updating a scene, and choosing File➪Revert from the File menu if you don't like how things turn out.

Updating scene properties selectively

Here's where things get complicated. At times in your SketchUp life, you'll want to update a scene without updating all its properties.

Updating scenes selectively involves making changes that you won't be able to see immediately; whenever you do this, you have the potential for disaster to strike. It's a good idea to make a copy of your SketchUp file before updating more than one scene at a time, just in case something awful happens.

Maybe you've used scenes to create a tour of the sunroom you're designing for a client, and you want to change the shadow settings to make your model look brighter. You have 30 scenes in your presentation, and your meeting's in 5 minutes. You don't have time to change and update all 30 scenes one at a time. What to do? Follow these steps (and have a look at Figure 10-8):

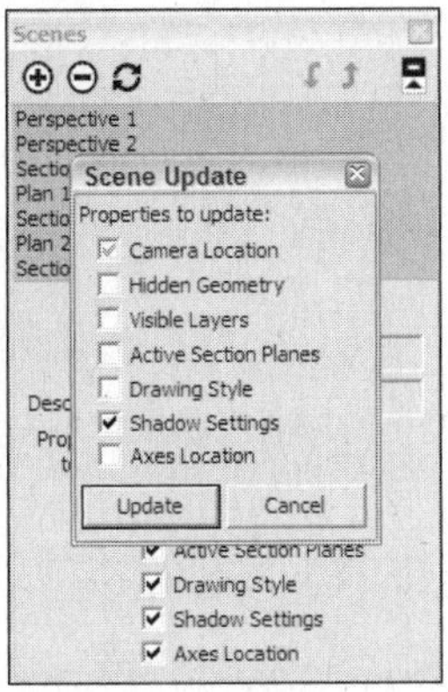

Figure 10-8:
Updating only certain scene properties is a little more involved.

1. **Adjust the shadow settings to where you'd like them to be for all the scenes you'd like to update.**

   While this example deals with shadows, this same method applies to any scene properties changes you'd like to make.

2. **In the Scenes dialog box, select all the scenes you'd like to update.**

   Hold down Shift to select more than one scene at a time.

3. **Click the Update button in the Scenes dialog box.**

   A Properties to Update dialog box appears.

4. **Select the Shadow Settings check box and click the Update button.**

   If all you want to update are the shadow settings, make sure that only that check box is selected. More generally, you would select the check box next to each of the properties you want to update. All the selected scenes are updated with those new properties, and all the properties left deselected remain unchanged.

Mastering the Sectional Approach

Software like SketchUp has a funny way of providing moments of perfect simplicity, moments when you sit back, scratch your head, and think to yourself, "That's it? That's all there is to it?"

Sections in SketchUp offer one of those moments. To put it simply, sections are objects that let you cut away parts of your model to look inside. You place them wherever you need them, use them to create views you wouldn't otherwise be able to get, and then delete them when you're done. When you move a section plane, you get instant feedback; the "cut" view of your model moves, too. If you want to get fancy, you can embed them in scenes and even use them in animations. Sections are the icing on the SketchUp cake: easy to use, incredibly important, and impressive as all get out.

People use sections for all kinds of things:

✔ Creating standard orthographic views (like plans and sections) of buildings and other objects

✔ Making cutaway views of complex models to make them easier to understand

✔ Working on the interiors of buildings without having to move or hide geometry

✔ Generating sectional animations with scenes

Cutting plans and sections

The most common use for sections is to create straight-on, cut-through views of your model. These are some of the views that often include dimensions, and are typical of the kinds of drawings that architects make to design and explain space. They're useful because they're easy to read and you can take measurements from them (if they're printed to scale), and they provide information that no other drawing type can. The following terms (which are illustrated in Figure 10-9) can help you create different views of your model more easily:

✔ **Plan:** A *planimetric* view, or plan, is a top-down, two-dimensional, non-perspectival view of an object or space. Put simply, it's every drawing of a house floorplan you've ever seen. You generate a plan by cutting an imaginary *horizontal* slice through your model. Everything below the slice is visible, and everything above it isn't.

✔ **Section:** Not to be confused with sections (the SketchUp feature about which this section of the book is written), a *sectional* view, or section, is a from-the-side, two-dimensional, nonperspectival view of an object or space. You would make a section by cutting an imaginary *vertical* slice through your model. Just like in a plan view, everything on one side of the slice is visible, and everything on the other side is hidden.

Figure 10-9:
A plan is a horizontal cut, while a section is a vertical one.

You cut plans and sections by adding section planes to your model. These are a little abstract, because nothing like them exists in real life. In SketchUp, section planes are objects that affect the visibility of certain parts of your model. When a section plane is active, everything in front of it is visible and everything behind is hidden. Everywhere your model is "cut" by a section plane, a slightly thicker "section cut" line appears.

If you're using Windows, now would be a good time to open the Sections toolbar by choosing View⊃Toolbars⊃Sections. If you're on a Mac, the Section Plane tool is in the Large Tool Set, which you can activate by choosing View⊃Tool Palettes⊃Large Tool Set in the menu bar. On both platforms, Section Plane looks like a white circle with letters and numbers in it.

Cutting like an architect

In architecture, the convention is to "cut" plans at a height of 48 inches, meaning that the imaginary horizontal slice is made 4 feet above the floor surface. This ensures that doors and most windows are shown cut through by the slice, while counters, tables, and other furniture are below it, and thus are fully visible. You can see what I mean in Figure 10-9. These things are important when you're trying to explain a space to someone. After all, architectural drawings are two-dimensional abstractions of three-dimensional space, and every little bit of clarity helps.

When it comes to architectural sections (as opposed to sections, the SketchUp feature), there's no convention for where to cut them, but you should follow a couple of rules:

✔ **Never cut through columns.** If you show a column in section, it looks like a wall. This is bad, because sections are supposed to show the degree to which a space is open or closed. You can walk around a column, but you can't walk through a wall (at least I can't).

✔ **Try your best to cut through stairs, elevators, and other "vertical circulation."** Showing how people move up and down through your building makes your drawings a lot more readable, not to mention interesting. Figure 10-9 shows what I'm getting at.

To add a section plane, follow these steps:

1. **Choose Tools⇨Section Plane to activate the Section Plane tool.**

   You can also activate Section Plane by choosing its icon from the Large Tool Set (Mac) or the Sections toolbar (Windows), if you have it open.

2. **Move the Section Plane tool around your model.**

   Notice how the orientation of the Section Plane cursor (which is quite large) changes to be coplanar to whatever surface you're hovering over. Check out Figure 10-10 to see this in action.

3. **When you've figured out where you want it, click once to add a section plane.**

   To create a plan view, add a horizontal section plane by clicking a horizontal plane like a floor. For a sectional view, add a vertical section plane by clicking a wall or other vertical surface. You can, of course, add section planes wherever you want; they don't have to be aligned to horizontal or vertical planes. Figure 10-11 shows a section plane added to a model of a house.

4. **Choose the Move tool.**

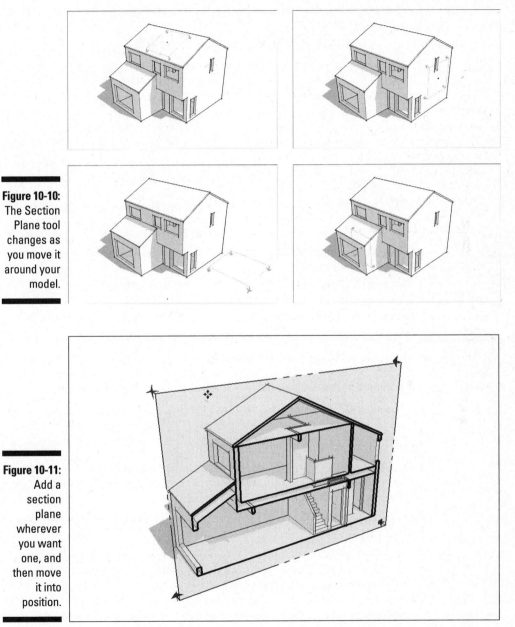

Figure 10-10:
The Section Plane tool changes as you move it around your model.

Figure 10-11:
Add a section plane wherever you want one, and then move it into position.

5. **Move the section plane you just added by clicking it once to pick it up and again to drop it.**

   You can only slide your section plane back and forth in two directions; SketchUp only allows section planes to move perpendicular to their cutting planes. When you're deciding where to locate your cut, the nearby sidebar, "Cutting like an architect," offers helpful pointers.

   After you've added a section plane and moved it to the desired location, you can rotate and even copy it, just like any other object in your model. It will never affect your geometry — just the way you view it.

6. **If you need to rotate your section plane, select it and use the Rotate tool (which you can read more about in Chapter 6).**

   Why rotate a section plane? In certain circumstances, rotating a section plane (instead of creating a brand new one) can help to explain a complex interior space. Showing a plan view *becoming* a sectional one is a powerful way to explain architectural drawings to an audience that doesn't understand them.

7. **To make a new section plane by copying an existing one, use the Move or Rotate tool to do it the same way you would make a copy of any other SketchUp object.**

   Chapter 2 explains these basic actions in detail.

   Copying section planes is a great way to space them a known distance apart; this can be trickier if you use the Section Plane tool to keep adding new ones, instead.

   Figure 10-12 shows moving, rotating, and copying a section plane.

When the section plane you've added is in position, you're ready to control how it impacts visibility in a number of other ways. See the following sections for details.

Figure 10-12:
Moving, rotating, and copying a section plane.

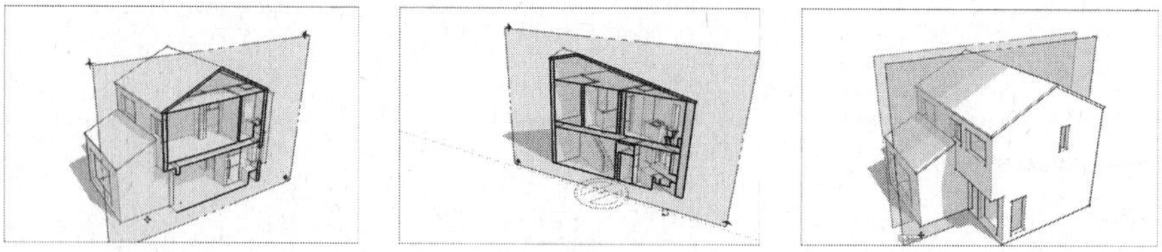

Controlling individual section planes

You can control the way section planes behave by right-clicking them to bring up a context menu that looks like the one shown in Figure 10-13. I show examples of what the following options do in the same illustration:

✔ **Reverse:** This option flips the "direction" of the section plane, hiding everything that was previously visible, and revealing everything that used to be "behind" the cut. Use this when you need to see inside the rest of your model.

✔ **Active Cut:** Although you can have multiple section planes in your model, only one of them can be "active" at a time. The "active cut" is the section plane that is actually cutting through your model; others are considered "inactive." If you have more than one section plane, use Active Cut to tell SketchUp which one should be active.

You *can* have more than one active section plane in your model at a time, but doing so requires that you nest, or embed, each section plane in a separate group or component. It's possible to achieve some pretty spiffy effects with this technique, but I'm afraid I don't have room to include more than this mention of it in this book. You can read all about groups and components in Chapter 5.

✔ **Align View:** When you choose Align View, your view changes so that you're looking straight on at the section plane. You can use this option to produce views like the ones that I describe in the section "Getting different sectional views," later in this chapter.

✔ **Create Group from Slice:** This option doesn't have much to do with the other choices in this context menu; it's really a modeling tool. You can use this to do exactly what it says: create a group from the active slice, or section plane. I don't use this very often, but it comes in handy for creating filled-in section cuts for final presentations.

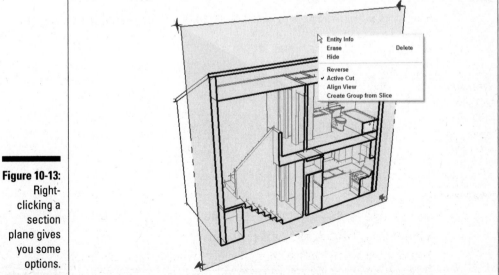

Figure 10-13:
Right-clicking a section plane gives you some options.

Setting section-plane visibility

If you want to control the visibility of all your section planes at once, a couple of menu options can help. You use both of these toggles in combination to control how section cuts appear in your model. These two options, shown on the View menu, are illustrated in Figure 10-14:

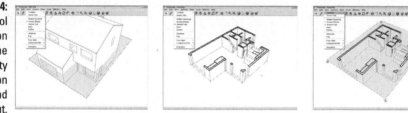

Figure 10-14: Control section plane visibility with Section Planes and Section Cut.

> ✔ **Section Planes:** This choice toggles the visibility of section-plane objects without affecting the section cuts they produce. More simply, deselecting Section Planes hides all the section planes in your model, but doesn't turn off the section cut effect, as shown in the middle image in Figure 10-14. This is how you'll probably want to show most of your sectional views, so this is a pretty important toggle.

> ✔ **Section Cut:** Deselecting this option toggles the section cut effect on and off without affecting the visibility of the section-plane objects in your model. This choice is sort of the opposite of Section Planes, in the previous point, but it's every bit as important.

Getting different sectional views

Using section planes, you can get a couple of useful and impressive views of your model without much trouble. The second builds on the first, and both are shown in Figure 10-15. A section perspective (left) is a special kind of way to view a three-dimensional space. The second type, an orthographic view (right), is straight on and doesn't use perspective.

Making a section perspective

If you imagine cutting a building in half and then looking at the cut surface straight on while looking inside, you have a section perspective. The *section* part of the term refers to the fact that the building has been cut away. The *perspective* part indicates that objects seen inside the space appear to get smaller as they get farther away.

Figure 10-15:
Turn
Perspective
on for a
section
perspective;
choose
Parallel
Projection to
produce an
orthographic
view.

Section perspectives are a great (not to mention incredibly cool) way of showing interior space in a way that's understandable to most people. To create a section perspective using the Section Plane tool in SketchUp, follow these steps (and check out this book's companion Web site for additional help; see the Introduction for details):

1. **Select the section plane you'd like to use to make a section perspective by clicking it with the Select tool.**

   When it's selected, your section plane turns blue, assuming that you haven't changed any of the default colors in the Styles dialog box.

2. **If the selected section plane isn't active, right-click and choose Active Cut from the context menu.**

   Active section planes cut through their surrounding geometry. If your section plane is visible but isn't cutting through anything, it isn't active.

3. **Right-click the selected section plane and choose Align View from the context menu.**

   This aligns your view so that it's straight on (perpendicular) to your section plane.

4. **If you can't see your model properly, choose Camera⇨Zoom Extents.**

   This zooms your view so that you can see your whole model in the modeling window.

Generating an orthographic section

Ever seen a technical drawing that included top, front, rear, and side views of the same object? Chances are that was an *orthographic projection,* which is a common way for three-dimensional objects to be drawn so that they can be built.

Producing an orthographic section of your model is pretty easy; it's only one extra step beyond making a section perspective. Here's how to do it:

1. **Follow Steps 1–3 in the preceding section, as if you're making a section perspective.**

2. **Choose Camera⇨Parallel Projection.**

   This switches off Perspective, turning your view into a true orthographic representation of your model. If you printed it at a specific scale, you could take measurements from the printout.

To print a plan or section view of your model at a particular scale, have a look at Chapter 12, where I explain the whole process.

Creating section animations with scenes

This is probably one of the most useful and impressive things you can do with this software, but some people who have been using SketchUp for years don't know about it. The basic idea is that you can use scenes to create animations where your section planes move inside your model. Here are a few reasons you might want to use this technique:

✔ If you have a building with several levels, you can create an animated presentation that shows a cutaway plan view of each level.

✔ Using an animated section plane to "get inside" your model is a much classier transition than simply hiding certain parts of it.

✔ When you need to show the relationship between the plan and section views for a project, using an animated section plane helps to explain the concept of different architectural views to 3D beginners.

Follow these steps to create a basic section animation. A simple example is illustrated in Figure 10-16 (and check out this book's companion Web site for additional help):

Figure 10-16:
Making a section animation is a fairly straight-foward process.

 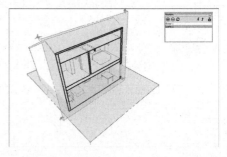

1. **Add a section plane to your model.**

   I give a complete explanation of how to create section planes in the section "Cutting plans and sections," earlier in this chapter.

2. **Add a scene to your model.**

   Check out the section "Creating scenes," earlier in this chapter, for a complete rundown on adding scenes.

3. **Add another section plane to your model.**

   You can add another section plane in one of two ways:

   - **Use the Section Plane tool to create a brand new one.** This is probably the easiest option, and it's the one I recommend if you're just starting out.

   - **Use the Move tool to copy an existing section plane.** I talk about copying section planes in the section "Cutting plans and sections," earlier in this chapter.

   Make sure that your new section plane is active; if it is, it'll be cutting through your model. If it isn't, right-click the section plane and choose Active Cut from the context menu.

4. **Add another scene to your model.**

   This new scene "remembers" which is the active section plane.

5. **Click through the scenes you added to view your animation.**

   You should see an animated section cut as SketchUp transitions from one scene to the next. If you don't, make sure that you have scene transitions enabled. You can verify this by choosing Window⇨Model Info and then choosing the Animations panel in the Model Info dialog box. The Scene Transitions check box should be selected.

If you don't like being able to see the section-plane objects (the boxy things with arrows on their corners) in your animation, switch them off by deselecting Section Planes on the View menu. You should still be able to see your section cuts, but you won't see any ugly gray rectangles flying around.

The hardest thing to remember about using scenes and section planes to make section animations is this: *You need a separate section plane for each scene that you create.* That is to say, SketchUp animates the transition from one active section plane to another active section plane. If all you do is move the same section plane to another spot and add a scene, this technique won't work. Believe it or not, it took me two years to figure this out, so don't feel dense if you need to come back and read this section a couple of times.

Part IV
Sharing What You've Made

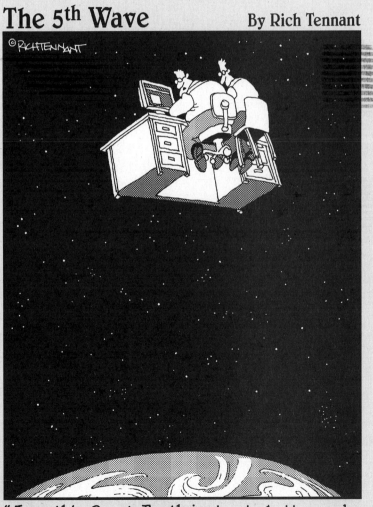

The 5th Wave   By Rich Tennant

"Jeez-this Google Earth just gets better and better, doesn't it?"

In this part . . .

1 suppose for some people in the world, 3D modeling is an intensely private endeavor; they build something in SketchUp, they burn the SKP file to a disk, and then they hide the disk in the crawlspace under their house.

If you're not one of these people, you're probably looking forward to *doing* something with the models you make — printing them, making animations, and sending them to other software programs. After all, for most folks, SketchUp is just the beginning of a process that includes lots of other steps.

The chapters in this part describe all the different things you can do with your models after you build them. Chapter 11 talks about using SketchUp with Google Earth. Chapter 12 is about printing, and Chapters 13 and 14 describe the process of exporting images and animations. Chapter 15 is a quick overview of LayOut, the brand-new presentation document design tool that comes with SketchUp 6 Pro.

Chapter 11

Working with Google Earth and the 3D Warehouse

*I*f you've ever used Google Earth, you know what it's like to look up from your computer and realize you just have no idea what time it is. There is no better way to spend several hours than to travel to Paris, Cairo, and the South Pole while checking out the peak of Mount Everest and looking at your old elementary school along the way. I love Google Earth because it does what Star Trek said computers are *supposed* to let us do — forget we're using technology and explore information in a way we never could before.

What if you could see 3D models of buildings and other man-made structures in Google Earth the same way that you can see aerial images and 3D topography? You can. What if you could build your own models, in SketchUp, and see them in Google Earth? You can do that, too. What if you could allow *everyone* who uses Google Earth — there are hundreds of millions of them — to see your models in *their* copies of Google Earth, no matter where they are? Now you're getting the idea. . . .

In this chapter, I talk about making SketchUp models that you and (if you want) anyone else can see on Google Earth. I also talk about the Google 3D Warehouse: a great big, online repository of free 3D models that anyone (including you) can contribute to or borrow from. It's a big, friendly 3D world out there, and this chapter is your Getting Started guide.

Getting the Big (3D) Picture

Okay. So there's SketchUp, which (I have to assume) you're pretty familiar with by now. Then there's Google Earth, which you've probably seen and which you probably think is pretty neat. Finally, there's the 3D Warehouse, which you probably don't know anything about — don't worry about that. Here's the "lay of the land" when it comes to the relationship among these three things and what they're supposed to do:

✔ **Google SketchUp:** Because SketchUp is especially good for architecture, you can use it to make buildings that you can look at in Google Earth. If you want, you can also *upload* (send) what you make to the 3D Warehouse, where anyone who finds it can *download* (borrow) your model and use it in his or her own copy of SketchUp.

✔ **Google Earth** (http://earth.google.com): Earth is a software program that lets you explore the world by "flying" around, zooming in on things that interest you. The more you zoom, the better the detail gets; in some places, you can see things as small as coffee cups. The imagery in Google Earth is anywhere from a couple of weeks to 4 years old, but it gets updated all the time. If you want, you can build models in SketchUp and view them in Google Earth. You can also see models that *other* people have made. Eventually, Google Earth will include entire 3D cities, built in SketchUp by people all over the world.

✔ **Google 3D Warehouse** (http://sketchup.google.com/ 3dwarehouse): The 3D Warehouse is a huge collection of 3D models that lives on Google's servers. The models all come from people just like you and me; anyone can contribute models, and anyone can use them in their own SketchUp projects. Some of the best models in the 3D Warehouse are used in a special layer where anyone can see them while they're flying around in Google Earth.

If you're the kind of person who likes diagrams (I know I am), Figure 11-1 might help; it shows the SketchUp/Earth/3D Warehouse workflow in a non-paragraphish way.

Taking the Ten-Minute Tour of Google Earth

Google Earth is a pretty deep piece of software, not because it's hard to use (it's not) but because you can use it to do an awful lot. I'm not even going to try to explain it in this section; this is the "zooming past it in a speeding car" tour that should be enough to get you started.

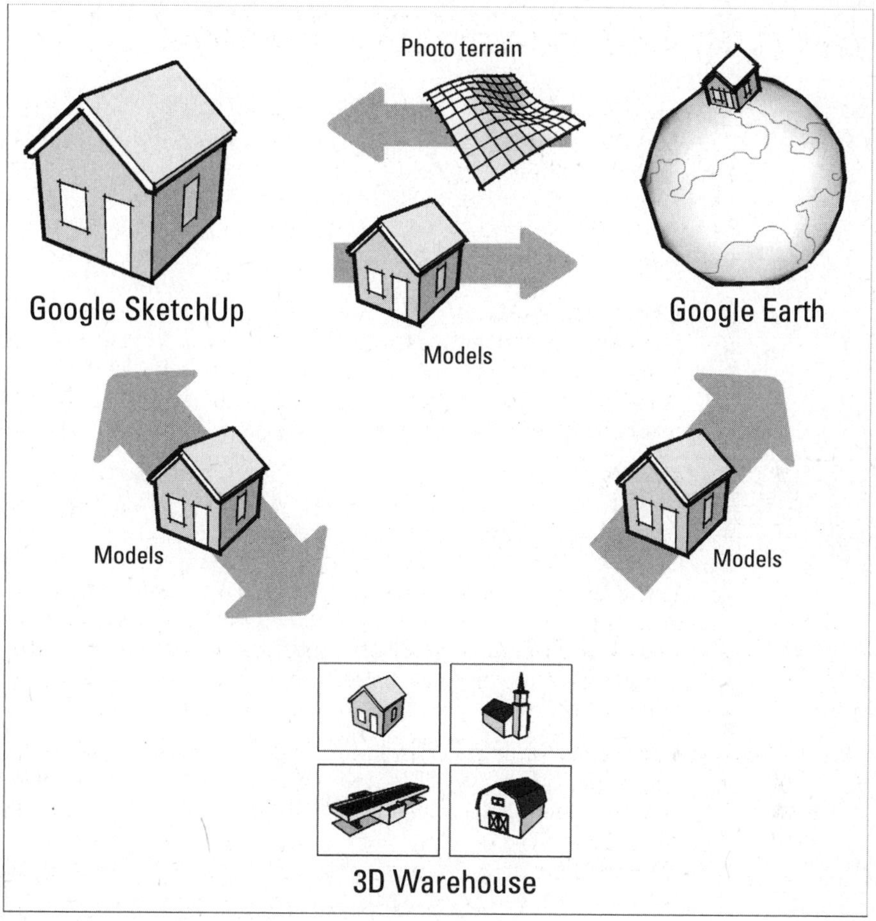

Photo terrain

Google SketchUp

Models

Google Earth

Models

Models

Figure 11-1:
SketchUp,
Google
Earth, and
the 3D
Warehouse
are all
related.

3D Warehouse

Getting Google Earth

Here's a piece of good news for you: Just like Google SketchUp, the basic version of Google Earth is free. Why? My mother always told me not to look a gift horse in the mouth, and Google Earth is the Secretariat of gift horses. All that matters to me is that people with a computer that can run SketchUp can also run Google Earth, and they don't have to pay for it. Here are some more things you need to know:

✔ **You get Google Earth by downloading it.** Just go to http://earth. google.com, click the Downloads link on the left, select your operating system, and then click the big Download button. While you're there, check out some of the other features of the site. You should be able to find answers to any other questions you have, as well as links to online help, user communities, and more. You can even find out about what you get in the fancier versions of Google Earth, if that's what floats your boat.

✔ **You need a fast Internet connection.** The magic of Google Earth is its ability to show you detailed imagery of the *whole world* — that's lots and lots of data that Google keeps on its servers until you "request" it by flying somewhere and zooming in. The faster your Internet connection, the faster you can stream imagery, 3D buildings, and topography into your copy of Google Earth. As you can imagine, Google Earth isn't worth a darn if you're not online.

✔ **You should clear your schedule.** If this is the first time you've used Google Earth, don't plan to do much of anything else for the next few hours. It's that much fun — and that addictive. If any geography nuts reside in your household, you might need to buy another computer.

Getting your first dose

Google Earth can do a bunch of stuff, but the following sections describe the first three things you should do with the software; have a look at Figure 11-2 for a view of the Google Earth user interface.

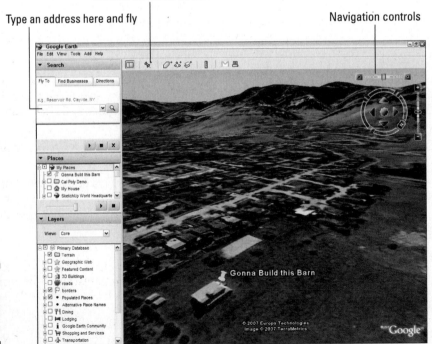

Create Placemark button

Type an address here and fly

Navigation controls

Figure 11-2:
Google
Earth in all
its glory.

Flying around

Check out the upper-right corner of the screen; you'll find the navigation controls for Google Earth conveniently grouped together. Notice how they appear when you hover over them? Go ahead and play around to figure out what they do. Here's some help:

- ✔ **Zoom:** Move this slider back and forth to zoom in and out on whatever's in the center of your screen. You can also use the scroll wheel on your mouse to zoom, just like you do in SketchUp.

- ✔ **Pan:** You can move around by clicking the arrow buttons, but the easier way is to use your mouse. Just click and drag to "spin" the world in whatever direction you want.

- ✔ **Rotate:** Turn the wheel to spin yourself around without moving. This works a lot like the Look Around tool in SketchUp. Click the N button to reorient the world so that north is up.

- ✔ **Tilt:** Google Earth is 3D! Move the Tilt slider back and forth to tilt your view. If you're looking at an area with mountains, they should look like a 3D image (if they don't, make sure that the Terrain layer is enabled in the lower-left corner). You can also tilt by holding down your scroll wheel button, the same way you do to orbit in SketchUp. (See Chapter 2 for more on orbiting.)

Going someplace specific

See the blank field in the upper-left corner that says "Fly To"? Go ahead and type in an address anywhere in the world, and Google Earth will fly you directly there. It works better for some places than others, but nobody's perfect. Here are some tips:

- ✔ **Use the right format.** If you're entering an address in the United States or Canada, use this format: Street Number Street Name, Zip (Postal) Code. Here's an example: 1234 Cherry Blvd, 64254. If it doesn't work the first time, try a few variations.

- ✔ **Type in landmarks.** Try typing **Eiffel Tower** or **Statue of Liberty**. I have no idea how Google does this, but it just seems to work.

- ✔ **Get directions.** Click the Directions tab (also in the upper-left corner of the screen), and then enter Origin and Destination addresses to see a list of driving directions along with a colored path on the ground.

Making some placemarks

You can stick "pins" into Google Earth to mark locations you'd like to come back to later; they're called *placemarks*. Follow these steps to create one yourself:

1. **Fly to where you want to create a placemark.**

2. **Click the Create Placemark button at the top of the screen.**

3. **Move your placemark (it looks like a thumbtack) to exactly where you want it (on top of your house, for instance).**

4. **Give your placemark a name in the Edit Placemark dialog box.**

5. **Click the OK button.**

Your new placemark should show up in the Places section on the left of your screen. No matter where you are in the world, double-clicking the name of your placemark in the Places list will fly you right there.

Building Models for Google Earth

Google Earth is fun and all, but you're interested in SketchUp, right? What you want to do is build a model of a building (maybe your house) and see it in Google Earth. After you've done that, you can e-mail the model to your friends (or clients) so that *they* can see it in Google Earth, too. And if you're especially proud of what you make, you can upload it to the 3D Warehouse so that the whole world can see it.

First things first. In this section, I talk about the basic procedure for making a model in SketchUp and viewing it in Google Earth. I also provide some tips for making buildings that are optimized for Earth; big models plus Google Earth can equal sluggish (like molasses in January) performance, and no one wants that.

Understanding the process

Very simply, building SketchUp models for Google Earth involves the following steps:

1. **Choosing a site in Google Earth**

2. **Importing the view into SketchUp**

3. **Building a model using the imported view as a guide**

4. **Exporting your model to Google Earth**

Simple, huh? Figure 11-3 is a handy diagram for the visually oriented among us.

Figure 11-3:
Making a
SketchUp
model for
Google Earth
is a four-step
process.

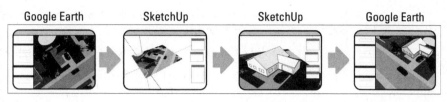

Google Earth   SketchUp   SketchUp   Google Earth

Finding a site and bringing it into SketchUp

Follow these steps to import a building site into SketchUp from Google Earth:

1. **Launch Google Earth.**

   Make sure that you're online when you launch Earth; if you aren't, you won't be able to see much of anything.

2. **In Google Earth, navigate to the area where you want to place a model.**

   It doesn't really matter how you get where you're going; the important thing is to fill your Google Earth window with the area that you want to import into SketchUp. Take a look at Figure 11-4 to see what I mean.

Figure 11-4:
Whatever
you can see
in Google
Earth (left) is
what gets
imported
into your
SketchUp
modeling
window
(right).

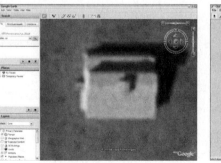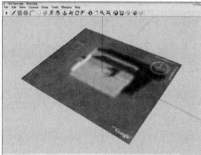

3. **Launch SketchUp and open a new file.**

   SketchUp opens a new file every time you launch it, so this step is pretty easy.

4. **Choose Tools⇨Google Earth⇨Get Current View from the menu bar.**

   When you do this, SketchUp imports a "snapshot" of whatever is visible in your Google Earth window when you choose Get Current View.

You can also access the Google Earth commands by opening the Google Earth toolbar; choose View⇨Toolbars⇨Google Earth to have at 'em.

If you want to import another snapshot from Google Earth into SketchUp, you can. SketchUp automatically tiles together all the snapshots you "take" (by choosing Get Current View) in your modeling window to form a kind of patchwork. This is super-handy if you find that you didn't get everything you needed the first time.

You need to wait until your Google Earth view is at least 95 percent loaded before you can capture a snapshot in SketchUp (patience is a virtue, after all). Just watch the little "Streaming" readout at the bottom of your Google Earth window to know when you've waited long enough.

Modeling on a Google Earth snapshot

Now that you've imported a snapshot from Google Earth, you can build a model on it. To do this, just go about your SketchUp business the way you always do — everything about SketchUp stays exactly the same, even after you import a snapshot.

To follow the steps in this section, you need to know how to do some basics, such as how to use the Line tool to trace a building's footprint, work with the drawing axes, and more. I cover these basics in detail in Chapter 2.

Building on top of a snapshot 101

Here are the basic steps for building a model on top of your Google Earth snapshot:

1. **Make sure that you have a flat view of your terrain.**

   Choose Tools⇨Google Earth⇨Toggle Terrain a couple of times to figure out which is the flat view, and then start from there.

2. **Trace the footprint of the building you want to model on the imported black-and-white image (see image A in Figure 11-5).**

   Of course, you're more than welcome to model something that doesn't exist yet; if that's the case, feel free to draw anything you like.

A   B

C   D

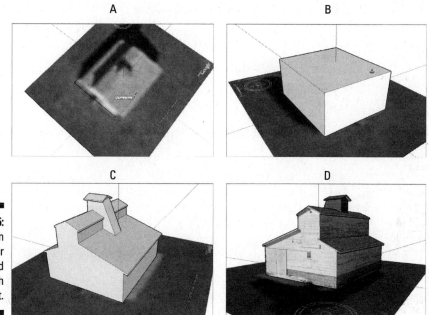

Figure 11-5:
Draw on
top of your
flattened
Google Earth
snapshot.

If the building you're trying to make doesn't line up perfectly with the colored axes, using the Line and Rectangle tools can be tricky. To fix this problem, reposition your main drawing axes by choosing Tools⇨Axes. Click once to set your origin, again to establish the direction of your red axis (parallel to one of the edges in your photo), and a third time to establish your green axis. I like to set my origin at the corner of the building I'm trying to make; I think it makes things easier.

3. **Use Push/Pull to extrude the footprint to the correct height (see image B in Figure 11-5).**

4. **Keep modeling until you're satisfied with what you have.**

5. **Flip to a 3D view of your terrain (choose Tools⇨Google Earth⇨Toggle Terrain), and then move your building up or down until it's sitting properly (see Figure 11-6).**

   Select everything you want to move, and then use the Move tool to move it up or down. You can press the up- or down-arrow key to constrain your move to the blue axis if you want.

If you have a SketchUp model you've already built that you'd like to export to Google Earth, just import it into the same file as your snapshot. Choose File⇨Import from the menu bar, find it on your computer, and bring it on in.

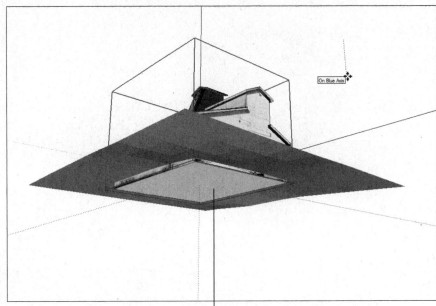

Make sure your building pokes through the ground

Figure 11-6: Move your model up or down until it's sitting properly on the terrain.

Letting SketchUp take care of the details

My favorite part of the whole Google Earth import process is how much time it saves. There's a whole bunch of information already in Google Earth, and SketchUp is smart enough to take advantage of it:

✔ **SketchUp *geolocates* your position automatically.** This means that it sets your latitude and longitude to match Google Earth, and orients your snapshot in the right cardinal direction. This means that any shadow studies you do with the Shadows feature will automatically be accurate for wherever you were in Google Earth when you took your snapshot.

✔ **Everything's already the right size.** Perhaps you take a snapshot of a football field in Google Earth; when you measure that football field in SketchUp, it will be exactly 100 yards long. That's because SketchUp scales your snapshot to the correct size as part of the import process.

✔ **There's more to snapshots than meets the eye.** The snapshot that SketchUp imports from Google Earth is more than just a black-and-white aerial photo — it also includes a chunk of topography called *terrain*. The terrain is flat when you first import it because it's easier to build on that way, but you can toggle between flat and 3D (not flat) views by choosing Tools➪Google Earth➪Toggle Terrain. Don't fret if you don't see any difference when you flip between the views — you probably just chose a flat site. Figure 11-7 shows the same snapshot with terrain toggled off (top) and on (bottom).

Toggle Terrain

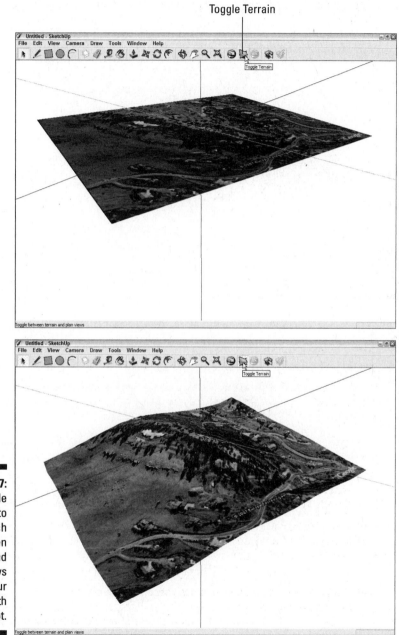

Figure 11-7:
Use Toggle
Terrain to
switch
between
flat and
3D views
of your
Google Earth
snapshot.

Thinking big by thinking small

When it comes to modeling for Google Earth, lightness is next to godliness. By light, I mean the file size of your model, and by file size, I mean the number of faces and textures you use to build it. The more complicated your model, the slower Google Earth will run, and the more likely you'll be to throw your computer through a window in frustration. Now more than ever, think about how you can do the most with the least — geometry, that is. Follow these tips:

✔ **Get rid of extra geometry.** Lots of times when you're modeling, you end up with edges (and even faces) that don't have a purpose. Figure 11-8 shows a prime example of the kinds of little edges you can erase to drastically reduce the number of faces in your model.

✔ **Reduce the number of sides in your extruded arcs and circles.** SketchUp's default number of sides for circles is 24. This means that every time you use Push/Pull to extrude a circle into a cylinder, you end up with 25 faces: 24 around the sides and the original one on top. Instead of using circles with 24 sides, reduce the number of sides by typing a number followed by the letter *s* and pressing Enter right after you draw a circle. For example, to draw a 10-sided circle (plenty for Google Earth), follow these steps:

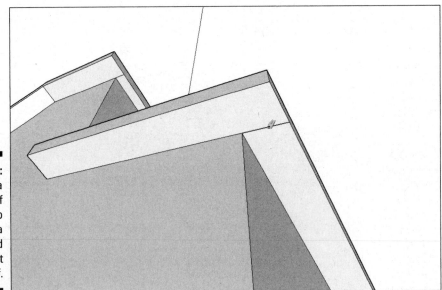

Figure 11-8:
Take a couple of minutes to erase extra edges and faces — it pays off.

1. Draw a circle with the Circle tool.

2. Type 10s **(this should appear in the lower-right corner of your modeling window), and then press Enter.**

The same thing goes for arcs; you change the number of sides in them in exactly the same way. I like to use 10-sided circles and 4-sided arcs when I'm modeling for Google Earth. Figure 11-9 shows the same pipe constructed by using Follow Me on two circles: one with 24 sides and one with only 10. Note the difference in the number of faces in each version.

✔ **When you can, use photo detail instead of geometry.** This really only applies if you're mapping photos (or using PhotoMatch) on the model you're making for Google Earth. If you are, it's a good idea to make as basic a model as you can, and let the detail in the photo "do the talking." Resist the temptation to model windows and doors. Figure 11-10 shows a model I built of a barn in my neighborhood. The view on the left shows it with photo textures visible; the version on the right is just the simple geometry. Surprised? You can read all about how to use photos to add detail to your models in Chapter 7.

24-sided circle   10-sided circle

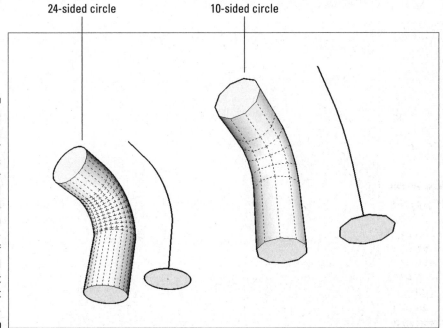

Figure 11-9:
Reducing the number of sides in your extruded circles and arcs can save hundreds of faces, and the object looks just as good.

Figure 11-10:
When a photo contains a lot of detail, you don't need to add geometry.

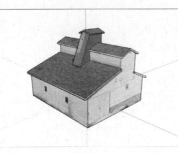

Viewing your model in Google Earth

After you've made a model on top of a snapshot, it's a simple operation to send it over to your copy of Google Earth. And after you've done that, you can save it as a Google Earth KMZ file and e-mail it to all your friends. If you're modeling for clients instead of friends, you can send it to them, too.

Exporting from SketchUp to Google Earth

This process is so simple you could probably figure it out while you're talking on the phone. Follow these steps to send your model from SketchUp to Google Earth on your computer:

1. **Choose Tools⇨Google Earth⇨Place Model.**

   Doing this sends everything in your modeling window (with the exception of the Google Earth snapshot) over to Google Earth. Your computer should automatically switch you over to Google Earth and fly you in so that you're looking at your model (see Figure 11-11).

2. **If you decide you want to make changes to your model, go back to SketchUp, make your changes, and then choose Place Model again.**

   Google Earth pops up a dialog box that asks you whether you want to overwrite the old version of the model you placed the first time.

3. **Click the Yes button if you're sure that's what you want to do.**

4. **Continue to go back and forth between SketchUp and Google Earth until your model looks exactly the way you want it to.**

Figure 11-11:
Your SketchUp model (actually my SketchUp model) in Google Earth.

Saving your model as a Google Earth KMZ file

You can save your SketchUp model as a Google Earth KMZ file that you can send to anyone. When someone opens the KMZ file, Google Earth opens on his computer (if he has Google Earth), and he is "flown in" to look at the model you made. Try sending directions to your next party this way; your friends will think you're related to Albert Einstein. Follow these steps to save your model:

1. **In Google Earth, select your model by clicking it in the Temporary Places list on the left of the screen.**

   Unless you've renamed it yourself, your model will be called SUPreview1. Click it once to select it.

2. **Choose File⇨Save⇨Save Place As.**

   The Save File dialog box opens.

3. **Give your file a name and figure out where to put it on your hard drive.**

4. **Click the Save button to save your model as a KMZ file.**

Becoming a SketchUp All-Star with the 3D Warehouse

If you've ever wondered where Google gets most of the realistic buildings that show up by default on the 3D Buildings layer in Google Earth, you should go take a look in the mirror. That's right: Google's strategy for building the whole man-made world in 3D is to rely on SketchUp users everywhere to model their local context. That's the biggest reason that SketchUp is a free program, and it's a pretty revolutionary way to think about tackling a massive project: millions of people working together to provide accurate, current information that can be used by anyone.

Getting to the Google 3D Warehouse

So how can you get your models into Google Earth so that everyone can see them? To do that, you need to upload your work into the 3D Warehouse. Residing wherever Google's other jillions of bits of data do, the 3D Warehouse is a huge collection of 3D models that is searchable and, most importantly, free for everyone to use.

The 3D Warehouse is basically a Web site; it exists online, and you need an Internet connection to access it. You can get there in two different ways:

- ✔ **From SketchUp:** Choose File⇨3D Warehouse⇨Get Models; when you do, a mini Web browser opens right in front of your modeling window. Voilà!

- ✔ **From the Web:** Browse to `http://sketchup.google.com/ 3dwarehouse`. This is a great way to hunt for 3D models without having to open SketchUp first.

Minding your modeling manners

People sometimes ask me if anyone at Google is paying attention to what gets uploaded to the 3D Warehouse. The answer to that question is a little bit complicated. For instance, nobody at Google minds if you refer to a Web site or enter tags that don't have anything to do with the model you upload — stuff like that is entirely up to you.

On the other hand, it's very frowned upon to go anywhere near the usual taboo subjects for public, G-rated Web sites: pornography and/or foul language will sound an alarm somewhere at Google that will get your model yanked off the 3D Warehouse quicker than you can say "First Amendment." Tens of thousands of impressionable, young eyeballs peruse Google's Web sites every day, so it behooves Google to keep those sites clean. If you have kids, I'm sure you understand.

Go ahead and poke around the 3D Warehouse. It's amazing what you'll find; thousands of people are adding new content every day. Most of it isn't very useful, but you'll still find plenty of interesting things to download and look at. I don't explain all the ins and outs of the 3D Warehouse in this book because I think it's pretty self-explanatory. However, if you need more information, check out the online Help — it's in the lower-right corner of your browser window when you're in the 3D Warehouse.

Uploading your models

You can break the models in the 3D Warehouse into two broad categories:

✔ **Geolocated:** Things like buildings, monuments, bridges, and dams exist in a specific geographic location; they never move around. These are the kinds of models that show up on the 3D Buildings layer in Google Earth, and the 3D Warehouse is where they come from. To upload your own geolocated models, you need to start with a Google Earth snapshot; this provides the geolocation information that Google needs to put your model in the right place. Check out the section "Building Models for Google Earth," earlier in this chapter, for a blow-by-blow account of how to build geolocated models that you can upload to the 3D Warehouse.

✔ **Nongeolocated:** Objects like toasters, SUVs, wheelchairs, and sofas aren't unique, and they don't exist in any one geographic location. No physical address is associated with a model of a Honda Accord because millions of them exist, and because Honda Accords move around. Stuff like this never shows up in Google Earth because the folks at Google wouldn't know where to put it. That doesn't mean it doesn't belong in the 3D Warehouse, though; models of nongeolocated stuff are incredibly valuable for people who are making their own SketchUp models. When I modeled my house, I furnished it with couches, beds, and other models I found in the Warehouse.

Follow these steps to upload your own model to the Google 3D Warehouse:

1. **Open the model you want to upload in SketchUp.**

2. **Fiddle around with your view until you like what you see.**

   When you upload a model to the 3D Warehouse, SketchUp automatically creates a preview image that's a snapshot of your modeling window.

3. **Choose File➪3D Warehouse➪Share Model.**

   A mini-browser window opens, and it shows the logon screen for the 3D Warehouse. If you want to upload models, you need a Google account. They're free; you just need a valid e-mail address to get one. If you don't already have one, follow the on-screen instructions to sign up.

When you're creating your Google account, be sure to type something in where the system asks for a "nickname." If you don't, everything you upload will be attributed to "Anonymous."

4. **Enter your Google account information and click the Sign In button.**

5. **Fill out the Upload to 3D Warehouse form as completely as you can:**

   • **Title:** Enter a title for your model. If it's a public building, you might enter its name. Something like "Royal West Academy" would do nicely.

   • **Description:** Models with complete descriptions are very popular with people who are hunting around the Warehouse. Try to use complete sentences here; the more you write, the better.

   • **Address:** This field only appears if your model is geolocated, meaning that you started with a Google Earth snapshot. If you know the physical address of the thing you made, type it in.

   • **Google Earth Ready:** You only get this option if your model is geolocated. If your model is accurate, correctly sized, and in the right location, and if you want it to be considered for inclusion on the default 3D Buildings layer of Google Earth, select this check box. If you do, the folks at Google will consider adding it to Google Earth. Keep your fingers crossed!

   • **Web Site:** If you have a Web-site address that you'd like people who view your model to visit, enter it here. For example, if your model is a historic building, you might include the Web site that provides more information about it.

   • **Tags:** Type in a string of words that describe the thing you modeled. Whatever you enter here will be used by the 3D Warehouse search engine to help people find your model. To increase the number of people who see what you made, add lots of tags. If I were uploading a modern coffee table, I'd enter the following tags: coffee table, table, coffee, modern, living room, furniture, glass, chrome, metal, steel. You get the idea — be exhaustive.

6. **Click the Upload button to add your model to the 3D Warehouse.**

If everything works properly, you should get a page with your model on it, along with all the information you just entered. The words "Model has been uploaded successfully" will be highlighted in yellow at the top of your browser window. Congratulations — you're now a member of the worldwide 3D community.

Chapter 12

Printing Your Work

As much as everyone likes to pretend that we all live in an all-digital world, the ugly truth is that we don't. People use more paper now than they ever have; I have a stack of junk prints on the coffee table in front of me as I'm writing this. It's not that I have anything against trees — it's just that printing is so *satisfying*. I love having something I can fold up and put in my pocket, or stick to the fridge, or mail to my Luddite relatives. Computer screens are nice, but in most people's minds, paper is *real*.

In this chapter, I talk about how to print views of your SketchUp model. Because the Windows and Mac versions of this procedure are so different, I dedicate a whole section to each platform. The last part of this chapter is devoted to scaled printing — a topic that can sometimes makes experienced architects nervous. SketchUp makes printing to scale a little harder than it could be, but it's still a whole lot better than drawing things by hand.

Printing from a Windows Computer

It's very easy to print from SketchUp, as long as you're not trying to do anything too complicated. By complicated, I mean printing to a particular scale, which can be a harrowing experience the first couple of times you attempt it. Fortunately, printing to scale is something most people almost never have to do, so I've included instructions for how to do it at the end of this chapter.

Making a basic print (Windows)

Most of the time, all you need to do is to print exactly what you see on your screen. Follow these steps to do that:

1. **Make sure that you have the view you want to print in your modeling window.**

   Unless you're printing to scale (which I cover in the last part of this chapter), SketchUp prints exactly what you see in your modeling window.

2. **Choose File⇨Print Setup.**

   This opens the Print Setup dialog box, which is where you make choices about what printer and paper you want to print to.

3. **In the Print Setup dialog box (see Figure 12-1), do the following:**

   a. Choose the printer you'd like to use.

   b. Choose a paper size for your print.

   c. Choose an orientation for your print; most of the time, you'll want to use Landscape, because your screen is usually wider than it is tall.

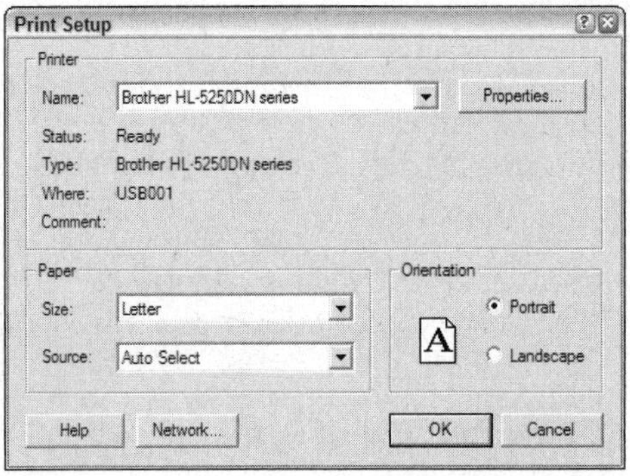

Figure 12-1: The Print Setup dialog box in Windows.

4. **Click the OK button to close the Print Setup dialog box.**

5. **Choose File⇨Print Preview.**

   This opens the Print Preview dialog box. As an exact copy of the Print dialog box, Print Preview lets you see an image of what your print will look like before you send it to a printer. Lots of trees will thank you for saving paper by using Print Preview every time you print.

6. **In the Print Preview dialog box, do the following:**

   a. In the Tabbed Scene Print Range area, choose which scenes you'd like to print, if you have more than one. If you need to, you can read all about scenes in Chapter 10.

   b. Tell SketchUp how many copies of each scene you need.

   c. Make sure that the Fit to Page check box is selected.

   d. Make sure that the Use Model Extents check box *isn't* selected.

   e. Choose a print quality for your printout (I recommend High Definition for most jobs).

   For a complete description of all the knobs and doohickeys in the Print Preview and Print dialog boxes, have a look at the next section in this chapter.

7. **Click the OK button to close the Print Preview dialog box and generate an on-screen preview of what your print will look like.**

8. **If you like what you see, click the Print button in the upper-left corner of the Print Preview window to open the Print dialog box.**

   If you *don't* like what you're about to print, click the Close button (at the top of the screen) and go back to Step 1.

9. **In the Print dialog box (which should look exactly like the Print Preview dialog box), click the OK button to send your print job to the printer.**

Decoding the Windows Print dialog box

Three cheers for simplicity! The Print Preview and Print dialog boxes in SketchUp are exactly the same. Figure 12-2 shows the former, because that's the one I advocate using first every time, but the descriptions in this section apply to both.

Printer

If you used the Print Setup dialog box first, you shouldn't need to change any of the settings in this section. If you want, you can choose which printer to print to from the drop-down list. If you know something about printers, you can even click the Properties button to make adjustments to your printer settings. (Because these are different for every printer on Earth, that's between you and your printer's user manual — I'm afraid I can't be of much help.)

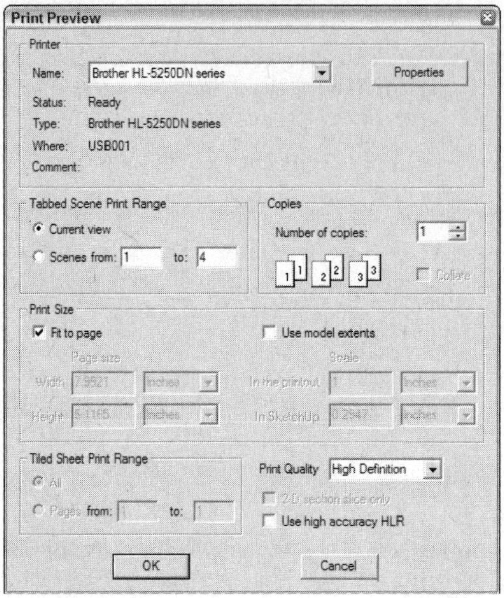

Figure 12-2:
The Print
Preview
dialog box in
Windows.
The Print
dialog box
looks exactly
the same.

Tabbed Scene Print Range

Use this area to tell SketchUp which of your scenes you'd like to print, if you have more than one. This is really handy for quickly printing all your scenes. Select the Current View option to only print whatever's currently in your modeling window.

Copies

This one's pretty basic: Choose how many copies of each view you'd like to print. If you're printing multiple copies of multiple scenes, select the Collate check box to print "packets," which can save you from having to assemble them yourself. Here's what happens when you're printing three copies of four scenes:

✔ Selecting the Collate check box prints the pages in the following order: 123412341234.

✔ Deselecting the Collate check box prints the pages like this: 111222333444.

Print Size

This is by far the most complicated part of this dialog box; you use the Print Size controls to determine how your model will look on the printed page. Figure 12-3 shows the effect of some of these settings on a final print.

My SketchUp screen

Fit to Page

Figure 12-3:
Different
Print Size
settings
applied to
the same
view in
SketchUp.

Fit to Page and Use Model Extents

The Print Size controls are as follows:

- ✔ **Fit to Page:** Selecting this check box tells SketchUp to make your printed page look like your Modeling Window. As long as the Use Model Extents check box isn't selected, you should be able to see exactly what you see on your screen — no more, no less.

- ✔ **Use Model Extents:** I have to admit that I don't like this option; I almost never select it. All this does is tell SketchUp to zoom in to make your model (excluding your sky, ground, watermark, and whatever else might be visible on your screen) fit the printed page. If I want this effect, I just use choose Camera⇨Zoom Extents from the menu bar before I print my model; it's easier, and I know exactly what I'm getting.

- ✔ **Page Size:** As long as you don't have the Fit to Page check box selected, you can manually enter a page size using these controls. If you type in a width or height, SketchUp figures out the other dimension and pretends it's printing on a different-sized piece of paper.

This option is especially useful if you want to make a big print by tiling together lots of smaller pages. See the next section in this chapter for more details.

- ✔ **Scale:** Here's where it gets a little complicated. To print to scale, you have to do two things before you go anywhere near the Print or Print Preview dialog boxes:

  - • Switch to Parallel Projection mode.

  - • Make sure that you're using one of the Standard views.

  Take a look at the section "Printing to scale (Windows and Mac)," later in this chapter, for a complete rundown on printing to scale in SketchUp.

Tiled Sheet Print Range

Perhaps you're printing at a scale that won't fit on a single page, or you've entered a print size that's bigger than the paper size you chose in the Print Setup dialog box. The Tiled Sheet Print Range area lets you print your image on multiple sheets and then attach them all together later. You can get posters from your small-format printer!

Print Quality

To be honest, I think there's a little bit of voodoo involved in selecting a print quality for your image. What you get with each setting depends a lot on your model, so you should probably try out a couple different settings if you have time. Draft and Standard are really only useful for making sure your model appears the way you want it to on the printed page; I recommend using High Definition first, then bumping up to Ultra High Definition if your computer/printer setup can handle it.

Other settings

You can control the following odds-and-ends settings in the Print Preview dialog box, too:

- ✔ **2-D Section Slice Only:** If you have a visible section cut in your model view, selecting this check box tells SketchUp to only print the section cut edges. Figure 12-4 shows what the same model view would look like without (on the left) and with (right) this option selected. I use this to produce simple plan and section views that I can sketch on by hand.

- ✔ **Use High Accuracy HLR:** The bad news is that I have no idea what HLR stands for. The good news is that it doesn't really matter. Selecting this check box tells SketchUp to send *vector* information to the printer instead of the usual *raster* data (check out Chapter 13 for a description of what these terms mean). Why should you care? Vector lines look much smoother and cleaner when printed, so your whole model will look better — with one condition: Gradients (those nice, smooth shadows on rounded surfaces) don't print well as vectors. If you have a lot of rounded or curvy surfaces in your model view, you probably don't want to choose this option. I'd try a print both ways, and choose the one that looks better. Thank goodness for Print Preview, huh?

  If your model view includes a sketchy edges style, don't use high accuracy HLR; you won't see any of the nice, sketchy effects in your final print.

Figure 12-4: Printing only the 2-D section slice yields a simple drawing that's easy to sketch over.

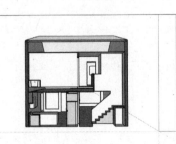 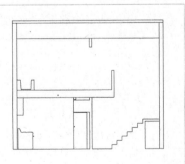

Printing from a Mac

If you're using a Mac, the printing story is a little simpler than it is for folks who use Windows computers, but only by a little. The first part of the following sections lays out a procedure for generating a simple, straightforward print of what you see in your Modeling Window. The second part could be called "Gross anatomy of the Mac Document Setup dialog box"; this is where I go into some detail about what each and every setting does.

Making a basic print (Mac)

Follow these steps to print exactly what you see in your Modeling Window on a Mac:

1. **Make sure that your Modeling Window contains whatever you want to print.**

   SketchUp prints exactly what you see in your Modeling Window, unless of course you're printing to scale. This is considerably more complicated, so I gave it a whole section at the end of this chapter.

2. **Choose File➪Page Setup.**

   This opens the Page Setup dialog box, where you decide what printer and paper size to use.

3. **In the Page Setup dialog box (see Figure 12-5), do the following:**

   a. Choose the printer you'd like to use from the Format For drop-down list.

   b. Choose a paper size for your print.

   c. Choose an orientation for your print. I usually end up using the second or third one (Landscape), because my Modeling Window is usually wider than it is tall.

4. **Click the OK button to close the Page Setup dialog box.**

5. **Choose File➪Document Setup.**

   This opens the Document Setup dialog box.

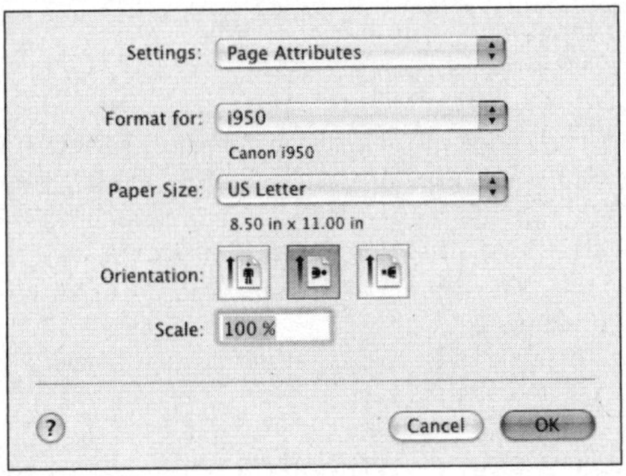

Figure 12-5:
The Page
Setup dialog
box on a
Mac lets
you select a
printer, a
paper size,
and a page
orientation.

Settings: Page Attributes

Format for: i950
Canon i950

Paper Size: US Letter
8.50 in x 11.00 in

Orientation:

Scale: 100 %

Cancel   OK

6. **In the Document Setup dialog box, make sure that the Fit View to Page check box is selected.**

   Check out the next section in this chapter for a full description of what everything does.

7. **Click the OK button to close the Document Setup dialog box.**

8. **Choose File⇨Print to open the Print dialog box.**

9. **In the Print dialog box, click the Preview button.**

   This generates an on-screen preview of what your print will look like on paper.

10. **If the preview suits you, click the Print button to send your print job to the printer.**

    If you're not happy with the preview, click the Cancel button and start again at Step 1. Isn't printing fun?

Deciphering the Mac printing dialog boxes

Because printing from SketchUp on a Mac involves two separate dialog boxes, I describe both in the following sections.

The Document Setup dialog box

You use the settings in the Document Setup dialog box (see Figure 12-6) to control how big your model prints. Here's what everything does:

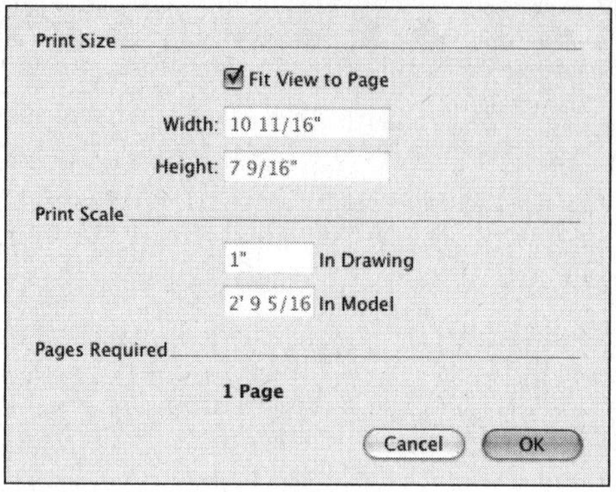

Print Size

☑ Fit View to Page

Width: 10 11/16"

Height: 7 9/16"

Print Scale

1"   In Drawing

2' 9 5/16 In Model

Pages Required

1 Page

Cancel   OK

Figure 12-6:
The Mac
Document
Setup
dialog box.

- ✔ **Print Size:** This one's pretty self-explanatory, but here are some details just in case:

  - • **Fit View to Page:** Selecting this check box tells SketchUp to make your printed page look just like your Modeling Window on-screen. It's really that simple.

  - • **Width and Height:** If the Fit View to Page check box is deselected, you can type in either a width or a height for your final print. This is the way to go if you want to print a tiled poster out of several sheets of paper; just enter a final size and you'll have a poster in no time flat.

- ✔ **Print Scale:** Use these settings to control the scale of your printed drawing, if that's the kind of print you're trying to make. Because printing to scale is a bit of an ordeal, I devote the last section of this chapter to the topic. Refer to that section for a description of what these settings do.

- ✔ **Pages Required:** This is really just a readout of how many pages you need to print. If you have selected the Fit View to Page check box, this should say 1. If your print won't fit on one sheet, it will be tiled onto the number of sheets displayed in this section of the dialog box.

The Print dialog box

The Print dialog box on the Mac is something of a many-headed beast; several more panels are hidden underneath the Copies & Pages drop-down list. Luckily, we only need to use two. Both are pictured in Figure 12-7 and described in the following list:

✔ **Copies & Pages panel:** The controls in this part of the Print dialog box are pretty straightforward; use them to tell SketchUp how many copies and pages you want to print:

- **Copies:** If you're printing more than one copy of a print that includes multiple pages, select the Collated check box to tell SketchUp to print "packets," which can save you from having to collate them yourself.

- **Pages:** If the Pages Required readout at the bottom of the Document Setup dialog box said that you need more than one sheet to print your image, you can choose to print all or some of those pages right here.

✔ **SketchUp panel:** You use the settings in this panel to control the final appearance of your print:

- **Print Quality:** I usually set this to High, but the results you get depend a lot on your printer model. In general, I never use Draft or Standard unless I'm just making sure my page will look the way I want it to. If you have time, try both High and Extra High and see which one looks the best.

- **Vector Printing:** When you select this option, SketchUp sends *vector* (instead of *raster*) information to the printer. Have a look at Chapter 13 for a description of these terms.

  The upshot here is that vector printing makes edges look much smoother and cleaner, but does a lousy job on gradients (the shadows on your curved surfaces). Use vector printing if your model view is made up of mostly flat faces, but try printing both ways (with vector printing on and off) to see which looks better.

  If your model view includes a sketchy edges style, don't choose Vector Printing; you won't see any of the nice, sketchy effects in your final print.

- **Line Weight:** This option only works if you've selected the Vector Printing check box. The number in this box represents the thickness of edges in your print; any edges that are 1 pixel thick in your model view will be drawn with a line as thick as what you choose for this option. The default is 0.50 points, but feel free to experiment to see what looks best for your model.

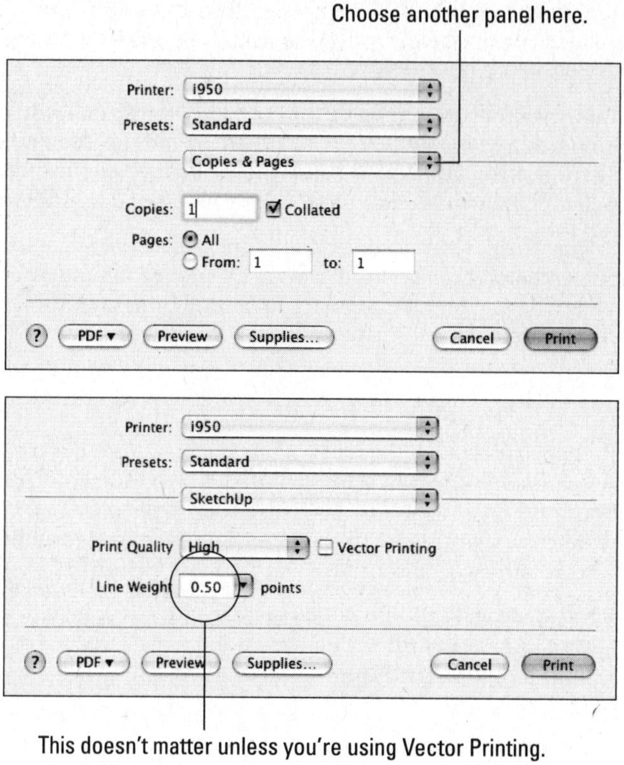

Choose another panel here.

Figure 12-7:
The Copies
& Pages and
SketchUp
panels of
the Print
dialog box.

This doesn't matter unless you're using Vector Printing.

Printing to a Particular Scale

Here's where printing gets interesting. Sometimes, instead of printing exactly what you see on your screen so that it fits on a sheet of paper, you might need to print a drawing *to scale.* See the nearby sidebar "Wrapping your head around scale" for more information about drawing to scale.

Preparing to print to scale

Before you can print a view of your model to a particular scale, you have to set things up properly. Here are some things to keep in mind:

✔ **Perspective views can't be printed to scale.** If you think about it, this makes sense. In perspectival views, all lines appear to "go back" into the distance, which means that they look shorter than they really are.

Because the whole point of a scaled drawing is to be able to take accurate measurements directly off your printout, views with perspective don't work.

✔ **Switch to Parallel Projection if you want to print to scale.** I know, I know — this is the same as the last point. But it's important enough that I figure it's worth mentioning twice. To change your viewing mode from Perspective to Parallel Projection, choose Camera⇨Parallel Projection. That's all there is to it.

✔ **You have to use the Standard views.** SketchUp lets you quickly look at your model from the top, bottom, and sides by switching to one of the Standard views. Choose Camera⇨Standard and pick any of the views except Iso.

Printing to scale (Windows and Mac)

The steps in this section allow you to produce a scaled print from SketchUp; I give Windows instructions first, and then Mac. When the user-interface elements are different for the two platforms, the ones for Mac are shown in parentheses. Figure 12-8 shows the relevant dialog boxes for printing to scale in Windows and on a Mac.

When printing to scale, don't worry about these numbers.

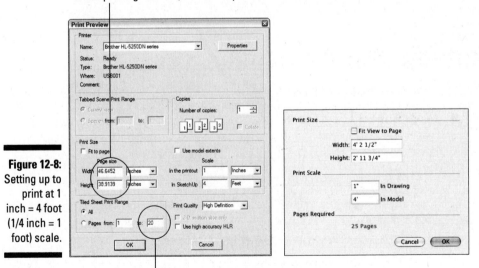

Figure 12-8: Setting up to print at 1 inch = 4 foot (1/4 inch = 1 foot) scale.

To print at 1 inch = 4 feet, you'll need 20 pages

Wrapping your head around scale

When you print to scale, anyone with a special ruler (called a *scale,* confusingly enough) can take measurements from your drawing, as long as he or she knows the scale at which it was printed. You can use three different kinds of drawing scales:

Architectural: In the United States, most people use feet and inches to measure objects. Most architectural scales substitute fractions of an inch for a foot. Three common examples of architectural scales are:

✔ ½ inch = 1 foot (1 inch = 2 feet)

✔ ¼ inch = 1 foot (1 inch = 4 feet)

✔ ⅛ inch = 1 foot (1 inch = 8 feet)

Engineering: When it comes to measuring big things like parcels of land and college campuses, U.S. architects, engineers, and surveyors still use feet, but they use engineering scales instead of architectural ones. Three common engineering scales are:

✔ 1 inch = 20 feet

✔ 1 inch = 50 feet

✔ 1 inch = 100 feet

Metric: Outside of the United States, virtually everyone uses the metric system. Because all measurement is based on the number 10, metric scales can be applied to everything from very small things (blood cells) to very big things (countries). Metric scales use ratios instead of units of measure; here are three examples:

✔ 1:10 (the objects in the drawing are 10 times bigger in real life)

✔ 1:100 (the objects in the drawing are 100 times bigger in real life)

✔ 10:1 (the objects in the drawing are 10 times smaller in real life)

The following figure shows the same drawing printed at two different scales.

Before you begin, make sure that you've switched to Parallel Projection and that your view is lined up the right way. See the previous section of this chapter for the lowdown on what you need to do to prepare your model view for scaled printing. Follow these steps to produce a scaled print:

1. **Choose File⇨Print Setup (Page Setup).**

2. **Select a printer, paper size, and paper orientation, and then click the OK button.**

3. **Choose File⇨Print Preview (Document Setup).**

4. **Deselect the Fit to Page (Fit View to Page) check box.**

5. **Make sure that the Use Model Extents check box is deselected.**

   Mac users don't have this option, so there's nothing to worry about.

6. **Enter the scale at which you'd like to print your model view.**

   If I wanted to print a drawing at ¼-inch scale, I would enter the following:

   - **1 Inches** into the In the Printout (In Drawing) box
   - **4 Feet** into the In SketchUp (In Model) box

   If I wanted to produce a print at 1:100 scale, I would enter the following:

   - **1 m** into the In the Printout (In Drawing) box
   - **100 m** into the In SketchUp (In Model) box

7. **Take note of how may pages you'll need to print your drawing.**

   If you're using Windows, you can check this in the Tiled Sheet Print Range area of the dialog box. On a Mac, the number of pages you'll need appears in the Pages Required section of the Document Setup dialog box. If you want to print on a different-sized piece of paper, change the setting in the Print Setup (Page Setup) dialog box.

8. **If you want to print your drawing on a single sheet and it won't fit, try using a smaller scale.**

   Using the ¼ inch = 1 foot example, try shrinking the drawing to ³⁄₁₆ inch = 1 foot scale. To do this, you would enter the following:

   - **3 Inches** into the In the Printout (In Drawing) box
   - **16 Feet** into the In SketchUp (In Model) box

9. **When you're happy with how your drawing will print, click the OK button.**

10. **(Windows only) If you like what you see in the Print Preview window, click the Print button (in the upper-left corner) to open the Print dialog box.**

11. **(Mac only) Choose File⇨Print.**

12. **In the Print dialog box, click the OK button to send your print job to the printer.**

Refer to the "Making a basic print" section for your operating system, earlier in the chapter, for the whole story on basic printing from SketchUp.

Chapter 13

Exporting Images and Animations

In This Chapter

▶ Creating 2D views of your model as TIFFs, JPEGs, and PNGs

▶ Learning about pixels and resolution

▶ Making sure that you export the right kind of image

▶ Exporting the kind of movie file you need

*W*ant to e-mail a JPEG of your new patio to your parents? How about a movie that shows what it's like to walk out onto that new patio? If you need an image or a movie of your model, forget about viewing or printing within SketchUp. Exporting is the way to go.

SketchUp can export both still images and animations in most of the major graphics and movie formats. Here's the part that's a little bit confusing: Which file formats you can export depend on the version of SketchUp you have. If you have regular ol' Google SketchUp (the free one), you can create *raster* image files as well as movies. If you've sprung for Google SketchUp Pro, you can also export *vector* files and a whole bunch of 3D formats; I talk about all of them in Chapter 14.

In this chapter, I talk about the export file formats that are common to both versions of Google SketchUp. Just in case you're not familiar with the terms *raster* and *vector,* I give brief definitions of each. Then I go into some detail about the 2D raster image formats that you can create with SketchUp. I spend the last part of this chapter talking about exporting animations as movie files that anyone can open and view.

Exporting 2D Images of Your Model

Even though the free version of SketchUp can only export 2D views of your model as *raster* images, I think it's helpful to know a little bit about graphics file formats in general. If you're already an aficionado about these sorts of things, or if you're in a big hurry, you can skip ahead to the section "Exporting a raster image from SketchUp."

Pictures on your computer are divided into two basic flavors: *raster* and *vector*. The difference between these two categories of file types has to do with how they store image information. Here's the one-minute version:

✔ **Raster:** Raster images are made up of dots. (Technically, these dots are called *pixels*, just like the pixels that make up images you take with a digital camera.) Raster file formats consist of information about the location and color of each dot. When you export a raster, you decide how many dots (pixels) it should include, which directly affects how big it can be displayed. SketchUp exports TIFF, JPEG, and PNG raster images; the Windows version also exports BMPs, although that's nothing to get excited about. You can read more about raster images in the sidebar "Understanding rasters: Lots and lots of dots," later in this chapter.

✔ **Vector:** Vector images consist of instructions written in computer code. This code describes *how* to draw the image to whatever software is trying to open it. The major advantage of using vector imagery (as opposed to raster) lies in its *scalability* — vectors can be resized larger or smaller without affecting their image quality, while rasters lose quality if you enlarge them too much. The free version of SketchUp can only export raster images, but SketchUp Pro can export vectors in both PDF and EPS file formats; you can read all about it in Chapter 14.

Exporting a raster image from SketchUp

The process of exporting a view of your SketchUp model is fairly straightforward. Depending on which format you choose, the export options are slightly different, but I address all of them in this section.

Follow these steps to export a raster image from SketchUp:

1. **Adjust your model view until you see exactly what you'd like to export as an image file.**

    SketchUp's raster image export is WYSIWYG — What You See Is What You Get. Basically, your entire modeling window view is exported as an image, so use the navigation tools or click on a scene to set up your view. Use styles, shadows, and fog to make your model look exactly the way you want it to. To change the proportions of your image, resize your SketchUp window. Follow these steps to do so:

    1. (Windows only) If your SketchUp window is full-screen, click the Minimize button in its upper-right corner.

    2. Drag the Resize tab in the lower-right corner of your SketchUp window until the modeling window is the right proportion.

In Figure 13-1, I want to export a wide view of a house I modeled, so I adjust the proportions of my modeling window until things look right.

Figure 13-1: Adjust your view and your modeling window until things look the way you want them to in your exported image.

SketchUp Modeling Window

Exported Image

You might be wondering whether *everything* in your modeling window shows up in an exported raster image. The red, green, and blue axes don't, which is good, but guides do, which is usually bad. If you don't want your guides to be visible in your exported image, deselect Guides in the View menu.

2. Choose File⇨Export⇨2D Graphic.

This opens the File Export dialog box.

3. Choose the file format you'd like to use from the Format drop-down list.

Before you go ahead and choose JPEG by default, you should know that this file type isn't always the best choice. For a complete description of each format (as well as recommendations for when to choose each), see the section "Looking at SketchUp's raster formats," later in this chapter.

4. Choose a name and a location on your computer for your exported image.

5. Click the Options button.

This opens the Export Options dialog box, where you can control how your image is exported. Figure 13-2 shows what this dialog box looks like for each of SketchUp's raster file formats.

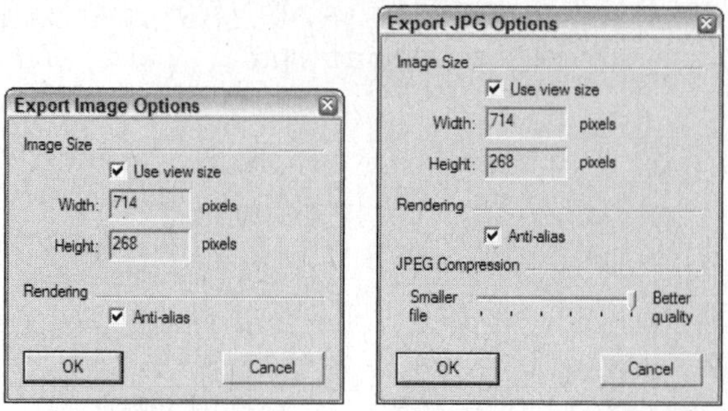

Figure 13-2:
The Export
Options
dialog boxes
for TIFFs,
PNGs, and
BMPs (left)
and JPEGs.

Export Options for
TIFFs, PNGs, and BMPs

Export Options for JPEGs

6. **Adjust the settings in the Export Options dialog box.**

   Here's a description of what the settings do:

   • **Use View Size:** Selecting this check box tells SketchUp to export an image file that contains the same number of pixels as are currently being used to display your model on-screen. If you're just planning to use your exported image in an e-mail or in an on-screen presentation (like PowerPoint), you select Use View Size, but it's still better to manually control the pixel size of your exported image. If you're planning to print your exported image, don't select this check box — whatever you do.

   • **Width and Height:** When you don't select the Use View Size check box, you can manually enter the size of your exported image. Because this process requires a fair amount of figuring, I've devoted a whole section to it; take a look at "Making sure that you're exporting enough pixels," later in this chapter, to find out what to type into the Width and Height boxes.

   • **Anti-alias:** Because raster images use grids of colored squares to draw pictures, diagonal lines and edges can sometimes look jagged and, well . . . lousy. *Anti-aliasing* is a process that fills in the gaps around pixels with similar-colored pixels so that things look smooth. Figure 13-3 illustrates the concept. In general, you want to leave anti-aliasing on.

   • **Resolution (Mac only):** This is where you tell SketchUp how big each pixel should be, and therefore how big (in inches or centimeters) your exported image should be. Pixel size is expressed in terms of pixels per inch/centimeter. This option is only available when the Use View Size check box isn't selected. Just like with the

Width and Height boxes, I go into a lot of detail about image resolution in the next section of this chapter.

No anti-aliasing   With anti-aliasing

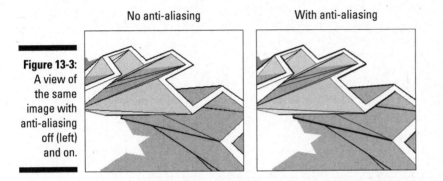

Figure 13-3:
A view of
the same
image with
anti-aliasing
off (left)
and on.

- **Transparent Background (Mac only, not for JPEGs):** Mac users can choose to export TIFFs and PNGs with transparent backgrounds, which can make it easier to "cut out" your model in another piece of software. Exporting your image with a transparent background is also a nice way to use image-editing programs like Photoshop to drop in a sky and ground plane later on. It's too bad this isn't available for Windows users; it's a really handy feature.

- **JPEG Compression (JPEG only):** This slider lets you decide two things at the same time: the file size of your exported image and how good the image will look. The two are, of course, inversely related; the farther to the left you move the slider, the smaller your file will be, but the worse it will look. I never set JPEG compression any lower than 8 — my models take too long to build for me to make them look terrible on export.

7. **Click the OK button to close the Export Options dialog box.**

8. **Back in the File Export dialog box, click the Export button to export your raster image file.**

You can find your exported file in whatever location on your computer you specified in Step 4, above. What you do with it is entirely up to you — you can e-mail it, print it, or use it in another software program to create a presentation.

Don't be alarmed if the export process takes longer than you think it should. If you're exporting a pretty big image (one with lots and lots of pixels), the export will take a while. Take the opportunity to call your mother — she'll appreciate it.

Looking at SketchUp's raster formats

So you know you need to export a raster image from SketchUp, but which one do you choose? You have four choices in Windows; three of them are available on the Mac. The following sections give you the details.

When you export a raster image, you're saving your current view in SketchUp to a separate file somewhere on your computer. As a raster image, that file consists of tiny, colored dots called *pixels* — more pixels than you can shake a stick at. When you look at all the pixels together, they form an image.

Understanding rasters: Lots and lots of dots

When you look at a photograph on your computer, you're really looking at a whole bunch of tiny dots of color called *pixels*. These are arranged in a rectangular grid called a *raster*. Digital images that are composed of pixels arranged in a raster grid are called *raster images,* or *rasters* for short. Have a look at the first image in the figure below for a close-up view of a raster image. Here are some things to keep in mind about rasters:

 ✔ **Rasters are everywhere.** Almost every digital image you've ever seen is a raster. TIFF, JPEG, and PNG are the most common raster file formats, and SketchUp exports all three of them.

 ✔ **Rasters are flexible.** Every two-dimensional image can be displayed as a raster; a grid of colored squares is an incredibly effective way of saving and sharing picture information. As long as you have enough pixels, any image can look good as a raster.

 ✔ **Rasters take up a lot of space.** If you think about how raster images work, it takes a lot of information to describe a picture. Digital images are made up of anywhere from thousands to millions of pixels, and each pixel can be any one of millions of colors. To store a whole picture, a raster image file needs to include the location and color of *each* pixel; the bigger the picture, the more pixels it takes to describe it, and the bigger the file size gets.

 ✔ **Rasters are measured in pixels.** Because every raster image is made up of a specific number of pixels, you use a raster's *pixel dimensions* to describe its size. If I told you that I'd e-mailed you a photograph that was 800 x 600, you could expect to receive a picture that is 800 pixels wide by 600 pixels tall. (See the following figure.) Pixels don't have a physical size on their own — they're just dots of color. You determine a picture's physical size by deciding how big its pixels should be; this is referred to as *resolution,* and is generally expressed in terms of *pixels per inch* (ppi). Check out the section "Making sure that you're exporting enough pixels," later in this chapter, for the whole scoop.

Why use pixels instead of inches or centimeters to describe the size of a digital image? It all has to do with how computer screens work. Because not all screens display things at the same size, it's impossible to predict how *big* an image will look when it shows up on someone's computer.

Depending on the person's display settings, an 800-x-600-pixel image might be a few inches across, or it might take up the whole screen. Giving a digital image's dimensions in pixels is the only accurate way of describing how "big" it is.

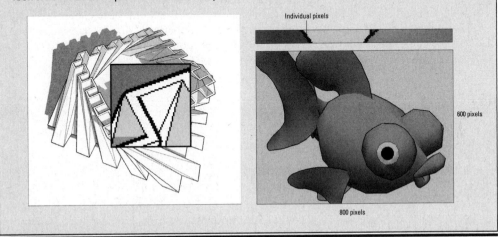

Tagged Image File (TIFF or TIF)

TIFFs are the stalwarts of the raster image file format world; everyone can read them and just about everyone can create them. TIFF stands for Tagged Image File Format, but that's hardly important. Here's everything you need to know about TIFFs:

- ✔ **When image quality is important, choose TIFF.** Unless file size is a concern (because, for example, you need to send an image by e-mail), always export a TIFF if you need a raster image. For everything from working in Photoshop to creating a layout in InDesign or QuarkXPress, a TIFF can provide the image quality you need.

- ✔ **TIFFs don't compress your image data.** That means they don't introduce any garbage like JPEGs do, but it also means that they're really big files.

- ✔ **Pay attention to your pixel count.** If you're exporting a TIFF, you're probably looking for the best image quality you can get. And if that's the case, you need to make sure that your TIFF is "big" enough — that it includes enough pixels — to display at the size you need. Have a look at the next section in this chapter for more information.

JPEG (or JPG)

JPEG stands for Joint Photographic Experts Group, which makes it sound much fancier than it really is. Almost every digital image you've ever seen was a JPEG (pronounced *JAY-peg*); it's the standard file format for images on the Web. Check out these JPEG details:

- ✔ **When file size is a concern, choose JPEG.** The whole point of the JPEG file format is to compress raster images to manageable file sizes so that they can be e-mailed and put on Web sites. A JPEG is a fraction of the size of a TIFF file with the same number of pixels, so JPEG is a great choice if file size is more important to you than image quality.

- ✔ **JPEGs compress file size by degrading image quality.** This is known as *lossy* compression; JPEG technology basically works by tossing out a lot of the pixels in your image. JPEGs also introduce a fair amount of pixel garbage; these smudges are called *artifacts,* and they're awful. Take a look at Figure 13-4 to see what I mean.

- ✔ **JPEG + SketchUp = Danger.** Because of the way the JPEG file format works, JPEG exports from SketchUp are particularly susceptible to looking terrible. Images from SketchUp usually include straight lines and broad areas of color, both of which JPEG has a hard time handling. If you're going to export a JPEG from SketchUp, make sure that the JPEG Compression slider is never set below 8. For more details, see the section "Exporting a raster image from SketchUp," earlier in this chapter.

Figure 13-4: A TIFF, on the left, and a JPEG, on the right; JPEGs compress file size by reducing image quality.

TIFF   JPEG

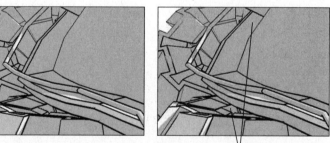

JPEG compression artifacts

Portable Network Graphics (PNG)

Hooray for PNG! Pronounced *ping,* this graphics file format is my hero. Unfortunately, it isn't as widely used as it should be. If I had my druthers (I keep leaving them on the subway), every raster export from SketchUp would be a PNG. Why? Because, at least as far as SketchUp is concerned,

PNG combines all the best features of TIFF and JPEG. Why don't more people use PNGs? Because standards are hard to change, and right now, it's a JPEG world. PNG details are as follows:

- ✔ **PNGs compress image data *without* affecting image quality.** As a *lossless* compression technology, PNGs are smaller files than TIFFs (just like JPEGs), but they don't mess up any pixels (totally unlike JPEGs). Granted, PNGs aren't as small as JPEGs, but I think the difference in image quality is worth a few extra bits.

- ✔ **If you're exporting an image for someone who knows a thing or two about computers, choose PNG.** The truth is, some software doesn't know what to do with a PNG, so there's a risk in using it. If you plan to send your exported image to someone who knows what he's doing, go ahead and send a PNG — he'll be impressed that you're "in the know." If the recipient of your export is less technologically sophisticated, stick with a JPEG or TIFF file; it's the safe choice.

The PNG file format wasn't developed to replace JPEG or TIFF; it was supposed to stand in for GIF (Graphics Interchange Format), which is a file type that SketchUp doesn't export. Without going into too much detail, folks use JPEG for images like photographs and GIF for things like logos. Because exported SketchUp views usually have more in common with the latter, PNG (the replacement for GIF) is the better choice. So why can't PNG replace JPEG and TIFF? For most photographs (which are the majority of images on the Web), JPEG is better than PNG because it produces smaller files, which in turn yields faster load times when you're surfing the Internet. TIFF is more versatile than PNG because it supports different *color spaces,* which are important to people in the printing industry. For reasons that are beyond the scope of this book, that isn't relevant to exports from SketchUp; PNG is still (in my opinion) the best — if not the safest — choice.

Windows Bitmap (BMP)

Windows Bitmap, or BMP, files are old school; they can only be used on Windows, and they're big. If a BMP were a car, it would be the old, rusty van in your parents' garage. As you can probably guess, I don't recommend using BMPs for anything, with a couple of exceptions:

- ✔ **To send your exported file to someone with a very old Windows computer:** If the person to whom you're sending an exported image has a Windows computer that's more than about 5 years old, I suppose I'd send her a BMP.

- ✔ **To place an image in an old Windows version of layout software:** If your layout person is using a copy of Word or PageMaker that's a few years old, he might need a BMP file.

Making sure that you're exporting enough pixels

When it comes to raster images, it's all about pixels. The more pixels your image has, the more detailed it is, and the bigger it can be displayed or printed. Figure 13-5 shows the same image three times. The first image is 150 x 50, meaning that it's 150 pixels wide by 50 pixels high. The second image is 300 x 100, and the third is 900 x 300. Notice how the image with more pixels looks a lot better? That's the whole point of this section.

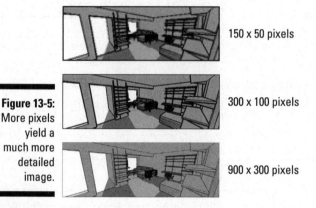

150 x 50 pixels

300 x 100 pixels

900 x 300 pixels

Figure 13-5: More pixels yield a much more detailed image.

Why not always export a truckload of pixels, just in case you need them? There are two reasons:

✔ Image exports with lots of pixels take a long time to process.

✔ Raster images are very big files.

How many pixels you need to export depends on what you're going to use the image *for*. Very broadly, you can do two things with your image:

✔ Display or project it on a screen, digitally

✔ Print it

In the next two sections, I talk about each of these possibilities in detail.

Exporting enough pixels for a digital presentation

If you plan to use your exported image as part of an on-screen presentation, it's helpful to know what computer monitors and digital projectors can display:

✔ The smallest, oldest devices currently in use have images that are 800 pixels wide by 600 pixels high.

✔ At the other end of the spectrum, high-end, 30-inch LCD monitors display 2560 x 1600 pixels.

So it stands to reason that, if you're exporting an image that will be viewed on-screen only, you need to create an image that's somewhere between 800 and 2500 pixels wide. Table 13-1 provides some guidelines on image sizes for different digital applications.

Table 13-1	Suggested Image Sizes for On-Screen Use
How the Image Will Be Used	*Image Width (pixels)*
E-mail	400 to 800
Web site, large image	600
Web site, small image	200
PowerPoint presentation (full-screen)	800 or 1024 (depends on projector)
PowerPoint presentation (floating image)	400

For images that will be shown digitally, leave the Resolution setting (in the Export Options dialog box) at 72 pixels per inch. For computer monitors and digital projectors, the image resolution is meaningless because the pixels in your image correspond directly to the pixels on your screen; inches and centimeters don't even come into play.

Understanding resolution: Exporting images for print

Images that you want to print need to have lots more pixels than ones that are only going to be displayed on-screen. That's because printers — inkjet, laser, and offset — all operate very differently than computer monitors and digital projectors. When you print something, the pixels in your image turn into microscopic specks of ink or toner, and these specks are smaller than the pixels on your computer screen. To make a decent-sized print of your exported image, it needs to contain enough *pixels per inch* of image. An image's pixel density, expressed in pixels per inch (ppi), is its *resolution*.

What kind of resolution you need depends on three things:

✔ **The kind of device you'll be printing to:** For home inkjet printers, you can get away with a resolution of as little as 150 ppi. If your image will be appearing in a commercially produced book, you need a resolution of at least 300 ppi.

✔ **How far away the image will be from the audience:** There's a big difference between a magazine page and a trade-show banner. For close-up applications, a resolution of 200 to 300 ppi is appropriate. Large graphics that will be viewed from several feet away can be as low as 60 ppi.

✔ **The subject matter of the image itself:** Photographic images tend to consist of areas of color that blur together a bit; these kinds of images can tolerate being printed at lower resolutions than drawings with lots of intricate detail. For images with lots of lines (like SketchUp models), it's best to work with very high resolutions — 300 to 600 ppi — especially if the image will be viewed close-up.

Table 13-2 provides some guidelines for exporting images that will be printed.

Table 13-2	Recommended Resolutions for Prints	
How the Image Will Be Used	*Image Resolution (pixels/inch)*	*Image Resolution (pixels/cm)*
8.5-x-11 or 11-x-17 inkjet or laser print	200 to 300	80 to 120
Color brochure or pamphlet	300	120
Magazine or book (color and shadows)	300	120
Magazine or book (linework only)	450 to 600	180 to 240
Presentation board	150 to 200	60 to 80
Banner	60 to 100	24 to 40

Keep in mind that the biggest raster image that SketchUp can export is 10,000 pixels wide or tall (whichever is greater). This means that the largest banner image, printed at 100 ppi, that SketchUp can create is about 100 inches wide. To make larger images, you need to export a *vector* file; check out the details on exporting to vector formats with SketchUp Pro in Chapter 14.

Follow these steps to make sure that you're exporting enough pixels to be able to print your image properly:

1. **In the Export Options dialog box, make sure that the Use View Size check box is deselected.**

   To get to the Export Options dialog box, follow Steps 1 through 6 in the section "Exporting a raster image from SketchUp," earlier in this chapter.

2. **Decide on the resolution that you need for your exported image. (Refer to Table 13-2.)**

   Keep the resolution in your head or scribble it on a piece of paper.

3. **Decide how big your exported image will be printed, in inches or centimeters.**

   Note your desired physical image size, just like you did with the resolution in the previous step.

4. **Multiply your resolution from Step 2 by your image size from Step 3 to get the number of pixels you need to export:**

   ```
   Resolution (pixels/inch or cm) × Size (inches or cm) = Number of pixels
   ```

   In other words, if you know what resolution you need to export, and you know how big your image will be printed, you can multiply the two numbers to get the number of pixels you need. Here's an example:

   ```
   300 pixels/inch × 8 inches wide = 2,400 pixels wide
   ```

   To export an image that can be printed 8 inches wide at 300 ppi, you need to export an image that's 2400 pixels wide. Figure 13-6 gives an illustration of this example.

TIP

SketchUp's default setting is to make your exported image match the proportions of your modeling window; that is, you can only type in a width *or* a height, but not both. If you're on a Mac, you can manually enter both dimensions by clicking the Unlink button (which looks like a chain). You can always click it again to relink the width and height dimensions later.

8 inches wide @ 300 ppi = 2400 pixels

Figure 13-6:
To figure out how many pixels you need to export, multiply the resolution by the physical size.

Enter 2400 here

5. **Type in the width *or* height of the image you'd like to export, in pixels.**

    It's usually pretty hard to know *exactly* how big your image will be when it's printed, and even if you do, you probably want to leave some room for cropping. For these reasons, I always add 15–25 percent to the number of pixels I figure I'll need. If my image calls for 2,400 pixels, I export 3,000 pixels, just to be safe.

    If you're on a Mac, things are a little easier because SketchUp's designers built a pixel calculator right into the Export Options dialog box. Just enter your desired resolution in the appropriate spot, change the width and height units from pixels to inches or centimeters, and type in your desired image size. SketchUp does the arithmetic for you.

6. **Click the OK button to close the Export Options dialog box.**

Making Movies with Animation Export

When it comes to having nerdy fun, I think exporting movie animations of your SketchUp models is right up there with iPods and store-bought fireworks. Like both of these things, what's so great about animation export is how *easy* it is to do. That's not to say that animation and digital video are simple topics — they're not. It would take a freight elevator to move the books that have been written about working with video on the computer, but I'm going to keep it simple. Because you and I are primarily interested in 3D modeling, what you'll find in the following sections are instructions for doing what you need to do.

Getting ready for prime time

The key to exporting animations of your SketchUp models is using scenes; if you haven't read it already, now's the time to check out Chapter 10. *Scenes* are saved views of your model that you can arrange in any order you want. When you export an animation, SketchUp strings together the scenes in your model to create a movie file that can be played on just about any computer made in the last several years.

Follow these steps to get your model ready to export as an animation:

1. **Create scenes to build the "skeleton" of your animation.**

2. **To adjust the animation settings in the Model Info dialog box, choose Window⇨Model Info and then select the Animation panel.**

    I explain all the controls in the section about moving from scene to scene in Chapter 10.

3. **Click the Enable Scene Transitions check box to tell SketchUp to move smoothly from one scene to the next.**

4. **Enter a transition time to tell SketchUp how long to spend moving between scenes.**

   If your Scene Delay is 0 (below), you can multiply your transition time by your number of scenes to figure out how long your exported animation will be.

5. **Enter a scene delay time to pause at each scene before moving on to the next one.**

   If you plan to talk about each scene, use this feature. If your animation is supposed to be a smooth walk-through or flyover, set this to 0.

6. **Adjust the proportions of your modeling window to approximate the proportions of your movie.**

   Unlike SketchUp's 2D export formats, the proportions of your exported movie don't depend on those of your modeling window; that is to say, making your modeling window long and skinny won't result in a long and skinny movie. You choose how many pixels wide and tall you want your movie to be, so to get an idea of how much you'll be able to see, make your modeling window match the proportions of your exported file (4:3 is common for video formats). Have a look at Step 1 in the section "Exporting a raster image from SketchUp," earlier in this chapter, for guidance on adjusting your modeling window.

7. **When your project is ready to go, move on to the next section to export your animation.**

Exporting a movie

Fortunately, you have only one choice if you want to export a movie from SketchUp. If you're using Windows, you create an AVI file; Mac users create QuickTime MOVs.

If you're paying close attention to the available file formats for exporting movies, you'll probably notice three more choices in the drop-down menu: TIF, JPG, and PNG. I don't go into detail about these formats for animation (movie) export in SketchUp because you probably won't need them; choosing to export in any of these formats will give you a pile of image files that each represent one frame in your animation. People who want to include their SketchUp animation in a Flash file should take advantage of this option, but explaining how to do so is beyond the scope of this book.

While exporting animations in SketchUp is a pretty simple operation, figuring out how to set all the animation export controls can seem like landing the space shuttle. What follows are step-by-step instructions for generating a movie file; settings recommendations are in the next section.

Follow these steps to export a movie file from SketchUp:

1. **Prepare your model for export as an animation.**

   See the section "Getting ready for prime time," earlier in this chapter, for a list of things you need to do before you export an animation.

2. **Choose File⇨Export⇨Animation.**

   This opens the Animation Export dialog box.

3. **Give your movie file a name, and choose where it should be saved on your computer system.**

4. **Make sure that the correct file format is selected.**

   In the Format drop-down menu, choose AVI if you're using Windows and QuickTime if you're on a Mac.

5. **Click the Options button to open the Animation Export Options dialog box. (See Figure 13-7.)**

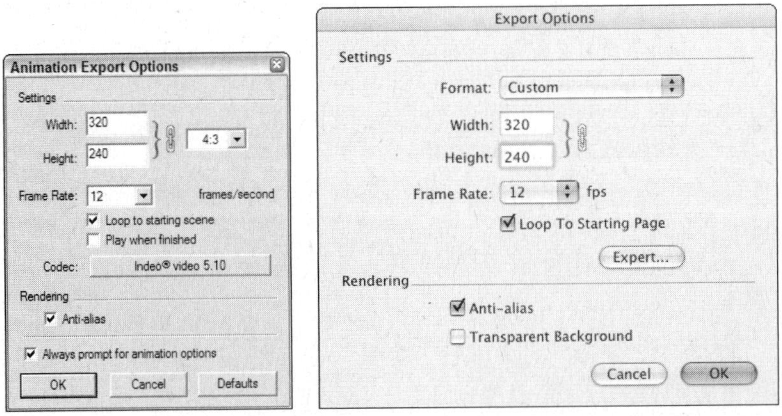

Figure 13-7:
The Windows (left) and Mac versions of the Animation Export Options dialog box.

6. **Adjust the settings for the type of animation you want to export.**

   How you set everything up in this dialog box depends on how you plan to use the animation you end up creating. Check out the next section in this chapter for recommended settings for different applications.

   If you're working on a Mac, there's an extra drop-down menu that you might find helpful: Format includes a short list of uses for your animation. Choosing one automatically sets most of the controls for you, though (as you see in the next section) you can improve things a bit by making some of your own selections.

7. **Select the Anti-alias check box, if it isn't already selected.**

Choosing this doubles the amount of time it takes for your animation to export, but it makes your edges look much better in the final movie.

8. **Click the Codec button (Windows) or the Expert button (Mac).**

    This opens the Video Compression (Compression Settings on a Mac) dialog box. (See Figure 13-8.) Choose the correct settings for the type of animation you want to export, again referring to the next section of this chapter for details about what the options mean.

9. **Click the OK button in the compression dialog box, and then the OK button again in the Export Options dialog box.**

    This returns you to the Animation Export dialog box.

10. **Check to make sure that everything looks right, and then click the Export button.**

    Because exporting an animation takes a while, it pays to double-check your settings before you click the Export button. When the export is complete, you can find your animation file in the location you specified in Step 3. Double-clicking it should cause it to open in whatever movie-playing software you have that can read it. On Windows computers, this is usually Windows Media Player; on Macs, it's QuickTime.

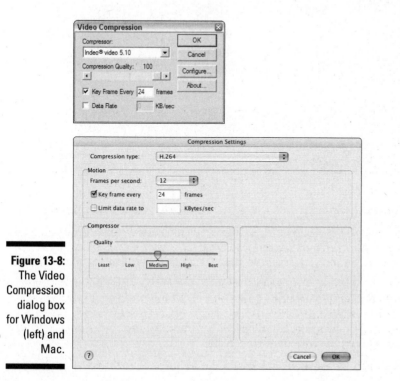

Figure 13-8:
The Video Compression dialog box for Windows (left) and Mac.

Figuring out the Animation Export options settings

As I said before, digital video is complicated. Lucky for us, you don't really have to know what everything means to export the right kind of movie; you just have to know how to set up everything.

What follows are a number of different things you might want to do with your animation, and recommended settings for getting good results. Feel free to experiment, but the following sections are a good place to start.

For sending in an e-mail

If you're going to e-mail someone an animation file, you have to make the file as small as you can. These settings can help you do just that:

Width and Height	160 x 120
Frame Rate	10 fps
Codec (Windows)	Indeo Video 5.10
Compression Type (Mac)	H.264
Key Frame Every	24 frames
Compression Quality (Windows)	50
Quality (Mac)	Medium

For posting on the Web

When you're creating a movie that will be placed on a Web site, you need to make sure that it's small enough to load quickly but big enough to look good. Try out these settings:

Width and Height	320 x 240
Frame Rate	12 fps
Codec (Windows)	Indeo Video 5.10
Compression Type (Mac)	H.264
Key Frame Every	24 frames
Compression Quality (Windows)	50
Quality (Mac)	Medium

For viewing on-screen (computer or projector)

If you plan to use your animation as part of an on-screen presentation (such as with PowerPoint or Keynote), you probably want it to look good full-screen. You'll probably be using a digital projector to present, and these days, most digital projectors come in two resolutions: 800 x 600 and 1024 x 768. If you know the resolution of the projector you'll be using, you're made in the shade. If you're unsure, export at the lower pixel count, just to be safe:

Width and Height	800 x 600 or 1024 x 768
Frame Rate	15 fps
Codec (Windows)	Indeo Video 5.10
Compression Type (Mac)	H.264
Key Frame Every	24 frames
Compression Quality (Windows)	100
Quality (Mac)	Best

You want your exported animations to look smooth — the transitions from one frame to the next shouldn't be jumpy or awkward. If your camera is covering a lot of ground (in other words, moving a large distance between scenes) in a very short time, you might want to experiment with increasing your frame rate to smooth things out. Doing so adds more frames between transitions, which means the camera isn't traveling as far between frames.

For exporting to DV (to be viewed on a TV with a DVD player)

If you need to export an animation that will be burned onto a DVD that will (in turn) be played in a DVD player, you should go all-in on quality and file size. The export process will take a long time, but you'll get the best-looking movie you can get. Try these settings first:

Width and Height	720 x 480
Frame Rate	29.97 fps
Codec (Windows)	Full Frame
Compression Type (Mac)	DV/DVCPRO
Compression Quality (Windows)	100
Quality (Mac)	Best
Scan Mode (Mac)	Interlaced

Chapter 14

Exporting to CAD, Illustration, and Other Modeling Software

. . . .

In This Chapter

▶ Finding out about vector graphics

▶ Generating 2D files for CAD and illustration software

▶ Exporting your model to other 3D software

. . . .

Don't you hate how airlines make you walk through the first-class section to get to your seat? I think the economy section is bad enough without having to see how much better some people have it — the big, cushy seats, the dinner entrees made with real meat — I'm usually in a bad mood by the time I sit down. But what does this have to do with export formats in SketchUp Pro? It's all about knowing what you're not getting.

If you don't have the Pro version of SketchUp, don't bother reading this chapter (or the next one, either). The stuff I talk about only applies to those folks who have sprung for the bells-and-whistles version of SketchUp. Now, if you're using Google SketchUp (free), and you're wondering what's in Pro, you might find it useful to peruse these pages to see what you're missing. Unlike the flight attendant on the last plane I was on, I won't yell at you for sticking your head through the curtain to take a look around.

SketchUp Pro users have access to a few file export formats that aren't available in the free version of SketchUp. These file formats let you share your work with other "pro-grade" software programs like Illustrator, AutoCAD, and 3D Studio MAX. Most people who design things for a living use a number of different pieces of software to get their work done, and they need the ability to move their data between them. That's where SketchUp Pro's exporters come in.

I've divided this chapter into two halves: The first part talks about SketchUp's 2D export formats, and the second part deals with the 3D ones. For each file format that SketchUp exports, I provide a description of what the settings do, and in some cases, why you might need them. Which format (or formats) you choose depends entirely on what other software you're using.

Exporting Drawings in 2D

It's all fine and well to have a 3D model in SketchUp Pro, but most people who design 3D objects (toasters, buildings, Volvos) eventually need to create 2D views of their designs. Sometimes these views are for presentations, and sometimes you need to import a 2D view into other software programs, where you can continue to work on it. You can use SketchUp Pro's 2D export formats to do both.

Sizing up the export formats

You can find a lot of other software out there, and luckily, SketchUp Pro provides enough export formats that you can interact with most of it. On the 2D export side, here's a brief rundown on what SketchUp Pro has to offer:

- **PDF:** Lately, you can't swing a cat (not that I ever would, Mom) without hitting a Portable Document Format file. On top of the fact that almost anyone can read them, PDF files are great for sending information to vector-illustration programs like Illustrator and FreeHand.

- **EPS:** Encapsulated Postscript files are what folks *used* to use to transfer vector information, but these days, more and more people are using PDFs.

- **DWG:** This is AutoCAD's native file format, and it's the best one to use for transferring information to that program and other pieces of CAD software. DWG can also contain 3D information, so I talk about it in the second part of this chapter, too.

- **DXF:** Document Exchange Format is another "flavor" of DWG. It was developed by Autodesk to be the file format that other pieces of software use to transfer data into AutoCAD, because they weren't supposed to be able to create DWGs. Trouble is, DWG has been *reverse-engineered* (taken apart, figured out, unlocked, and put back together again), so now most CAD programs can exchange both DXF and DWG files to their hearts' content.

- **EPIX:** You may have never heard of Piranesi, but you should know about it. It's a piece of software that lets you "paint" on top of 2D views of your model, but it's much cooler than that. Anyway, EPIX lets you open 2D views of your SketchUp model in Piranesi, if you have it.

In the sections that follow, I discuss each of the formats in more detail.

Exporting a 2D drawing

Regardless of which 2D format you choose to export, the procedure is always the same. Follow these steps to export a 2D image from SketchUp Pro:

1. **Adjust your model view until you have the view you want to export.**

2. **Choose File⇨Export⇨2D Graphic.**

   This opens the File Export dialog box.

3. **Choose the file format you'd like to use from the Format drop-down list.**

   I describe each format in a fair amount of detail later in this chapter.

4. **Choose a name and a location on your computer for your exported image.**

5. **Click the Options button.**

   This opens the Export Options dialog box for the file format you chose in Step 3. The options are unique to each file format, so check out the section on the one you're using for details on that particular format.

6. **Adjust the settings in the Export Options dialog box, and click the OK button.**

   This closes the Export Options dialog box.

7. **Click the Export button to export your 2D image file.**

Getting to know PDF and EPS

Here's what you need to know about these two common *vector* file formats. (Have a look at the sidebar "Vectors: Pictures made of math," later in this chapter, to find out what vectors are all about.)

Portable Document Format (PDF)

You've probably already heard of PDF files. Back in the old days (a few years ago), it was hard to send someone a digital graphics file because so many different kinds were available, and because the person to whom you were sending the file had to have the right kind of software to be able to open it. If I made a brochure in QuarkXPress and wanted to send it to you to review, you had to have QuarkXPress, too — and chances were, you didn't (QuarkXPress cost $1,000).

Vectors: Pictures made of math

Remembering the location and color of millions of tiny dots isn't the only way that computers save images; it just happens to be the most common. The alternative to raster imaging is *vector graphics,* or *vectors* for short. In a vector, lines, shapes, and colors are described by mathematical functions. Before you run screaming off into the distance, know that it's not as scary as it sounds. You don't need to do any math to create a vector. Your hardware and software do it for you. Here are some things to think about when it comes to vectors:

✔ **Vectors don't take up much space.** Imagine a straight line drawn using pixels. In order to draw the line, your computer has to be told where to put each and every pixel. In a vector image (which doesn't use pixels), a mathematical function is used to tell your computer how to draw that same line. Instead of having to provide details for every single pixel, only two instructions are needed: the function

that defines the line and its color. Of course, actual vector graphics programming is a zillion times more complicated than this, but you get the general idea. Vector files are much smaller than raster files.

✔ **Vectors are scalable.** With a raster, you're limited by the number of pixels you have in your image. If you don't have enough, you might not be able to print or otherwise display your image very big. If you have a large number of pixels, your image might look terrific, but your file might be too huge to work with. Because vectors are math-based instructions that tell your software how to draw an image, there's no size limit to how big — or small — your image can be. With the same vector file, you could print your company logo on your business card and on the side of a blimp, and they would both look great. The figure that follows shows what I mean.

Raster

Vector

Adobe developed PDF to solve this problem, and it's been wildly successful. Because PDF reader software is already installed on tens of millions of computers, anyone can open and view a PDF file created by anyone else. Lots of programs (including SketchUp Pro) can export PDFs, so now there's an easy way for people to share graphics files.

Here are some things to consider about PDF and SketchUp:

- **PDF is universal.** Anyone with Adobe Reader (which is free from Adobe's Web site: www.adobe.com) can open and view a PDF you create with SketchUp. In fact, anyone with a Mac can open a PDF just by double-clicking it; the picture-viewing software that comes with the Mac operating system uses PDF as its native format.

- **PDF is consistent.** When you send someone a PDF file, you can be 99 percent sure that it will look just like it looks on your computer. The colors, line weights, and text will all stay the same, which is important if you're showing someone a design.

- **When you need to send a vector graphic file, use PDF unless someone specifically requests an EPS file.** Here's the thing — just about every piece of software I can think of handles PDFs with no problem. If you or someone else needs a vector export from SketchUp, PDF works just about every time.

Encapsulated Postscript (EPS)

Postscript is a computer language that was developed to describe graphical objects. An EPS is an *encapsulated* Postscript file, meaning that it's a self-contained bundle of instructions for a how to draw an image. Back before PDFs existed, this was the best way to move vector information around. The key here is "back before PDFs existed" — nowadays, you don't have much reason to use EPS when you could export a PDF file instead. Here are some things you should know about the EPS file format:

- **EPS is complicated.** Without boring you with all the details, EPS files are different depending on what software and what operating system made them. What's more, you won't find any free, commonly used programs that can open them. You need something like Illustrator or a layout program like InDesign, which most people don't have.

- **Use EPS if your other graphics software is more than a couple of versions old.** PDF support has only been widely incorporated in the last few years, so if you're using older image-editing, illustration, or layout software, you might need to use EPS.

- **If someone you're working with insists on EPS, go ahead and send an EPS file.** Some workflows have been designed with EPS files in mind, which is why SketchUp exports EPS in the first place. It's good to know that EPS is there if you need it.

Navigating the PDF/EPS Options dialog box

Figure 14-1 shows what this dialog box looks like. Careful — it's ugly. Luckily, it's the same for both PDF and EPS exports, so that's something, I guess.

Figure 14-1:
The PDF/
EPS Options
dialog box
for Windows
(left) and
the Mac.

In Windows, the name of this dialog box, as written in its title bar, is PDF (or EPS) Hidden Line Options, but that makes no sense. I think it's probably a remnant from when SketchUp could only export vectors in the Hidden Line Face style, but those days are over. The folks who make SketchUp are sharp as tacks, but everybody makes mistakes sometimes.

Drawing (Image) Size

You use these settings to control the physical dimensions of your exported image. If you want to produce a PDF that's a particular size, this is where you do it. You have these options:

- ✔ **Width and Height:** These controls are for telling SketchUp how big you want your exported image to be. Because the proportions of your image will be the same as those of your modeling window, you can enter a width or a height, but not both.

   If you're on a Mac, you can click the Maintain Aspect Ratio button (it looks like a chain). Doing so allows you to enter both width and height, which is useful for exporting to common document sizes like letter and tabloid.

- ✔ **Match View Size:** (Mac only) Sometimes certain features just don't work; it's not even worth explaining what the Match View Size check box is supposed to do. *Always* leave Match View Size deselected — that's all you need to know.

✔ **Full Scale (1:1):** (Windows only) Selecting this check box tells SketchUp to export a drawing that's the same size as your model. You can use this option if you want a full-scale image of something relatively small, like a teapot or a piggy bank. If you end up using Full Scale, remember to follow Steps 1 through 3 in the nearby sidebar, "Setting up for scaled drawings," to make sure that your drawing exports the way you want it to.

Drawing (Image) Scale

Perhaps you're designing a deck for your neighbor's house, and you want to export a scaled PDF file so that the lumberyard can take measurements right off the printed drawing. You want your drawing scale to be ⅛ inch = 1 foot, and this is how you would specify that:

1. **Enter 1" into the In Hidden Line Output (In Image) box.**

2. **Enter 8' into the In SketchUp (In Model) box.**

If you want to export a scaled drawing from SketchUp Pro, you have to set up your model view a certain way. See the nearby sidebar, "Setting up for scaled drawings," for details. If you're not set up properly, the Scale controls are grayed out.

I should probably point out that you can choose to set the Drawing (Image) Size or Scale, but not both. You can't, for instance, tell SketchUp to export a ⅛-inch drawing as an 8½-x-11-inch PDF file.

Setting up for scaled drawings

To export a scaled drawing from SketchUp Pro, you have to set up your model view properly. It's pretty simple — just follow these steps:

1. **Before you go anywhere near the 2D Graphic dialog box, switch from Perspective to Parallel Projection view.**

   You do this by choosing Camera⇨Parallel Projection. In case you're wondering, it's impossible to make a scaled perspective view — drawings just don't work that way.

2. **Switch to one of the standard views.**

   Choose Camera⇨Standard and pick a view from the submenu to see a straight-on top, side, or other view of your model.

3. **Use the Pan and Zoom tools to make sure that you can see everything you want to export.**

   Whatever you do, don't orbit! If you do, you can always repeat Step 2.

Profile Lines (Windows only)

I don't think profiles end up exporting very well to PDF and EPS, so I only use this option if I'm going to be tweaking my image in a vector drawing program like Illustrator or Freehand. You have the following options:

- ✔ **Show Profiles:** Select this check box to export profile lines in your image, assuming that you're using them in your model.

- ✔ **Match Screen Display (Auto Width):** Selecting this check box tells SketchUp to make the exported profiles look as thick, relative to other edges, as they do in your modeling window. If this check box isn't selected, you can type in a line width (thickness).

Section Lines (Windows only)

If you have section cut lines in your model view, these options become available:

- ✔ **Specify Section Line Width:** I'm not entirely sure why this option even exists, because *not* selecting it is the same as choosing Match Screen Display (see the next point). Software's funny sometimes.

- ✔ **Match Screen Display (Auto Width):** Select this check box to export section cut lines that look like they do on your screen. If you have another thickness in mind, don't select this check box; just enter a width right beside it.

Extension Lines (Windows only)

As the only edge-rendering effect (besides profiles) that SketchUp can export to PDF and EPS, extensions are pretty special; this is where you control them. You have the following options:

- ✔ **Extend Edges:** Even if you have edge extensions turned on in your model, you can choose not to export them by deselecting this check box.

- ✔ **Match Screen Display (Auto Length):** Select this check box to let SketchUp make your extensions look like they do on your computer screen. To put in a custom length, type one into the box on the right.

Line Quality (Mac only)

Whereas Windows users get to be very specific if they want to, Mac users only have one point of control over exported line thickness, or weight. For very detailed models, knock the Line Weight setting down to 0.5 or 0.75 points; otherwise, leave it at 1.00 and see whether you like it. This setting depends on the complexity of your model, and on your personal taste.

Other Windows-only controls

You have a couple of other options in this dialog box; both can be very helpful:

✔ **Always Prompt for Hidden Line Options:** Do yourself a favor and select this check box; it never hurts to look over your options before you do an export.

✔ **Map Windows Fonts to PDF Base Fonts:** Even though PDF almost always preserves the original appearance of your image, fonts are tricky. For this reason, the PDF file format comes with a set of "safe" fonts that will work on any computer, anywhere. Choosing this option tells SketchUp to "map" — substitute — PDF-safe fonts for the ones in your SketchUp file. Unless you're really in love with the fonts you originally chose, it's not a bad idea to select this check box. Better safe than sorry.

Coming to terms with DXF and DWG (in 2D)

What can you say about these file formats? When it comes to CAD, DXF and DWG are the 800-pound gorillas; they're also the only 2D CAD formats that SketchUp can export. Just about every CAD program in existence can do *something* with either DXF or DWG, so your bases should be covered, no matter what you're using. Here are some things to keep in mind:

✔ **DWG is more capable than DXF.** Because the former is AutoCAD's *native* (private) file format, and DXF was developed by Autodesk to be an *exchange* (public) file format, DWG has more bells and whistles. For exporting 2D drawings from SketchUp to use in other CAD applications, using DWG usually yields better results.

✔ **Don't be afraid to experiment.** I'll be saying this a couple more times in this chapter. Data export from *any* program is kind of a hit-or-miss endeavor, and you never know what you're going to get until you try. Whenever I'm sending my information from one piece of software to another, I leave myself an extra hour for troubleshooting. I fiddle with settings until things work.

✔ **Don't get confused by all the version numbers.** Which version of DWG or DXF you decide to export depends on what CAD software you're using. In general, it's a good idea to use the most recent version available, which is DWG/DXF 2004 in SketchUp Pro 6. As long as your CAD program isn't older than that, you should be fine. If it is, try exporting an earlier version.

This is a chapter about exporting and not importing, but I thought I'd slip this in anyway: The most recent version of DXF or DWG that SketchUp Pro 6 can *import* is 2004. If you're working in AutoCAD 2007, you'll need to save your file as version 2004 to bring it into SketchUp.

What you see isn't always what you get

With their ability to scale without losing detail and their (relatively) tiny file sizes, vector images seem like a panacea, but unfortunately, there's more to the story. Whereas exported raster images look just like they do on-screen, vector images don't. Most of SketchUp's spiffy graphic effects can't be exported as vector information. Here's a list of what you give up with PDF and EPS:

- Photo textures and transparency on faces
- Edge effects like depth cue, endpoints, and jitter
- NPR (Sketchy Edge) styles
- Shadows and fog
- Background, ground, and sky colors
- Watermarks

Take a gander at Figure 14-2; this is what the DWG/DXF Hidden Line Options dialog box look like, which contains your export options. Blessedly, the options are the same for both DWG and DXF, so the following explanation (the figure and the text), does double duty.

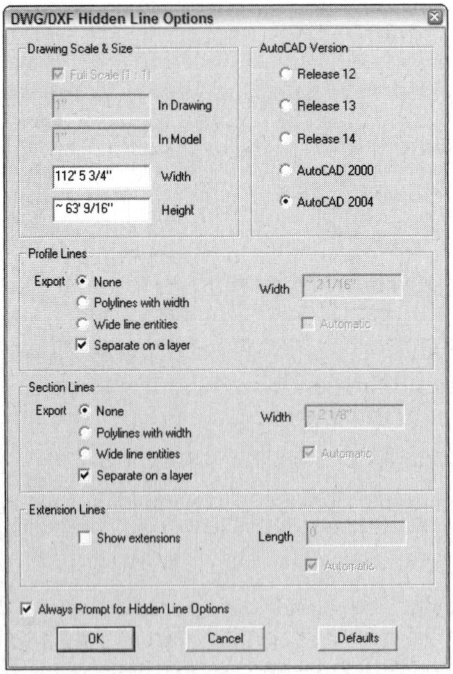

Figure 14-2:
The DWG/
DXF Hidden
Line Options
dialog box.

Drawing Scale & Size

These settings let you control the final physical size of your exported drawing. If you're in Parallel Projection view, you can assign a scale; if you're in Perspective view, scale doesn't apply. You have the following options:

✔ **Full Scale (1:1):** Most people use SketchUp Pro's DXF/DWG Export feature to produce nonperspectival, orthographic views of their models that they can use in their CAD programs. If that's what you're trying to do, you should select this check box; it'll make opening your exported file in another program that much easier.

To export a scaled view of your model, you need to set things up properly in your modeling window before you begin the export process. You need to be in Parallel Projection view, and you have to be using one of the standard views from the Camera menu. I talk all about this in the sidebar "Setting up for scaled drawings," earlier in this chapter. Keep in mind that unless you're set up properly, this option will be grayed out.

✔ **In Drawing and In Model:** If you're exporting a scaled drawing, and you haven't chosen the Full Scale option (see the previous point), you can set your drawing's scale using these controls. If you're not set up to export at scale, these settings won't be available. As an example, for a drawing at ⅟₁₆-inch scale, you would do the following:

　• Enter **1"** in the In Drawing box

　• Enter **16'** in the In Model box

✔ **Width and Height:** You can use these settings to determine the dimensions of your exported drawing, as long as you're not printing to scale.

Profile Lines

This is where you control how profile lines in your SketchUp model view are exported. You have the following options:

✔ **None:** Exports profiles the same thickness as all your other edges.

✔ **Polylines with Width:** Exports profiles as polylines, which are a different kind of line object in CAD programs.

✔ **Wide Line Entities:** Exports profiles as thicker lines.

✔ **Width:** You can enter your own line thickness for exported profiles, or you can select the Automatic check box to tell SketchUp to match what you see in your modeling window.

✔ **Separate on a Layer:** Puts your profiles on a separate layer in the exported file. This is handy for being able to quickly select all your profiles and give them a line weight when you open your exported file in a CAD program.

Section Lines

Section lines occur where section planes create section cuts in your model. Traditionally, these lines are thick, which is why SketchUp gives you special control over how they export. The options in this section are identical to those for exporting section lines in the PDF/EPS Export Options dialog box. Have a look at the section "Section Lines (Windows only)," earlier in this chapter, for information on what everything in this part of the dialog box means.

Extension Lines

Extensions are the little line overruns you can choose to display in the Styles dialog box. If you want to include them in your exported file, you can. Just select the Show Extensions check box, and then either enter a length or select the Automatic check box to let SketchUp try to match how they look on your screen. Just so you know, extension lines are exported as lots and lots of tiny, individual edge segments.

If you're using the Windows version of SketchUp, you have an extra option in this dialog box: Always Prompt for Hidden Line Options. This just means "Do you always want to see this dialog box when you're exporting to DXF or DWG?" Selecting this check box reminds you to look at these settings every time you export, so I'd go ahead and do it.

Peeking at EPIX

You only need to use the EPIX file format if you're using Piranesi, a great artistic rendering program that you can buy. Basically, EPIX is kind of a hybrid, strange-o raster format that keeps track of pixels, just like other raster formats. But it also remembers another piece of information: the *depth* of each pixel in your scene. If you have a tree in the foreground, the pixels that make up that tree "know" they're, say, three feet away. Cool stuff, to be sure.

It slices, it dices. . . .

SketchUp's Section Plane tool is pretty neat. If you don't know much about it, check out Chapter 10. If you have a section cut in your model that you'd like to export to a CAD program, you're in luck; just follow these steps:

1. **Make sure that the section cut you'd like to export is active.**

2. **Choose File⇨Export⇨Section Slice.**

3. **Click the Options button to open the Section Slice Export Options dialog box.**

4. **Set the export options the way you want them, and then click the OK button.**

5. **Click the Export button.**

The most important part of the Export Options dialog box is right at the top: You need to choose either True Section or Screen Projection. Have a look at the following figure to see what happens when you choose each. Chances are, you'll want to pick True Section; it yields the most useful information. The top image is a screen shot of my modeling window in SketchUp. The lower-left image shows what a file export as a true section looks like in AutoCAD. The lower-right image is an AutoCAD view of the same file exported as a screen projection. For a description of the controls in the rest of this dialog box, see the section "Coming to terms with DXF and DWG (in 2D)," earlier in this chapter.

SketchUp modeling window

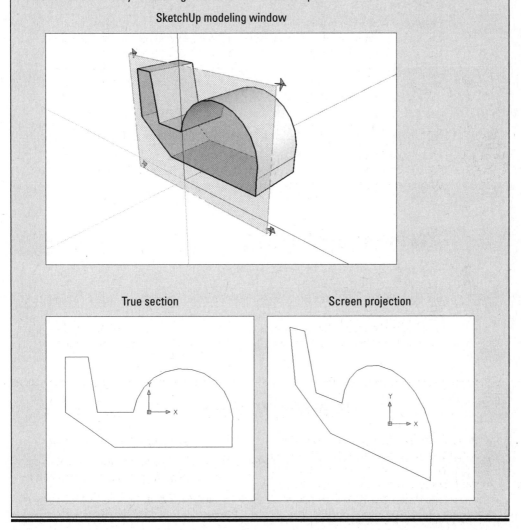

True section

Screen projection

Figure 14-3 shows the Export Epx Options dialog box in living, um, black and white. (Note that Epx and EPIX are the same thing.) Here's what all the doohickeys do:

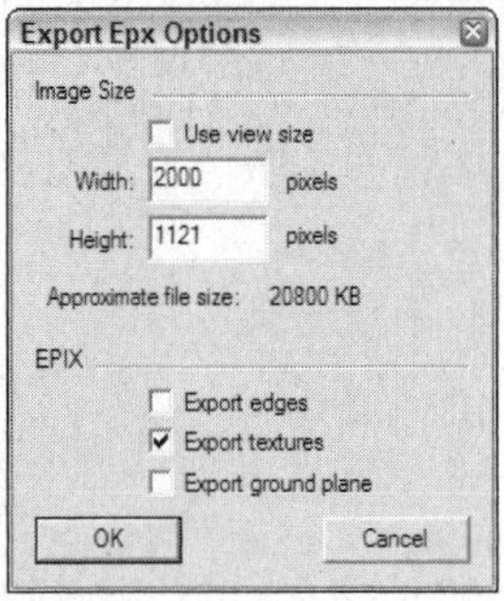

Figure 14-3:
The Export
Epx Options
dialog box.

- ✔ **Image Size:** This part of the Export Epx Options dialog box is just like the Export Options dialog boxes you use for exporting 2D raster images (like JPEG, TIFF, and PNG). I give a full rundown on what everything means, and how to set things up properly, in Chapter 13.

- ✔ **Export Edges check box:** Choose this option to export the edge-rendering settings you currently have applied to your model.

- ✔ **Export Textures check box:** Piranesi can do some pretty terrific things with the textures you apply in SketchUp; select this check box to export those textures as part of your EPIX file. Just a note: You need to have a style applied to your model that displays textures for those textures to be exported properly.

- ✔ **Export Ground Plane check box:** Exports a ground plane in your model view, regardless of whether a ground plane is in your currently applied style.

Exporting 3D Data for Other Software

To be perfectly frank, I've been dreading having to write this part of this book since I started. The process of exporting 3D data from *any* program to *any* program is fraught with equal parts mystery and despair. There are so many pieces of software, with so many versions, and so many different file types that finding a "step-by-step" recipe for success is practically impossible. The simple truth is that 3D file export from SketchUp Pro is about 50 percent knowing where to start and 90 percent trial and error after that.

Gathering your marbles (so that you don't lose them later)

I'll focus on the "knowing where to start" part. First, I provide a list of 3D file types that you can export with SketchUp Pro — I hope you can use it to make some decisions about which format you should use. Second, I lay out a general procedure for how to export a 3D model from SketchUp Pro.

Examining your 3D file format options

"Alphabet soup" is how some people describe the world of file types that exist for 3D models. Here's a bit of information about the 3D file formats that SketchUp Pro 6 can export:

- **DAE (Collada):** Every couple of years or so, a new 3D file format comes out that promises to be "the one." More capable than 3DS (which is getting on in years), Collada is being adopted all over the place by 3D software and gaming companies; Google has even chosen Collada as the file format for the 3D buildings in Google Earth. If you're using a recent version of any of the most popular 3D modeling programs, you might well be able to deal with Collada files; you should try it and find out.

- **DWG/DXF:** "But aren't these 2D formats?" I hear you asking. Yep, they are. But ever since AutoCAD went 3D a few versions ago, its formats have gone 3D, too. These are a pretty safe bet for most of the CAD-type programs out there, but not as safe a bet as 3DS. You need to know that, given the choice between the DXF and DWG, you should usually pick the latter.

- **3DS:** This has become one of the few standard 3D file formats in the industry. When in doubt, export a 3DS file and see whether your program can open it. SketchUp Pro's options for 3DS export are kind of complicated, so be sure to have a look at the section about it later in this chapter.

- **OBJ:** OBJ is probably your best option for sending your data to Maya, which is now owned by Autodesk. While it doesn't offer some important things that 3DS does, it's still a pretty common 3D format.

- **XSI:** The folks at SketchUp built XSI export into SketchUp Pro so that it would be more useful to people who use Softimage, a nifty modeling/rendering/animation program from Canada.

- **VRML:** Though it's getting on in years, plenty of people still use VRML to exchange 3D information.

- **FBX:** The FBX format is used primarily by people in the entertainment industry who use Maya, 3ds Max, or Autodesk VIZ. Depending on what you're doing, you might want to use it instead of DAE (Collada), 3DS, or OBJ; try it and see whether you like it.

- **KMZ:** This is the Google Earth file format. Technically, the ability to export KMZ files isn't restricted to the Pro version of SketchUp; anyone with regular, old free SketchUp can export them, too.

Keep an eye out for plugins

Sometimes, two software companies figure out that they have a large number of users in common, and set out to make it easier for these users to transfer files back and forth between their products. These file-exchanging solutions are usually called *plug-ins,* because they're little pieces of software code that you can download and install (plug in) separately. Some handy plug-ins are available for SketchUp Pro. If you're using ArchiCAD, MicroStation, VectorWorks, Architectural Desktop, or ESRI ArcGIS, you should check out Google's SketchUp Plugins Web page — they're all there, and they're free. It's worth visiting just to see what's available. Go to `www.sketchup.com/downloads` and click the SketchUp Plugins link at the top of the page.

A great place to go for help with exporting 3D files is the SketchUp Pro Forum. The experts who hang out there have "been there and done that"; consulting with them can save you hours of frustration. Check out Chapter 18 for more information on this (and other) forms of further SketchUp edification.

Exporting your 3D model

The process of exporting your 3D data from SketchUp Pro is the same no matter what file format you choose. Follow these steps to export a 3D model from SketchUp Pro:

1. **Choose File⇨Export⇨3D Model.**

   This opens the File Export dialog box.

2. **Choose the file format you'd like to use from the Format drop-down list.**

3. **Choose a name and a location on your computer for your exported image.**

Whenever you're exporting a 3D model from SketchUp, it's a *very good* idea to create a new folder for your exported file. A lot of the file formats that SketchUp Pro exports save the textures in your model as separate files alongside your model. If you don't have everything in a single folder, you can end up with a big mess.

4. **Click the Options button.**

   This opens the Export Options dialog box for the file format you chose in Step 2. Check out the sections in the rest of this chapter for more information about all the controls in the Export Options dialog box — they're anything but intuitive.

5. **Adjust the settings in the Options dialog box, and then click the OK button.**

   This closes the Export Options dialog box.

6. **Click the Export button to export your 3D model file.**

Getting a handle on OBJ, FBX, XSI, and DAE (Collada)

I am pleased to report that the Export Options dialog boxes for each of the aforementioned file formats are almost identical, even if the file formats themselves aren't — this means that I'm lumping them together into one section. Here are a few reminders about using OBJ, FBX, XSI, and DAE (Collada):

✔ **Try using Collada first.** Because it's relatively new, not all 3D programs support it yet, but you never know — your software might.

✔ **If Collada doesn't work, use OBJ for Maya, XSI for Softimage, and FBX if someone you respect tells you to.** I'm sorry I can't be more specific, but the sheer number of programs and versions out there means that it's impossible to give hard-and-fast rules.

✔ **Experiment.** Leave yourself some time to try exporting your model in more than one format. Then open each one in your other piece of software and see what works best.

Figure 14-4 shows the Export Options dialog boxes for all four file formats. Here's some help with what everything does:

✔ **Export Only Current Selection:** Tells SketchUp Pro to only export the geometry you currently have selected in your model.

✔ **Triangulate All Faces:** Some programs don't support faces with cutouts in them, so selecting this check box carves things into triangles so that you don't end up with any holes. Experimentation will tell you whether you need to use this; don't choose this option if you don't have to.

✔ **Export Two-Sided Faces:** SketchUp's faces are two-sided, but not all 3D programs' faces are. Choose this option if you've spent a lot of time *texture-mapping* (painting with textures) your model in SketchUp, and you want it to look the same in the program you're sending it to. If you plan to use another piece of software to add textures to your model, don't select this check box.

✔ **Export Edges:** SketchUp models *must* include edges and faces, but some programs' models only support the latter. Select this check box if you want to export the edges in your model; leave it deselected if you don't. Programs that don't support edges (and that includes most of them) will leave them out, anyway. The Export Edges option isn't available for FBX files.

✔ **Export Texture Maps:** Includes the textures you used in your SketchUp model in the exported file. If you plan to "paint" your model in another program, deselect this check box.

✔ **Generate Cameras from Pages (Scenes):** The Collada file format can store information about different views of your model. Selecting this check box exports each of your scenes (if you have any) as a separate camera object. Note that this option doesn't exist for OBJ, FBX, or XSI.

✔ **Swap YZ Coordinates (Y Is Up):** If your model ends up oriented the wrong way when you open it in another piece of software, try selecting this check box and exporting it again. Some programs set up their axes differently. This option isn't available for Collada.

✔ **Units:** Leave this option on Model Units unless something is wrong when you open your model in another program. If it is, make an adjustment and export again.

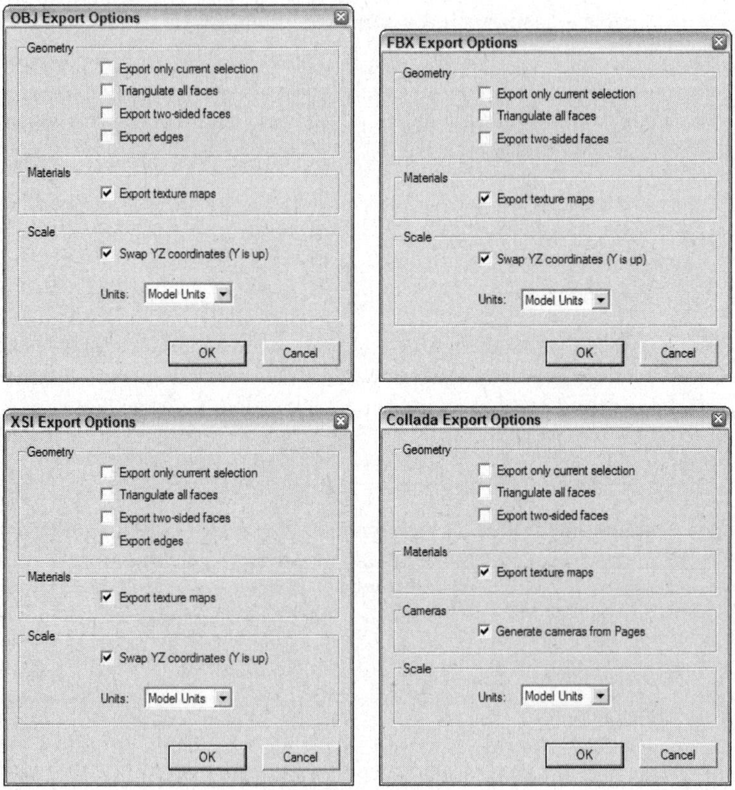

Figure 14-4:
The Export Options dialog boxes for OBJ, FBX, XSI, and DAE (Collada).

Wrapping your head around 3DS

Ah, 3DS — the Old Faithful of 3D modeling file formats. 3DS is almost a shoo-in to work with just about any other piece of 3D software you're using, which is good. What's bad is that this flexibility comes at (what I perceive to be) a terrible price: a seemingly infinite number of options. Here are some things you should know about the 3DS file format:

✔ **You'll lose your layers.** 3DS doesn't support 'em, so you might be better off exporting a DWG file (if your other software can open it and if you aren't using textures). Another option is to use the Color by Layers option, which I describe in a moment.

✔ **You'll lose your edges, too.** You can always choose Export Stand Alone Edges, but few people recommend doing that.

✔ **Only visible faces get exported.** None of your hidden faces, or faces on hidden layers, will go along for the 3DS ride, so make sure that you can see everything you want to export before you reach for the File menu.

✔ **Make sure that you paint the correct side of your faces.** Faces (or the equivalent) in 3DS are one-sided, so only materials you apply to the front side of your faces in SketchUp will end up getting exported. If you have materials on both sides of your faces, you might consider choosing the Export Two-Sided Faces option, described later in this section.

Figure 14-5 shows the 3DS Export Options dialog box in all its complicated glory. Your options are as follows:

✔ **Export:** You have four choices here:

- **Full Hierarchy:** This option tells the 3DS exporter to make separate *meshes* (surfaces made out of triangles) for each "chunk" of geometry in your SketchUp model. Chunks are things like groups, components, and groupings of connected faces.

- **By Layer:** This option tells the exporter to create separate meshes based on two things: chunks of geometry and what layer things are on. If a bunch of faces are connected and they're on the same layer, they get exported as a single mesh.

- **By Material:** When you choose this option, you get a separate mesh for each grouping of connected geometry that shares the same material.

- **Single Object:** Choosing this option exports all your geometry as one, big 3DS mesh.

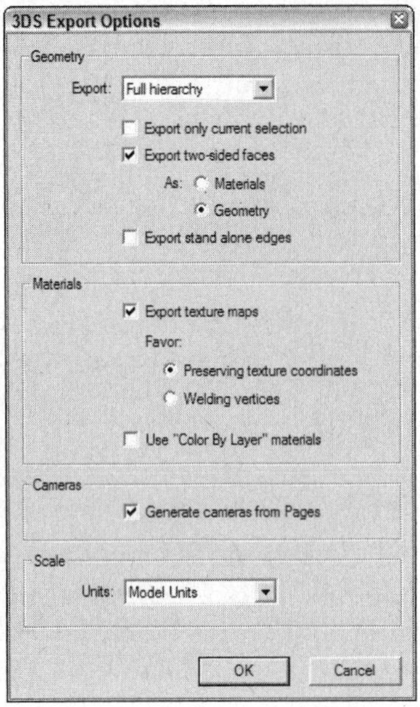

Figure 14-5:
The 3DS
Export
Options
dialog box.
Better get
out your hip
waders. . . .

3DS Export Options

Geometry
Export: Full hierarchy
☐ Export only current selection
☑ Export two-sided faces
As: ○ Materials
● Geometry
☐ Export stand alone edges

Materials
☑ Export texture maps
Favor:
● Preserving texture coordinates
○ Welding vertices
☐ Use "Color By Layer" materials

Cameras
☑ Generate cameras from Pages

Scale
Units: Model Units

OK   Cancel

✔ **Export Only Current Selection:** Only exports the geometry you've selected in your SketchUp model.

✔ **Export Two-Sided Faces:** Selecting this check box exports two faces (back to back) for every face you have in your SketchUp model. Because 3DS supports only single-sided faces, this is necessary to preserve the appearance of your textures in your exported model. If you don't care about preserving your SketchUp textures, or if you didn't apply any in the first place, don't bother choosing this option:

   • **As Materials:** Choose this option to export your back-side materials as 3DS materials without corresponding geometry.

   • **As Geometry:** Choose this option to export your extra set of faces as actual geometry. Folks I know who do this a lot recommend that you choose this option if you're wondering what to do.

✔ **Export Stand Alone Edges:** 3DS doesn't support edges the way SketchUp does — you don't have a good way to export edges as "lines" to 3DS. When you select this check box, the exporter substitutes a long, thin rectangle for every edge in your model. The appearance is (sort of) the same, but this can cause major problems in your file. I don't recommend selecting this check box. If you really need to be able to see your edges, you should probably try another export format altogether.

✔ **Export Texture Maps:** If you have photo textures in your model (this includes the photo textures from the Materials dialog box), you might want to include them in your exported model file. 3DS handles these textures very differently than SketchUp does, so you have to decide on an export method:

   • **Favor Preserving Texture Coordinates:** Choose this option if you've spent a lot of time getting the texture "maps" right in your SketchUp model.

   • **Favor Welding Vertices:** Choose this option if it's more important that your geometry export as accurately as possible. In some cases, your textures won't look right, but your geometry will be correctly *welded* (stuck together) and smoothed.

✔ **Use "Color by Layer" Materials:** Because the 3DS file format doesn't support layers, you can choose to export your model with different colors assigned to the faces on each layer in SketchUp.

✔ **Generate Cameras from Pages (Scenes):** Select this check box to export your file with a different camera position saved for each scene in your SketchUp file. An extra scene (called Default Scene) is also exported to reflect your current model view.

✔ **Units:** If you leave this set to Model Units, most other 3D programs will understand what you mean — your geometry will appear the right size when you open your exported 3DS file. In some cases, it won't, and the best thing to do is to manually choose the units that you'll be using in the other program. Sometimes this doesn't work either, and you'll just have to fiddle around until something works. Hooray for 3DS!

Dealing with VRML

The VRML file format is pronounced *vermal,* which ties it with Collada for the title of Hardest Format to Use in Everyday Conversation without Giving Away the Fact That You're Nerdy Enough to Know What VRML and Collada Mean. Virtual Reality Modeling Language is used by a large number of people around the world. There are newer, arguably better, formats out there, but VRML's been around long enough that it's tightly integrated into lots of professional workflows.

Figure 14-6 shows the VRML Export Options dialog box; what follows is some help with all the controls:

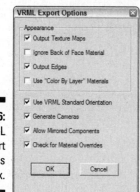

Figure 14-6:
The VRML
Export
Options
dialog box.

✔ **Output Texture Maps:** If you don't select this check box, you'll get colors instead of textures in your exported VRML file.

✔ **Ignore Back of Face Material:** Go ahead and select this check box unless your faces have different materials painted on either sides of them.

✔ **Output Edges:** VRML supports edges, so select this check box if you want to export your edges (along with your faces) as part of your VRML file.

✔ **Use "Color by Layer" Materials:** VRML doesn't do layers, so if your layers are important to you, you should consider selecting this check box. All the faces in your exported model will be painted with the colors in the Layers dialog box (Chapter 5 has more information on assigning colors to layers).

✔ **Use VRML Standard Orientation:** You should select this check box to convert your model's "up" axis to match VRML's "up" axis.

✔ **Generate Cameras:** If you have scenes in your SketchUp model, you might want to select this check box. It tells the exporter to create a separate camera view for every one of your scenes, and an extra one for your current view.

✔ **Allow Mirrored Components:** If you have components in your model whose instances you've *mirrored* (flipped over), you should select this check box. Because this is a standard technique for building symmetrical things like vehicles (as I talk about in Chapter 6), this might apply to your model.

✔ **Check for Material Overrides:** This option makes sure that the materials in your exported model end up looking like they do in your SketchUp model.

Handling DWG and DXF (in 3D)

As 3D file formats go, these two are a little anemic. You should use them if you need to export your 3D data to AutoCAD, but for other programs, you're probably better off getting the right plug-in (see the sidebar "Keep an eye out for plugins," earlier in this chapter). Here are a couple of tidbits about DXF and DWG:

- ✔ **Say goodbye to materials.** Your materials won't export to DXF/DWG, so pick another format if they're important to you.

- ✔ **We'll always have layers.** The one great thing about exporting to DXF/DWG is that you get to keep your layers.

- ✔ **Go with DWG.** If you can, pick DWG instead of DXF; it's more robust, which means that it saves more of your data.

Figure 14-7 is a screen shot of the AutoCAD Export Options dialog box; it's an oasis of blissful simplicity compared to the one for 3DS. In fact, it's so self-explanatory that I won't bother going through the options one at a time. Just select the kinds of things you want to export, and then click the OK button. And just so you know, "Construction Geometry" means Guides; that's what Guides used to be called.

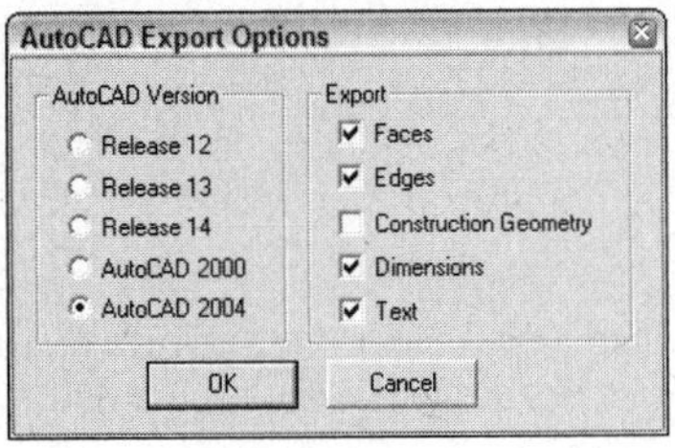

Figure 14-7:
The AutoCAD Export Options dialog box.

AutoCAD Export Options

AutoCAD Version
- ○ Release 12
- ○ Release 13
- ○ Release 14
- ○ AutoCAD 2000
- ● AutoCAD 2004

Export
- ☑ Faces
- ☑ Edges
- ☐ Construction Geometry
- ☑ Dimensions
- ☑ Text

OK   Cancel

Chapter 15

Creating Presentation Documents with LayOut

- -

- -

People who design things in 3D have to present their ideas to other people, and most of the time, they have to present in a 2D format. Creating these presentations almost always involves the use of layout or illustration software like InDesign, Illustrator, or QuarkXPress; these programs are great, but they can be expensive and tricky to get the hang of, especially if you're not a graphic designer.

If you're lucky enough to have the Pro version of Google SketchUp 6, you have access to a whole separate piece of software called Google SketchUp LayOut, or LayOut for short.

LayOut is a program that lets you create documents for presenting your 3D SketchUp models, both on paper and on-screen. LayOut was designed to be easy to use, quick to learn, and tightly integrated with SketchUp. The people who built it want you to use LayOut to create all your design presentations; here are some examples of what you can make:

- ✔ Information sheets
- ✔ Storyboards
- ✔ Design packs
- ✔ Presentation boards and posters
- ✔ Banners
- ✔ On-screen, PowerPoint-style slide shows

LayOut gives you the tools to create cover pages, title blocks, callouts, and symbols — whatever you need to accompany views of your model. You can create presentations that are just about any physical size, and you can export them as PDF files to send to other people. Best of all, when your design changes in SketchUp, you can easily update your model views in LayOut to reflect the changes. If you make your living designing and presenting ideas in 3D, LayOut can save you boatloads of time.

In this chapter, I give a pretty high-level overview of what you can do with LayOut — there's a lot of information to convey, after all. I start out with a couple of pages about the different things you can use LayOut to accomplish. I follow that up with a quick tour of the LayOut user interface, explaining where everything is and what it's supposed to do. Next, I take you through the process of creating a simple presentation drawing set from one of your SketchUp models — not exhaustively by any means, but it should be enough to see you through a tight deadline.

Getting Your Bearings

Even though LayOut comes with SketchUp Pro, it's not just a SketchUp feature — LayOut is a full-fledged, gets-its-own-icon program. As such, LayOut has its own menus, tools, dialog boxes, and Drawing Window. A couple of versions from now, LayOut will probably have its own *For Dummies* book. (Maybe I'll even get to write it!)

Even though LayOut's user interface is pretty standard, I want to give you a quick overview of the different elements. Knowing that it's a lot like other software you've used (including SketchUp) should help you come up to speed quickly. Figure 15-1 shows the LayOut user interface. The following sections explain the various parts in more detail.

Some menu bar minutiae

Just like almost every other piece of software in the universe, LayOut has a menu bar. And just like SketchUp, you can use LayOut's menu bar to access the vast majority of its tools, commands, settings, and dialog boxes. Here's a brief description of each of LayOut's nine menus:

- ✔ **File:** No big surprises here — you use the items in the File menu to create new LayOut files, save and adjust settings for the document you're working on, and insert SketchUp and other graphics files.

- ✔ **Edit:** You use the items in the Edit menu to copy and paste, work with clipping masks (LayOut's version of cropping), and control object grouping.

In the Windows version of LayOut, the Edit menu includes Preferences, which is where you can do some things to customize LayOut.

✔ **View:** Besides standard stuff like controls for zooming, the most interesting item here is Full Screen, which lets you view your LayOut as a PowerPoint-style slide presentation.

✔ **Text:** Fifty bonus points if you can figure out what the items in the Text menu are for — there's nothing out of the ordinary here.

✔ **Arrange:** Because LayOut documents are basically well-organized collections of images, inserted SketchUp models, text, and callouts, you need to be able to control everything's place on the page. In the Arrange menu, you find commands for controlling the horizontal, vertical, and stacking-order position of every element in your document, as well as controls for telling LayOut what snap settings to use.

Stacking order refers to the fact that all elements on the same layer in your document are either in front of or behind other elements. When one thing is overlapping another, their stacking order determines which one you see and which one is hidden.

Snap settings help you position elements on your page by making it easier to line things up with a grid or with other elements. Depending on what you're trying to do, you might choose to work with both kinds of snap settings, just one, or none at all; I usually switch between them while I'm working.

✔ **Tools:** Here's where you'll find all of LayOut's tools (big surprise); there are a lot more of them than you think. Luckily, most are pretty specialized, so you don't need to know them all before you get started.

✔ **Pages:** Given the complexity of most of the software we all have to use, it's almost adorable how few items live in the Pages menu. Your LayOut presentation can have many pages, and here's where you add, delete, duplicate, and move among them.

✔ **Window:** In the Window menu, you find links to all of LayOut's dialog boxes; take a look at the next section in this chapter for a rundown on all of them.

✔ **Help:** Just like SketchUp, the Help menu should be the first and last place you go when you're stuck. It's also a great place to look for resources (besides this book) that can help you get started; I highly recommend watching the video tutorials — they're great.

✔ **LayOut (Mac only):** The Mac version of LayOut includes a LayOut menu, which is standard operating procedure for Mac applications. The important thing in this menu is Preferences, which lets you set up the program the way you want it.

Toolbar

Menu bar   Drawing window   Dialog boxes

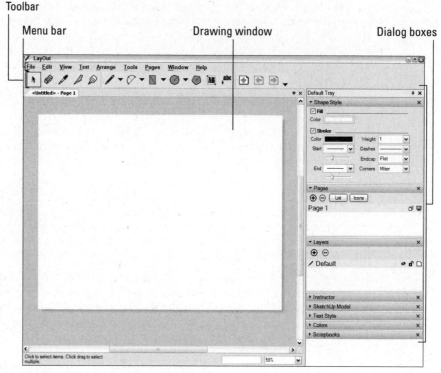

Figure 15-1:
The LayOut
user
interface.

A dialog box discourse

You can find most of LayOut's knobs and switches in its eight dialog boxes. In Windows, most of LayOut's dialog boxes are contained in a "tray" that appears on the right side of your screen by default. On the Mac, your dialog boxes float around willy-nilly, but you can "snap" them together if you want.

Here's a one-minute description of each:

> ✔ **Colors:** Just about all your LayOut documents will use color in some way, so you'll need this dialog box most of the time. The nice thing about Color is that it appears when you need it; clicking any color well in LayOut pops it open (if it wasn't already open).
>
> To hide a dialog box without closing it, click its title bar once to minimize it. Click again to see the whole thing.
>
> ✔ **Shape Style:** A lot of the graphic elements in your presentation can have color fills and strokes (outlines). The Shape Style dialog box is where you control the appearance of those fills and strokes. Check out the options in the Start and End drop-down menus — you won't find callout styles like these in most other layout programs.

✔ **SketchUp Model:** The greatest thing about LayOut (at least with respect to other software like it) is its ability to include 2D views of your SketchUp models. In the SketchUp Model dialog box, you can control all sorts of things about the way your "placed" SketchUp model looks, including camera views, scenes, styles, shadows, and fog. For folks who spend a lot of time laying out presentation drawings that include SketchUp models, the SketchUp Model dialog box is a godsend.

✔ **Text Style:** If you've ever used another piece of page layout or illustration software, you should be pretty familiar with what the Text Style dialog box lets you do. You use it to control the font, size, style, color, and alignment of text in your document.

✔ **Pages:** You use the Pages dialog box to manage the pages in your document. You can add, delete, and rearrange them to your heart's content. The List and Icon buttons at the top let you toggle between views of your pages; I prefer to use the former and give my pages meaningful names as I work. The little icons on the right control visibility for shared layers and full-screen presentations.

Shared layers are somewhat unique to LayOut; they let you automatically place elements on more than one page. For more detail, see the section "Simplifying Layout with Layers and Master Layers," later in this chapter.

✔ **Layers:** You can have multiple layers of content in every LayOut document you create.

I like to work with at least four layers, organizing content on each as follows:

- Elements that should appear in the same place on almost every page, like logos and project titles

- Things that appear in the same place on most pages, but that change from page to page, like numbers and page titles

- Content (like images and SketchUp model views) that only appears on a single page

- Unused stuff that I'm not sure I want, but that I don't want to delete

Use the Layers dialog box to add, delete, and rearrange layers in your document. The icons on the right let you hide (and show), lock, and share individual layers.

✔ **Scrapbooks:** This one's a little trickier to explain; scrapbooks are unique to LayOut, so you probably haven't worked with anything like them before. Scrapbooks are LayOut files that live in a special folder on your computer system. They contain colors, text styles, and graphic elements (like scale cars, trees, and people) that you might need to use in more than one of your LayOut documents. To use something you see in a scrapbook, just click it, and then click again in your drawing window to "stamp" it in (if it's a graphic element), or to apply something (if it's a color or a text style).

You can create your own scrapbooks if you want. Just choose File⇨Save as Scrapbook from the menu bar to save any LayOut file as a scrapbook that will show up in your Scrapbooks dialog box.

✔ **Instructor:** The Instructor dialog box works just like it does in SketchUp; it shows information on whichever tool you happen to be using. If you're just starting out with LayOut, make sure that this dialog box is open.

Setting up LayOut preferences

In LayOut, as in SketchUp, you have two kinds of preferences to worry about: those that apply to *every* LayOut document you work on and those that only apply to the document you happen to be working on at the moment. Settings for the former are made in the Preferences dialog box; controls for the latter reside in Document Setup. The following sections describe what I mean.

Preferences

The LayOut Preferences dialog box is made up of six panels. You open it by choosing Edit⇨Preferences in Windows or LayOut⇨Preferences on the Mac. Here's what you'll find on each panel:

✔ **Applications:** Tell LayOut what programs you want to use to edit image and text files when you right-click them (in LayOut) and choose Open with Image (or Text) Editor from the context menu.

✔ **Backup:** Work smart by letting LayOut auto-save and create automatic backups of your file. Here's where you tell it where and how often to do so.

✔ **Folders:** Let LayOut know where to look for the templates and scrapbooks on your computer. Templates show up when you start LayOut or open a new document; scrapbooks appear in the Scrapbook dialog box.

✔ **Scales:** This is a list of scales you can choose from for a SketchUp model view you've placed in your LayOut document. If you want to use a certain drawing scale and it doesn't show up in the Scales pane of the SketchUp Model dialog box, feel free to add it here. This is *not* the drawing scale for the document you're currently working on, so don't worry about that.

✔ **Shortcuts:** Just like SketchUp, you use this panel to define a keyboard shortcut for any tool or command in LayOut.

✔ **Startup:** In this panel, tell LayOut how to behave every time you launch it.

Document Setup

The Document Setup dialog box includes five panels. You open it by choosing File⇨Document Setup in the menu bar. Here's the skinny on each panel:

✔ **General:** Feel free to enter information about yourself and your document; this might be important if you're working on a team.

✔ **Grid:** Nothing beats a grid for helping to line up elements in your presentations. Use the options in this panel to control the visibility and size of the grid in your document, if you want one. For Major Grid, type in an interval for the darker grid lines. For Minor Grid, enter the number of divisions between dark lines you'd like to have. For ¼-inch squares, you would enter 1 inch for the former and 4 for the latter.

✔ **Paper:** Here's where you tell LayOut the size and color of the sheet of paper you'd like to use for your document. You can also control the width of your margins and the resolution at which you'd like your SketchUp model views to print. See the section "Creating a new, blank document," later in this chapter, for a list of recommended resolutions.

✔ **References:** When you insert a SketchUp model or an image in your LayOut document, LayOut creates a file reference that keeps track of where it came from.

If you edit the original file (which you probably will), this panel lets you know whether LayOut is showing the most currently saved version. For people who go back and forth between design and presentation documents a lot (sound familiar?), the References panel is a gift from the heavens.

✔ **Units:** Depending on where you live and work, you might use a different system of measurement. Use the Units panel to pick the right one for your workflow.

Tooling around

LayOut has lots of tools, but as with most software, you spend most of your time with only a handful of them. You can find the complete list in the Tools menu, but it's easier to get at them on the toolbar. This strip, across the top of your Drawing Window, includes icons for the most commonly used tools (and commands), but you can easily add others if you want to. Here's a bullet point on each of the tools in the LayOut toolbar's default set. (See Figure 15-2, which shows the toolbar for the Windows version of LayOut.)

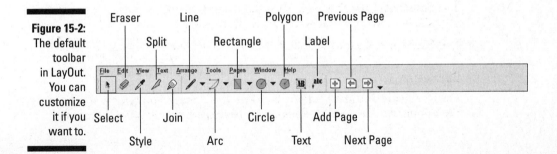

Figure 15-2: The default toolbar in LayOut. You can customize it if you want to.

✔ **Select:** Select, rotate, move, copy, and scale elements in your document. Double-click to edit text and SketchUp model views.

✔ **Eraser:** Click or drag over any unlocked elements to erase them.

✔ **Style:** Click any element to *sample* (soak up) its fill, stroke, and other attributes. Doing so turns the tool into the Bucket, which you use to apply those attributes to other elements in your document by clicking them.

✔ **Split:** Cut one line segment (whether curved or straight) into two by clicking where you want the split to occur. Turning Object Snap on (in the Arrange menu) is very helpful for splitting shapes at their corners.

✔ **Join:** Turn two line segments (curved or straight) into a single one by clicking each in turn. Both are highlighted blue when they're joined.

✔ **Line:** Draw a straight line by clicking to define start points and end-points. Press Esc to stop drawing a line.

✔ **Arc:** Draw an arc by clicking once to define the arc's center point, again to start the arc (which defines its radius), and a third time to end the arc. You can draw an arc in four ways; check out the Tools menu to see all of them.

✔ **Rectangle:** Draw a rectangle by clicking to define opposite corners.

✔ **Circle:** Draw a circle by clicking once to define a center and again to define a radius.

✔ **Polygon:** Draw polygons by first entering a side count and then using your mouse. Select the Polygon tool, type the number of sides followed by the letter *s* (*8s* for an octagon), and then press Enter. Now click once with your mouse to define a center point and again to draw the shape. Whew.

✔ **Text:** Draw an empty text box into which you can enter text. If you need to edit text you've already typed, double-click it with the Select tool or the Text tool.

✔ **Label:** Draw a text label with a leader line by clicking to define the end of the line (where it's pointing), clicking again to define the beginning, and then typing in some text.

✔ **Add Page:** Add a page after the one you're on.

✔ **Previous Page:** View the previous page in your document.

✔ **Next Page:** View the next page in your document.

Adding more tool icons to your toolbar is easy; just right-click the toolbar and choose Customize to bring up the Customize dialog box. Now drag tool icons into your toolbar. (If you're on Windows, you'll have to select the Command tab first.)

Switching to LayOut from similar software

If you're used to using other page-layout or illustration software, some things about LayOut are useful to know when you're just getting started. The folks who designed LayOut did things a little differently on purpose, hoping to do for page layout in 2007 what they did for 3D design seven years earlier — make it easier for motivated people with no experience to produce good work, quickly.

Here, I point out the five things you should keep in mind when you're exploring LayOut:

✔ LayOut includes templates that help you get up and running in no time. See the nearby section "Starting out with templates" for details.

✔ You can insert models from SketchUp, skipping the process of exporting your model as an image file. Importing has the added benefit of helping you automatically update model views in your presentation. See the

section "Bringing In Everything You Need," later in this chapter, for details.

✔ The Layers feature in LayOut is a powerful tool for organizing your content. In particular, you can place content that appears on more than one of your pages on a master layer, so you only have to position it once. The section "Simplifying Layout with Layers and Master Layers," later in this chapter, outlines just what you need to know.

✔ In LayOut, you have enormous flexibility to crop images, including model views, with ease using clipping masks. The section "Cropping with clipping masks," later in this chapter, explains how in four easy steps.

✔ When your presentation is ready to go, LayOut enables you to set up digital slide shows in full-screen mode, as well as to create printouts and PDF files.

Getting Set Up

Every time you launch LayOut, and every time you choose File⇨New, you're presented with a dialog box that asks you how you want to start out. (See Figure 15-3.)

The theory is that when you open most programs, you usually want to do one of two things:

✔ **Start a new document:** The New tab at the top of the dialog box presents you with a list of templates that come preloaded in LayOut. There's nothing special about these templates — they're just ready-made LayOut files you can use as a starting point for your presentation. Expand the items in the list on the left to see the available templates broken down by category.

✔ **Open a document you've already started:** Click the Recent tab at the top of the dialog box to show a list of LayOut files you've worked on most recently. Select one and click Open (Choose, on a Mac) to open it. To open an existing document that doesn't appear in the Recent list, click the Open an Existing File button to pop up the Open dialog box.

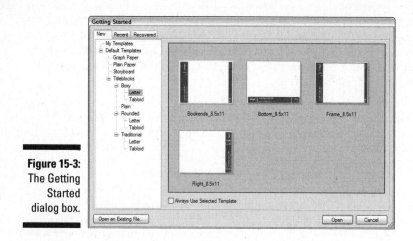

Figure 15-3:
The Getting
Started
dialog box.

Sometimes you see a third tab in your Getting Started dialog box: Recovered. If LayOut has crashed on you, or if you ever had any LayOut files that weren't saved when things went awry, the document you were working on should show up in the Recovered tab. It's still a good idea to save often, though.

Starting out with templates

More often than not, you can find a template to use as a starting point for your presentation. Browse the list, select one you like, and click Open (Choose, on a Mac) to begin working with a template. You can also create a custom template, as I explain in a moment. In my experience, templates are the quickest way to get up and running with a new LayOut project.

Here are a few things you should know about templates (while I'm on the subject); Figure 15-4 points them out in a screen shot:

✔ **Pay attention to the layers.** Many of the templates that come with LayOut have multiple layers, and some of these layers are locked by default. They're locked so that you can't accidentally move things around, but you can always unlock them if you need to. In the Layers dialog box, click the lock icon to lock or unlock a layer; knowing you need to unlock a layer is especially handy when you want to swap in your logo instead of using the generic "Logo Design" that comes preinstalled.

✔ **Have a look at the pages.** Most of the more interesting templates include at least two pages; the first one's a cover page. Don't forget to look at the all the pages when you're working with a template.

✔ **Double-click to edit text.** One of the really neat things about LayOut is that you can edit text on locked layers. Using the Select tool, just double-click any text you want to edit (and in some templates, you'll want to edit all the text), type in new text, and then click once somewhere else to finish the edit.

✔ **Feel free to change colors.** LayOut's templates are designed so that you can easily change the overall color scheme. Just unlock all the layers, open the Shape Styles dialog box, and go nuts. For more information about changing colors, see the section "Drawing something from scratch," later in this chapter.

Most of the design presentations that you (or your firm) put together probably look a lot alike — after all, they're part of your brand identity. If the presentation documents you make are all variations on a couple of themes, why not build your own templates and use them every time you need to start a new project? You can set things up so that your templates appear in the Getting Started dialog box, making it easier to build consistent presentations, quicker.

You can use whatever colors you want

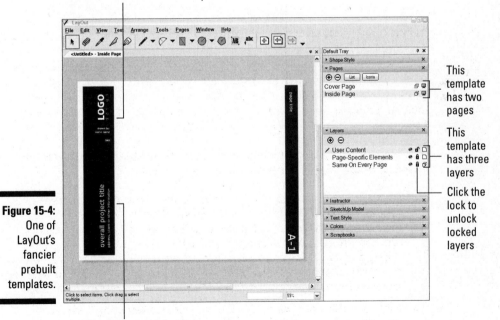

Figure 15-4: One of LayOut's fancier prebuilt templates.

This template has two pages

This template has three layers

Click the lock to unlock locked layers

Double-click on text to edit it

Follow these steps to turn any LayOut file into a template:

1. **Build a LayOut file that includes all the elements you want.**

   These elements might include a title block, a logo, a page number, and a cover page.

   Make sure that you're viewing the page you want to use as the thumbnail preview in the template list, before you move on to Step 2.

2. **Choose File⇨Save as Template.**

   The Save as Template dialog box opens.

3. **Type a name for your template.**

4. **Choose a location for your new template.**

   In the list at the bottom of the dialog box, click the folder (they're all folders) in which you want to include the template you're adding.

5. **Click OK. On a Mac, click Save.**

   The next time the Getting Started dialog box appears, your new template will be in it.

Creating a new, blank document

If you decide not to start with one of LayOut's handy-dandy templates, you'll need to set up a new document from scratch.

Follow these steps to create a fresh, new LayOut document:

1. **Launch LayOut.**

   Keep in mind that LayOut and SketchUp are separate software programs, so you need to launch them individually. If you've already launched LayOut, choose File⇨New to open the Getting Started dialog box.

2. **In the Getting Started dialog box, click the New tab.**

   This shows a list of available templates on the left, with thumbnail previews of each template on the right.

3. **Click My Templates (All on the Mac) in the list on the left.**

4. **Select a Plain Paper template on the right and click Open (Choose, on a Mac).**

   The plain paper templates are completely white.

   When a new, blank document that you can set up however you like appears, you then need to set up your new document the way you want it.

5. **Choose File⇨Document Setup.**

   This opens the Document Setup dialog box.

6. **Click Units in the panel list on the left, and select the type of measurement units you prefer to use, as shown in Figure 15-5.**

   The Units panel lets you choose which units you'd like to use.

7. **Click Paper in the list on the left, and set your paper size and color.**

   If you know you'll be printing on paper that isn't white, you can simulate the color by choosing one here. I don't recommend trying to print out a paper color; most printers don't print *full bleed* (right to the edges), so the effect really isn't that great.

8. **Set up some margins, if you want to.**

   Margins are useful if you know how close to the edge of your paper you can print.

9. **Set the rendering resolution according to your document size.**

   Basically, the rendering resolution you choose depends on the physical size of your printed document. As long as your paper size isn't any bigger than 11 x 17 inches, you should probably choose 300 dpi. For bigger presentations (like boards and posters), use a setting of 100 or 150 dpi. The goal is to limit the size of the file (in megabytes) that gets sent to your printer — if it's too big, things can get ugly. For more information on image resolution, have a look at Chapter 13.

10. **Click Grid in the list of panels on the left, and set up your grid options the way you want them.**

    Now you're in the Grid panel. For more information about this section of the Document Setup dialog box, see the section "Getting Your Bearings," earlier in this chapter.

11. **Click the Close button to close the Document Setup dialog box.**

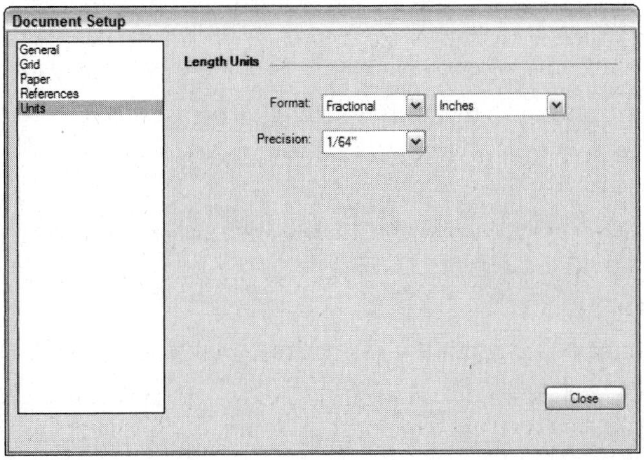

Figure 15-5:
The Units panel in the Document Setup dialog box.

Adding pages to your document

Follow these steps to add a few blank pages to your document:

1. **If your Pages dialog box isn't already open, choose Window⇨Pages to open it.**

2. **Choose Pages⇨Add.**

   This adds a page to your document. You can also add pages by clicking the little button that looks like a plus sign (in the upper-left corner of the Pages dialog box). Add as many pages as you want.

3. **In the Pages dialog box, double-click the name of your new page, and then type in a name for it.**

   Press Enter when you're done. Repeat to give all your pages meaningful names.

Moving around your document

You move around on the pages in your document just like you do in SketchUp — except in 2D instead of 3D. Here's how to move around:

✔ **Panning:** Hold down your scroll wheel button while moving your mouse around to slide your page around in your Document Window. This is called *panning*.

✔ **Zooming:** Roll your scroll wheel back and forth to zoom in and out on your page. To fill your Document Window with the page you're viewing, choose Scale to Fit (Zoom to Fit on the Mac) from the Zoom drop-down list in your window's lower-right corner.

✔ **Moving from page to page:** Click the Next Page and the Previous Page buttons on your toolbar to move among the pages in your document. You can also click your pages' names in the Pages dialog box.

Simplifying Layout with Layers and Master Layers

You use layers to create multipage documents with elements that are consistent from page to page. You can have two different kinds of layers in LayOut:

✔ **Unshared:** Unshared layers are like layers in every other software program. Any element (text, graphic, or otherwise) that you put on an unshared layer exists only on one page: the page you're on when you put the element on the layer.

✔ **Shared (Master Layers):** LayOut introduces the notion of *master layers;* anything you put on a master layer appears on every page of your document, as long as those pages are set up to show master layers.

It's all a little confusing at the beginning, so here are a few quick tips about how you organize content on layers — including master layers — as you create presentations in LayOut:

✔ **You can make an element (like a logo) appear in the same spot on more than one page by putting it on a master layer.** For example, the logo and the project title need to appear in the same spot on every page; I put these two elements on the master layer called "On Every Page." In Figure 15-6, note how the logo and project title appear in exactly the same place in the pages labeled B and C.

✔ **Put content that appears on only one page on an unshared layer.** Again, in the pages labeled B and C, the image boxes and page titles are different on each page, so I put them on the unshared layer called "Unique."

✔ **You can make any layer a master layer by clicking the Sharing icon to the right of its name in the Layers dialog box. (See Figure 15-7.)**

✔ **You decide which pages should display master layers by toggling the Sharing icon to the right of their names in the Pages dialog box.** For example, I don't want the logo and the project title to be on the cover page (labeled A in Figure 15-6). I toggle the Show Master Layers icon beside the cover page to Off, as shown in Figure 15-7.

When you're manipulating elements on individual layers in LayOut, keep these points in mind:

✔ **To add a new layer,** click the plus sign icon in the Layers dialog box.

✔ **To change which layer something's on,** select the destination layer in the Layers dialog box, right-click the element you want to move, and choose Move to Current Layer.

✔ **To see what layer an element is currently on,** select the element and then look for the tiny blue dot in the Layers dialog box. If you select two elements on two different layers, you see two blue dots.

✔ **To lock layers you're not using,** click the Lock icon. I know it's annoying to have to go and unlock a layer before you can modify its contents, but it's even more annoying to accidentally move the wrong things around, or even delete them.

✔ **To hide layers and improve your performance,** make liberal use of the Hide icon next to the name of each layer; this can really improve LayOut's performance, especially on slower computers. Hide any layers you're not working with, and you'll notice the difference.

A

B

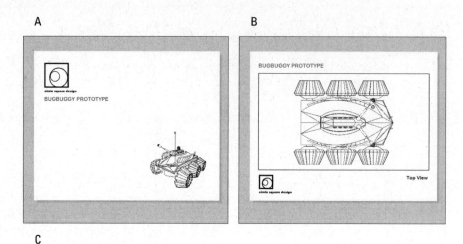

C

Figure 15-6:
A simple
document
with two
layers: one
that's shared
(master) and
one that's
not.

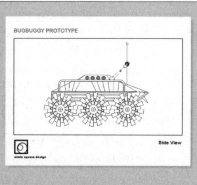

Sharing icon is toggled
off, which hides the
Master layer on this
page

Sharing icon
shows this is
a Master layer

Figure 15-7:
Click the
Sharing icon
to control
master
layers.

Bringing In Everything You Need

After you have your document set up the way you want it, you probably want to start bringing in images. Some programs call this *importing,* and others call it *placing.* LayOut calls it *inserting.*

Vive la différence!

You can insert two kinds of images into your LayOut documents:

✓ **Raster images:** This means TIFFs, JPEGs, GIFs, BMPs, and PNGs — these are all graphics file formats that save pictures as lots of tiny dots. Unfortunately, LayOut can't insert *vector* images in its first version. Check out Chapter 13 for a full description *raster* and *vector* images.

✓ **SketchUp models:** To get a SketchUp model view into your presentation, LayOut lets you insert SketchUp models directly into your document.

With every other page-layout program in the universe, the only way to include a view of a SketchUp model is to export that view from SketchUp as an image file, and then place it in the layout program. Changing the SketchUp file means having to go through the whole process again, and if your presentation includes lots of SketchUp model views, it can take hours.

This brings us to LayOut's *raison d'être:* Instead of exporting views from SketchUp to get them into LayOut, all you do is insert a SketchUp file. From within LayOut, you can pick the view you like best. You can also use as many views of the same model as you want. When your SketchUp file is modified, LayOut knows about it and (using the References panel in the Document Setup dialog box) lets you update all your views at once by clicking a single button.

In sections that follow, you find out the best tips and tricks for working with models, as well as how to insert other images and text.

Inserting images and model views

Regardless of which kind of image you want to insert, the procedure is the same; follow these steps to bring an image into your LayOut document:

1. **Choose File⇨Insert.**

   This opens the Insert dialog box.

2. **Find the file on your computer that you want to insert, and click the Open button.**

   This closes the Insert dialog box and places the image (or SketchUp model) you chose on your current LayOut document page.

3. **Use the Select tool to resize your image.**

   You can resize an image by clicking and dragging any corner.

   If your image is a TIFF, JPEG, GIF, BMP, or PNG file, hold down Shift while you drag to resize *proportionally;* you probably don't want to distort your image by stretching it out. To resize an inserted SketchUp model view proportionally, hold down Alt (Command on the Mac).

4. **Use the Select tool to move your image around.**

   Click and drag to move any element in your document around on the page.

5. **Use the Select tool to rotate your image, if you want to.**

   This is probably best explained with a picture; Figure 15-8 shows the Rotate Circle (I call it the Steering Wheel) that shows up in front of any element when you click to select it with the Select tool. You rotate an element by clicking and dragging its Steering Wheel. To rotate about a different point (a different center of rotation), just move the Steering Wheel by clicking its center point and dragging it around.

   See the next section for tips on working with inserted SketchUp model views.

The "Steering Wheel"

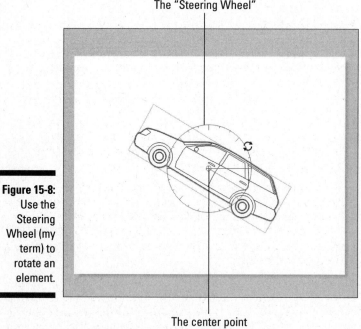

Figure 15-8:
Use the Steering Wheel (my term) to rotate an element.

The center point

Working with inserted model views

Figure 15-9 shows a view of a LayOut drawing window with a SketchUp model I inserted. The following are some things I think you should know:

- ✔ **Double-click to change your view.** When you're using the Select tool, double-clicking a SketchUp model view allows you to orbit, pan, and zoom around your model. When you like what you see, click anywhere outside the view to exit.

- ✔ **Right-click 'til the cows come home.** The key to working with SketchUp models you've inserted into LayOut is to right-click them; this opens a context menu full of useful options.

- ✔ **Display your model views at scale.** One of the options in the context menu that pops up when you right-click on a model view is "Scale". Click on it, then choose a scale from the long list. Keep in mind that only *non-perspectival, orthographic* model views can be displayed at a true scale. Check out Chapter 12 for more information on this.

- ✔ **Do your dimensioning in SketchUp.** This may seem strange, but the first-ever version of LayOut doesn't have a way to add dimensions to your drawings. Dimensions you add in SketchUp show up in LayOut, though, so feel free to add them there.

- ✔ **Create scenes in SketchUp to make life easier in LayOut.** In the context menu that appears when you right-click an inserted SketchUp model view, you can pick a scene. This is incredibly convenient, because getting just the right view is easier in SketchUp than it is in LayOut. If you know which views you need, create scenes in SketchUp and then choose them in LayOut. See Chapter 10 for details about creating scenes.

- ✔ **Tweak your line weights.** In the Styles pane of the SketchUp Model dialog box, you find a setting at the bottom called Line Weights. Reduce that number from 1.00 to 0.25 and you'll like what happens — your inserted SketchUp models will look a whole lot better.

- ✔ **Don't forget to check the document setup.** When a SketchUp model you've inserted is modified, LayOut knows about it — but it doesn't automatically update your views to reflect the changes. You have to do it yourself: Choose File⇨Document Setup and then click to open the References panel. (See Figure 15-10.) Select each model view you want to update, and then click the Update button.

While I'm talking about the References panel in Document Setup, I want to mention the Purge button. Click it to dump references to external files you're not using anymore. It can't hurt anything to click it, and doing so reduces the size of your LayOut file and keeps it from getting corrupted.

✔ **Choose Open with SketchUp to avoid the Document Setup dialog box.** Choosing Open with SketchUp from the right-click context menu opens your model in SketchUp, where you can make any edits you want. When you're done, save your SketchUp file, and then come back to LayOut; your view will have changed to reflect the edits you made in SketchUp.

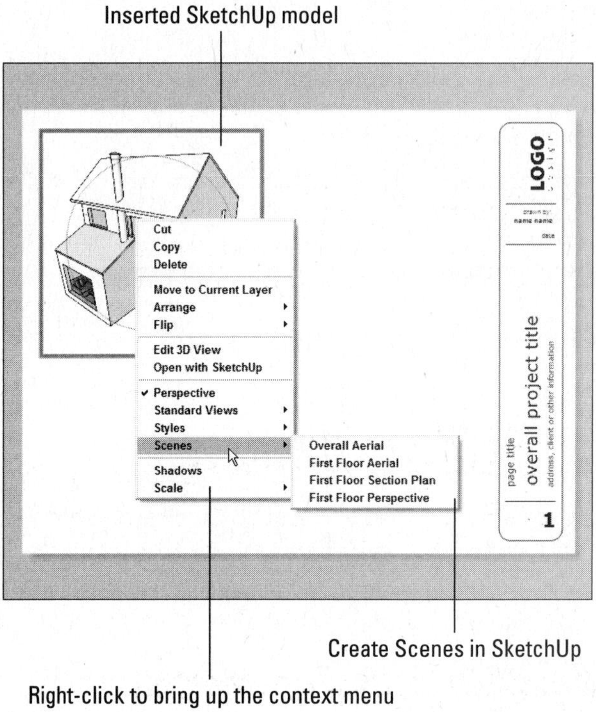

Inserted SketchUp model

Figure 15-9:
A SketchUp
model view
inserted in a
LayOut
document.

Create Scenes in SketchUp

Right-click to bring up the context menu

Inserting text

You can insert a third type of content into LayOut documents: text. This is useful if the text you want to use is already typed, spell-checked, proofread, and ready to present.

Insert a text file the same way you do an image, but keep in mind that it has to be an RTF or TXT file. Luckily any text editor (like Word or Text Edit) can save to these formats.

Check to make sure your inserted images are current

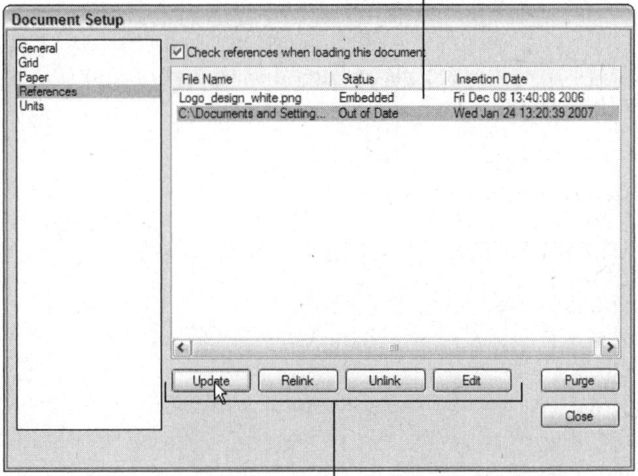

Document Setup			
General	☑ Check references when loading this document		
Grid			
Paper	File Name	Status	Insertion Date
References	Logo_design_white.png	Embedded	Fri Dec 08 13:40:08 2006
Units	C:\Documents and Setting...	Out of Date	Wed Jan 24 13:20:39 2007

[Update] [Relink] [Unlink] [Edit] [Purge]

[Close]

Figure 15-10:
The References panel, inside the Document Setup dialog box.

Use these controls to manage your References

Presentation-Perfect Images

After you import content, it's generally not quite presentation-ready. You may want to crop images or use the drawing tools to create a professional-looking, well-organized layout. The following sections show you how.

Cropping with clipping masks

Cropping an image means reframing it so that you can only see part of it; every page-layout program on the planet allows you to crop images, and each one insists that you do it a little differently. LayOut is no exception.

In LayOut, you use *clipping masks* to hide the parts of images that you don't want to see. Follow these steps to use a shape as a clipping mask (see Figure 15-11):

1. **Draw the shape you want to use as a clipping mask.**

2. **Make sure that it's positioned properly over the image you want to crop.**

3. **Use the Select tool to select both the clipping mask object and the image you want to crop.**

   Hold down Shift while clicking to select more than one object.

4. **Right-click the selected elements and choose Create Clip Mask from the context menu.**

Here are some fun facts about clipping masks in LayOut:

- ✔ **Clipping masks work on inserted images.** These include pictures and SketchUp models that you place in your LayOut document.

- ✔ **Deleting clipping masks is easy.** To see a whole image again, you need to "release" its clipping mask. Select the image and then choose Edit⇨Remove Clip Mask.

- ✔ **Edit clipping masks by double-clicking them.** When you double-click a clipping mask, you can see the whole image and the shape you used to create the mask. Now you can modify the shape, the image, or both. Clicking somewhere else on your page exits the edit mode.

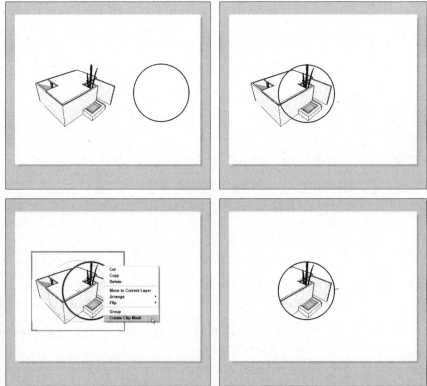

Figure 15-11: Use clipping masks to hide parts of images you insert.

Drawing something from scratch

LayOut includes a full slate of drawing tools that you can use to create logos, title bars, north arrows, graphic scales — anything you want. The drawings you create are *vectors,* meaning that you can do the following:

✔ Scale them without losing quality

✔ Change their fill and stroke (outline) colors

✔ Split lines and then rejoin them to make new shapes

Because I don't know what you want to draw, a step list would be pretty pointless here. Instead, here are a few pointers to get you started:

✔ **Use the right kind of snaps.** It's easier to draw exactly what you want if you let the software help a bit. Just like SketchUp, LayOut includes an elaborate (but easy-to-use) *inference* system of red and green dots and lines to help you line things up. LayOut also allows you to use a grid (that you define) to help you keep things straight:

• **Snap to objects:** Choose Arrange⇨Object Snap to turn on object snapping; this gives you colored "hints" to help you draw.

• **Snap to grid:** Choose Arrange⇨Grid Snap to turn on grid snapping. Now your cursor automatically *snaps* to (is attracted to) the intersection of grid lines in your document — whether your grid is visible or not. See the section "Getting Your Bearings," earlier in this chapter, for more information on using grids in LayOut.

You can use any combination of snapping systems (Object or Grid) while you're working, but I prefer to use one or the other — it all depends on what I'm trying to do. To save time, I assign a keyboard shortcut that toggles each system on and off. (To do that, use the Shortcuts panel in the Preferences dialog box, which you can find in the Edit menu — on a Mac, it's in the LayOut menu.)

✔ **Build complex shapes out of simpler ones.** I'll use an example here: Figure 15-12 shows how I would draw a simple arrow. You can follow these steps to build one just like it:

1. Make sure that Grid Snap is turned off and Object Snap is turned on.

2. Draw a rectangle with the Rectangle tool.

3. Draw a triangle with the Polygon tool (Type in **3s** and press Enter before you start drawing to make sure that you're drawing a triangle). Hold down Shift to make sure that the bottom of the triangle is a horizontal line.

4. Use the Select tool to select both shapes by holding down Shift as you click them.

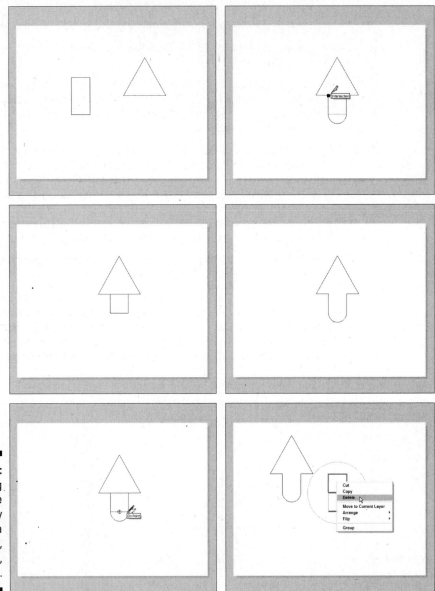

Figure 15-12:
Drawing
a simple
arrow by
combining a
rectangle,
a triangle,
and an arc.

5. Choose Arrange⇨Align⇨Vertically to line up the rectangle and the triangle vertically.

   Don't forget that you can always use the Undo feature to go back a step; it's in the Edit menu whenever you need it.

6. Deselect both shapes by clicking once somewhere else on your page.

7. Select one of the shapes and move it up or down on the page (by pressing the up- and down-arrow keys) until the two shapes overlap.

8. Use the Arc tool to draw a half-circle at the bottom of the rectangle.

9. Using the Split tool, click and *hold down* each of the points of intersection in the figure; don't let go until all the lines stop flashing blue. Do this for all four intersection points to split the shapes into a series of line segments.

10. Use the Join tool (it looks like a bottle of glue) to connect all the line segments by clicking once on the "arrowhead" part, once on each half of the "stem" part, and once on the half-circle. Now you have one shape instead of three; verify this by clicking the shape once with the Select tool. You should see one red "selected" rectangle around your new shape. If you don't have one shape, try using the Join tool again; sometimes it takes a couple of tries to get things to work.

11. Move your new shape somewhere else, and then delete the left-over lines segments you don't need.

✔ **Open the Shape Style dialog box.** You use the Shape Style dialog box to change the fill and stroke characteristics of elements in your document. (See Figure 15-13.) In plain English, this is where you pick colors for the things you draw. The controls are pretty straightforward, so you don't need much help from me; just experiment and see what happens.

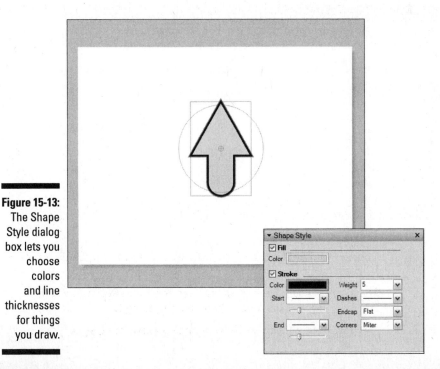

Figure 15-13:
The Shape Style dialog box lets you choose colors and line thicknesses for things you draw.

Life after LayOut

After you've created your LayOut document, you can do the following three things:

✔ Print it

✔ Export it as a PDF file

✔ View it as a full-screen presentation

Simple, huh? The next three sections provide some more detail on each of these options.

Printing your work

Follow these steps to print your LayOut document:

1. **Choose File⇨Page Setup.**

   In the Page Setup dialog box, choose a printer and a paper size and orientation.

2. **Click the OK button to close the Page Setup dialog box.**

3. **Choose File⇨Print.**

   In the Print dialog box, choose which pages to print and how many copies you want.

4. **Click the OK button to send your document to the printer you chose in Page Setup.**

Exporting a PDF file

Anyone with Adobe Reader software (which is free and is already loaded on millions of computers) can look at a PDF document you create; all you have to do is e-mail it to him or her. Follow these steps to export your LayOut document as a PDF file:

1. **Choose File⇨Export PDF. (It's just Export on the Mac.)**

   This opens the Export dialog box.

2. **Give your PDF file a name, and figure out where to save it on your computer.**

3. **Click the Save button (in Windows) to open the PDF Export Options dialog box (see Figure 15-14); click the Options button if you're on a Mac.**

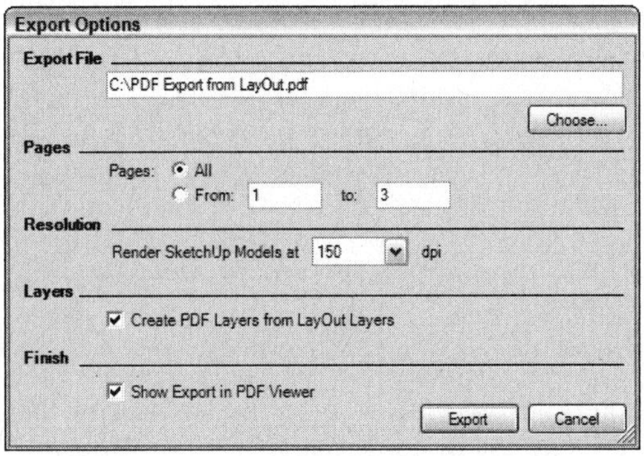

Export Options

Export File

C:\PDF Export from LayOut.pdf

Choose...

Pages

Pages: ● All
○ From: 1 to: 3

Resolution

Render SketchUp Models at 150 ▼ dpi

Layers

☑ Create PDF Layers from LayOut Layers

Finish

☑ Show Export in PDF Viewer

Export | Cancel

Figure 15-14:
LayOut's
PDF Export
Options
dialog box.

4. Set the PDF options the way you want them.

Here's what everything means:

- **Pages:** Choose which pages you want to export.

- **Resolution:** See the section "Creating a new, blank document," earlier in this chapter, for a brief discussion of resolution. Here's a good rule of thumb: For documents that are small enough to be hand-held, I recommend a setting of 300 dpi. For anything bigger, go with 150 dpi.

- **Layers:** PDFs can have layers, just like LayOut documents do. If it makes sense to do so, you can export a layered PDF so that people who view it can turn the layers on and off.

- **Finish:** Select this check box to view your PDF after it's exported.

5. (Mac only) Click the OK button to close the PDF Options dialog box.

6. Click the Export button (Save button on a Mac) to export your document as a PDF file.

Going full-screen

Many times, design presentations for clients go beyond printed boards and booklets; they include a digital slide show that usually involves a few hours of work in a program like PowerPoint or Keynote (if you're on a Mac).

LayOut was designed to help you skip the PowerPoint step by letting you display your presentation in a full-screen view. You can move back and forth between pages with the arrow keys on your computer, and you can even double-click SketchUp model views to orbit them around. Follow these tips:

✔ **Switching to full-screen mode takes less than a second.** Choose View⇨ Full Screen to view your presentation full-screen. Press Esc to exit full-screen mode.

✔ **Move from page to page.** Use the left- and right-arrow keys to flip through pages.

✔ **Choose which pages to show full-screen.** You can decide not to show certain pages in full-screen mode by toggling the Show in Presentations icon to the right of those page names in the Pages dialog box (make sure that you're in List view to be able to do this).

✔ **Double-click to change your view of a SketchUp model.** When you're in full-screen mode, you can double-click any SketchUp model view to orbit and zoom around inside it. Just use your mouse's scroll wheel button the same way you do in SketchUp. Click anywhere outside the view to exit.

✔ **Draw while you're in full-screen mode.** Try clicking and dragging while you're in full-screen mode; doing so lets you make red annotations right on your presentation. If a client doesn't like the porch you designed, scrawl a big, red *X* over it to let him know you understand.

✔ **Play scene animations right in full screen mode.** You can double-click, then right-click on a model view with scenes that you've set up in SketchUp and choose Play Animation. LayOut will transition from scene to scene, just like SketchUp does. You can read more about scenes in Chapter 10.

Part V
The Part of Tens

The 5th Wave   By Rich Tennant

"So this is your design? I didn't know Google SketchUp had an 'overkill' function."

In this part . . .

Let's face it; everybody loves lists. The last part of this book (and of every *For Dummies* book out there) is dedicated to presenting useful information in short, bite-sized chunks that you can read while you're standing in the elevator. Or using the bathroom. Or waiting for your turn in the shower.

Chapter 16 is a list of the problems that every new SketchUp user runs into — check here when you're ready to pour acid all over your keyboard and move to Amish country.

The list in Chapter 17 is mostly about promoting consumerism, but it's also handy if you're wondering what else is available that can improve the way you use SketchUp.

The last chapter in this book is, fittingly, about ten ways that you can keep discovering more about SketchUp — places to go, books to read, DVDs to watch. I'm a firm believer that the best way to figure out anything is to see it presented in more than one way, so I highly encourage you to check out at least a couple of these resources.

Chapter 16

Ten SketchUp Traps and Their Work-arounds

The bad news is that every single new SketchUp user encounters certain problems, usually in his or her first couple of hours with the software. I guess you could call them growing pains. The good news is that such predictability means that I can write a chapter that anticipates a lot of the bad stuff you'll go through. I can't prevent it from happening, but I *can* help you make sense of what's going on so that you can get on with your life as quickly as possible.

SketchUp Won't Create a Face Where I Want It To

You've dutifully traced all around the boundary of where you'd like SketchUp to create a face, but nothing's happening. Try checking whether your edges aren't all on the same plane or whether one edge is part of a separate group or component.

To check whether you have a component problem, try hiding groups or components and checking the edges to make sure that they're all in the group or component you think they're in. See Chapter 5 for details.

However, 90 percent of the time, when SketchUp won't create a face where you think it should, an edge isn't on the *plane* you think it's on. To check whether your edges are coplanar, draw an edge that cuts diagonally across the area where you want a face to appear. If a face appears now, all your edges are not on the same plane. To fix the problem, you have to figure out which edge is the culprit. I call my favorite method for doing this the Color by Axis method; Color Plate 20 shows images of the steps that I describe below:

1. **In the Styles dialog box, change your edge color from All Same to By Axis.**

   See Chapter 8 for details. Doing this step tells SketchUp to draw the edges in your model the color of the axis to which they're parallel; edges parallel to the red axis will be red, and so on.

2. **Look carefully at the edges you were hoping would define a face.**

   Are all the edges the color they're supposed to be? If they're not all supposed to be parallel to the drawing axes, this technique doesn't do much good. But if they are, and one (or more) of them is black (instead of red or green or blue), that edge (or edges) is your problem child. Fix it and switch back to All Same when you're done.

My Faces Are Two Different Colors

In SketchUp, faces have two sides: a front and a back. By default, these two sides are different colors. When you do certain things like use Push/Pull or Follow Me on a face, sometimes the faces on the resulting geometry are "inside out." If it bothers you to have a two-tone model (I know it bothers me), just right-click the faces you want to flip over and choose Reverse Faces from the context menu. If you have lots of them, you can select them all and then choose Reverse Faces to do them all at once.

Edges on a Face Won't Sink In

This tends to happen when you're trying to draw a rectangle (or another geometric figure) on a face with one of SketchUp's shape-drawing tools. Ordinarily, the Rectangle tool creates a new face on top of any face you use it on; after that, you can use Push/Pull to create a hole, if you want. If your shape's edges look thick instead of thin, they're not cutting through the face they're drawn on. When that happens, try these approaches:

✓ **Retrace one of the edges.** Sometimes that works — you'd be surprised how often.

✔ **Select Hidden Geometry on the View menu.** You're checking to make sure that the face you just drew isn't crossing any hidden or smoothed edges; if it is, the face you thought was flat might not be.

✔ **Make sure that the face you drew on isn't part of a group or component.** If it is, undo a few steps and then redraw your shape while you're editing the group or component.

SketchUp Crashed, and 1 Lost My Model

Unfortunately, SketchUp crashes happen sometimes. The good news is that SketchUp automatically saves a copy of your file every five minutes. The file that SketchUp autosaves is actually a *separate* file, which it calls `AutoSave_your filename.skp`. So if your file ever gets corrupted in a crash, there's an intact one, ready for you to find and continue working on. The problem is that most people don't even know it's there. Where?

✔ If you've ever saved your file, it's in the same folder as the original.

✔ If you've never saved your file, it's in your My Documents folder — unless you're on a Mac, in which case it's here:

```
User folder/Library/Application Support/
        Google SketchUp 6/SketchUp/Autosave
```

Keep in mind that normally, SketchUp cleans up after itself by deleting the autosaved file when you close your model, and nothing untoward happens.

 To minimize the amount of work you lose when software (or hardware) goes south, you should always do two things: save often (compulsively, even), and save numbered copies as you're working — I use Save As to create a new copy of my work every half-hour or so. When I'm building a big model, it's not uncommon for me to have 40 or 50 saved versions of it on my computer, dating back to when I first started working on it.

SketchUp 1s Sooooo Slooooooooow

The bigger your model gets, the worse your performance gets, too. What makes a model big? In a nutshell, faces. You should do everything in your power to keep your model as small as you can. Here are some tips for doing that:

✔ **Reduce the number of sides on your extruded circles and arcs.** See the sidebar in Chapter 6 for instructions on how to do this.

✔ **Use 2D people and trees instead of 3D ones.** 3D plants and people have *hundreds* of faces each. Consider using 2D ones instead, especially if your model won't be seen much from overhead.

Some models are just big, and you can't do much about it. Here are some tricks for working with very large SketchUp models:

✔ **Make liberal use of the Outliner and layers.** Explained in detail in Chapter 5, these SketchUp features were specifically designed to let you organize your model into manageable chunks. Hide everything you're not working on at the moment — doing so gives your computer a fighting chance.

✔ **Use substitution for large numbers of complex components.** For example, insert sticks as placeholders for big sets of 3D trees, cars, and other big components. See the tips for replacing components in Chapter 5 for details.

✔ **Turn off shadows and switch to a simple style.** It takes a lot of computer horsepower to display shadows, edge effects, and textures in real time on your monitor. When you're working, turn off all that stuff.

✔ **Use scenes to navigate between views.** Scenes aren't just for presenting your model — they're also great for working with it. Creating scenes for the different views you commonly use, and with different combinations of hidden geometry, means that you don't have to orbit, pan, and zoom around your gigantic model. Better yet, deselect Enable Scene Transitions (in the Animation panel of the Model Info dialog box) to speed things up even more.

1 Can't Get a Good View of the Inside of My Model

It's not always easy to work on the inside of something in SketchUp. You can do these things to make it easier, though:

✔ **Cut into it with sections:** SketchUp's Sections feature lets you cut away parts of your model — temporarily, of course — so that you can get a better view of what's inside. Take a look at Chapter 10 for the whole story on sections.

✔ **Widen your field of view:** Field of view is basically the amount of your model you can see on the screen at one time. A wider FOV is like having better peripheral vision. You can read all about it in Chapter 10.

A Face Flashes When I Orbit

If you have two faces in the same spot — maybe one is in a separate group or component — you see an effect called *Z-fighting*. What you're witnessing is SketchUp trying to decide which face to display by switching back and forth between them. It's not a good solution, but certainly a logical one, at least for a piece of software. The only way to get rid of Z-fighting is to delete or hide one of the faces.

I Can't Move My Component the Way I Want

Some components are set up to automatically *glue* to faces when you insert them into your model. A glued component instance isn't actually glued *in one place*. Instead, it's glued to the plane of the face you originally placed (or created) it on. For example, if you place a sofa component on the floor of your living room, you can only move it around on that plane — not up and down. This behavior comes in handy when you're dealing with things like furniture. It allows you to use the Move tool to rearrange things without having to worry about accidentally picking them up.

If you can't move your component the way you want to, right-click it and check to see whether Unglue is an option — if it is, choose it. Now you can move your component around however you want.

Every Time I Use the Eraser, Bad Stuff Happens

It's pretty easy to delete stuff accidentally with the Eraser tool. Basically, just because you can't see an edge (like because it's behind something else) doesn't mean that you can't erase it. Worse yet, you usually don't notice what's missing until it's too late. Here are some tips for erasing more accurately:

  ✔ **Orbit around.** Try to make sure that nothing is behind whatever it is you're erasing; use SketchUp's navigation tools to get a view of your model that puts you out of danger.

✔ **Switch to Wireframe mode.** Choose View➪Face Style➪Wireframe when you're going to be using the Eraser heavily. That way, you won't have any faces to obstruct your view, and you'll be less likely to erase the wrong edges.

✔ **Double-check.** I've gotten into the habit of giving my model a quick once-over with the Orbit tool after I do a lot of erasing, just to make sure that I didn't get rid of anything important. Put a sticky note on your computer monitor that says something like CHECK AFTER ERASE! just to remind yourself.

All My Edges and Faces Are on Different Layers

I'll be blunt — using Layers in SketchUp is a dangerous business. Chapter 5 has tips you should follow when using layers, so I won't repeat them here, but here's the short version: You should always build everything on Layer0, and only put whole groups or components on other layers if you really need to.

If you used layers, and now things are messed up, here's what you can do to recover:

1. **Make sure that everything is visible.**

   Select Hidden Geometry on the View menu then (in the Layers dialog box) make all your layers visible. Just make sure that you can see everything in your model.

2. **Choose Edit➪Select All to select everything.**

3. **In the Entity Info dialog box, move everything to Layer0.**

4. **In the Layers dialog box, delete your other layers, telling SketchUp to move anything remaining on them to Layer0.**

5. **Create new layers, and follow the rules in Chapter 5.**

Chapter 17

Ten Plugins, Extensions, and Resources Worth Getting

*T*he really great thing about SketchUp's price is how much room it frees up in your budget for nifty add-ons. This chapter is a list of ten such nifty add-ons, along with a little bit of information about them, and where you can go to find them. I've split them up into four categories, just to make things clearer: components, Ruby scripts, renderers, and hardware.

Components

Hooked on components? If you do any amount of modeling with SketchUp, you'll quickly realize how much time you can save by having the right components to "populate" your work with people, cars, trees, furniture, and other stuff like that. Why make your own sofa when you can grab one from somewhere else? If the components that you can download from SketchUp's Web site aren't enough for you (see Chapter 5 for more information about this), the following sections provide some additional Web sites where you can buy what you need.

Form Fonts

`www.formfonts.com`

Form Fonts is a Web site that sells components "all you can eat, buffet style." You pay a (surprisingly low) monthly fee, and you have access to *thousands* of high-quality models of just about anything you can think of. Form Fonts' international team of modelers even takes requests — if you need something that they don't have, they can probably make it if you ask nicely. In addition to components, Form Fonts also has tons of extra materials you can apply to your work, as well as a growing library of styles. Even if you're not interested in signing up, it's worth checking out the Web site just to see the beautiful models Form Fonts makes.

Sketchupmodels.com

`www.sketchupmodels.com`

Along the same lines as Form Fonts, Sketchupmodels.com is an online spot where you can buy SketchUp components. This place isn't a buffet, though; you only buy what you need, *à la carte*. Some of its models might seem a little expensive, but when you consider how much time it would take you to make them yourself, it might be worth it to buy them — especially if you use SketchUp for work.

Ruby Scripts

What's a Ruby script, you ask? Basically, Google provides a way for people to make their own plugins for SketchUp. These plugins are just mini-programs (scripts) written in a computer programming language called Ruby. The best thing about Ruby scripts (Rubies, for short) is that you don't have to know anything about Ruby, or programming in general, to use ones that other people have created.

To install Rubies, you just drop them into a special folder on your computer:

- ✔ **Windows:** `C:/Program Files/Google/Google SketchUp 6/ Plugins`
- ✔ **Mac:** `Hard Drive/Library/Application Support/Google SketchUp 6/SketchUp/Plugins`

The next time you launch SketchUp, Rubies you put in the preceding location become available for you to use. How you use them depends on what they do. They might show up on one of the toolbar menus or on your right-click context menu. The more complex ones even come with their own little toolbars. Helpfully, most Rubies also come with a set of instructions that tells you how to use them.

Luckily for those of us who aren't programmers, plenty of smart folks out there develop and (in some cases) sell Rubies that anyone can use. Smustard.com (www.smustard.com) is a Web site run by a few of these smart folks. You can choose from dozens of helpful Rubies that add functionality to SketchUp, and best of all, they're *very* inexpensive. Here are some of my favorites:

✔ **Weld:** This Ruby takes edges you've selected and "welds" them together to make a single edge that you can select with a single click. This is *super*-handy when you're using Follow Me.

✔ **PresentationBundle:** This is a package of five Rubies that help you use scenes to create better presentations. You can customize the transition time between individual scenes, for instance, and even create really elaborate fly-by animations.

✔ **CAD cleanup scripts:** If you routinely import 2D CAD drawings to use as a starting point for SketchUp models, you need these scripts. Cleaning up imported CAD drawings is a real drag, but the following Rubies make the whole process immeasurably easier:

  • **StrayLines:** Run this script to figure out how much work you'll have to do to a CAD file after you've imported it — it goes through and labels stuff you'll probable have to fix.

  • **CloseOpens:** Imported CAD drawings almost always have one glaring problem: Their edges don't meet precisely, which means that you can't create faces. You end up hunting around with the Zoom tool, looking for all the tiny gaps and filling them in. Yuck. This script does it for you, which makes it worth a lot more than Smustard charges for it.

  • **MakeFaces:** When you import a 2D CAD drawing, you get edges but not faces. Trouble is, you need faces for working in SketchUp, so you end up retracing a bazillion little lines to make faces appear. Run this Ruby, and you don't have to.

  • **IntersectOverlaps:** You know how edges that cross don't automatically cut each other? If you use this script they will. Be careful to read the instructions (on the Web site); this Ruby can cause some unexpected results.

- **Flatten:** Sometimes (who knows why), imported CAD lines don't all come in lying on the ground. You probably want them to be (so that they're all coplanar), and this Ruby makes sure that they are.

- **DeleteShortLines:** When people make CAD drawings, they often accidentally overshoot their targets, creating hundreds of tiny, annoying edge segments that you need to get rid of in SketchUp.

Renderers

One thing SketchUp does not do is create photorealistic renderings. Its styles are great for making your models look hand-drawn, but none of them can make your work look like a photograph. Most SketchUp users are okay with that, but for those who aren't, you can find some nice solutions out there.

Of course, SketchUp Pro's 3D export formats make it possible to render SKP files with just about any of the dozens of über-powerful renderers on the market, but the ones that I describe in the following list have three important things in common: They work with the free version of SketchUp, they were developed with SketchUp in mind, and you don't have to work for George Lucas to figure them out. Here's the list:

- ✔ **SU Podium** (www.suplugins.com)**:** If you're using a Windows computer, you should probably check out Podium first. It's a plugin that lets you create photorealistic views right inside SketchUp. It's really too bad that Podium isn't available for the Mac, but it might be sometime in the future. Regardless of which platform you're on, it's definitely worth checking out.

- ✔ **TurboSketch** (www.turbosketch.net)**:** The good news about TurboSketch is that it's available for both Windows and the Mac, and that it (like Podium) also runs as a plugin inside SketchUp. The bad thing is that a lot of folks I know think Podium's a bit better. You should try both (if you can) and make up your own mind.

- ✔ **Artlantis R** (www.artlantis.com)**:** If you're really serious about making images that look like photographs, take a good look at Artlantis R. Instead of running as a plugin inside SketchUp, it's a fully functional, separate piece of software that works with lots of other 3D modeling programs. The results it produces are out of this world.

Like I mentioned earlier, lots of rendering applications are out there, and depending on what you want to do, different ones might work better than others. If photo rendering is your thing, try plugging these names into your favorite search engine: Kirkithea, Maxwell, Cheetah3D, and Vue. They're hardcore, but they all work great.

Hardware

All you really need to use SketchUp is a computer with a decent video card, a keyboard, and a mouse. On the other hand, having specialized hardware can come in handy — especially if you find yourself using SketchUp all the time:

✔ **A second monitor:** Having a dual-monitor setup makes using SketchUp a lot easier. All of a sudden, you have space for all your dialog boxes and toolbars on one side of your setup, and you still have a whole screen just for your SketchUp modeling window.

✔ **SpaceNavigator from 3Dconnexion:** Using a scroll-wheel mouse to fly around in three-dimensional space works great for most people, but lots of SketchUp power users swear by dedicated 3D navigation tools like the SpaceNavigator. It looks a little like an enormous button that sits on your desk, connected to your computer via a USB cable. You use it with whichever hand you aren't using for your mouse; it's an add-on (and not a replacement) for any of the other peripherals in your system. Basically, the SpaceNavigator lets you orbit, pan, and zoom with subtle movements of your hand — it really is a much more natural way to interact with a 3D model. You'll find a bit of a learning curve, but that's nothing for serious SketchUp users. Anything that makes software easier and more fun to use is worth the time it takes to master it.

Chapter 18

Ten Ways to Discover Even More

In This Chapter
▶ Checking out some great, free ways to find out more about SketchUp
▶ Discovering other helpful resources

Don't get me wrong — it's not that I think this book is woefully incomplete. It's just that I don't think it's possible to get too many different *forms* of information, especially about something as dynamic as SketchUp. You can find some great help resources out there, and I'd be remiss if I didn't point you to some of them.

The first half of this chapter is devoted to the free stuff; it's all online and it's all available to anyone who wants it. In the second half of the chapter, I list some of the best nonfree SketchUp resources I know of. If you're willing to shell out a few bucks, you won't be sorry — nothing beats seeing the same information presented in different ways.

Put Away Your Wallet

I have a confession to make: At fancy receptions, I'm the one stuffing my suit pockets with hors d'oeuvres wrapped in napkins. I love free stuff *that much.* So without further ado, what follows are six *complementary* sources of SketchUp help.

Everything in this section requires that you have an Internet connection, so make sure that your computer's online before you try any of these.

If you take a peek at SketchUp's Help menu, you'll see a bunch of different options (see Figure 18-1) — these are my favorites, in order of favoriteness:

> ✔ **Video Tutorials:** When SketchUp was first launched in 2000, it became known for its excellent video tutorials. I can't recommend them highly enough; there's nothing like *seeing* SketchUp in action.

- ✔ **Self-Paced Tutorials:** These are SketchUp files that use scenes to teach different aspects of the program in a "follow along with me" style. If this is how you like to figure things out, have a look.

- ✔ **Online Help Center:** Google maintains big, extensive help centers (Web sites, basically) for all its products. These include hundreds of articles in question-and-answer format, created specifically to help new users along. The SketchUp one is terrific.

- ✔ **SketchUp Community:** This consists of two online "places." Though they're intended for different kinds of SketchUp users, I think you'll find good stuff in each of them:

    • **Google SketchUp User Groups:** This option uses Google's Groups feature to let SketchUp users from all over the world get help, ask questions, and show off their work.

    • **Google SketchUp Pro User Forums:** Plenty of people out there use SketchUp to make a living — and a lot of them hang out in the SketchUp forums. These are a lot like the groups (in the previous point), but they're for people who use SketchUp *a lot*. SketchUp's forum users are legendary for their generosity. Post a question (remember to be polite), and you'll see what I mean.

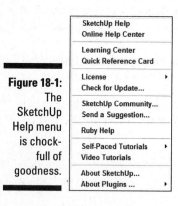

Figure 18-1:
The
SketchUp
Help menu
is chock-
full of
goodness.

Here are a couple of great online destinations for people (like yourself) who are SketchUp beginners:

- ✔ **School Podcasts** (www.go-2-school.com): These guys have a terrific Web site. Check out the Podcasts area for a list of great, free online videos they've put together. They also have a great learning DVD you can buy, and I talk about it in the next part of this chapter.

- ✔ **SU Wiki** (www.suwiki.org): This is a Web site built by SketchUp users, for SketchUp users. It's a goldmine of tutorials, tips and tricks, plugins, and other resources that I'm sure you'll find useful.

Now Get Out Your Wallet

Really. These resources cost a bit of money, but they're worth every penny:

✔ **Bonnie Roskes' books:** Bonnie's *The SketchUp Book* was the first one available, and now she has two new titles. If you think you'd like to get another, bigger book about SketchUp (written with architects and other design pros in mind), check out Bonnie's books at: `www.f1help.biz`. (Notice the `.biz` suffix — `.com` takes you somewhere else.)

✔ **School DVD:** I mention School's videos in the previous section, but School's designers have also produced the world's first SketchUp educational/training DVD, which you can order from its Web site (`www.go-2-school.com`). The production quality on this thing is outstanding, and Mike and Alex (the School guys) do an amazing job of teaching SketchUp for both Windows and the Mac.

✔ **Dennis Fukai's books:** One word: jaw-dropping detail (okay — three words). Dennis's books are hard to describe. He has written three of them, each is fully illustrated in SketchUp and each teaches a different subject. If you want to discover more about using SketchUp in building construction or more about construction itself, or you just want to be completely inspired by what you can do with SketchUp, have a look at these books. Search for his name on Amazon (`www.amazon.com`) or go to his company's Web site, `www.insitebuilders.com`.

✔ **SketchUp Pro training:** If you think you might benefit from being able to spend a few hours with a real-live trainer and a handful of other SketchUp students, Google's SketchUp training might be for you. Its trainers travel around to different cities, giving training seminars that you can sign up to attend. Check out its Web site for more information: `www.sketchup.com/training`.

Index

Google SketchUp For Dummies

• T •

SPORTS, FITNESS, PARENTING, RELIGION & SPIRITUALITY

0-471-76871-5   0-7645-7841-3

Also available:
- Catholicism For Dummies
  0-7645-5391-7
- Exercise Balls For Dummies
  0-7645-5623-1
- Fitness For Dummies
  0-7645-7851-0
- Football For Dummies
  0-7645-3936-1
- Judaism For Dummies
  0-7645-5299-6
- Potty Training For Dummies
  0-7645-5417-4
- Buddhism For Dummies
  0-7645-5359-3

- Pregnancy For Dummies
  0-7645-4483-7 †
- Ten Minute Tone-Ups For Dummies
  0-7645-7207-5
- NASCAR For Dummies
  0-7645-7681-X
- Religion For Dummies
  0-7645-5264-3
- Soccer For Dummies
  0-7645-5229-5
- Women in the Bible For Dummies
  0-7645-8475-8

TRAVEL

0-7645-7749-2   0-7645-6945-7

Also available:
- Alaska For Dummies
  0-7645-7746-8
- Cruise Vacations For Dummies
  0-7645-6941-4
- England For Dummies
  0-7645-4276-1
- Europe For Dummies
  0-7645-7529-5
- Germany For Dummies
  0-7645-7823-5
- Hawaii For Dummies
  0-7645-7402-7

- Italy For Dummies
  0-7645-7386-1
- Las Vegas For Dummies
  0-7645-7382-9
- London For Dummies
  0-7645-4277-X
- Paris For Dummies
  0-7645-7630-5
- RV Vacations For Dummies
  0-7645-4442-X
- Walt Disney World & Orlando
  For Dummies
  0-7645-9660-8

GRAPHICS, DESIGN & WEB DEVELOPMENT

0-7645-8815-X   0-7645-9571-7

Also available:
- 3D Game Animation For Dummies
  0-7645-8789-7
- AutoCAD 2006 For Dummies
  0-7645-8925-3
- Building a Web Site For Dummies
  0-7645-7144-3
- Creating Web Pages For Dummies
  0-470-08030-2
- Creating Web Pages All-in-One Desk
  Reference For Dummies
  0-7645-4345-8
- Dreamweaver 8 For Dummies
  0-7645-9649-7

- InDesign CS2 For Dummies
  0-7645-9572-5
- Macromedia Flash 8 For Dummies
  0-7645-9691-8
- Photoshop CS2 and Digital
  Photography For Dummies
  0-7645-9580-6
- Photoshop Elements 4 For Dummies
  0-471-77483-9
- Syndicating Web Sites with RSS Feeds
  For Dummies
  0-7645-8848-6
- Yahoo! SiteBuilder For Dummies
  0-7645-9800-7

NETWORKING, SECURITY, PROGRAMMING & DATABASES

0-7645-7728-X   0-471-74940-0

Also available:
- Access 2007 For Dummies
  0-470-04612-0
- ASP.NET 2 For Dummies
  0-7645-7907-X
- C# 2005 For Dummies
  0-7645-9704-3
- Hacking For Dummies
  0-470-05235-X
- Hacking Wireless Networks
  For Dummies
  0-7645-9730-2
- Java For Dummies
  0-470-08716-1

- Microsoft SQL Server 2005 For Dummies
  0-7645-7755-7
- Networking All-in-One Desk Reference
  For Dummies
  0-7645-9939-9
- Preventing Identity Theft For Dummies
  0-7645-7336-5
- Telecom For Dummies
  0-471-77085-X
- Visual Studio 2005 All-in-One Desk
  Reference For Dummies
  0-7645-9775-2
- XML For Dummies
  0-7645-8845-1